ONE
LAST
STRIKE

Fifty Years in Baseball, Ten and a Half
Games Back, and One Final
Championship Season

TONY LA RUSSA
with Rick Hummel

wm
WILLIAM MORROW
An Imprint of HarperCollins*Publishers*

HarperCollins books may be purchased for educational, business, or sales promotional use. For information please write: Special Markets Department, HarperCollins Publishers, 10 East 53rd Street, New York, NY 10022.

A hardcover edition of this book was published in 2012 by William Morrow, an imprint of HarperCollins Publishers.

FIRST WILLIAM MORROW PAPERBACK EDITION PUBLISHED 2013.

Designed by Jamie Lynn Kerner

Library of Congress Cataloging-in-Publication Data has been applied for.

ISBN 978-0-06-220754-8

13 14 15 16 17   DIX/RRD   10 9 8 7 6 5 4 3 2 1

To Elaine, Bianca, Devon, and our four-legged family
You made it all possible

To the ARF staff, volunteers, sponsors, and donors
You created the ARF season and pushed the dream
way beyond our original goals

Also, to all those special people I've met over the years
who have become friends. The closer the bond,
the greater my appreciation

And finally, to all those involved with professional baseball,
especially everyone associated with MLB
and our teams in Chicago, Oakland, and St. Louis

CONTENTS

FOREWORD

ABOUT A DECADE AGO, WORD FILTERED DOWN THAT TONY La Russa was looking for me. I had never met him, but given his high profile in the game, I felt as though I knew him. He managed the Cardinals, my team, and for that reason alone he rated pretty high. We eventually hooked up by phone and had a long talk. Tony is a voracious reader and had just finished *A Painted House*, my highly fictionalized childhood memoir and a story brimming with Cardinal baseball. I told Tony that being a Cardinal fan was in the blood. My father, grandfather, and everybody else in the family had followed the team for as long as anyone can remember. Growing up in small towns in Arkansas and Mississippi, the highlight of our day was the nightly broadcast on KMOX out of St. Louis with Harry Caray and Jack Buck on the radio. Bob Gibson, Lou Brock, Curt Flood, Orlando Cepeda, Tim McCarver—those were my heroes, and I knew their statistics, birth dates, and hometowns. My grandfather's team had been the Gashouse Gang with Dizzy Dean, another Arkansas farm boy, and my father revered Stan Musial.

Satisfied with my credentials, Tony graciously invited me to come to St. Louis, watch a game, hang out with the team, and have a late dinner. I collected my dad, Big John, and away we went. It was a memorable visit, the highlight being Big John and Stan the Man sitting together for two hours watching the Cardinals and reminiscing. Leaving St. Louis the following day, my dad informed me that he had now reached the pinnacle, his life was complete, and he was ready for the hereafter. Thankfully, he's still around and doesn't miss a Cardinal game on television.

A friendship was born, one that Tony and I have maintained over the years. On many occasions, I've visited him at spring training, in St. Louis, and even on the road. Long after the games were over, we dined for hours and solved many of the world's problems. He always wanted to talk about books and writers, while I preferred to get the gossip on players and managers. Over the years I have marveled at his passion for the game, his dogged pursuit of perfection, his commitment to his players, his endless quest to learn even more, his determination to win, his complete inability to accept defeat (even in spring training), and his breathtaking knowledge of the intricacies of baseball. Every baseball fan thinks he or she is an expert on the game, but an hour with Tony and the average fan would feel like a T-baller.

Through Tony, I've been lucky to meet and spend time with Bob Gibson, Lou Brock, Ozzie Smith, Mike Shannon, Red Schoendienst, Jack Buck, and Stan Musial. He's a tireless networker and relishes friendships with other great coaches. I once walked into his office in Florida after a spring game and was introduced to Bobby Knight and Bill Parcells, two of his old chums. Tony pushed the right buttons, got the two bickering over something, and for the next hour I laughed until I cried. During a long dinner at Nick's Tomatoe Pie, one of his favorite restaurants in Jupiter, I listened as the great John Havlicek regaled us with stories of his days with the Celtics.

Over the years, Tony challenged me to write a baseball novel, and I said I planned to as soon as I found the right story. I challenged him to write a book that would dissect the game and reveal its many layers of complexity. In 2005, he worked with Buzz Bissinger on *Three Nights in August,* a masterful analysis of a crucial three-game series with the Cubs.

In late spring of 2011, I called Tony and told him I finally had an idea for a baseball novel. The central plot involved a beanball and baseball's unwritten code of dealing with it. Talk about a hot-button topic. Nothing torments Tony like a hit batter. Was it intentional? Do we retaliate? If so, when? And who do we hit? In his dugout, he makes the call, and by doing so takes the pressure off his players. Other managers refuse to touch the issue, instead allowing their players to handle things. More than once I've heard Tony describe how a perfectly civilized baseball game can change in an instant by a fastball up and in.

In August of last year, Tony called to check on the novel. The Cardinals were ten games behind the Brewers and the season looked rather bleak. Typically, though, he had a plan to win the wild card and he was optimistic his team was buying into it. I had my doubts, though I kept them to myself. The odds of closing from ten games back with only thirty to go were slim. He reminded me that I had not been to see a game the entire year, beginning in Florida in February, and hinted there may not be another season, at least not for him. Shortly after that conversation, the Cardinals slowly came to life, and the Braves, their wild-card rivals, began to fall apart.

When I arrived in St. Louis on Friday, September 23, the Cardinals were two games out with only six left, and they had blown a win the day before against the Mets. The fifth-place Cubs were in town, but win-loss records mean nothing in that rivalry. Statistically, the Cardinals were still alive, but the mood in Busch Stadium that night was far from festive. Someone forgot to tell the team they were still in the hunt. They lost 5–1 to the Cubs and went to the locker room down three games with only five to go. It would take a miracle.

In St. Louis, the postgame dinner was always at a wonderful Italian restaurant called Tony's—no connection other than great food. It's downtown and a short walk from the stadium. Mr. La Russa had his table there, regardless of the late hour. He invited some of his St. Louis pals, all rabid Cardinal fans, and we set about the task of trying to cheer him up. Dinner after a win was a celebration, but after a loss, especially to the Cubs, it was another matter. The mood was generally upbeat, though everyone at the table knew the season was practically over. We talked about beanballs, retaliation, baseball's codes, headhunters, famous brawls, and the like. There was no discussion of the playoffs or the World Series.

No one at the table, including Tony, could have foreseen the magical and memorable ride the Cardinals were about to take. Their gutsy run from ten games out had come to an end with two straight bad losses. It was time to think about next year.

There was no reason to suspect the miracle was just beginning.

After the Cardinals beat the Rangers in game seven, Tony announced his retirement. He had made the decision weeks earlier and had quietly informed the ownership. Like all his friends and fans, I was saddened by the end of an era, but I was also proud to see him walk away on top.

Almost immediately he began talking about a book, this book. He was eager to tell the story of his team, of a close, familylike bunch of players who coalesced and pulled themselves up from the mat, believed in one another and their coaches, followed their leader, and refused to lose.

Here is their remarkable story.

John Grisham
July 23, 2012

PART I

One more game.

Those three words had been going through my head since the moment I'd awakened in my Houston hotel room.

Game 162 loomed, and finally—unbelievably—we were tied with Atlanta in the National League wild-card race. How did we pull this off? Barely a month ago we'd been ten and a half games back in the wild card. Now, on Wednesday, September 28, we had our fate in our hands. Win tonight and, at the very least, we'd be in a one-game showdown for the wild-card slot in the playoffs. A series of tough and dramatic wins and losses the final weeks of the regular season had us on the brink of joy or despair.

An impressive come-from-behind win on Tuesday, coming on the heels of Monday's tough loss, simply demonstrated the formula that had come to define our season: when faced with a serious adversity, the team always found a positive response. I'd seen that pattern so many times throughout the season. Those kinds of wins never feel routine, but this season, each time we pulled it off it felt better than ever, another jolt that had me thinking, "Hey, we can do this."

I've always liked the drama of having your magic number at one or two games and walking to the ballpark knowing you could be a champion. That's a helluva motivator.

Normally I don't look back. I keep my focus on the one ahead. Yet, on this morning, as I prepared to head over to the stadium, the emotional surge of it all was too much, and I broke one of my golden rules.

You take that pause to think back or look too far ahead and suddenly you've lost focus. Save that for after the game, and look back to learn from your past wins or losses. I've heard it said don't break your arm trying to pat yourself on the back. Well, don't break your neck looking behind goes right along with that.

I'd always stressed this with our players, telling them that the second they started being content with what they'd done, they weren't focusing on what they were going to do. You can't truly savor what you're doing while you're doing it. Our goal every day was to enjoy the experience of dedicating all of our mental and physical efforts to the next game's competition. In fact, the most enduring impression I have from the 2011 team is the give-it-all attitude the players brought to the games. The fame and fortune would be by-products of the winning. The real fun was how we competed.

I risk having to call B.S. on myself. Memories of the season and what our team had endured to be in this position snuck through my defenses. I figured there had to be an exception to the golden rule when a team played through the kind of season that we'd had. At seemingly every point, we'd experienced setbacks—pitching problems; injuries to essential players; our bench depth replacing injured regulars, who then had to be covered by our minor league depth when they were hurt; slumps; falling ten and a half games back. You name it, we faced it. We never really got down, despite the fact that there were several points when we were nearly out. We'd been written off by just about everyone but ourselves at one point or another. After Adam Wainwright's season-ending injury in Florida, the consensus was that we were a second-division team watching a two-team race between the Brewers and the Reds. Every season each team faces challenges. I'd been managing for thirty-three years and part of two World Series Championships, but I'd rarely seen a team or a season like this.

I glanced over at the clock on the dresser and silently counted the minutes until it was time to leave. I was proud of what we'd accomplished to that point. Who wouldn't be? That's not bragging, it's just telling it like it is.

But then I added heresy to rule-breaking: I knew we were going to beat Houston. Atlanta was going to win as well. We'd see them at our place on Thursday in St. Louis, winner take all.

My prognostications aside, I knew the game had to be played, and anything could happen. The baseball gods punish you for not respecting the game and your opponents—I've learned that the hard way. My hope was that maybe on September 28, 2011, when three other games around the major leagues had playoff implications, the gods would be distracted enough to let my sins go unnoticed.

Still, there was another potential distraction, one I'd been better at controlling because it belonged to me alone: if we lost and the Braves won, this would be my last game managing in Major League Baseball.

Several months before, in the middle of the summer when no one, especially me, had any idea what was going to happen with our year, I had decided that after thirty-three seasons in the major leagues, this was going to be my last as Cardinals manager, or manager of any team.

I'd been preaching the importance of focus for years. I'd been expecting our players to tune out some of the most important things in their lives so that their play would stay at a high level. Could I practice what I'd preached? If the season began to go downhill, if we fell out of playoff contention, would I be able to maintain my focus, or would I get caught up in memorializing each moment?

The funny thing is, I never had to answer those questions. Not long after my decision was made, our comeback began. As we climbed back into contention, the elephant in my room grew smaller. As we closed in on the wild card, it had been reduced to a barely audible mouse's squeak.

Now, on the verge of game 162, I had a lot of questions, but anxiety over the end of my career wasn't one of them. I knew we would continue to enjoy playing the game that night because there was something special about this team: they liked it when the stakes were high, and I'd seen *a lot of the players deal with situations like this one before. "Take it one game at time" is something you hear players and coaches alike spout almost daily. The thing is, these guys actually had fun doing that. They knew how to deal with the game they had in front of them. They knew not to think too far ahead. After all, that's pretty much the only way a team can claw back into the playoff race from ten and a half games back.*

I knew a moral victory wasn't enough for them; they'd come too far to settle. They wanted to finish the Astros and finish the comeback. In a few hours, I would remind them of what I believe they already sensed: that our regular season made for a very good story, but only a win, followed by several more, would make it a great story. You always want to be great.

One more game. That's all you can ever ask for.

CHAPTER ONE

Going the Distance

FOR A PROFESSIONAL BASEBALL MANAGER, THE ONLY THING WORSE than driving home 2,000 miles in October with your season over is having a 2,000-mile drive home when your season ended like ours did in 2010—a legitimate contender falling short. It's not the distance; it's the disappointment.

As it turned out, the distance was a plus; it gave me an opportunity to sort out 2010 and examine my uncertainties about 2011. On September 28, 2010, we'd been officially eliminated from a playoff berth. The excitement of counting down your "magic number" as the front-runner is replaced by the despair of seeing your "tragic number" being reduced to zero and elimination. The word *eliminated* is very appropriate—it feels like the whole season has been flushed down the toilet.

This was not my first postseason trek. My wife, Elaine, and I along with my daughters, Bianca and Devon, live in California. Following the 1996 season, my first in St. Louis, I'd made the same drive—three and half or four days—back home. In 1996, I was excited yet exhausted. That year had been the most difficult I'd ever had as a manager. We hadn't made it to the World Series, but we'd won the National League Central, swept the San Diego Padres in the Division Series, and gone to the National League Championship Series, where the Braves beat us. The loss to the Braves just shy of the World Series stung, yet there was plenty to be satisfied with, especially given where we'd been at the start of the year. We'd begun the season as twenty-five players and eight staff members wearing the same uniform, but we weren't really a team. After some very difficult challenges, some our staff had never before dealt with, we'd become a single unit. If we hadn't, we wouldn't have advanced as far as we did.

The drive in '96 had been the perfect bookend to the season—I was dog tired when I got into my car, but when I emerged on the West Coast I felt refreshed and inspired by what lay ahead.

I knew before my foot had even touched the gas pedal that this drive would be different, because 2010 was not 1996—not on the calendar and not on the field or in the clubhouse.

If I compared the story of the 2010 season to a drive back home, the difference between what I saw and what I'd hoped to see was slight. It wasn't like I'd viewed war-torn cities, derelict houses. Instead this city was one where the neighbors had let their lawns grow shaggy, hadn't pulled all the weeds, and maybe the kids had left their bikes outside in the grass.

The 2010 team didn't have the same level of intense focus, pitch by pitch and at-bat by at-bat, that had marked the successful clubs we'd had in St. Louis since the 2000 season. We hadn't been horrible. And maybe in another organization our performance might have been acceptable or the falloff that I saw would have been imperceptible to another pair of eyes. However, we'd slipped on my sliding scale from our customary 10 in 2009 to a 7 or 8 in 2010.

From about the 2000 season on, the Cardinals were really good a majority of the time. Many things contributed to our success, the first and most critical was the intensity that we brought to the competition. That's just one cornerstone. It got our team playing hard for nine innings, every day, all year long. Sure, we didn't embarrass ourselves in 2010, but we didn't get to the same level as teams like Atlanta, San Diego, San Francisco, and Cincinnati. They wanted it more than we did; that was not acceptable. The intensity hadn't disappeared altogether—it lurked beneath the surface—but it didn't have the same presence in the locker room, in the dugout, or on the field.

As I wound my way to California, I listened to the static-crackled accounts of the Phillies and Reds in the Division Series. I couldn't help but think about the nature of that radio signal's interference and how it affected communication. I wondered if maybe I hadn't done the right things to get through to people. You know, there's the expression that managers have to push the right buttons. Well, with the exception of the ones they wear on their uniforms, players don't have buttons. They aren't machines. They're human beings, and increasingly the number-one duty of a baseball manager and staff is to understand and relate to the diverse personalities of the players. Since the 1980s, that job had become even more critical, more time-consuming, and more challenging.

The issues we'd encountered as a team in 2010 were more than just pragmatic problems that any team might face. They felt more substantial, more systemic. I had a decision to make that was bigger than just making personnel changes around the diamond: I had to decide whether I would return in 2011 to manage again or retire.

After thirty-two years, I couldn't take the decision lightly. By July, I'd been thinking about it for weeks, but I still didn't have a good answer. Much of my indecision had to do with distance and perspective. Though the St. Louis Arch had long since receded in my rearview mirror, I was still back in the clubhouse and my office, still trying to figure out what to say to the guys that would fix the team's problems. Clearly, what we'd tried hadn't worked. Did that mean that it was time for me to go, to let someone else with a different approach reach this club a different way? I wasn't sure. So I sat there in my car, with the quiet hum of the play-by-play of the Division Series leaking out of my speakers, and reviewed everything about 2010, hoping to find my answer.

FOR YEARS, WHAT WE'D ALWAYS DONE AS A COACHING STAFF— equipment men to video guys, the strength and fitness coach, public relations people, the director of travel, everybody—was to personalize our relationships with the players. Whoever you were, my coaching staff and I wanted to establish a relationship with you. Not every player is the same, and not every position they play is the same. Our goal was to create an environment where the ballplayer looked forward to coming to work and knew that a bunch of people were trying to put him and his teammates in the best position to succeed.

You demonstrate that effort in a lot of ways—the strength of the drills, the quality of the facilities, the care and attention paid to every part of the workday—all of it adds up to a big positive. Wherever I'd managed, the ownership and front office supported those efforts. Without exception, the management—Bill Veeck, Jerry Reinsdorf, and Roland Hemond in Chicago; the Haas family and Sandy Alderson in Oakland; Bill DeWitt's group and Walt Jocketty and John Mozeliak in St. Louis—stayed this course through good times and tough times.

The new Busch Stadium, with all its upgrades for fans and players, complemented the "personalizing" philosophy. Our players totally appreciated the improved indoor batting cages, training equipment, weights, video room, dining facilities, meeting spaces, and locker rooms. I could go on, but the point is that all the thought put into those details—from batting practice to the blades of grass in the field—sent a positive and simple message to the players: we care. Whether a guy is on a hot streak or going through a slump, we want him to anticipate coming to the park knowing that he has our full support.

This simple concept of personalizing had been at the heart of my survival as a rookie manager in August 1979. As soon as I was actually standing in front of a major league team, I realized nothing was automatic about the attention they would pay to me and how well they would follow me. At first, I simply related to players as I remembered good managers relating to me. I remembered the style of those who'd made me feel better as a player, teammate, and competitor. John McNamara, Loren Babe, and Gus Niarhos all established a personal bond with their teams. They focused on having players respond with energy and competitiveness, and part of how they ensured that was to connect with the players on a personal level. Every season since my first this had become more and more the controlling philosophy of my management style with the players, the staff, and myself.

My awareness and emphasis on personalizing coincided with a shift in the players and in sports culture. During the 1980s, professional baseball was changing dramatically compared to my introduction to the major leagues in the '60s and '70s. The distractions of fame and fortune were a constant adversary to a manager focusing on team matters. The players were hearing many more voices than just their coach's, and those voices were telling them to get their numbers up to earn more money and attention. If the team wins, that's nice; if not, that's how it goes. In this changing landscape, the only effective way to lead was to personalize my interactions with the players, to form bonds with them individually. When it came to pushing our team message through all of those distractions and rhetoric, establishing a personal connection with all of my players was the only effective solution. It was hard, and it was time-consuming, but it worked.

Toward the end of my White Sox years and early on with the A's, I began to really understand personalization and why it met so well the leadership challenges of professional sports. Every team and every season has its own set of problems. By personalizing, I was creating a pattern of feedback that would address those problems—both big and small—that we faced as a team and as individuals. Together with the coaches, we would find the points that needed attention and craft messages to specific players, groups of players, or the whole team. In the process of personalizing these messages, we'd develop a number of "edges" that would help us compete individually and collectively. These edges ranged from the macro—team chemistry, handling adversity, making players' families feel welcome at the clubhouse—to more individual issues like physical and mental toughness, feeling comfortable in pressure situations, emphasizing process over results, and dealing with distractions. Depending on what needed to be emphasized in a given year, we would hone our relationships with the players to promote these edges as much as possible.

The edges gave us a competitive advantage, but we could only produce those edges by providing individual feedback. Those competitive edges all start with and come back to your relationships with your players.

Over the years I kept refining this personalizing philosophy and formalizing how I'd apply it to my leadership responsibilities. Before I could ask the players to take personal responsibility, I had to personalize my own efforts. The theory is only powerful if it works in *both* directions.

At the same time, personalizing with players never meant that everything they did was okay. We didn't sign any blank checks. You're kidding yourself if you think you'll win players' trust that way. You win them over with your honesty. In fact, one of the ways we'd show this throughout the season was in how we reacted when they made mistakes. Whatever the problem was, we'd tell them what they'd done—whether it was throwing to the wrong base, making a bad turn, or laying back on a ball—and we'd deal with it as a fact and not a judgment. We created an environment that recognized that mistakes would happen and would be corrected.

By the same token, I'd ask our players that if they had an issue with something to tell a member of the staff or me directly. It's a part of human nature to grouse about things, and long ago we'd designed a system to deal with complaints. Of course, it wouldn't always work, leading to frustration. The clubhouse is private, but sometimes we'd hear someone being critical and complaining about the organization—maybe it was the quality of the food we offered, the way a coach had waved a runner around to take another base, or how we handled travel arrangements. We don't allow those kinds of behind-the-back complaints. We expected everyone to be honest and direct. If something wasn't working, then it was up to us to keep experimenting to find ways to improve things. But for that to work, we needed everyone's candor.

When you create that kind of environment, the guys look forward to coming to the park. They come early, and they respond well to the various assessments and input coaches have for them.

In a system like ours, where I was constantly giving and receiving feedback from players, coaches, and everyone on staff, I was forced to pay attention to everything. I'd look at the clubhouse or the dugout every day to see if a different feeling existed than previously. I'd read into our interconnected relationships. I'd observe when people were getting to and leaving the ballpark. Would they work on things or just hang out? Maybe the weight room wasn't as active as it once was.

I was constantly on the alert for those kinds of things. As I thought about the 2010 season, the problem was that I couldn't find anything quantifiably different. It wasn't like I was taking attendance every day and noting down who was arriving when, who was in the weight room, and for how long. I was doing what we called "sniffing"—just testing the air. On the surface, things appeared to be as they had been the year before; the trouble was more a *feeling* than anything tangible I could point to. If you've ever come home after a trip away and everything looks like it's still in place, but something smells different, then you know what I'm talking about.

Whether on a baseball club or at your house, that's a tough thing to address and an even tougher thing to fix. In 2010, as we moved into the second half of the season, the best way to put it was that the environment in the clubhouse was colder, more clinically professional than it had been. The guys were there, and they were going about their business the right way, but it felt more like they were doing what they needed to do and less like they were doing what they really *wanted* to do.

Also the team's on-field performance didn't decline dramatically, but just enough to make me wonder if we could have finished higher. When you're with a group of guys for a full season and you're intently observing the whole time like I was, then some obvious issues emerge in the playing of the game. On a game-to-game basis, the at-bats we took were not consistently at the level that we'd expected. At times guys weren't having quality at-bats, whether it was waiting for a good pitch to hit, making adjustments for the count, or learning from how the pitcher had thrown to them the first time around. As a result, we'd see guys making the same outs over and over again. This slight degrading of the process also affected our pitching and defense.

Something happens once you give players the benefit of the doubt. It's a long season. Guys get fried. You try to rest them to help them take a fresh approach to the game. But when the same drop-offs happen with greater frequency, then the first thing that pops into your mind is that the team, individual by individual, is not as excited about competing to its best level.

That's one of the things we demand of our players, and that's one of the things that was elusive about 2010. Because our intensity was down, the executions were not as good as we were capable of.

After the All-Star break, we had the last of our four regularly scheduled team meetings. In that last meeting, probably the most important point I made was that we had to understand there were teams in our league that were really excited about their chances of winning. One was Cincinnati. Cincinnati hadn't had a winning year in a while, but they were playing well and brought a lot of heat to the competition. It was clear that the Padres and Giants also liked their chances and were doing everything possible to exploit them. In Atlanta, Bobby Cox was in his last year, and they were into the competition as well. As I told our club in that post–All-Star break meeting, we were missing an edge compared to these other clubs, and we needed to make sure that nobody got into the competition more than we did.

Unfortunately, my speech seemed to provide only a short-term boost, but I didn't let it go. As part of my daily routine after the All-Star break, I'd talk with the guys individually, personalizing player by player and rotating through the roster to be certain that I spoke with everyone at one point or another. In this capacity, I ended up talking with individuals, small groups, and, a few times, the entire team—all while trying to get that *feeling,* that drive, back. We went on little hot spurts here and there, but nothing sustained.

A legitimate question would be whether the loss of intensity ever caused a loss of temper. It never did. The effect on me was real concern, but that concern never led to me ripping into them. Intensity at a 7 or 8 level was respectable. As a consequence, we'll never know how many extra wins we could have earned if we had been a 9 or a 10.

Over the years I've had the occasional after-game clubhouse explosion. It was always caused by a game that lacked at least the minimum amount of effort and competitive fire. In the old days, mostly in Chicago and Oakland, I'd walk into the clubhouse and toss the postgame spread on the floor. Finally, it dawned on me that I was penalizing the wrong guys. After all, it was the clubhouse staff who had to clean up the mess. So, in the second half of my career, I changed tactics.

After an interleague game against Detroit when we lost 10–1, I went into the clubhouse and locked the doors to the eating room. By the looks on their faces, I knew they were thinking, *Okay, let's get this over with so we can go eat.* I stepped in front of them and said:

"This is unacceptable. What the hell is going on? One day we compete. The next we don't. My bottom line is this: tonight's Saturday night in Detroit. Since you didn't compete during the game, I want you to have to compete to get a reservation in a really nice restaurant, because you're not going to eat this food. I locked the door. You're not going to get it. So you shower and get out of here as soon as you can. You didn't compete today, but you will compete for food tonight.

"And by the way, tomorrow we leave here. If anybody short-changes the clubhouse guy on tips because you didn't eat your meal in here tonight and I find out, then I'm going to fine you about five times what the dues are and give it back to him. So in other words, in my opinion, we mailed it in today, and it's not acceptable. It isn't the clubhouse guy's fault; it's our fault."

The next day I was in the visiting manager's office, and one of the coaches said to me, "Hey, you've got to see this."

I went out in the clubhouse thinking this was a new day and a new game. And there in Eric Davis's locker I see a paper bag. Now, Eric Davis was a quality pro. He'd already won a title in 1990 with the Reds. He always kept in great shape, and he was a veteran presence— witty, smart. I looked at Eric and asked him what was in there.

He says, "Hey, skip, I know I'm not playing today. If these guys pull that same shit as they did yesterday and you shut that door, I brought myself a sandwich. I'm going to eat."

I couldn't help but bust out laughing.

THE ANNOUNCER'S VOICE POPPED THROUGH THE RADIO FUZZ AS I wound my way home to California on Saturday, October 9. I'd just driven across the Colorado border listening to Game 3 of the American League Division Series (ALDS) between Texas and Tampa Bay. Texas had impressively won the first two games on the road. Early in the game the commentators were praising the Rangers and counting the Rays out. Their words got my adrenaline going because they were disrespecting the Rays' well-earned reputation for competing in the tough AL East. Down 2–1, the Rays scored two in the eighth inning and three more in the ninth to win 6–3. I started honking my horn to honor their tenacity.

Even as I was caught up in my reaction to the Rays' comeback win, including the manager's moves late in the game and the media comments, the game also brought me back to our own 2010 season. Mostly I couldn't shake the fact that the responses to my efforts to increase our intensity had been only sporadic. What I kept coming back to was the possibility that I wasn't the right messenger anymore.

As is usually the case with most really significant problems, some extra considerations made the solution harder to find. In recent years, we'd developed a hard-edged rivalry with the Cincinnati Reds. We'd played them eighteen times in 2010, and even though they won the division, we had finished with twelve wins and only six losses. In fact, the next-to-last series in August featured some on-field scrapes and the ugliest incident I had ever witnessed. Johnny Cueto, their young pitcher, had spiked Carpenter in the back and kicked Jason LaRue in the head. Jason suffered a concussion that ended his career. We'd responded by sweeping the Reds in August and taking two of three in September. At least in that series, our intensity was exactly where it needed to be.

Yet, after the Reds series, we were back below our intensity standard, and even now there wasn't a good answer why. I finally decided to trust the end-of-year process that I'd begun near the end of my time in Oakland. I'd review the season and the future with people in the front office, with a small group of veteran players, and with myself. I wanted to make sure that I was still the right man for the job the next year.

I'm the first to admit that, at least on the surface, it's an odd system. Throughout the years there's been a lot of confusion in the sports media about why I do this. Some people said it was because, before committing to return, I wanted to create drama or because I wanted to have my ass kissed or some nonsense like that. Not true.

The correct answer was this: if I were a fan, I would want these questions answered about the next year's manager. I wanted to make sure that everyone in the organization—including myself—still believed I was the right man for the job. To me, anything less than this thorough evaluation would mean I was a fraud—because I'd have my job based on my work from the past, not the present.

Each year the process I'd go through was the same. The season would end—whether it was where we wanted it to or not—and shortly after that, my first stop would be the front office to find out if they wanted me back. At the end of the 2010 season, before my drive back, I'd sat down with owner Bill DeWitt and general manager John Mozeliak, who I most often refer to as "Mo," and they both indicated that they wanted me to return.

Once I had the decision from the front office, my second stop was the players. The question that the players needed to answer was "Am I still the leader you will follow?" Every year I was there, this became more and more important, because at some point the players get tired of listening to you. They're looking for a new voice—that's just kinda the way it is. And if you have determined that the players are really no longer listening to you, then even if you've been offered a job, you're taking the owner's money on false pretenses.

I always broached this question the same way: I would meet with a committee of guys who I thought were respected in the clubhouse. This leadership committee—I called them our "co-signers" because they were responsible for "co-signing" onto the team's priorities—was something I used throughout the season for all kinds of team issues. This group was made up of guys like Chris Carpenter, Albert Pujols, Matt Holliday, and several others. I liked using the term *co-signers* because it implied that they'd made a binding agreement to be on board with what we were trying to do as a club. I can't claim this idea as my own. Bill Walsh, the great San Francisco 49ers coach, shared it with me. When I was in Oakland, I would go to breakfast or lunch with him two or three times an off-season. He explained how you take the guys who are respected as leaders and you convince them that what you and the coaches are selling is legitimate and they have a right to challenge it. He always said that he did 75 percent of his talking to 25 percent of this team.

This leadership committee would be responsible for determining whether or not I was still the one they thought the team wanted to follow.

So after management said they wanted me back, I spoke to the co-signers, and to a man the guys told me that there wasn't anything that I could have done. They agreed with the assessment about both the loss of edge on the field and the coolness in the clubhouse. But there was something else, something they hadn't told me about until then.

The co-signers told me that there had been a problem within our clubhouse involving team unity, especially in the second half of the season. I was disappointed at this news for many reasons, but mostly because if the relationship between the co-signers and the manager and coaching staff is going to work effectively, they need to tell me explicitly what is going on when it's actually happening. By "going on" I don't mean that they told me something insidious was happening in the clubhouse, like a drug or alcohol issue or anything like that. It was more that the players hadn't come together in a productive way—and the co-signers felt that this lack of cohesion contributed to the lack of intensity. Perhaps the worst part was that a number of them said that they didn't look forward to coming to the ballpark as much as they had in the past. I thought that was key.

Personally, I was also disappointed that I hadn't detected precisely what was going on and so, without a heads-up from the players, our staff hadn't had a chance to fix things. Frustrated as I was, I understood their reluctance to come forward. A clubhouse is a kind of sanctified space where teammates want and need to feel a kind of immunity from being forced to testify against one another. They have to be able to trust in those bonds that define being a teammate.

One thing to understand: none of this is about pointing fingers. I never do that. I worked very hard in my years as a big league manager to earn a reputation for addressing players privately, not publicly, and for stressing how very much like a family a team needs to be. Part of the respect and trust we'd earned as a staff working together came from our duty to put our asses on the line and, on rare occasions, to cover one another's asses. We did that because we believed it was the right thing to do as leaders. I'm not going to throw all of that out the window and talk here to any great degree about specific incidents involving particular players as they relate to this issue of a decline in team cohesiveness and that unsettling feeling we all acknowledged. I know that as fans you get frustrated when you read that a player, coach, manager, or member of the team's management has said that the matter is going to be handled internally; however, that's how families handle problems.

The bottom line with 2010 was that we ended the season with team chemistry issues. How that figured into our season numerically is difficult to say. What I can tell you is this, and I believe it: Roland Hemond—the most beloved guy still alive in baseball—once told me, "If you have true chemistry on your team, it will be like tomorrow I added a superstar to your roster—a twenty-game winner, a top closer, or a 30/30/30 middle-of-the-lineup hitter."

Would that help your team? Oh yeah, it would, and over the years there's no doubt in my mind that chemistry contributes or detracts to that significant of a degree.

On the other side, rarely does a team without the chemistry edge win unless they have a real superiority in talent. In some ways that was true of the Oakland A's of the glory days of the 1970s. They were a dysfunctional bunch, to be sure, but what people forget is that they had a unifying force working for them—their dislike and distrust of their owner, Charles O. Finley. In chemistry terms, Finley was a catalyst, crystallizing all the divergent interests and egos on the team for those few hours when the players were on the field. As a teammate of most of those players in either the minor or major leagues, I can attest that they had terrific competitive chemistry. In fact, I believe they enjoyed their mystique.

You need chemistry to win ball games—it's as simple as that. I knew it, and the co-signers knew it, and now we were all aware that it had been an issue in the second half of 2010. But despite these revelations that came out of my meeting with the co-signers, their answer to the question of whether I was the right person to lead the team was "yes." They were unanimous.

This led to the third and final step: my own personal gut check to see if the competitive fires were still burning as hot as ever. Was I ready for another season? Was I hungry for it? These were the questions that I'd been asking myself for years, and almost always I'd answered yes without hesitation. This year, though, was different, and that was where I found myself as I sped toward California.

As I pushed my way to the edge of Nevada, the playoffs were in full swing. The series that excited me the most involved the Braves and Giants, two teams led by outstanding managers I admired and respected, Bobby Cox and Bruce Bochy.

I was feeling every pitch and situation from both sides. At the end, I was sad for Bobby and glad for Bruce. Feeling that close to October baseball had ignited my competitive fire.

Looking out at the vast expanses of land all around the four-lane highway, I found myself visualizing the fun of October and thinking about how much I liked our ball club. Next year would be a fresh chance, especially if we could make a couple of off-season moves. I knew that things would have to change. If we were going to win, as a club this problem of intensity would have to go away. But I kept coming back to the fact that the co-signers had been united in their certainty that these problems could be fixed. Replaying our conversations, I found myself starting to believe as well. This group was capable of amazing things; given the right setup and the right chemistry, they could accomplish an enormous amount.

With each mile that passed, I felt more certain that I was not done, not by a long shot. I'd been in this too long, and cared about these players too much, to find myself done in by something like chemistry.

When I finally arrived in California, my fire was full burn. My gut check complete. I got out of my car, stretched my legs, greeted my family, and called Mo, telling him that, yes, as a matter of fact, I would love the opportunity to manage another year.

CHAPTER TWO

Spring Starts at Zero

B Y THE TIME THE GIANTS WERE WRAPPING UP THE SERIES, I WAS
as eager as I'd ever been to start work on next year's Cardinals
team. I liked, respected, and trusted the group of players who would
form the core of the team, but throughout the organization I could
sense dissatisfaction with our second-place finish and a determination to do whatever necessary to improve our 2011 championship
chances.

Some of my optimism sprang from an outstanding meeting that
Mo conducted at the end of the season. The group included Bill
DeWitt, Mo's front-office staff, and our major league staff. We agreed
that our team, coming off the Division Championship in 2009 and
contending in 2010, needed tweaking in several areas, but not a complete overhaul. We evaluated our talent as measured by whether we
thought they were of championship quality.

Each of our two top-of-the-rotation guys, Adam Wainwright and
Chris Carpenter, could have been a number one on just about any
other club in either league. They were that good. That's a great position to be in. Dave Duncan, our pitching coach and resident genius,

and I have gone around and around on this issue for most of the nearly three decades we've worked together. A former major league catcher, Dunc's insights into the art and craft of pitching are justifiably legendary. We play a kind of "who would you rather have on your staff?" speculation game. This isn't about individual players but about slots on the staff. Dunc would rather have a top-of-the-rotation ace like Wainwright or Carp—not just an innings muncher but a guy who can shut down the opposition. He believes that the Carps, the Wainwrights, the Roy Halladays—in other words, the perennial Cy Young contenders—are a must-have in comparison to a top-flight closer.

I agree, but if you can only have one of those two, I think it's the other way around, and the Dennis Eckersleys, Bruce Sutters, and Mariano Riveras—the Hall of Fame closers—are more important to a pitching staff and a team's success. Ideally, you'd have both kinds of pitchers, and the teams that do generally fare pretty well.

Last year my buddy Jim Leyland of the Tigers had the Cy Young winner and Most Valuable Player in Justin Verlander and the Rolaids Relief Pitcher of the Year in Jose Valverde (who was a perfect 49-for-49 in saves in the regular season), and won their division and knocked out the Yankees in the Division Series. Another example that you can be good enough to get into the playoffs but that doesn't guarantee that you can win it all.

Staffing decisions are complicated and crucial. That's why, in our postseason evaluations, we are so tenacious in assessing our needs. Add to that the economic realities of the game and the payroll limits that every owner and management team has to acknowledge, and suddenly the setting of priorities for off-season acquisitions can make for a lot of late nights hashing over the input from scouts and analytics (numbers) people, as well as from the uniformed staff, the accountants, and the executives.

Armed with that meeting's input, Mo and his staff went to work on the off-season process. I was impressed by Mo's grasp of our internal issues: he was considering our chemistry with every addition to the club. First, we needed another middle-of-the-lineup bat to join Matt and Albert. One of the issues we'd dealt with in 2010 was having to push one of our young players, David Freese, Allen Craig, or Colby Rasmus, into the middle of the order sometimes. For young guys, the demands of hitting in the four and five spots can be too much of a load too soon. Those guys had done well, but we thought we could be better there, and those three, among others, could really thrive hitting elsewhere in the order.

The second thing we had to address was our bullpen. We knew we wanted to have some protection at the end of the game. Ryan Franklin had just completed a very good year—twenty-seven saves out of twenty-nine opportunities—but you're always better with depth. We had a lot of youth in our bullpen, but you just never know for sure how quickly they're going to mature. We'd learned a long time ago that it's much better to bring them along at their own pace than to force them because you have no further alternatives. With that in mind, we wanted to look for a real quality setup guy who could pitch the eighth inning as well as the ninth on days when Ryan wasn't available. We wanted to add another left-handed specialty guy, the one- or two-out man so critical to a team's ability to hold leads or keep it in position to win a game late.

The third position we needed to solidify was shortstop. Brendan Ryan, our shortstop from the 2010 season, would be used to acquire a young power arm to add depth to our minor league system. And last but not least, because of the unfortunate incident in Cincinnati, we were looking for a backup catcher to replace Jason LaRue.

The first move we made in the 2010–2011 off-season was to get shortstop Ryan Theriot from the Dodgers. We'd seen and liked him a lot when he was in our division playing for the Cubs. In what proved to be a key move—not only because it met our first priority but because of the quality of the player and the individual—we signed Lance Berkman, who was a free agent. The Yankees had picked him up in a kind of rent-a-player deal in 2010, and even by his own admission, he hadn't done as well as he would have liked in New York. We were willing to take a chance on him, knowing that a switch-hitting power hitter with a near-.300 career average who was closing in on 400 home runs doesn't become available every day. Over the years we had been beaten many times by a healthy Berkman playing for the Astros. Besides having seen for ourselves that Berkman was a clutch, winning player, we also knew that in 2010 he'd taken many at-bats hitting on one leg due to a knee injury. We gambled, but we were certain about his intangibles.

We addressed our other needs by signing Gerald Laird at catcher to back up Yadi Molina and Nick Punto as a utility infielder. On the mound, we improved ourselves by keeping Jake Westbrook as a starter and signing Miguel Batista and Brian Tallet for our bullpen.

With his focus on the chemistry priority, Mo really hit a grand slam. Each player we added had a well-deserved reputation as a tough competitor and a good teammate.

For me, February 1 has always been the time when I'd feel the off-season ending and the preseason beginning. Usually that means working up a checklist of *t*'s to cross and *i*'s to dot. I was determined to honor one of my pet philosophies—no regrets. Once a challenge is complete, I want to know that there is nothing else that could have been done.

I didn't want to leave any stone unturned, so I detoured to Pebble Beach to meet with New England Patriots coach Bill Belichick. My purpose was to get Bill's thinking on competitive urgency. For years I had marveled at how season after season Bill's team approached each game with the same great intensity. Despite how busy he was, I met with him to get his latest thinking on three elements of our approach: team concept, game-to-game intensity, and the relationship between the staff and the players. His words struck home, and I'll never be able to thank him for the long hours he spent with me.

I had one last thing to do before camp began. I had to go to St. Louis to meet with state legislators about a puppy mill proposition on behalf of the Animal Rescue Foundation (ARF) that my wife, Elaine, and I began in 1991. We started it after a stray cat wandered onto the field in 1990. The cat was threatened with being put down, and Elaine and I found a home for her.

WE TAKE SPRING TRAINING VERY SERIOUSLY. JUST LIKE SCORING early in games and getting in the first strike are about firsts, so is spring training.

This was always the first chance we had to set the tone for the up-coming season for the players. We did that from the very beginning when we met as a staff on the day the pitchers and catchers first officially reported. Mo, other front-office people, and the various minor league coordinators would join the major league staff, and we'd go over the camp roster, focusing on the players whom we believed had a legitimate shot at making the club.

I reminded everyone of something John Madden taught me: spring training starts at zero. We were going to take nothing for granted—on several levels. One step at a time, all the coaches needed to establish that the players respected and trusted us. All the coaches need to demonstrate competence, a passion to teach, a work ethic, and the understanding that this was the players' time—we had to emphasize the personal.

Then we established the priorities we wanted to focus on in the camp and throughout the season. For example, the way 2010 had ended, we wanted to improve our situational at-bats, beginning with better strike zone discipline, so we structured drills and constantly emphasized it in camp in 2011. The same was true with one of the keys in pitching—first-pitch strikes. On defense, we wanted to continue our defense-first mentality. Last but not least, we were going to drive home the point about maintaining our competitive urgency. I was going to present that last item to the co-signers when I met with them.

The following day pitchers and catchers were in uniform for their first practices. We held a quick meeting to reassure them that we felt our best way to win was by stopping the other club first—that starts with them. We were also going to maintain our philosophy of the position players spending more time working defensive drills than offensive drills to support their efforts. Dunc spoke to the pitchers about the need to be smart in camp—take advantage of Pete Prinzi, the strength and conditioning coach, don't avoid using the training room, and especially pitch to their current level of conditioning. Don't show us the best you've got until you are 100 percent there physically. I added that they had the toughest spring training challenge because they had a comparatively small number of drills that they'd have to do ad nauseam. The staff saw this as the first challenge they faced in competing—maxing out those repetitions showed us they were into it. We'd learned not to fall in or out of love early in camp. Overthrowing wouldn't show us anything but that you were overthrowing.

For four days, we had the pitchers only, so we had additional time to map out how we'd conduct things once the position players arrived. From early in the off-season to the day of the first meeting of the full squad, the challenge of coming up with a message or theme that would set the right tone was constantly on my mind. I'd been through a lot of springs, so had many of the players, including a few with me, so coming up with something fresh was difficult. That's why I met with other coaches and other leaders trying to get new approaches and insights. I couldn't assume that the players were into the idea of competing to the extent that we wanted and needed them to be.

Delivering a message that would energize today's players was the first critical hurdle I faced. If I could get them enthused, then all the work they'd do the rest of the camp would take on new meaning. Their energy would translate into winning. I'd delivered a similar message for years: "Sometimes winning just means finishing above .500." But delivering that message was not nearly as much fun as talking about a realistic shot at the postseason.

Some years, the message is easy to come by. For example, in 1989, the year after the A's lost to the Dodgers in the World Series, we were a team on a mission. We wanted to get back to the Series and not be denied the championship. For 2011, I decided to tell the guys that we had to be aware of the uniform we all put on and the history and the meaning associated with it. That meant that because of all those years of past success, we came into camp with a chance to be successful. Since 2000, I'd been able to say that every year. Each year the torch had been passed on. With few exceptions we'd carried that flame into October. One exception was last year. So not only did we have a bunch of players who'd participated in that October history, we'd added a number of players who fit our club real well with their talents and their pedigree for being gamers and winners. The only thing missing from that equation was how we'd embrace this opportunity.

The lesson I'd repeated for quite a few years was that, in the end, it came down to how we got into the competition. Everything else sprang from that. Money, security, and fame were by-products of competing as hard as we could. *They were not right next to it and they were not ahead of it—they came after it.* If you get the players excited for the right reason, then they'll be eager to hear how you're going to get this all done.

When I finally delivered those words, I then asked several veterans if they agreed or disagreed with this statement: Were they ever disappointed by a winning experience? To a man they said, "No."

How we were going to make this happen had a lot to do with the great facility we had. Having six and a half diamonds meant that we'd be able to get a lot of work done in a short amount of time. I next asked a few guys how many big league camps they'd been to. Two. Five. One. I then turned to Red Schoendienst and asked him the same question.

"Sixty-six."

I watched the eyebrows go up.

"What was it like for most of them?"

"One diamond. A nine-to-five day. You maybe got four to six swings if you were a new guy, a dozen for the veterans. Old balls, too, maybe a half dozen new ones to start, not so new the next."

I then summed up the point. Don't take these facilities for granted; take advantage of them. I knew that I'd never do that because I had too many memories of another spring training facility. My first full spring as the manager of the White Sox in 1980, we started at the minor league camp that had four fields. After that, when the games started, we moved to the big league camp that had just one diamond. To compensate for that, we set up a diamond in the parking lot to do bunt defense drills and a few others. I had to organize the program around the fact that at 11:30, cars started to come into the lot. Necessity truly is the mother of invention, and those deficits back then, in comparison to today, made me a more creative and flexible manager.

That first full spring training I was lucky enough to have Chuck Tanner, who'd just managed the Pittsburgh Pirates to victory in the 1979 World Series, mentoring me. This had come about because our general manager, Roland Hemond, had a long association with Chuck, and because the White Sox were playing in Sarasota, Florida, and the Pirates were headquartered right next door in Bradenton. Chuck laid out a three-pronged approach for me.

The first aspect was physical: make sure that everything about your players—their legs, their core, their arms, their hands—is in shape. All the baseball activities—taking ground balls and fly balls, batting practice, were a part of that conditioning. We sometimes had the guys take upward of two hundred swings a day, toughening their hands and their muscles.

The second of Chuck's keystones was the fundamentals. All those "routine" plays, all those pieces that get executed hundreds of times over the course of a season—they all needed to be practiced mercilessly. The way you make those fundamentals sound is to do the right thing over and over to the point where it becomes automatic and you can make the plays by pushing that figurative button that allows you to execute them. As a result of that kind of preparation, you won't get bogged down by those routine plays. You can then concentrate on the uniqueness of that day's game. If you're finally called on to execute a bunt to win a game or a pennant, all that work on bunting fundamentals in spring training will make that possible. The same can be said for any other basic offensive or defensive play.

The third and final preparation that Chuck convinced me was a crucial part of spring training was also the most important: you want to walk out of spring training mentally strong. Part of this mental strength comes from players having a good baseball IQ. If a player doesn't understand the rationale for, say, moving a runner over or guarding the line, he's not going to be as big of an asset to the club as someone who understands all parts of the game. The litmus test is if you can look at the scoreboard and have it tell you what you should be thinking.

The second part of the mental side, the more critical aspect, is getting players to understand that "mental toughness" is something they can acquire. *If they decide to make something important, then they can make it happen.* It's all about making a choice—you can be tough, you can play through a minor injury, you can get through a slump. It's all about control and knowing that you possess it, but it's your choice whether or not you activate it. Players also have to recognize that if they choose not to activate it, they aren't going to play for the Cardinals.

In keeping with this plan, I told the guys that we were going to get ready in the three ways—physically, fundamentally, and mentally. In that first meeting, I highlighted some of the things we were going to do to prepare them physically. Then I let them know that over the course of the next couple of days, we'd transition into those other emphases.

I would always wrap up that first-day meeting by reminding them that the Cardinal way means effort and execution. What I'd explain was that a whole lot of spring training was about putting total effort into the practices and the games. Two types of players called our locker room home—those who had a choice and those who didn't. A certain number of players knew they would be in St. Louis for opening day. For a lot of spring training work, those players would choose the level of their effort and execution. They'd earned that choice and we trusted that they were going to use their experience to peak on opening day. The majority, though, were in the no-choice category— they had no choice about effort and execution. They had to max out all the time, or our choice would be that they were going to the minor league camp. Given these two groups, we had a huge advantage; that group of guys who had a choice always chose to max out, so others followed their lead.

After two full days of workouts, I held a second meeting. There, the emphasis was on the concept of what it meant to be a team. We were going to come together as a family. One of the examples we used to let the players know how that gets done was not to show one another up publicly, be it on the field or in comments made after the game. If we scored seven runs and lost, no one would bitch about the pitchers not getting anyone out. If we scored no runs, no one would bitch about the hitters not getting any runs. They could think that. They chould challenge one another in the clubhouse, but not in the media.

Also, to keep the team together, we were going to discuss how we protect our hitters if the other side attempts to intimidate us.

We stressed the team chemistry component and how that related to three important words: *Respect. Trust. Caring.* If chemistry can have the effect that Roland Hemond said, that "superstar" added to the roster, then we all had to work on establishing those three components. The players had to demonstrate that they earned respect and trust and cared for their teammates and the team. They earned respect by having enough talent to help us win, but more than that, by proving that they were willing to put what the team needed ahead of their own interests. They earned trust by being ready to contribute every day. They were going to be there whenever they were needed.

Caring is something some people don't really consider when thinking about a baseball team, but it's an essential part of our team concept. That said, we've had selfish individuals who cared more about themselves than the team. They earned respect and trust and contributed to us winning. But the selfish player is the one who misses out. If he's not included in that team feeling, then his experience pales in comparison to what the other guys do. The "I" or "me" player just doesn't have as much fun.

The last point I made that day was that if we did this camp right, then the first twelve days for the pitchers and eight days for the position players would involve a lot of effort and repetition. They'd do a lot of work and they'd get tired. By the time they were sick of those drills, the games would begin. Everyone would get excited and a natural kick of adrenaline arrives. The workouts would be shorter before the games and then they'd get to have some fun playing. The point here was that we didn't want the players to pace themselves. We'd do that for them.

Toward the end of the meeting, the guys sent a message to me and to one another. We have a no-cell-phones rule during these meetings: Turn them off or risk a one-hundred-dollar fine. As I was rounding third and heading for home in my remarks, a cell phone started bleating. Along with that ring tone, you could hear a pin dropping. Much turning around and patting of pockets ensued. I looked out and there was Gerald Laird, a holy crap look of indignation and shock on his face. He sat there staring at his phone like it was an alien artifact. Beyond him, I could see a group of veterans snickering like little boys. That will teach you to go to the head and leave your phone behind so someone could turn your phone on.

While Chuck's three points didn't include preparing for practical jokes, they were general rules that I followed each year. I also used Lou Piniella's notion of dividing spring training into three sections in order to get off to a fast start. The first, the "happy to be back" phase, can be high-energy and intense. You've got the guys' attention, they've been away from the game for a while, and they're eager to go, so you work them. In the second phase, about two weeks into the games, you give them a bit of a break. The games have begun, and you back off on some of the intense drill work, shorten the day, all in preparation for phase three. As the squad is reduced and the pitchers go deeper into games, with about a week to ten days to go, you get back to regular work, review the fundamentals one last time, and begin to point toward opening day. Lou had a winning career as a player and a manager and is a good friend. His three-phase spring training insight is the perfect fit for the energy level of camp.

During our third meeting, day five for the position players, the subject was the priorities we'd set in the staff's pre-camp meeting— at-bats, first strikes, and reestablishing the competition edge that we'd had for so long. That relentless competing asset of ours is completely a part of our makeup—the mental side of the game. Just as we'd worked on hitting, pitching, and defense, we were going to have conversations about this subject. Primarily the point was not to have any regrets at the end of the season.

The edges that separated us from the rest of the competition would be our keys to walking away without regrets and to winning, things like our execution and our effort.

Just to keep the guys on their toes and to keep it light, I concluded that meeting by asking Tony Cruz, our young backup catcher, this loaded question, "Are you willing to do everything it takes to help this club win?"

Tony nodded very seriously and said, "Yes."

"Would you go down to AAA Memphis?"

He looked shocked for a few seconds until the other guys laughed. Got 'em.

At subsequent meetings, we usually discussed gaining additional edges, such as dealing with mistakes and handling adversity. Adversity was always huge, and normally, I concluded the camp by talking about it. Unfortunately in 2011, we had to deal with it immediately.

On February 21, a week into camp, Adam Wainwright felt some discomfort in his right elbow. A week later, he underwent Tommy John surgery to replace his ulnar collateral ligament. His season was over before it had even begun. We were stunned. Adam seemed opening day ready, was that sharp, and then bam!, we got the bad news.

Telling the ball club was tough. We all felt bad for Adam, and he did his part to help us get over the shock and disappointment of losing a frontline starter for the year. He sent an email around to everyone, letting us know that he'd still be with us, in body and spirit. He would do most of his rehab from the surgery in St. Louis. Adam is a great guy, a devout family man, and a real competitor.

We had some major league shoes to fill, but as difficult as it is to say this, if he had to go down for the season with that injury, at least it happened early enough in spring training that we could regroup mentally, find another guy in the rotation to take up the slack, and have enough time to reset the rotation that had had Adam starting opening day. That's a few small blessings to count in comparison to the coolness under pressure, the command of the strike zone, and the strong work ethic that Adam possesses. That said, we were fortunate that we'd have Jake Westbrook with us for the full season. Dunc could work his magic on him. We'd also added a valuable veteran presence in the bullpen with the Renaissance man Miguel Batista, a hard-nosed writer of poetry who we hoped would also bring his artistry to painting the corners. Things were looking so good with the bullpen that we ended up sending down Fernando Salas and Eduardo Sanchez, young talents who had improbable springs.

Still, it's an understatement to say that Adam's loss was a huge blow to the club. After his injury, the sports media began to write our obituary for the season. No one thought we could do it without him. *Devastated* was the word that we heard most often from our fans. The media experts were more objective and less dramatic, but their ominous tone was similar. A national magazine stated that we were out of the division race and it would be either the Brewers or the Reds. Later, they ran another piece that picked us to finish fourth because Wainwright was that irreplaceable. What none of them realized was the power of having a huge chip on your shoulder. Our team took being counted out personally, and the character of the group started to show itself.

Though it was hard to keep the guys from dwelling on the media's ominous predictions, I reminded everyone of Lou Holtz's line that we had to think about what we had and not focus on what we didn't have. Every club faces adversity. The games still count. Nobody cares—they still want you to win.

The intensity that Adam's injury inspired followed us through much of spring training. Hard as it was, I had to like how the squad handled his loss, and it was then that I started to see that there was something special about this group. It was then that I started to feel certain that the problems that had dogged us in 2010 had been an aberration of that year. We were getting our message across in 2011. Unfortunately, this wasn't the only bit of adversity we'd have to overcome.

When it came to communicating those spring training priority messages, I always handled it the same way: the co-signers were the messengers. Regardless of the specific priorities, motivations, and personalities of a given team or season, that committee of respected players would reinforce the message. One of the things we always took a lot of pride in was the mentoring system we put in place wherever I was coaching: our veterans would take the responsibility to show the young guys that they were welcome and part of the team, but they would also stress that the new guys had to live up to our standards of competing—the respect, the trust, the caring. So I'd tell the leaders what I thought our priorities were and give them an opportunity to challenge me or add on anything they wanted to bring up from the year before. And once they'd accepted the priorities of the team, they'd help carry that message to the other players.

In our co-signers' meeting that spring of 2011, I brought two major priorities for spring training to them: One was about the urgency issue. The second priority, for the first time ever, was about a specific player.

I told our committee: "If this guy gets on board and joins what we're trying to do to the best of his ability, he could take us from good offense to really good and from really good to great. That's because he's got the qualities of an impact player. And that's Colby Rasmus."

I had never focused on one player before.

Colby was the classic example of a young, talented player who had to learn a lot about success in pro ball while playing with the extra burdens of being a number-one draft choice and the high expectations that come from that, while also contributing to a contending team. In some ways that is a unique challenge. Accepting personal responsibility meets that challenge.

Now, I've coached a lot of young players. Some I've clicked with right off the bat, and there have been very few I never managed to connect with at all. With some, things started off slowly and got better over time. My rule of thumb with young guys is this: three years. We've got three years to reach a young player when he first arrives in the major leagues. After that it's too late; the player acquires more power over his career through forces such as salary arbitration and free agency. Those early years provide you the best opportunity to impress upon him the values of competition, excellence, team, and other responsibilities. What you see all too often when this window is missed is a player and an organization suffering as the player gives in to selfishness and accepts less than his best.

With some players, you can tell after two years that it's going to be hard to turn them around, but with Colby I was still optimistic.

For one thing, I'd seen a handful of times when he did respond well to feedback. In those moments, it was clear what he could do if we were able to focus him better. I remembered well those moments when it was clear we hadn't lost him yet, that he was still worth the team's effort, the co-signers' effort, the coaches' effort, and my effort.

After some discussion, the co-signers agreed to commit themselves to a fresh approach to getting Colby to be a part of what we did. If it worked, we'd be a better team for it. If it didn't, we would know that we'd done everything we could to bring him on board.

Having a three, four, and five of Albert, Matt, and Lance was looking good as spring training went on. Berkman wasn't hitting a ton, but he was making good, solid contact, and his bat speed was where it needed to be. We knew he was an offensive force, but we didn't really appreciate his solid defensive play until we witnessed it day in and day out in spring training. He was getting good jumps on the ball in the outfield, and he had a really accurate arm with a quick release and always hit the cutoff man. Playing for Rice University as a collegian had helped make him fundamentally sound.

What pleased us almost as much as his play was his demeanor. Lance is a Texan, and I can't quite say that he possessed that stereotypical "good ole boy" demeanor, but he was an engaging presence. From the very beginning of spring training, guys just seemed to gravitate toward him. He was quick with the quip, the well-timed, well-aimed put-down, and the story, but unlike a lot of ballplayers who can bring the funny and not much else, he was also great on the field. He seemed to have a switch that not a lot of fun players have— turning it on, he could go from clubhouse comedian to cold-blooded competitor instantly and effectively. His kind of veteran presence was exactly what we needed to help warm up a clubhouse environment that had ended 2010 on a cold streak.

I don't know if it's mathematically possible, but by starting from zero again that spring, our new additions and our renewed commitment had me feeling like we were already more than just plus two.

CHAPTER THREE

Opening Day

FOR A GAME THAT IS ONLY ONE-162TH OF A SEASON, OPENING DAY gets an inordinate amount of attention. That doesn't just come from fans and the media—the players feel it too. Your home opener is a big deal, and 2011 was no different. Any time you line up along the baselines, anytime the club brings out some of its stars from the past, and, in St. Louis, anytime the majestic Clydesdale horses take their ceremonial lap around the field, the atmosphere before the game becomes magical. You want to savor opening day, but you also need to get through it and over it so that you can get into the flow of the season. Still, opening day is an important touchstone: it gives you a chance to enjoy the game and to recognize your good fortune to be a part of it. You feel almost overwhelmed with a sense of anticipation and arrival.

As I walked through the clubhouse a few hours before game time, I stopped to have brief chats with a few of the guys. I could see from their eyes that they were into it. Berkman was clearly carrying his attitude from spring training into the regular season. Gerald Laird, a catcher, was another guy with a terrific sense of humor and a real passion for and knowledge of the game. Skip Schumaker, our second baseman, was as tough as nails and always worked his tail off. David Freese was a great story and a great individual—a guy who once gave up the game completely but was now on the verge of being one of its real stars. He had gone through a rough patch in his life and had injured his ankles in a car accident, so we had to be careful with him, monitoring him regularly and resting him when needed. He had worked harder than ever in the off-season and felt he was back on track and getting healthier.

He and Allen Craig were a lot alike offensively and temperamentally. Both were hard-nosed guys who were going to battle in every at-bat, and both had the added value of having the knack of producing in rally situations. Ryan Theriot was another gamer, a gritty player with a championship pedigree, having played on LSU's national championship squad while in college. He and Schumaker, our middle-infield double-play combination, spent a lot of time working together and became good friends. At one point they started buying each other gag gifts—snow globes, the tackier the better—from each of the cities we went to on the road. That's a part of good team chemistry—having guys who appreciate one another and who also give each other a lot of crap. Nothing is sacred, and no one's ego is immune from the barbs that are exchanged between teammates throughout a season.

Chris Carpenter was our starter for that first game. We'd originally had conversations about making Adam Wainwright the opening day starter in 2011 in recognition of his having won twenty games for us in 2010. I'd been leaning toward Carp for the opener. The matchups seemed better that way. Carp's response at that time had been to say that he felt—and Dunc agreed—that Wainwright had earned the opening day honor. This was a classic example of Carp being not only the number-one starter but also a true leader and teammate.

On opening day Albert Pujols was his usual quietly intense self.

The man knows how to prepare, and because of his unique position in the game as one of the most sought-after interviews, he has to isolate himself a bit from the press in order to keep his intense focus. No one I've seen went about getting ready any better than Albert. That's not to say that he's not a great teammate—he'll always join in a conversation or a verbal dog pile when a guy is catching grief from his teammates for whatever reason—but he's got this no-nonsense look about him when it's time to go to "the Dungeon" for a video study session.

Some of Albert's conscientiousness might spring from the fact that he was a thirteenth-round draft choice, the 402nd player overall. From the beginning, scouts expressed some concern about his build. He played shortstop in high school, which gives you some idea of his agility, but as he matured questions were raised about his range and quickness. I first heard about him in the off-season between the 1999 and 2000 campaigns. At our organizational meetings in Florida, the site also of our winter instructional league, we went over the players who had been recently drafted and were now in the system, and the staff highlighted the players who had made a special impression. Albert was the first player mentioned. After watching his first game, I remember thinking only that he seemed to carry himself well.

In his first year in the minors, Albert was with the Cardinals' low A team in Peoria. Fortunately for him and for us, Dave Duncan's son Chris was also on that team. In talking with his dad regularly to let him know how things were going, he mentioned Albert and Yadier Molina a few times, always saying something glowing about him. Because of that, Albert was on our radar.

In 2000 we were putting together a good season, closing in on a division win. When September call-ups rolled around, we brought up a few guys from AAA in Memphis. As a result, there were a few slots that needed to be filled at that level. The Memphis team had also had a good year and earned a playoff spot. Our organization was always keen on recognizing success at every level and would reward their efforts by promoting from the lower clubs to give them their best competitive chance. Albert became one of those late-season call-ups to AAA straight from A ball, and he did well, hitting a home run in the thirteenth inning of the game that got Memphis the Pacific Coast League Championship. Later that fall he was in the Arizona Fall League, where I saw him bat three times and I liked what I saw.

Based on his impressive first full year, Albert was invited to our major league spring training camp in 2001. Our intention was to provide him with some exposure to major league techniques, practices, teammates, and game experience, since it's an ideal method for preparing a top prospect for his minor league season. His work was immediately impressive in the early drills, in all phases. One of the subtleties of training camp is that, on almost a daily basis, you can increase the challenges for the players, especially the younger prospects, through various drills, such as batting drills. When I saw that Albert was hitting well, I started putting him in hitting groups with our frontline players, just to see how he handled himself. The same result. In fact, it was difficult to see any difference between Albert and our top guys. Some younger guys either try to do too much to impress or prove they belong; others get intimidated. Albert did neither; he just impressively went to work.

We threw many tests like that at Albert, and he passed every one with flying colors. Very quickly he became the talk of our camp at daily staff meetings. The evaluations were so glowing that everyone, including groups of scouts and instructors, started gravitating to Albert's work area to really scrutinize him. The discussions within the organization that spring reminded me of those that the White Sox had about Harold Baines; the A's about Jose Canseco, Mark McGwire, Walt Weiss, Terry Steinbach, and Jason Giambi; and the Cardinals in earlier years about Brian Jordan and J. D. Drew. Impact players (or pitchers) developed within your system can stoke dreams of championships to come.

At that point, practice was important, but taking it into the games was the litmus test. When the games began, we saw exactly the same kind of outstanding overall play by Albert. Normally, when a young player has a spring like this, you try to give him just enough opportunity to maintain his belief in himself and to send him to the minor leagues full of confidence, but in the middle of the exhibition schedule we started seriously thinking about putting Albert on our 2001 roster. His playing time was becoming an issue because those who were sure to be major leaguers needed to start playing more. Fortunately, Gaylen Pitts, the Memphis manager from 2000, recommended playing him in left field so that he could still get at-bats. As Gaylen said, Albert got an excellent jump on fly balls and ran better than most thought.

He seemed too good to be true. Paul Richards, one of my baseball mentors, had always warned me not to fall in or out of love with a player during spring training. The idea was to wait as long as possible before taking the plunge or taking a hike. So I increased the pressure assignments. I challenged Albert more than any young player I had ever coached. A key fact was that we were coming off a Division Championship and felt we could win again. The challenges I gave Albert were tough enough that some of our staff and veteran players felt I was looking to make him fail to justify sending him out.

Here's a good example: Later that spring we were scheduled to face Javier Vazquez of the Expos, a guy with nasty stuff. I put Albert in the cleanup spot to see what he would do. First time up, he flails at a Vazquez slider well off the plate—looking just terrible—and I think, *Aha. Got you.* In my mind, Albert needs some additional seasoning, he has to work on that small thing—seeing the ball and being better disciplined at the plate. Next time up, Vazquez throws him that same slider and Albert hits a bullet to right-center. I think, *Holy crap, what an adjustment.* Making an adjustment is not something you see in many hitters, let alone younger ones. Even hitting cleanup didn't bother him.

Now, according to the legend Bobby Bonilla, who'd been signed that season to be our veteran switch-hitter to play first, third, and outfield and come off the bench, he hurt his hamstring, thereby supposedly creating a spot for Albert. But in reality, we had already decided that if I could find him enough playing time where he wouldn't just be a bench player, Albert was going to make the team. Originally, we were going to figure out how to do that with Bobby on the roster too, but when he got injured, the question became academic.

The record book shows that not only did Albert earn playing time (156 games played—52 at third base, 37 in left field, 33 in right field, 32 at first base, and twice at DH), but he also earned the National League Rookie of the Year Award.

And it had been that way ever since. If Albert was physically ready to go, then I was penciling in his name on the lineup card, and being able to do so on April 2, 2011, gave me a good feeling. For the past decade-plus, Albert had been a kind of sun around which so much of the team orbited. And just as you can count on the sun to rise each morning, Albert might dim for a bit now and then, but he'd always be back again shining brightly.

If spring training is all about promise, then opening day is about promise fulfilled or unfulfilled. I spent a lot of time thinking about what I would say to the club during our opening day meeting. I wanted to set the right tone, get the guys in the proper frame of mind. The meeting always takes place the day before the opener. On game day the players need to be totally focused on getting off to a good start. The idea is to talk the day before, then start the action on game day. Since we were opening in St. Louis, the meeting's venue was our clubhouse dining area. It's big enough for the team to fit comfortably and small enough to feel intimate. More important, the room was filled with memories and reminders of years of winning game celebrations, sending the message that competing is fun but having the final score go your way is true joy.

Over the years I had painfully learned that ten minutes tops is as long as this session should go. A meeting that goes longer than that becomes less effective. Coming off spring training, I devoted my first comments to a quick review of the "edges" we were going to pursue to separate ourselves from our competitors; the heart of the message, though, was that nothing good is automatic or just happens. We were going to control our minds and compete together with urgency and toughness. Consistent effort and execution were going to be the priorities for each of the more than fifty series we would play over the course of the season. Each of us would "personalize" how we earned respect and demonstrated caring for one another and our team. Finally, I emphasized that we had a legitimate chance to play in October. Why not us? It would be us.

I COULDN'T HAVE KNOWN THIS THEN, BUT IN A LOT OF WAYS OPENING day 2011 served as a microcosm for much of our season—we were going to have to overcome adversity time and time again.

We started out the first inning exactly as you'd want to. Carp got the Padres out one-two-three. In our half, Colby hit a triple with one out, and Matt Holliday had a two-out base hit to center to drive him in. Two-out RBIs are a huge boost for a club, and Holliday delivered for us.

In the top of the fourth, the Padres tied it, but we came right back in the bottom of the inning—exactly what you want your team to do in response to that challenge. We got three straight hits from Berkman, Freese, and Yadi to start off the inning, which resulted in another run, but in the fifth the Padres tied it again. And it stayed tied until the bottom of the eighth, when Matt Holliday showed how strong he was by going after a hard ninety-two-mile-per-hour sinking fastball from Mike Adams and driving a ball that never got more than thirty feet off the ground over the right-center-field wall. The dugout erupted, and I loved seeing that. This wasn't just an opening day thing—we always expected the guys on the bench to really be into it.

The previous year, our closer, Ryan Franklin, had gone 27-for-29 in save situations. He'd been an outstanding setup reliever before that, but in 2008, when Jason Isringhausen went down with an injury, Ryan really stepped up for us. With the momentum of that Holliday home run on our side and a very dependable closer heading out there, I really liked our chances to pull out a great late-inning victory. That's not to say that my guts weren't churning, because they always are. A one-run lead in the ninth inning. Three outs to get. Get them and feel great for a few moments. Miss them and feel lousy for a lot longer.

Ryan got the first two guys out, so we were down to the last out, the out that in a lot of people's estimation is the hardest to get. That proved true this time. Cameron Maybin, a guy with nowhere near the track record of Matt Holliday, hit one 420 feet into the wind to tie the game on a decent first pitch—a get-me-over curve.

We wound up losing 5–3 in eleven innings. Talk about your highs and lows. Even the two runs the Padres scored in the eleventh were gut-wrenching. A two-out bloop single, a couple of ground balls through the infield, a misplayed outfield relay, and we were down two. Frustrating as that was, you think, *Tough loss, come back and get them next time.* Only it didn't work out quite that way.

We dropped two of three to the Padres, and then two of three to the Pirates, who came in for our second series of the year.

Not much changed as we traveled to San Francisco to play the defending World Champions in their home opener. Living in the Bay Area, I had an up-close view of the Giants' exciting playoff run in 2010, which culminated in their first World Series Championship in San Francisco. Now, you always look at the early-season schedule to see if you're going to be on the road for any opposition openers. Home teams are excited to be in front of those big crowds at any time, but when they're hoisting the championship banner, that's even more you have to overcome as a visitor. I knew they would come to play, and sure enough, we were trailing 3–2 going into the top of the ninth, when they sent in Brian Wilson, their outstanding bearded closer, to save the game.

Over the years Brian has received a lot of attention about his beard, his tattoos, and his personality. Our problem was that he's a tough competitor with quality stuff and command. Sure enough, two outs later, we were down to our final out and last strike, when that toughest out in baseball phenomenon popped up again and Wilson walked Molina. Great at-bat. Remembering our old rallying cry of "just get something started," even with two out, we got a couple of breaks: an infield single (putting the ball in play is almost never a bad thing), a hit batter, and then a great at-bat from Theriot, who fought hard, fouling off several two-strike pitches before delivering a two-out single to drive in two for a 4–3 lead. The rally led to the type of late comeback to win that can jump-start your season.

Unfortunately, Ryan Franklin got victimized again. With the tying run on second base, Buster Posey on first, and two outs, a ground ball to first base to end the game became a freakish hit to tie. On the pitch that tied it, Yadi had signaled for a fastball in off the plate and a pickoff at first base. It's a play he and Albert had perfected and executed at least twenty times, including two that had ended a game.

Somehow Pablo Sandoval put the ball in play right through the spot that Albert had just vacated. Base hit, and suddenly the game is even. When Albert came into the dugout at the end of the inning, he was shaking his head.

"We had him picked off at first," he said. Buzzard luck, someone once called it.

So Ryan got the blown save, and San Francisco scored one in the twelfth, and we lost. What was almost forgotten was how we'd battled back against their closer in the ninth—not an easy thing to do during the home opener for the defending World Series Champions.

After a situation like that, you want to get your closer back out there as soon as possible to let him compete again, and we did just that. Unfortunately for Ryan and for us, the buzzard reappeared. We had a 2–1 lead the next day when we brought him in to close it out, and he gave up a walk-off double to Miguel Tejada. It was scored a double, but our center fielder, Colby Rasmus, usually makes that play. Walk-offs are always tough to deal with, but coming on the heels of that blown save the day before, this was especially tough on Ryan. Three blown saves in four chances. There was an explanation for each game that got away, but no excuses, except invoking the buzzard's curse. No matter how they were presented to Franklin, the bottom line rules, and he was suffering.

The blown save is a tough statistic for any pitcher to deal with. Think about it: who else in baseball gets hung with the idea that something was blown? The umpires blow calls, but they're not playing the game. When a fielder makes a bad play, it's an "error." A pitcher hits a batter, it's a "hit by pitch." Runners are thrown out stealing. Those are about the only real negative statistics you find in a typical box score, with the exception of BS, for "blown save." "Blown save" makes it sound like the pitcher did something really egregious, something he somehow willfully intended, like we're in a court of law and this statistic proves that, with malice aforethought, he went out there and ruined the game.

Over the years I'd dealt with plenty of closers going through tough stretches, and because of how I personalized my interactions with my players, I came to understand just how hard closers could take blown saves. No matter how skilled the pitcher, closing is a tough job, both mentally and physically. The pressure that accompanies it is enormous. From 1987 to 1997, first with the A's and then the Cards, we enjoyed the huge edge of managing a team that had Dennis Eckersley as the closer. Whitey Herzog, in the mid-'80s, told me that no manager is regarded as smart or capable unless he has a legitimate closer. Eck proved that point many times over. He brought several talents to that awesome responsibility, but one facet the public never saw was the hurt he felt on those rare occasions when he failed to secure the win.

One night we had a getaway game on the road, and Eck didn't close the win. As he boarded the bus to the airport, on the airplane, and then busing to our next hotel, it was clear he was beating himself up and struggling to let it go. Usually personalizing involves talking, but this time I didn't want to intrude on his space, so I wrote a note explaining how great he was and what he meant to our team. It wasn't anything dramatic, I just wanted to remind him of what he knew to be true: anyone could see what an amazingly talented pitcher he was. I slipped the note into his room key envelope as we checked into the hotel. Years later Eck mentioned what I did, and it must have helped because he told others what an effect it had on him.

The thing is, every closer deals with those kinds of issues at one point or another, and my role as manager was always to figure out how I could help them compete. Ryan took losses and blown saves hard. He started out 1-for-4 in 2011, and I could tell it was eroding a bit of his soul to let his teammates down. When this happens with a player, Dunc is the master at getting into his head and tinkering. Still, you feel for a guy in that situation, and we were concerned.

We were at 2-6, and we already had three blown saves and three bullpen losses. That's not a stellar way to start out the season. More than that, though, we were in an 0-fer. We hadn't won a series yet; we'd lost all three we played. That was weighing as heavily on my mind as the bullpen issues—the fact that to that point we hadn't scored more than four runs in any game—and just about anything else that I worked my worry beads over. Above all else, we preached three words: Win the series. Win the series. Win the series.

Why?

Because we play a 162-game season, we want to create a sense of urgency throughout that long span of six months of grinding. You need to create urgency in April because you can't wait until September to win. So how do you create that sense of urgency? How do you bring the same level of intensity to a weekday game in April in front of 5,000 people as you bring to a weekend game in Chicago or St. Louis with 40,000 screaming fans? It's about the series; the goal of each series is to win it. If you do that, you keep the intensity up no matter who, when, or where you are playing.

To achieve this goal, we coached this idea of manageable bits: a three-game series, do this; another three-game series, do that. Every off-season I spent a lot of time reading all kinds of books—on history, on leadership, on management—and one of the concepts I'd picked up over the years was about goal-setting. If you want to lose forty pounds, you have to start by losing a certain number every week. You use small, attainable goals that add up to the whole. The same is true with winning each series. Wins will accumulate—so will home runs, RBIs, strikeouts, and just about every individual statistic that matters.

We were only eight games in, and although being four under .500 was concerning, I'd have slept a lot better if we'd won a series. After Wainwright, this was our first real adversity, and even though it was early, I had to wonder how we would respond. I also had to weigh what was best for Ryan and for the club. Pulling him from the closer role would damage his confidence. But if we kept running him out there, hoping he'd reverse the trend and he didn't, we'd dig ourselves an even deeper hole that we'd have to climb out of.

Over the course of the final game in San Francisco and in our next two series against the Diamondbacks and the Dodgers, the bats woke up in a big way to bring us back to .500. Seeing the team climb back into things made me hopeful that Ryan would rebound as well. For a seven-day stretch, we didn't need to use him, and I hoped that would be enough time for him to gather his head and refocus. But when we finally called upon him to close out a 1–0 game against the Dodgers in the bottom of the ninth, Matt Kemp crushed a 2-2 pitch 422 feet for a walk-off home run.

I stood there for a moment, watching Ryan come off the field, feeling the collective disappointment of the team. The most frustrating thing was that I loved how we were competing to that point. They'd responded to that tough start and climbed back to .500, just as they'd bounced back from the preseason loss of Wainwright. We were also scoring runs late to tie and to take the lead. Winning like that came from character, the will to win, and team unity more than talent.

At the same time, I couldn't ignore the fact that we'd blown four save opportunities and our late bullpen performance was a concern. If we were going to win over the long haul, those issues were going to have to be resolved somehow, or it would likely cost us the season.

CHAPTER FOUR

The Surge

As concerned as I was about those early obstacles we'd faced in 2011, the fact that we never let ourselves get too far down had me thinking that there was something different about this club, something special. The teams we'd had over the years that were special had all shared that quality of toughness when faced with challenges. This impression was solidified by the fact that after that tough start, the 2011 club turned it around, fast.

From April 10 through early June, fifty-six games, we went 36-20 for a plus-sixteen during that span. That put us at plus-twelve overall and in first place with a two-and-a-half-game lead. That span covered eighteen series plus that one final game in San Francisco. During that stretch, we won fifteen out of eighteen series during what I now see was a really nice surge.

In retrospect, it's clear that one of the keys to the surge was the decision to change the scenery for Franklin by adjusting his responsibility and experimenting with Mitchell Boggs, Fernando Salas, Eduardo Sanchez, and Jason Motte in his place. Again, Ryan did a great job for us in 2010, and he cared about how his performance affected the team and felt for the pitchers who might have won their games if he had come through better for them.

"Do you know why the closer is my favorite player?" I asked him.

"No," he said.

"The difficulty of the closer position is that he is the only player about whom you can say this: if he has a good day, the team wins. No other player's good day carries that guarantee."

I went on to tell him that I'd also gone through similar stretches with Eck when he was really hurting and we had to talk through it.

Ultimately, I dealt with Ryan the same way I would have if he'd been a position player. If Ryan was a hitter and was struggling, I would have moved him down in the order to give him a change of scenery. And that was what we were going to do with him.

Boggs, Salas, Sanchez, and Motte were all right-handers, and though most fans might not have understood the reasoning, it made good sense to have them all coming in at different times to close out games. They were all still developing as major leaguers, and each had much to learn. The unfair pressure of such a situation usually retards rather than assists careers. If possible, the idea is to expose developing pitchers to pressures slowly. The problem is that, in the major leagues, you sometimes do what you have to do rather than what you want to do.

In a six-game span beginning on April 20, Boggs earned three saves before losing on April 26 against Houston. Mitchell Boggs is a big, strapping guy from Georgia who was a very good starter in the minor leagues and could be either a reliever or a starter in St. Louis. He's healthy, and he throws heat—he runs it up there at ninety-four to ninety-seven miles per hour and it's hard and heavy, but his command is a work in progress. So, even though he was a starter in the minors, he took on a role in our bullpen—not an easy thing to do.

After Boggs had his turn as closer, Salas and Sanchez took over that role, with Salas doing the bulk of the work. Salas earned eleven saves and Sanchez five, with Salas going 7-for-7 in save opportunities to start out. That's sixteen saves from two guys not projected at the start of the season to be closers. They both simply stepped into the role and took command of it. That's not to say our bullpen issues were over, but when it comes to looking at what you have instead of what you don't have, those nineteen saves out of twenty-four opportunities from the bullpen helped us get back on even footing.

Just looking at those totals and how the bullpen stepped it up, you'd think that we enjoyed a really smooth ride during this period, that things were going our way in all phases of the game, but what that overview of the surge doesn't show is that while our bullpen may have settled down, we had to battle through some major injury issues.

Injuries are a part of the game, an adversity you have to get accustomed to overcoming because one way or another they factor into every season. As much as you try to prepare guys physically—and for the most part guys are much more conscientious than ever about off-season workouts and taking care of their bodies—they are still going to break or break down. I make that distinction because bodies "break" when something like Adam Wainwright's torn elbow ligament occurs without there being an immediate kind of cause and effect. It wasn't like one pitch he threw tore that ulnar collateral ligament.

The thing with arm injuries and pitchers is that you just really can't ever predict who will get hurt. There are some time-tested thoughts about what makes for good mechanics—such as not throwing across the body, getting out over the lead leg, and staying on top of the ball. Yet you see guys with great mechanics get hurt while guys with less than ideal and sometimes even lousy mechanics stay injury-free. A lot of that has to do with genetics, and we aren't at a stage in the game where we can factor that in when drafting and developing a player.

With some types of injuries, you know immediately the why for the what, and we suffered a couple of those early in the year. On May 1, David Freese got hit on the hand when Scott Linebrink of Atlanta came inside on him. He was done for fifty games. Three weeks later, Gerald Laird, our backup catcher, had a finger in his right hand fractured on a bunt attempt against Kansas City in a game we won 9–8 in the tenth inning. As I said at the time, "You never really have a completely happy day at the ballpark. Great win like this, but to lose him, a key part of the squad, there's no celebrating." We would celebrate his return forty-two games later.

When bodies "break down" it's a bit different, and we had our share of those as well. It started when Brian Tallet went on the disabled list for fifteen days beginning April 13, and that same day, and for the same period, we also lost reliever Bryan Augenstein. On April 16, Allen Craig strained his groin, which sidelined him for fifteen games, and Nick Punto sprained his elbow on May 10, putting him out for forty games. Matt Holliday was gone for fifteen games after straining his left quadriceps on May 18, and Kyle McClellan strained his groin on May 30, forcing him out for fifteen days as well. Berkman also sprained his wrist sidelining him for a bit. When Allen Craig finally came back and started doing a good job for us, he then fractured his patella on June 7 and was out for another forty-five days.

With all of these injuries, and the number of games missed by these guys, there were really two things happening simultaneously. On the one hand, we were losing guys like flies, including some of our biggest contributors, but on the other hand, other guys were stepping up enough so that we were winning. As a manager, nothing makes you prouder than seeing guys do that. You never want to see somebody get hurt, but it is really inspiring to see other guys get their chance and take advantage of it. Since every club is affected by injuries, we always preached the edge of not giving in, making excuses, or giving up.

Certainly these injuries were tough to take, but I'd been on plenty of teams that had struggled through their share of injuries and still found success. In the A's 1989 World Championship year, we played the first half without Eck (elbow) and Canseco (hamate bone). In 2002, besides mourning the death of Darryl Kile, we had to use fourteen different starting pitchers. And in 2006, we could not have won it all without our depth, especially from guys like Chris Duncan (twenty-two home runs) playing the games missed by Jim Edmonds, Scott Rolen, and Albert Pujols.

The surge was our response to this kind of adversity. Not only because of the injuries but because I believe in playing as much of the roster as possible, the surge featured huge contributions from our depth. In a late April series in Atlanta, Nick Punto, who barely had played because of a sports hernia on which he had surgery in the spring, tripled home two runs to win the first game in the eleventh inning of a game in which Trever Miller got his first save of the year. The next day Gerald Laird tripled home the winning run in the ninth inning. Two days, two reserves, two clutch performances late in the game, and eventually two guys on the disabled list. In May, Daniel Descalso, our valuable backup infielder who wound up playing 148 games, drove in game-winners in back-to-back games in San Diego, in the ninth inning one day and then the eleventh inning the next day.

Then we also had veterans like Holliday and Berkman contributing. Though they both did get injured as well during those months in the first half of the season, when they were healthy they were helping. I can't say enough about the starts each of these players got off to. Holliday hit a clutch home run on opening day and then was out for seven games after surgery to remove his appendix. He came back strong, leading the league in hitting after the first month of the season on April 30.

For his part, Lance Berkman got hot early, winning the NL Player of the Week Award on April 18 for hitting .417 and leading the league with six homers, twelve RBIs, and slugging at a rate of 1.167. He was third behind Matt in hitting after the first month. And those two weren't alone. As a team, we were hitting .295, which led the league, and we'd scored more runs, had more total hits, and had more total bases than anybody. We also struck out the least through the end of April. The more the injuries piled up, the more focused these guys seemed to become. They were a team that really understood that you have to pick up your teammates when they're struggling.

This was true not just because of the injuries but also because of Albert, who got off to a slow start, going through the longest homerless period in his career, at 105 at-bats. Albert being Albert, we knew he'd come around, and he did, the first week of June, as the surge drew to a close. He hit five home runs the week ending June 5 and won NL Player of the Week honors for that accomplishment. Prior to that Mark McGwire, our hitting coach, told him that he was falling into the trap that a lot of hitters do when they're not producing the way they were used to. He told Albert to stop expanding his zone, take his walks, and the better pitches to hit would come his way.

The bats, though, were only part of our response to Wainwright's injury—our starting pitching was also clicking during that time. Kyle Lohse started the surge with a victory and wound up winning seven times during that span while losing only one. He'd struggled with injuries in the previous two seasons. To Kyle's credit during those two years, he'd pitched a number of innings with less than his full arsenal of weapons. He took the ball because we needed him, and while his statistics suffered, he gained a great deal of respect from his teammates.

Jake Westbrook also pitched well during that stretch. He lost his first start, had a no-decision, and was part of the surge, starting April 13 with his first victory and ending up at 6-3 to that point.

Jaime Garcia really set the tone for his season with that two-hit shutout in the first week. You always want to start off strong, and boy, did he ever. By June 9, he was 6-2. Jaime was only in his second year, and for a guy to have that kind of a start defies the old story of the so-called sophomore slump. Jaime had a great rookie year, and we were excited to see how he'd develop. He has special stuff, but probably more important, he is sometimes unflappable and sometimes erratic in pressure situations because he's still learning.

Guys just kept coming in and bridging the gap for us. In Wainwright's absence, Lohse, Garcia, and Westbrook had all taken up a good bit of the slack, but having a fifth starter could have arguably given us our biggest lift. During spring training, the competition for that spot had been between two young guys, Brandon Dickson and Lance Lynn, and one of our veteran bullpen guys, Kyle McClellan.

To be honest, I was rooting against Kyle being that fifth starter. I even told him so. I said, "You're going to be in the competition for that spot, but I hope you don't get it."

Here's why, and it goes back to my old debate with Dunc: I'd take the closer, and he would take the starter. I was hoping one of those two young guys would grab that fifth spot because I didn't want to lose McClellan from the bullpen. He was too valuable there. I figured that having a guy in the bullpen who could get out left-handers and right-handers was more important than having him in the rotation. In addition to the lefty/righty dimension, if we needed him to, Kyle could be an innings guy out of the pen, not just a "one-or-one" specialist (one out, one inning). Having that kind of flexibility is important to a manager making the late-game decisions that really determine whether you win or lose. From the start of spring training, though, Dunc believed that McClellan should be the guy in the rotation. Why? Kyle is a four-pitch pitcher—he has a late-moving fastball that tops out at ninety-two or ninety-three miles per hour, a good curveball, a little changeup, and a little slider. As a reliever, he wasn't required to throw all four pitches very much, but because he had those four pitches, he was good against both left-handed and right-handed hitters. Dunc said that was what would make him an effective starter, and that's true, but I saw that versatility as more of an asset in the bullpen.

In the end, he was outstanding in the spring and won the spot in the rotation, becoming an anchor through the surge and winning his first five decisions. And by the end of the surge, he was 6-2, tied for the team lead in wins to that point. Great. Nothing against the job he did as a starter, but like I said before, there's never completely good news after a day at the ballpark. Because we took such a valuable guy out of the bullpen and put him in the rotation, we lost a good lefty/righty man, an innings man, and a really effective one-or-one guy. We lost versatility.

Nothing on a team during the season happens in a vacuum. Someone just observing this debate over McClellan's role from the outside might say, "Hey, you lost Wainwright, but McClellan really filled in nicely." True enough. But that observer might not make the connection between Wainwright's injury and its effect on the bull-pen. So, in a sense, Wainwright's going out for the season gave us two holes to fill.

Another maybe misunderstood or unnoticed part of the Wain-wright and pitching staff issues was their role in putting Salas and Sanchez on the roster. Neither Salas nor Sanchez, who accounted for those sixteen saves during the surge, was with the club when we headed north after spring training. Salas and Sanchez were originally called up because both Bryan Augenstein and Brian Tallet went on the disabled list on April 13, and with McClellan in the starting rotation, suddenly we had a bunch of holes in the bullpen. Once again, injuries had pre-sented us with adversity and we had guys who were able to meet it.

The team's ability to handle adversity also extended to games they had to play without me. Apparently being the manager didn't make me immune from the rash of injuries. In fact, it was my immune sys-tem's failure to adequately protect me that caught up with me. Before we started a road series in Chicago, I was in Arizona seeking treat-ment for shingles at the Mayo Clinic there; things had gotten to the point when I had to do what was best for me so that I could continue to do what was best for the team.

Shingles is a benign name for a viral infection related to the childhood disease chicken pox. It usually causes a skin rash of blistering welts. Before I had it, I was only aware that it could occur somewhere on a person's torso. Once the virus was activated in my own body, owing to stress and being run-down, my right eye and the area around it got inflamed. Now I know that's not terribly common, but it's common enough. I didn't need anyone to tell me that it was incredibly painful. The area around the eye and the eye itself are rich in nerve endings, so when the first symptoms showed up in mid-April, I was hurting.

At first I didn't know what was wrong with me—I thought it was a sinus infection. By the time we arrived in L.A. for a series in April, it was clear that this thing was kicking my ass. The Dodgers' team physician diagnosed it as shingles. Still, I wanted to just gut it out. On the road, we're short one coach, so during pregame batting practice I'd go out on the field to try to hit fungoes one-eyed to the infielders. With one eye nearly shut, I was a bit of a circus act out there. I noticed that I was tiring really quickly as well, both because of the virus and because it was so tough to sleep at night with the pain. I'd gotten some pain medication, but one of the side effects was drowsiness. I couldn't risk nodding out during a game, so I didn't take anything for the pain for a month until I finally went to Mayo.

I was wiped out and hurting during that series in L.A., but I remember it clearly even though I couldn't see straight. In Dodger Stadium the visiting team manager's office has a little alcove set off from where the desk is. After batting practice, I'd retreat into that little alcove area, lean against the wall, and just kind of collapse there. A couple of times I heard Vin Scully had come to visit, but he didn't see me at my desk. I felt bad about missing his visits, since it's not every day you get to talk to a legend.

People have asked me if in my years in the game I've seen it all, and I tell them no. Every game is different, and every now and then I've seen something happen in a way that I hadn't seen before. During that stretch when I had shingles, every game I saw was different. It was like watching a game through a periscope and I was in the darkened bowels of a submarine running silent. My eye was very sensitive to light, so peering out of the dugout from the darkness into the high-watt brightness of the field was agonizing. The last day in L.A., a day game, was even worse.

Between pitches, I'd have to look down and then back up with one eye when I sensed the pitch was about to be delivered. I was literally getting through it one pitch at a time, inning by inning. Classic proof that I was more prone to relying on guts than brains. With the adrenaline of the game pumping through me, I was able to forget about the pain for a while, but before and after were both really rough.

Finally, when we returned to St. Louis from L.A., I visited our team internist, Dr. John Ellena, who confirmed I had shingles. He gave me antibiotics, but still I wouldn't take the pain meds. That went on for a month, and the lack of sleep and being run-down dragged things out. My wife, Elaine, and the girls all have had to deal with migraines, and when I told them I was feeling like a nail was piercing my right eye and head, they said welcome to that sad little corner of their world. They were sympathetic, as I was to their plight, but being able to really feel something like they were going through gave me a whole new appreciation for their experience.

Dunc, who always sat near me on the bench, could tell that I was hurting, and it was impossible not to let on that I had something going on with my eye since I looked like I'd gone a few rounds with Manny Pacquiao. Ballplayers being ballplayers, I'm sure the guys were talking about me, saying something like I was a little troll hiding under a bridge when I was back in the darkness of the runway and then popping out. I cut them off at the pass by telling them that pain wasn't so bad, but that making little kids cry and women faint was starting to get to me.

In the end, all that mattered was that we kept the surge going. After a month the shingles had still not run its course, and I had to leave the team and take the pain medication. I was still involved, obviously, but not being in the dugout wasn't easy. We got swept in Cincinnati, so I didn't have to hear any Wally Pipp remarks upon my return. Pipp is legendary for being the guy who was injured and re-placed by Lou Gehrig, who went on to play 2,130 consecutive games after that.

I REFER TO THIS PERIOD AS A SURGE, NOT A STREAK, BECAUSE DURING that span the longest winning streak we had was four games and the longest losing streak was three. Everyone loves it when a team gets on a roll and starts racking up win after win. It makes for good press, and it gets the fans excited, but I've never really liked streaky clubs—the kind that would win eight and then lose the next five. At the end of that thirteen-game stretch, you are still 8-5, a plus-three. Between the four in a row we won and the three in a row we lost, I think the more important number was by far the three. The fact that we never lost more than three in a row, given all the injuries, the turnover among bullpen personnel, the loss of a top-of-the-rotation starter, and the slow start for our top hitter and pitcher, really showed the character of our club. A lot could be learned about this team from how it demonstrated urgency and never let a big slide happen. A couple of games in Chicago showed exactly what we were about.

In many ways, Chris Carpenter embodied that refusal to let losses of any kind dictate future outcomes. Carp's start to the season was rough. He didn't get his first win until May 10, and before then he'd been racking up losses in a way that would have been frustrating for any pitcher but was downright baffling for someone of his talent. If you'd predicted, coming out of spring training, that Carp wouldn't get his first win until May 10, in his eighth start, and his second on June 23, I would have said, "No chance," but still, I wasn't shocked that it had taken him that long. Baseball is just that unpredictable.

To his credit, Carp had pitched better in most instances than that

1-7 start reflected, but more important, he'd continued to go about his business the same way he would have if he'd been 8-0. He may have pitched better than his numbers, but the buzzard had bitten him as well. The true test of a player is how he handles himself when things aren't going well. Thankfully for us, he reported to 2011 for the whole season—not just the start—and in that first victory against the Cubs, Carp demonstrated his tenacity.

What with the wind off the lake and the cozy dimensions, pitching in Wrigley Field isn't easy. That day Carp had to fight from the first inning. Unfortunately, I wasn't in the Friendly Confines; instead, on May 10, I was watching the game through one eye from my office in St. Louis. He wound up throwing 116 pitches in seven innings, giving up thirteen hits but only four runs: two in the first and then another two in the seventh. We went into the eighth tied at four, and Descalso, who figured so prominently in so many wins, drove in two runs to put us up 6–4. Another late rally. Another positive early experience. Another sign that there was something to this club.

Benign as this game might have appeared, it served as a good example of the fascinating nature of baseball itself. Carp didn't cave. Of course he didn't. But the point is, he limited the damage. Carp didn't have a single one-two-three inning. It's incredibly hard on a pitcher to be constantly pitching with runners on base. The mental strain of that takes a toll, as does the physical strain of having to reach back and get something extra. A lot of pitchers are what we call "max effort" guys: they throw every pitch with the same intensity, and then they also frequently "over-throw"—they try to get too much on a fastball and either release too high or too low, or they try to snap off the wickedest of curveballs and bounce one in, or they don't take enough off a changeup and groove a batting-practice fastball.

The great Tom Seaver, who pitched for Chicago when I was there with the White Sox, is the pitcher who had the best grasp of the pitching game and talked about some of these issues with me. By the time he was with us, Tom was well into the tail end of his career.

He's a really bright, articulate guy, a USC guy, and very, very astute about the art of pitching.

Tom explained that, as he got older, he didn't max out his fastball because he wanted to save that good plus fastball for key situations. He'd throw an eighty-four- or eighty-five-miler up there and hold the eighty-eight to ninety-one pitches in reserve. As a youngster, he'd be in the nineties regularly. I learned this from Tom the hard way. Everybody charts velocity, and even though I'm not sure it's the best indicator of whether or not a pitcher is losing it, it's certainly a factor. I'd see Tom's velocity dropping, and I'd hop out of the dugout at Comiskey or wherever and go out to the mound to talk with him later in a game to see how he was feeling. He was the only pitcher I asked and didn't tell. Normally, I followed Paul Richards's advice and had my mind made up before going out there. Tom's a great and gregarious guy with a smile as wide as the strike zone, except during the competition. I'd come out there with my hands in my back pockets, kind of slouched over a bit, and look up at him, and I'd see him grinning after I asked him how he was feeling.

He'd say, "I'm saving it. I've got a little extra."

He's the only guy I ever trusted when he told me that. The why for that what is because we'd talk pitching a lot. He'd convinced me that not every out in the game is the same in a pitcher's mind, or at least not in his. To him, there were key outs that occur at a handful of points throughout a game, and what he wanted to do as a pitcher was to be ready for those with his best stuff. This meant not only having those extra few miles per hour behind his fastball but also keeping a more acute sense of concentration and focus so he could give that key situation his best shot.

One obvious example of a key out is facing a leadoff hitter in a one-run game and the guy's got good speed. Or the situation might be that you're winning by three or four and there are runners on second and third with two outs. If you get that out, you keep the three- or four-run lead, but if you give up a base hit, your lead is down to only one or two and they're still hitting. So Tom believed that there were a few outs like that every game. He talked to me about those things in 1984, when I was just starting out, and I used that and my lineup to try to figure out ahead of time what those key outs and situations might be in a given game.

I know that for most baseball fans this discussion of key outs may not sound that earth-shatteringly new. Of course there are key outs, of course pitchers try to put a little more on or take something off to disrupt a hitter's timing, but Seaver was the first pitcher I talked to who spoke about those things together. He talked about how to get any hitter out in a particular key situation. More than that, though, we were talking about saving his best stuff for those situations.

SOMETIMES YOU HAVE TO MAKE UNORTHODOX DECISIONS, AS WE DID during that same series in Chicago, though I was in St. Louis. Before that series, I'd looked at how we were using guys, and it occurred to me that we could put Allen Craig at second base, though he had played first base and the outfield primarily. I called Joe Pettini, the bench coach, who was handling the lineup while I was away and, along with Dunc, making the pitching decisions. Joe was a bit baffled when I told him about my plan, thinking that we would be at a defensive disadvantage with Craig at second. He was right. However, I wanted Craig's bat in there. I figured that all Craig had to do was make the routine plays and on any double plays just get the force and get out of the way of the sliding runner. We didn't need any more injuries. I also studied the Cubs lineup against our left-hander Garcia on May 12. The Cubs were sure to load their lineup with righties against Garcia. Most guys tend to pull the ball, so Craig was likely to get fewer chances than usual at second base.

This was a case where having a better offensive player in the game meant more than having the stronger defensive player. I learned this from Loren Babe, a minor league manager and scout for the White

Sox. Loren had also played in the major leagues, and in 1983 he was scouting for Chicago but ended up on our coaching staff. Loren taught me, as his player-coach for him in '75, this offense-defense lineup strategy: use the better offensive player from the start and count on getting some production out of him in those first three at-bats so that you have a lead and then substitute a better defensive player for him in the fifth or sixth inning.

In Craig's first at-bat he singled. His second time up he hit a sacrifice fly that scored a run. He later walked and popped out, but by the sixth, with a comfortable 6–0 lead, Nick Punto went in to replace him.

In the end, the gamble paid off, and while it was only one game, it was moves like that and wins like we had in that Chicago series that kept us not just competing but getting all the way to first place by mid-June. Whether it was pitching or hitting, the surge demonstrated an underlying characteristic of the team. The guys routinely proved themselves to be inspired by adversity. To win as they were doing—with players constantly rotating on and off the DL, with the many times they came back late in the game, and with a manager who was out for six games—was a tough thing to do, especially early in the season after a rough start. And yet, during the surge they did just that, providing the urgency, showing careful attention to the process of playing baseball, and displaying a mental toughness that was impossible to ignore.

When I looked at the attitude of the club, it started to make sense: it wasn't just that this team seemed to have shrugged off the malaise of 2010; they seemed wholly changed. We were seeing contributions from every guy on the roster—young and old alike were taking this seriously. We'd had stretches where our luck was a problem, but none of that went to anyone's head. They just kept lacing up their shoes, going out there, and playing the best ball they could. And it was working. June is early in any baseball season, but it felt like we had been tested and come out stronger for those tests.

CHAPTER FIVE

The Storm

ONE REASON WHY *SURGE* SEEMED LIKE THE RIGHT WORD TO ME for our mid-April to June 9 strong start is that I grew up in Florida, home to orange groves and hurricanes. I'm not going to compare what happened to us in the weeks after the surge to the tornado that tore through Joplin, Missouri, that week. No disrespect in using this metaphor, but storms of all kinds were definitely on our minds as we headed back home after concluding one of the longest road trips of the year.

What I can say is that an ocean's surge, its rising tide, comes before a period of difficulty really begins. During the surge, the skies are clear and the sun shines, but somewhere in the distance, maybe still not discernible on anyone's radar, the weather forces have something stirring in the air or churning under the sea.

The "storm after the surge" analogy makes sense because it's rooted in the realities of the baseball season. Rarely does a team win by leading its division wire to wire. My best personal example was in 1988, when the Oakland A's got off to a franchise record early-season winning streak and sprinted to a 104-win season. We stayed relentlessly hot, with only one hiccup, when we lost nine of eleven, in June. Our lone period of struggle coincided with both our top two catchers getting hurt. Still, one season like that in thirty-plus years is just the exception that proves the rule that almost always your season will have its ups and downs. Part of the edge your team seeks is the ability to handle both the good and the bad effectively.

Coaches in every sport talk about overcoming obstacles—that's the classic feel-good story that we all love. Look around the sports world and tell me: how many people really want to see a team, loaded with all the best talent, winning from wire to wire during a season and having very little go wrong for them? Maybe because most of us think of ourselves as the "little guy" or the underdog, we root for teams and individuals with whom we can relate.

As much as I admire the Yankees organization and what they achieved over the years, I can understand why many people outside of New York pull against them. Look at the Red Sox. They went eighty-six years without a World Series title, and they were lovable losers, a team people's hearts went out to, the whole Bill Buckner ball-between-the-legs fiasco and all. (What a lot of people forget is that the Red Sox had a chance the next game to redeem themselves and didn't. Bill Buckner did not lose that series for them.) Now that they've won two titles, now that they have a reputation for amassing high-priced talent, they've lost some of their charm. In fact, I just heard that on a sports website fans listed them as one of the most reviled franchises in sports.

If fans around the country have a soft spot for teams that struggle, we had a full bandwagon of non-Cardinal fans on our side for a while. From June 10 through June 26, 2011, we lost our first seven in a row, went 3-12 over that span, and saw our record go from plus-twelve to plus-three. You can't be in this game if you can't handle losing. If you go out and bust your ass and put in a solid effort and the other guy beats you, you should be able to sleep well that night and move onto the next day understanding that you got beat plain and simple. That's how I felt on the night of June 10, when we went into Milwaukee and got throttled 8–0.

Maybe it's just because the two words rhyme, but *June* and *swoon* have always seemed to go together. I'm not a big believer in the inevitability of a team going through a rough patch in that month, but I am a believer in evaluating your team within the context of a season divided into thirds. In April and May, the scene is fresh and optimistic. Teams are eager to get into the season's routine. In August and September, especially if you're in contention, the end is in sight. Teams are excited to play the schedule out and try to earn a playoff spot.

The middle third is a different story. June and July, I think, are the toughest to play. The season is no longer new, and nearly 100 games remain. The weather gets hotter, and the schedule is more demanding, with fewer off days and more night games on travel days. In my opinion, it's this period that requires a team to dig the deepest to scratch out wins.

Losing the next night, 5–3, to the Brewers' newly acquired former Cy Young winner, Zack Greinke, was another case of nothing to be ashamed about. Okay, we didn't win the series, but we also stress to the guys the importance of ending a series on a high note if possible—win the last one, get on the bus to the airport, get on the flight, get on another bus to the hotel—feel good about yourselves following a win. Nobody wants to be swept, especially by a division opponent, since your loss and their win has a doubling effect in the standings. We didn't do it. We lost the last game of the set with the Brewers 4–3. They had a good offense in 2010, the upgrades to their rotation with Greinke and Shaun Marcum and their bullpen (especially with John Axford) made us aware that they were a solid club.

It was not a particularly fun flight to D.C. that evening. All things considered, I'd rather be in first place, and that loss on getaway day had put the Brewers ahead of us. Hoping the players were getting the rest they might have needed, I took the off day to think about what

I'd been seeing in that Brewers series. Miller Park is a tough place to play, and the Brewers were playing well and had a solid club, one that most experts had picked to finish ahead of us after Wainwright went down. The more I thought about it, the more it seemed like the guys were putting in the same time and effort they had been doing since the start of the year.

The next day was another tough loss—we came out fresh, added on, set the tempo, and were up by five runs with four innings left, only to end up losing the game in the bullpen. It was our fourth in a row, officially our longest losing streak of the season, and my staff and I could tell that everyone was feeling it. We also lost Allen Craig to the disabled list.

We were going to have to continue to battle through these games to survive.

Over the next two games we started each night at zero, thinking this would be the end of our slide, only to find ourselves in one hapless situation or another—whether it was Kyle McClellan's start just off the fifteen-day disabled list, when the Nationals ended up scoring ten runs in all, or the night that Salas, who at that point had twelve saves and three wins without a loss, gave up a home run in the tenth. When you're winning, the game seems to flow and fall into place so that it feels like it's hard to lose. When you're in a losing stretch, it's like swimming against the tide, and it's hard to put together the good things you need to win.

We flew back to St. Louis in near-silence. We were now only plus-six and still just a game behind Milwaukee, but we were only a game up on Cincinnati and two ahead of the Pirates. The good news was that we were headed home to play the Royals in our park. The fans had been clamoring for interleague play, and with our regional rivals coming in, all signs were pointing toward the guys really not needing to be reminded of the importance of maintaining or lifting their intensity level. Our history with the Royals dated back to the

1985 Interstate 70 World Series. "Win the series" stayed in place as the mantra.

And then we lost again.

Seven in a row.

I heard a few grumbles from the faithful after that one. Fans were hoping that Albert could do what he did on both June 4 and 5 during the surge, when he'd beat the Cubs with dramatic, extra-inning, walk-off home runs on consecutive days, something only one other Cardinal had done, the amazing Stan Musial.

Win the series, boys, I told them, but I was also thinking, *Just win.* The players' mysterious and complicated victory handshakes had gone dormant. We needed to do something about that.

We won the next two games of the series by identical scores of 5–4. Important as those wins were for us, the bigger headline coming out of those two games was the fact that we lost Albert to injury in the final game against the Royals. Albert, in reaching for a wide throw from second base in the top of the sixth, was run into by the batter, Wilson Betemit. Albert went down in a heap, and our hearts went up into our throats. As bad as it turned out to be—a slight fracture of a bone in his forearm—it could have been much worse, according to Barry Weinberg, our trainer. Instead of being out six weeks, as projected, Barry said that if Albert had broken a bone in his wrist, one of the most complicated joints in the body, not only would he have been out much longer but his return to form would have been hampered.

There was little that could brighten us after Albert went off the field, but in the bottom of the ninth Skip Schumaker did his best to try. After Descalso got thrown out trying to stretch a single into a double, Schumaker came up and, after taking the first pitch for a ball, drove one high into right-center for a walk-off homer. At this point, I wasn't sure of the nature of Albert's injury, but I knew it likely wasn't good. Albert had been 3-for-3 with his seventeenth home run mixed in among those hits that Sunday afternoon. He was hitting more Albert-like all the time, and he had those seventeen dingers and fifty RBIs, but his average was misleading. After his slow start early in the season, he was in the midst of a typically impressive prolonged stretch of productive hitting. Watching Schu's ball climb and then drop over the fence matched my mood that night—rising expectations and elation and then the return to the reality that one of the game's greatest players was likely to be out for a considerable period of time.

It was a classic good day/bad day at the ballpark.

You have to make all the statements after the game. Injuries are a part of the deal. "We'll have to step up and fill the void." You say those things and you believe them, while simultaneously saying to yourself, *Why the heck now and what the hell does this mean for us?* I let my guard down a bit the next day at a charity golf tournament for our canine and feline rescue foundation ARF when I said, within earshot of the press, "I'm going to go find a place to cry." I was being honest, if overly dramatic, by saying that. Even Mo, our general manager, couldn't put much of a positive spin on it: "You can't replace a player of his magnitude."

That's true.

What Mo said next is also true: "We still have to find a way to win games, and that's what we'll do."

After the golf tournament, Mo and I had a candid conversation about the effect of Albert's loss on our team, especially in this trying situation. Our biggest concern was that even if the injury buzzard left us alone, our team would still run out of gas and spirit. We both agreed that to this point our team had been valiant, and we would keep working with them. Then prepare for the worst and hope for the best.

I mentioned the 1992 A's to Mo. We played a few critical games against Toronto and Minnesota in late July. Our starting outfielders— Rickey Henderson, Dave Henderson, and Jose Canseco were injured. To replace them, we used Randy Ready, Eric Fox, Willie Wilson, and Jerry Browne. Despite the changes, we went 6-1 in those games. Though Toronto would later beat us in the ALCS (and Atlanta in the World Series), sweeping the Twins on that trip moved us into first place, which we refused to relinquish in the second half.

How did we do it? Baseball rewards effort and execution. It's meant to be played "hard" and "right." If you do, you can compete and win your share.

Mo was impressed and suggested that would be a good story to refresh our team. I agreed, but I decided to save it for just before the last two weeks of the first half—our last four series versus Baltimore, Tampa Bay, Cincinnati, and Arizona. In retrospect, maybe I should have shared it right away, because we lost five of the last six games before that meeting.

As THE END OF JUNE APPROACHED, WE WENT TO BALTIMORE FOR OUR final series of the month. We were 3-12 in our last fifteen, and we were all feeling how tough the previous couple of weeks had been. In addition to the loss of Albert, Eduardo Sanchez, who had been on a streak of nine straight scoreless outings, went on the fifteen-day DL with a mild shoulder strain. He wouldn't return until September 27.

With the start of July looming, we knew we were staring down the barrel of two big points of the season—the All-Star break and the trading deadline—so we started to make adjustments that we knew we had to make. At the end of June, we released Ryan Franklin and Miguel Batista. I hated to see Ryan and Miguel go. Ryan had meant so much to the club's personality in 2010 and was a great presence in the clubhouse and a wonderful person. He was also a thirty-eight-year-old player who had enjoyed a taste of success late in his career, and I could only hope that he walked out of the clubhouse with the taste of that vintage in his mouth and not the bitterness of 2011.

Personalization sometimes includes the general manager. Mo and

I both spoke to Ryan individually. We told him to go home for a while, get away from the game for a bit, spend time with his family. Later in the summer, if he wanted to start throwing again, we'd be willing to look at him again. I was pulling so much for him, that I told him that since he had a good knuckleball and had gotten some outs with it, he should consider throwing it more often. I wanted him to know that he'd earned the right to end his career with no regrets.

Hard as those decisions were, we knew we had to prepare ourselves for the All-Star break and the psychological shift that would come with it. For years we'd emphasized the importance of finishing the first half strong. Marking the halfway point, the All-Star break is like that proverbial cartoon oasis in the desert toward which some clubs are crawling as they grind out the first half. Crawling is good. Why? Because you're taking your time step by step to get there. Worse are the teams that go running toward the halfway point, stumble, and end up regretting the games they skipped in their rush. I'd seen that kind of thing happen time and time again.

We had the four series left—thirteen games—and we needed to reward intensity level with a healthy dose of winning. We had an unscheduled meeting to relate the 1992 A's story and its message that we could play through anything. I then tried to add some of the "how" to our approach for the last thirteen games. I came back to the idea of manageable bits. I've heard people who run marathons talk about the fact that not all 26.2 miles of the race will "fit" in a runner's brain. They say that if you try to cram it all in there, you end up overstuffing your brain and not allowing it to function properly. So some runners think of a marathon as a series of four ten-kilometer races (a marathon being forty-two kilometers long).

So we couldn't go to the guys and say: "We want to go X out of thirteen." That would have been looking too far ahead and focusing on results. We still needed to focus on winning the series. If we did that, the math would tell us what the record was. We had to focus on the process of winning, not the result of winning. Focus on the series as the what and then look at individual players and their contributions as the why and the how.

To prepare for this final sprint we went to each player or pitcher personally to remind him of what his keys to success were. For example, David Freese and Allen Craig both have an RBI mentality. Our coaches would review their success keys as a way to refocus them in their last stretch of first-half games and as a way to renew our confidence in them. We did the same, usually informally, with players throughout the rest of the roster. We would also continue giving clear feedback like this about the process of success. It's a lot different than saying to a guy, "Hey, over the next two series I want you to drive in six runs." Focusing on a predetermined result like six runs doesn't take into account the many things that can come into play to negatively or positively affect a player's ability to reach that goal. In some ways, a predetermined goal with a set number, such as six runs, is arbitrary and distracting. We don't want distractions. We want focused effort on the process, i.e., how to do it.

In addition, the informal process of setting expectations and giving feedback was how we could evaluate whether or not individual guys as well as the team on the whole were buying into the program. This was important all the time, but we felt it would be absolutely vital during those final games before the All-Star break, because we felt that those last four series would be a litmus test to see where we were.

The question of intensity as we made the crawl to the All-Star break was crucial because another question was looming in our minds, this one about the trading deadline at the end of July: Were we going to be buyers or were we going to be sellers? Were we going to acquire talent in the hopes of competing or unload it because we felt our season had more or less run its course?

As much as we preached focusing on the game and the series at hand, this buyer or seller decision controlled the early part of the season's second half. Changing the makeup of the squad, potentially messing with the chemistry of what we saw as a very gritty and determined team, was not something that we could take lightly. As we traveled to Baltimore for a three-game series, I was curious to see how this club was going to respond. We'd just gone 3-12. After Baltimore, were we going to be 3-15 or 6-12 or what? And after that? And after that?

We didn't need to see a specific outcome; we needed to see guys buying into what we were selling in the same way they had to this point. The next stretch of games had the potential to change the course of the season for good or bad—the only question was which it would be.

CHAPTER SIX

Buyer or Seller

AS IT TURNED OUT, THOSE FINAL THIRTEEN GAMES GAVE ME MORE than enough information to turn over as we went to the All-Star break. For their part, the players had been simply concentrating on a strong finish to the first half. I don't think they seriously considered that we were approaching such a crucial make-or-break decision.

For my part, I knew we weren't going to rush the decision about whether to be buyers or sellers at the July 31 trading deadline. That said, Mo had made it clear following the series with Toronto that he wanted us to give him an answer soon. His management style was always direct and to the point, and as we got into July he began conversations with his peers. I shared Mo's message with my coaching staff. They needed to know that these next few series would impact whether we played the second half for next year or for this one.

Overall, we went 8-5 during those final thirteen games. Good but not great as those results might appear at first glance, two gutcheck games were particularly instructive and held the key to my thinking about whether we were in or out.

The first occurred five games before the break, when we got

Albert back. Given all the tough luck that we'd had with injuries, it came as a surprise to us all that he returned more quickly than anticipated, after just a fifteen-day trip to the disabled list. We'd gone 7-7 during his absence, keeping us at plus-six.

Albert's first game back was July 6, the final night of our series against the Reds. We'd taken the first two games from them, and maybe we expected that with Albert back things would come easy. Jake Westbrook really struggled, so we wound up trailing 8–0 going into the bottom of the sixth. You want the urgency to be there at all times, but the fact is that in the middle of the grind, on a hot night in July, and down by 8–0, it's the rare player and the rarer team who can envision much else besides a cool shower and a colder beer after a loss like that. Take your lumps and go home, right?

Not this group.

It started with two in the bottom of the sixth. Then Holliday led off the seventh with a home run, 8–3. We could feel the energy level rising in the dugout as the temperature cooled. Maybe we could make this interesting.

We wound up scoring four more runs that inning on big hits by Descalso, Theriot, and an Albert two-out single. With each run that crossed the plate, I looked over at Dunc and we shrugged our shoulders. What was going on here? Were these guys *really* going to do this?

8–7.

We went into the last three outs trailing by a run. Jon Jay started off the ninth for us with a home run, and a feeling started creeping in:

We believe that we are going to pull this comeback off.

Unfortunately, we didn't. In the thirteenth, the Reds pushed across a run, and we "failed" to respond. I put "failed" in quote marks because that loss said a lot about our ball club, and that game loomed large in my mind in assessing whether or not we were in or out. This was hardly a failure except in the harshest win-loss terms. *Part of a winner's philosophy is that there's a win somewhere in every loss if you search for it.* For this loss that win was easy to find. We'd come all the way back from an eight-run deficit. Our bullpen threw seven shutout innings. Sure, we had a longer night than we might have liked on a typically muggy July 6 in Missouri, but I can't really say we mugged that loss. We had some fun, and as Albert said later in a postgame interview, "That was awesome, man. For us to be a winning team you're going to have to do things like that. We're not going to give up." Does that sound like a guy after a typical loss?

I don't know if it was a hangover from that long extra-inning game, but we lost the next two in a row of a four-game set with the Diamondbacks, who were on their way to a Western division championship. With two games left before the All-Star break, we were at plus-four. We reminded the guys again of the need to be vigilant about not starting the break too early. I was concerned about how the second game played out. Another late rally fell short, and we lost 7–6. You can only come back from behind so many times before fatigue sets in.

Apparently we weren't that tired, because the same pattern came into play the next day. Down 6–3 going into the bottom of the eighth, we scored three to tie, aided by a couple of errors and Albert's first home run since his return. In the ninth, another rookie produced for us when Tony Cruz doubled for a walk-off victory. Another contribution from a bench player, and another opportunity to pour out of the dugout to celebrate a comeback victory.

The last day we ended the first half on a good note with a win to end that stretch of thirteen games at 8-5. Now I had to use the next few days to catch my breath and figure out where we were as a club. The discussion was going to include three key pluses. Not only had Albert come back after missing only fifteen days, but he was playing to his usual MVP form. Also, almost unnoticed, Carp had started his chase. His tenacity was paying off. He had won three straight games, including a complete-game victory against the Orioles and a close 1–0 win over the Reds on July 4. The patient was showing signs of life—we just had to read them correctly. Once again, we had responded to a crisis point. We had gone plus-three for the last thirteen games. Most impressively, we'd closed with two wins and that was key; if we'd lost the last two, I don't know if we'd have had the same answer to the question we faced.

WITH THE FIRST HALF BEHIND US, I KNEW IT WOULDN'T BE LONG before Mo was waiting for the answer to his question: are we buyers or sellers? If I was going to be ready with my answer, I had a lot to factor in. First I consulted with the coaches, and we talked about the makeup of the team and how hard we'd competed.

As we sifted through it all, one of the things we kept coming back to, one of the edges that we felt this team had, was our chemistry. As a manager, you sense chemistry by watching how guys relate to each other, and in our case, all kinds of signals were evident that the players were enjoying and caring for one another. I found myself remembering a game early in the season, on April 22. That night we had just started a game at home against the Reds when the rains came and we had to endure a long delay. I walked through the clubhouse while we were waiting, and wherever I went—the locker room, the dining room, the video room, the training room—I saw guys hanging out, the cardsharps playing, the domino fanatics going at it, the scoreboard watchers catching some innings on TV, pitchers, position players all intermingled. I made a second pass; different guys had circulated through the groups. No cliques. I felt then and continued to feel that these players had established the respect, trust, and caring edge.

This chemistry thing doesn't just happen. As I've pointed out, we look for good character guys in trades and in free agent signings. That work doesn't end there. In most cases, players are good people who can go either way. They can become distracted by fame and fortune and make it all about themselves, or they can focus on the team. We hope that they will use their ego to become a contributor without going to the extreme of being an egotist. For example, at the beginning of the season the guys had made an informed decision about who would ride with whom on the bus trips. We have two buses, and the veterans wanted their own to avoid crowding. That meant that the guys with fewer years of service—not just rookies and second-year players—would have to ride the second bus with the media and non-uniform staff. Seeing this, I took it up with the co-signers, telling them that those kinds of divisions weren't going to contribute to the goal of gelling and truly becoming a team. I explained that bus trips to airports, hotels, and stadiums were golden opportunities to build the cohesiveness we needed. By the way, that tightness often came, curiously, from some very pointed kidding around. Everyone, including the coaching staff, was fair game. Over the years some of my favorite moments have involved watching the players getting on one another.

I went to the extreme and prepared a seating chart that gave extra room to the veterans but made sure all the young players and coaches were on the first bus. To their credit, though they could have objected, the players accepted my reasoning when we made the switch. They groused about it, of course, and I had to take a lot of good-natured kidding about the seating chart (Berkman and Laird were particularly good at asking me every time where they were supposed to sit), losing parent permission slips for the "field trips." In the end, though, I think that move paid off for us. They wound up enjoying having every teammate on the bus. Imagine the bus trip vibes leaving the stadium for the airport before we took a "happy flight."

The team's good chemistry made the trading deadline decision that much more complicated, and our 2011 staff recommendation was more difficult than usual. Mo had shared with us that, in his early discussions with other teams, the only trading chip we had was

Colby Rasmus. Trading our best young player prospect was a tough call. Still, we had some holes to fill.

In-season additions can really help sometimes. In Oakland, Sandy Alderson had traded for Rickey Henderson in 1989. In St. Louis, Walt Jocketty had routinely acquired stars like Mark McGwire, Woody Williams, Will Clark, Chuck Finley, Scott Rolen, and Larry Walker in late July or early August. In all those instances, we'd been buyers because we knew we were in the race, so it was a matter of learning who was available and at what cost. This year, though, there was nothing clear about our situation except that our group had become a team.

In the end, the coaches and I believed that, despite the setbacks we'd faced in the first half, this group could compete and make a run at the playoffs if we filled those holes. I really liked how, for the most part, guys were taking the things we stressed with them seriously. They seemed to be buying into the program. I can't emphasize how critical that was to our success.

While we were debating all this, our staff's opinion about whether to recommend a trade became more serious when Mo, correctly evaluating the situation, raised the stakes. Ownership understandably was reluctant to trade a young talent like Colby Rasmus unless a likelihood of a happy ending to our season existed. One day Mo came into my office and asked me the make-or-break question: "Can we win if we trade Rasmus for the help we need?" This was a perfectly straightforward expression of what we faced. Now, winning is different from making a playoff run, but I understood that Mo was facing a career decision and was asking the appropriate question.

Putting Colby on the table was a big deal. He is a real five-tool player: he can run, throw, hit for average, hit for power, and cover some ground in the outfield. Management, in particular our owner Bill DeWitt, was reluctant to let him go, for two reasons: one, he's that five-tool player, and two, the economics of the game make guys like Colby high-value players. They don't have a lot of years in the league and aren't making as much money as other players. The economic reality of the business of baseball dictates that you keep as best you can to the budget you've set. Young guys help offset the higher salaries.

Mo needed our opinion, so I immediately put the question to my staff: Could this team go further than a playoff run? Could this team win? On a pragmatic level, Colby was our center fielder, and we had good depth in the outfield. By moving a few players around, we'd be able to make up for his absence there. Looking beyond the tangibles, though, we went over everything: how we'd hung in despite our adversities, the heroes who had emerged when we needed them, the resurgence of Albert and Carp. All that added to our biggest asset and ultimately our main deciding point: the competitive guts and closeness our team had shown. Simply put, we believed in their character, chemistry, and will to win, so we bet on it. I gave Mo my answer: yes, we can win.

It was a close call, a kind of bang-bang play that, when we looked at all the factors, could have gone either way. If we hadn't won those last two games against Arizona, if we'd gone 6-7 instead of 8-5, I would have still told management that I thought we could be in it, but I'm not sure I would have had enough ammunition to make that case as strongly as I was able to. Like I said, the players didn't know this. Given how things played out down the road, any one game here or there could have made the difference between a World Championship and a long drive home empty-handed and empty-hearted.

Everybody could see the importance of every game in September, but who would have thought a home stand at the start of July could have mattered so much? This was one of those quiet yet defining moments in the season that most people probably weren't even aware of, despite the fact that it changed the course of the season and eventually Cardinals history.

With the decision made that we were in this thing, the question then shifted to what we were going to do about it. At the All-Star break, we were 49-43; we were tied for first place; Lance Berkman was leading the league to that point with twenty-four home runs; and despite his slow start and the injury, Albert was third at eighteen. Our three-four-five hitters were doing everything we'd hoped they were capable of, except staying off the disabled list, and the other guys had stepped up when needed. Offensively, we were in great shape.

Our starting pitching was good but not great. Our 4.27 runs allowed per game put us in the middle of the pack, the same place we occupied in most team pitching categories. We were concerned about fatigue and how some of the guys would perform down the stretch. Starting pitching was certainly something we needed, just like everyone else around the league. Defensively, we were struggling as well, a trend that would continue over the second half as we wound up the year with the second most errors and a fielding percentage of .982, just below the league average.

On top of those two pieces, we couldn't forget the bullpen struggles that we'd had and the shifts that we'd had to make there to compensate. Wearing guys out was a real concern, and so we had to say the bullpen was vulnerable too. We may have made our analysis, but now Mo had to go to work to find a trade that would satisfy all our various needs and bring in the needed reinforcements.

THE DAY AFTER THE BREAK, LIKE OPENING DAY OF THE SEASON, WAS another microcosm game. We were in Cincinnati and trailing going into the top of the eighth, 4–3. Aroldis Chapman, the Reds' "Cuban Missile" who has absolutely electric stuff that tops out sometimes more than a hundred miles per hour, faced Albert in one of those classic power versus power matchups that get everybody's attention. Colby had walked to lead off the inning, and then Chapman fell behind, 2-0. There's a reason why 2-0 is called a hitter's pitch, and Albert demonstrated the truth of that by drilling a Chapman fastball 407 feet to left. I don't know the physics of that exchange of power in and power out, but Albert proved that a big league hitter looking for a fastball in a spot in a given count can reverse just about any heat a pitcher brings up there.

You see that amazing demonstration by major league hitters all the time. They can time anyone's fastball, even those at a hundred miles per hour. This has been true forever.

The thrill of seeing those kinds of confrontations was one of the things that kept me coming back year after year. Ted Williams said that the most difficult feat in all of sports was hitting a baseball. A ninety-five-mile-an-hour fastball travels from the pitcher's hand—less than the sixty feet, six inches from the rubber to home plate because of the pitcher's stride—in about four-tenths of a second. Typically, a hitter has about one-tenth of a second to determine if the pitch is worth going after and getting his swing in motion. None of those numbers really make any sense unless you've stood in there yourself, and even then the speed and the fraction of time are nearly impossible to comprehend. The answer to how they do it isn't just physical talent. The courage to make a positive move with the body into the strike zone before you can determine its location is more essential than your talent, mechanics, or your hitting smarts.

I could admire Albert's home run for only a short while. The bottom of the ninth was coming up, and we went with Fernando Salas in another save situation. I'd really been hesitant to "anoint" anyone our closer officially. Though Salas had done some fine work in saving sixteen games prior to the break, naming him the go-to guy in all situations just wasn't something I was comfortable with, and I didn't think he'd be comfortable with it either.

He was going to get the bulk of the work in the save situations, but he still had to continue to demonstrate that he could handle it. That night he couldn't. A two-run home run in the bottom of the ninth let us know that even though we were post–All Star break and coming off a good few days of rest, some things hadn't changed.

That kind of back-and-forth, both in terms of wins and losses and in terms of the bullpen's performance, continued as we neared the trading deadline. Salas gave up a home run in the bottom of the tenth against the Mets on July 20 and then came back and got his eighteenth save on July 22. We lost another in the tenth two days later to the Pirates, this time with Motte taking the loss. This pattern kept driving home the point about what our top priority was.

We were essentially treading water—at plus-five, never dipping too far below the surface, but not launching ourselves onto the safety of dry land either. Depending on whether or not you're a strong swimmer, treading water for a long while can either exhaust you or help you store up some energy for the swim to shore.

One of the ways that you can get back to shore is with the aid of personnel moves. For example, the off-season signing of Berkman, when many thought that his legs and his bat were serious question marks, was proving to be a genius move. Historically, as an organization, we'd also made some pretty good in-season moves as well. Mo had gotten Matt Holliday from the A's midseason in 2009. Mo's predecessor, Walt, had also picked up a slugger. In July '97, he brought over Mark McGwire, who belted twenty-four home runs in the two months we had him that season. The list goes on.

Much has been made of the trade that was finally consummated on July 27. Colby Rasmus was the key piece in that trade. Mo will tell you that he was the one piece, with the exception of some of our minor league talent, who we had considered untouchable and who other clubs had inquired about. Colby wasn't being shopped around. The interest came from other parties first.

Colby was a good young ballplayer who sometimes struggled with doing the things necessary to focus on elements of the game, especially self-accountability.

Colby had the benefit of all the pluses that we provided for the players on our roster: personalization, a positive environment, chemistry built on respect, trust, and caring, and veteran mentoring. In fact, he'd received extra mentoring because we could see flashes of what he might become. With all that, for two and a half years in the majors, he didn't consistently embrace it. That said, he was traded because we had a chance to win and his trade helped improve our chances. If we had not been in the race, he might still be a Cardinal.

Colby clearly had value and an upside, and several other clubs, including the Padres and the White Sox, expressed interest in him. In the end, we traded Colby to Toronto, after convincing our owner of the advisability of doing so, because we thought the players we'd get in return would meet our needs and give us a better chance to win.

We knew we were taking a risk in dealing him, but obviously we were willing to take that risk.

The only way that trade was going to be made, the only way we were going to be able to improve the pitching staff, was if Colby was included. He is now with Toronto, and at any point, now or in the next several years, he could do all the things he needs to do to realize his potential. More often, as a young player acquires experience a bunch of things start to make sense and things come together.

We made a three-team deal that had us sending relievers Trever Miller and Brian Tallet to Toronto along with Colby, while we got starter Edwin Jackson from the White Sox and reliever Octavio Dotel and left-handed reliever Marc Rzepczynski from Toronto. When the guys learned that we were getting Rzepczynski, Berkman asked if we were getting cash considerations as well for all the lettering we'd have to put on his jersey. Even I couldn't afford to pronounce all those letters, so he became "R-zep" from day one with us. Gerald Laird wanted to pass the hat in the clubhouse to buy R-zep another vowel or two.

Shoring up the bullpen with Octavio Dotel and then later signing another veteran, Arthur Rhodes, proved a key to our success. They had an added value to the club. Their sense of urgency was heightened by where they were in their career. Neither of them had won a ring before. In fact, Arthur had just been released by Texas, making him available for us to sign. These guys were great in the clubhouse, and they were also very hungry.

Some young guys may not have that same do-or-die sense that a veteran brings. We all think we're going to be young forever, that we're going to have unlimited chances to succeed. Often, young guys have that "happy to be here" attitude, which on the one hand is great, but on the other, might detract from the sense that now is as crucial a time as any and they may not get another chance to do something special. I would like it if I could gather together the hundreds if not thousands of guys who never got to play for a champion and who really, really wanted it so badly but fell short of the mark. I'd have them talk to the young guys, let them know that things can slip away so quickly, that seemingly in the blink of an eye their careers could be over.

We try to impress this idea of the fleeting nature of their careers on our young players. Some get it. Some don't. We did. We always believed in seizing the moment.

CHAPTER SEVEN

Tough Decisions

IT IS IMPOSSIBLE TO CALCULATE THE NUMBER OF DECISIONS I'VE had to make as a manager of more than 5,000 games that either directly or indirectly affected the outcome of a baseball game.

During the 2011 season, I was faced with another decision, one that I'd encountered for the last several years in my career as a big league manager: did I want to do this anymore? In 2010 I'd gotten closer to ending my managerial career, but in the end I'd decided to come back for 2011, and I was grateful for the fact that the choice had been mine.

I've been blessed with a great family—my parents, my sister, her husband, and Elaine's and my extended families included, and with all the baseball people who form that family of friends, colleagues, and employers. The plus to that is, beginning with my parents, I was taught one thing: do your job to the best of your ability and take responsibility for your actions. In my baseball life, I was "raised" by some wonderful men who taught me how to play the game right and later how to go about managing a team.

Loren Babe was one of my earliest mentors. Loren was our AAA manager at Denver in 1975 and Des Moines in 1976. Toward the end of my career, I became a player-coach for him. Loren encouraged me to ask any and all questions that came to mind. He was very shrewd and provided me with pointers and strategies that were much deeper than I had imagined. As a player, you think you understand what the game is about and what role the manager plays, but it isn't until you actually start managing that you come to see what that role fully entails. From time to time Loren allowed me to manage a few minutes just to try it out and see how it fit.

In 1976 I was player-coach for Loren with the White Sox in Des Moines. Loren was sick, and I had to manage the game and play third base. That game, I went 6-for-6 at the plate, tying a league record, but we lost in the tenth inning when Andre Dawson hit a walk-off home run over the light tower in left field. Still, the game was a huge awakening for me. I usually didn't get six hits in a week, and that should have been my highlight for the evening. Instead, after the game I realized I was more fired up about managing the game than I was about the six hits.

Paul Richards was another early mentor to me. He was a legendary figure in his seventies when I first met him, and in 1978 and 1979 he was the White Sox farm director, with a résumé that included many of the top major league jobs as well as being a top-flight catcher. He was well known for being creative. He'd mentored all the young managers, and he took special interest in my baseball education. To my last managing days I was still applying Paul's lessons. One of his best was that your game decisions should be based on "Trust your gut, don't cover your butt!"

All those people stressed the important message that my integrity as a person and as a leader was crucial. Who I was as a person would be reflected in the players I put out in the field and in how they performed. I took that responsibility very seriously. I also understood that there was something reciprocal about the relationship I had with the teams and organizations that trusted me as a manager. In trying to give each organization my best efforts, I received support many times over from the White Sox, A's, and Cardinals. The last sixteen years in St. Louis had a special meaning for me because of the historic nature of that franchise. The St. Louis Cardinals is an organization with a long tradition of success. In fact, my decision to accept the offer to manage there in the first place was influenced by the idea that I was being given an opportunity to become part of an organization in which a lot of other people had invested their hearts and souls to make something they could be proud of.

All that being said, I didn't take the decision to retire lightly. I also had to consider so many other factors besides my own interests. Since at least 2005 or so, I would show up at spring training every year when we brought our uniform staff together, from the major league team down through the various levels of A-ball, and I'd feel guilty. We had some wonderful coaches and managers in the organization who deserved a shot at being a part of the major league club. Stability in an organization is something that has tremendous benefits, but it can also hamper the growth and development of the next wave. I felt like I was clogging up the coaching pipeline. I wondered if maybe a new voice was needed in the clubhouse. I always speculated that maybe I'd said the same things too many times and a fresh perspective was needed to really get guys' attention. I'd talked to coaches in a lot of other sports—Bill Parcells of the NFL, Don Nelson of the NBA, Bob Knight, and many others. We'd all pick one another's brains about this profession we share, and it was always helpful to get their insights.

Many felt that five to seven years was about the longest you could go as a professional coach. You may not lose the team's respect after that, but they may just tire of hearing your voice.

I can say this: the shingles episode played a role in my decision only in that it was such a distraction and had me so exhausted that I knew I couldn't really think much about retirement while I was still dealing with it. I would be irresponsible if I made a professional decision about my future and its potential impact on the organization—and to an extent, the players—in the middle of that medical situation.

As a result, just as we did in assessing the club and its needs in the run-up to the trading deadline, I seriously began the same process of assessing myself and my own career after the All-Star break. I knew I'd been feeling different from before, but only then did I start to seriously analyze it. As I said, I was glad that I'd earned the right to make this choice instead of having the decision made for me. That isn't always the case.

I WAS, AND ALWAYS WILL BE, GRATEFUL TO THE WHITE SOX ORGANIzation and in particular Bill Veeck, the owner in 1979; Roland Hemond, the general manager; and Jerry Reinsdorf, who bought the club in 1981, for giving me a chance to manage when I'd had only limited experience. Looking back on it, I can see that they probably had more trust in me than I did in myself. Or maybe as Harry Caray claimed: They were too cheap to hire a real manager.

That first spring as manager of the White Sox, the task of organizing spring training fell to me for the first time. I'd gotten the job temporarily back in August 1979, but at the end of the season Bill Veeck and Roland Hemond told me the club was mine the following year. Shortly thereafter, Paul Richards, who at that point was with the organization as an adviser, called and asked me about my plans for the following spring.

Seeing as how the season had just ended, I hadn't spent too much time thinking about it, but I was definitely leaning toward letting our third-base coach, Bobby Winkles, lead the camp. He had been responsible for running the spring training program and had done an outstanding job. Fundamentally, he was really sound, with solid experience. The way I figured, if you have somebody who does something well, you let him do it.

Paul heard me out, but then he made these points:

1. It was easy to admit that on a scale of 1 to 10, I was pretty far down the scale in terms of respect and credibility with the players. I had only fifty-four games of experience as a big league manager, and I'd been a lousy ballplayer, hitting only .199 for my career. I needed every possible opportunity to show them that the right guy was managing the club.

2. If I came in with the attitude that spring training is important, put Bobby Winkles in charge of the camp, and it was run well with a good program, then Bobby Winkles would get the credit in the players' eyes. Similarly, if I put Bobby in charge and it was a poor camp and the club wasn't ready to play, I'd be held responsible, even though I hadn't been in charge of the program. It was a lose-lose for me as far as the team was concerned. I needed to earn points with the players, and I was missing an opportunity. Paul was clear, "You've got to do it."

So that was what I did—and I organized the camp every year since. What made sense in my first year made sense in my last. By running the camp myself that first year, I earned some much-needed credibility with the team.

Because I was neither a great player nor an experienced manager who could draw on years and years of time-tested strategies and a data bank of situations to use in making decisions, I knew the team questioned the basis for my authority. So did I.

During my early years, the best managers were so successful that they were known by their first names—Sparky, Billy, Earl, Gene, Chuck, and Whitey. I was confident that they were doing more for their teams than I was for the White Sox. So I prepared more, tried to learn more, and grinded out every pitch hoping to narrow the gap.

Every time I faced a first—first postseason game (Baltimore, 1983), first league championship game with Oakland (Boston, 1988), first World Series game (Los Angeles, 1988), and first All-Star Game (Anaheim, 1989)—the same confidence problems would crop up. What I lacked in confidence I made up for with aggressiveness, and I always tried to learn from my mistakes so the next time I would be better.

There were some people in Chicago who didn't question whether I was right for the job—they were sure I wasn't. They made those beliefs known in let's just say socially and legally inappropriate ways. In 1982, we started off hot, going 8-0. I don't know if that ignited the fever in some people's minds, but in late July the team was hovering around .500 and the fans were clamoring for me to be fired.

Rumors were flying, and I walked into one of my favorite restaurants in Chicago, a place where I ate regularly, and saw a WELCOME, BILLY! sign hanging up. I'd already heard a rumor that the baseball genius and tortured soul Billy Martin was in town. The word on the street was that he was there to meet with Jerry Reinsdorf and Eddie Einhorn, the owners of the club. That same day, I went to the ballpark and talked with Roland Hemond, the general manager. Roland was one of my staunchest defenders. When I saw him, I told him that if they wanted to get rid of me, that was fine. I just didn't want him sticking his neck out for me and getting fired as a result.

I asked him to make that pledge to me, and, reluctantly, he did. I asked him to tell Jerry one thing: I wanted to have the weekend at least. I couldn't do more than hope that they'd agree to let me at least do that. I figured we had a shot at winning those games. Little did I realize, but that choice of words was prophetic. Roland told me before the game that I just needed to manage the club. There was nothing imminent, he said, so go out there and do your job. Hardly the kind of reinforcement you want, but okay, I would do that.

Before the game, David Shaffer, the head of security for the White Sox, came up to me and told me, "Hey, it happens every now and again, but this one sounded different. A guy called in to the switchboard and said that if you're in the dugout tonight, he's going to shoot you."

They had decided not to take chances. He held out a bulletproof vest and said, "You have to wear this." The thing wouldn't fit underneath my uniform, so I had to wear it over my jersey. The last thing I wanted to do was have anyone see me with that thing on. The only other uniform item I had that could cover it was my quilted jacket, the one I'd worn early in the season when the snow was flying. This was June, and it was hot enough without those added layers, but what are you going to do?

With that jacket on, I wasn't exactly inconspicuous, so I had to tell our coaches what was going on. Of course, this being baseball, we made it into a joke. When I went to sit on the bench next to them, they got up and moved away. So I'd get up and move toward them, saying, "Hey, come here. I've got to talk to you."

"No, no. You're on your own."

Obviously nothing happened with the death threat, but we won three out of four that weekend against the Red Sox and went on a hot streak, winning fifteen of eighteen. The cries for my head stopped.

I tell that story because of all the different elements of it, but mostly because despite all that nonsense, I was fired up just to be managing major league games. Even with those literal and figurative threats hanging over me, we were able to laugh a bit and win some ball games.

A couple of postscripts to that story. If you're a big baseball fan, you probably know that baseball players are a superstitious bunch. Because we won three out of four when I had to wear that jacket, I kept wearing it. You couldn't have torn that thing off me. I can tell you exactly when it finally came off. On August 16 we won in Texas. Imagine a hot Texas night in high summer with me sitting there with a heavy jacket on, sweating bullets. By that time, my sweat had eaten holes in the armpits, and the thing was as nasty-looking and foul-smelling as an end-of-the-year game hat. After the game, about two in the morning, I got a phone call from my mother-in-law telling me that my wife, Elaine, was about to give birth to our second child, Devon.

I hustled back to Chicago, but missed her birth by just a few hours. She was, and is, a beautiful girl. Elaine delivered Devon naturally, at our apartment with Dr. Bill White assisting. Bianca was thrilled to have a little sister. That night, when the game came on television, we all sat there watching it. The legendary Charley Lau took over managing duties. The team was behind, and on the broadcast they showed a shot of the dugout, and Ken Silvestri, the interim pitching coach, was sitting there wearing my lucky jacket. We were a tight group, and they really wanted to win one to celebrate Devon's birth, and even though we tied it late, in extra innings, the club fell. So did the jacket.

I did survive that year, only because Bobby Winkles and Charley Lau both spoke up for me, telling the owners that I hadn't lost the club, that there were other reasons we were losing. The next year, '83, we won ninety-nine games and the Western division championship. Imagine, in those days winning a best-of-five series was all it took to earn a World Series shot. We didn't—the Orioles did. Still, these were the first tangible accomplishments I could point to that said, both to others and to myself, that hey, maybe I could do this thing.

None of that changed after the White Sox fired me in June 1986. Despite the tenuous nature of being a coach or manager in any sport, the near-constant threat of being let go never really got to me. I was too excited about being involved with the game. That threat was simply part of the job, and after getting fired the first time, I had to discipline myself to just keep getting into the flow of the game. I had learned to work my job and the game. The wins, money, and security would either come from that or they wouldn't. Probably because I knew I was so close to the edge from day one, I never worried about getting fired. All my worrying was directed at winning the game.

In relating that story, I'm reminded that missing the birth of my daughter was tough, and also that Elaine had to do more than her share of raising the kids. There's a plus and a minus to that as well. The girls have an amazing relationship with their mother, who was there for them and with them through everything while I was away eight months out of the year. In fact, Elaine did such great work that every year on Father's Day they give her a card or gift as well. Since she home-schooled them, they should also have been giving her an apple on Teacher Appreciation Day. I'll have to give them some grief for that.

I understood how important family was, and the kinds of sacrifices players and, more important, their wives, kids, and other family members make. I learned that by committing the errors that result from giving baseball too much of my attention and my family not enough. I couldn't ever have done what I did for as long as I did without the kind of support I got from Elaine. Our extended families in Virginia, Tennessee, and Florida would have helped, but they were often too far away. Elaine had to do it herself. Baseball takes a toll, and I was beyond fortunate to have a wife who understood me, my passionate commitment to doing things right, and what that meant for all of us. I know it wasn't easy, and I know the load she had to carry. She never asked me to step down or to rethink a decision that meant we had to move, and her priority was always doing what was best for the girls.

Some of my fondest memories are of the looks that we used to get from airline personnel when we were living in the East Bay and traveling down to Arizona for spring camp. Not only did we have our own piles of luggage to carry around, but we had the crates for all our animals. The La Russa family traveling menagerie in those days probably still brings tears of frustration to porters and baggage handlers. We couldn't go anywhere without our four-legged friends.

I used to tease Elaine and the girls that I'd come home on an off day during the season and they'd ask me about, say, why I'd pinch-hit with Craig in that situation when a right-hander was on the mound. The dogs and cats would just run up to me, do their little serpentine butt wiggle at my feet, and jump up. I'd sit on the floor, and the pile of them would wash over me like furry surf. I'd say to them, "You know, you never second-guess me, do you?" Their response was always tail wagging and joy to see me.

THE MEDIA EVOLVED OVER THE YEARS TO THE POINT WHERE SECOND-guessing and a lot else besides recapping the games took over. I want to make it clear that I understand that media people have to make a living and that, like me and our players, they have to survive in a highly competitive environment. Still, just because I understand all that doesn't mean that I enjoyed it. It was more like I tolerated it as part of the dues you pay to stay in the game.

One consequence of media proliferation was it seemed as if some members of the media were trying so hard to make a name for themselves that they began to compete with the very players they were interviewing for the attention of the public. Toward the end of my career, these competitive individuals were becoming more the rule than the exception, and as in most competitions, hostilities were a natural result. Being stuck in the middle between the players and the media when this occurred was a taxing and irritating part of my job.

Having to manage the media, though not my full-time job, took up a considerable amount of time and energy and also took some enjoyment out of managing.

And that's not to say that the players themselves don't add to a manager's list of responsibilities and irritations. We play a team sport, and as time has progressed, I've seen more and more examples of individual players falling victim to all kinds of distractions in order to "get theirs." In that sense, they're not that different from the media types who seek notoriety, and that's what I mean about the players being in competition with some members of the media. The players' attention is being pulled away from the game by that. I'll admit I watch *SportsCenter* as much as anybody, but I'm not out there on the field doing things that I hope will get me on "Plays of the Day" when I should be doing some small thing to help the club win. Those plays don't have to be that kind of big deal. Your teammates know what you did, and that should be enough.

David Freese is a terrific ballplayer, a clutch hitter with a good, strong arm. He didn't have the best range, owing to some nagging injury issues, so for most of 2011, I took him out in late-game situations to put in a better defensive player. This was not an easy decision. It goes against Managing 101, which tells you that you build confidence in a player by what you do *for* him, not what you do *against* him. So I personalized things and went to David and told him honestly, "We are concerned about your range while you get back to 100 percent, and we also worry that you won't be able to play for us all season without getting hurt if we push you. So not only does substituting for you make sure we don't run you into the ground, but we're hoping this approach will help you regain your quickness and your good footwork. Because of all that, I'm going to play Descalso late in games."

David said that *he* understood, but that he was taking a lot of heat from "other people." They kept telling him that I was taking him out late in games because I thought he was a poor defender. Those other people might have been friends, family, his agent, but whoever they were, in addition to managing our player, did that mean that I had to manage them? No, not directly, but in a sense yes. I kept this personal. I told David that he was going to have a hard time in this game if he took to heart everything he heard and read. He was going to have to get used to criticism. I asked him if he was tough enough to stand up to his friends or whatever he was reading or seeing.

"Yes, I'm tough enough," he said.

"Well, then," I said, "tell your friends, just ask them, who started the game and where did you hit in the lineup? If I don't have confidence in you, why am I hitting you in the middle of the lineup, and for that matter, why are you even in the starting lineup?"

Keep this in mind. This is a *minor* example of the larger point about how distractions and that "gotta get mine" attitude come into play regularly. Even though in this example I didn't have to deal with the player's agent, with greater and greater frequency coaches do just that. Agents are in their players' heads, telling them that they need to start instead of relieve, that they have to hit for more power, that they should be playing more—anything and everything to make them focus on themselves and not the team. It's exhausting having to manage the expectations and demands of agents. At its worst, you have a player you and the coaches have worked hard to develop, and all of a sudden everything becomes about him—not about the team or the game. You feel betrayed when that happens, and that tears you up.

The media also contributes to these attitudes with what I think of as baiting players. For example, I have two guys in the bullpen—let's call them Bob and Tom. Going into the ninth inning, I decide to use Bob to close out the game. Why? Because Tom has had a lot of work recently, and Bob hasn't. So I go with Bob to get him an inning in a game situation instead of throwing on the side again. After the game, a reporter tracks down Tom and asks, "Hey, why didn't La Russa go with you in that last inning? Do you think he's lost faith in you?" Tom now starts to think about it. He may say something to the reporter, or come to me or one of the other coaches later, or bitch to his pen mates, and now we've got a problem that wouldn't have existed if the seed hadn't been planted by someone else. That happens all the time, and now the staff is out there putting out fires set by an arsonist. All that detracts from the focus on the game and the preparation for the opponent, not to mention the pleasure you get from the game.

Sounds a bit like high school, doesn't it? Having to squash baseless rumors and worrying that someone's nose is out of joint because of something that someone else said behind your back. To be honest, after a while those kinds of things bothered me less and less. Too much time and attention was being paid to them. I'd long since stopped thinking, *This isn't what I'd signed up for,* and instead I just kept adding new tasks to my to-do list. But it did take away from the excitement of competing.

Now, I don't want to paint with too broad a brush here, because looking at the span of my career, I have known plenty of appreciative and respectful players, as well as media members who were responsible and loved the game. Call it the squeaky wheel syndrome, the bad apple or whatever, but human nature being what it is, you tend to remember the really good and the really bad, and the big middle becomes a kind of blank. What I was taught, and followed religiously, was not to grease the squeaky wheel. Instead, our staff gave our best care and attention to those teammates who took care of our team.

Over the years there have been really good players who really understood what we coached when it came to building a sense of team and not putting themselves first. They also never forgot what it was like to be the young guy, the one not making a lot of money and being in unfamiliar cities and trying to get the hang of what it means to be a big leaguer. Every now and then on a road trip, veterans like Kile, Morris, and Carp would announce before the game that they'd made reservations at some nice restaurant. Anybody who wanted to come, the meal was on them. That was a great way for the guys to get together, talk a little baseball, get to know one another better, that kind of thing. It also helped incorporate the new players and the rookies into the fold. The point wasn't that they were popping for the other guys' meals, it was that they cared enough to take the time and make the effort to arrange these things.

Early on, I'd seen that team meals could have a strong effect on camaraderie, and at the very real risk of sounding like an old fart longing for the days of his youth, I have to say that, as I thought about my decision to retire, I found myself thinking about those early years I had as a manager and remembering them wistfully. When I first started managing in the White Sox organization, as far back as 1978, I remember something we did when I was a player-coach for the White Sox AAA affiliate, the Denver Bears. This was before the Rockies franchise was awarded, and the folks in Denver really wanted to make a good show of it so that they could get a big league club there.

In 1975 we were scheduled to start the season off with a twelve-game road trip. That's a tough schedule, and the Denver Bears' legendary general manager, Jim Burris, was concerned about those two things—making a good show of it with a good start and dealing with that tough early schedule. Not starting off strong would hurt early ticket sales, and that could carry over to the rest of the season and at the gate. At a team dinner before we opened in Evansville, he told us that every time we had a winning road trip, he'd buy us dinner.

As it turned out, we went 10-2 on the trip, won all four series, and dined very happily and very inexpensively on the club's dime. That worked so well that Jim continued the program for the rest of the year. We got so far ahead on dinners owed that he realized he could never get them all in, so he sprang for a huge team dinner, families and all. That meant Elaine and I got to go together and didn't have to dip into my $10,000 a year salary.

It was from guys like Jim that I borrowed some of my ideas for team-building and treating families well. When I started officially managing in the White Sox organization in 1978, at Knoxville in the Southern League, I used Jim's motivator. If we won a road trip, I'd have the bus driver stop someplace, usually an all-you-can-eat equivalent of a Pizza Hut or whatever, and pay for the guys' meals. When the owner found out, he decided that wasn't right and said that he would foot the bill.

This was not only a motivator but, as I also learned, a good team-builder. You may not have heard this expression, but some clubs are "twenty-five taxi" teams. That means that when a road game is over, in the big leagues, each guy gets his own cab and goes his own way to his own place. That may not literally be true (well, I've heard that some teams actually are like that and guys won't share cabs with one another), but the point is obvious. So is this one: teams whose players like each other and hang out together are often very successful. You may think that my "dinner's on me" plan wouldn't work in the big leagues, but it did. When I got to the White Sox in the last half of '79, and for my entire tenure there, we occasionally held team get-togethers on the road. We'd organize a group, feed them, and let them talk and rip on one another, insults being the standard means of communication among ballplayers. We had a lot of fun doing it.

Probably the high point of this was 1983, when the White Sox won the division. Two great veterans, Jerry Koosman, who was a starter with the 1969 "Miracle Mets" and was just a stellar individual, and Greg "The Bull" Luzinski, who was part of the 1980 World Champion Phillies, used to rent a suite at whatever hotel we were staying in just so the players would have a place they could get together. After every night game on the road, an open invitation was extended to anyone who wanted to go to the suite, and they'd order bags of burgers or a pizza and hang out and talk baseball and talk crap about one another.

When I moved on to Oakland, the White Sox players would ask the A's if we had a lot of parties. We had some, but not as many. Times were changing, and when I got to the Cardinals, we didn't do those kinds of things very much at all, and there were some good reasons for that. Guys were taking better care of their bodies and watching what they ate and drank. On the negative side, we had to be careful about team-"sponsored" events where alcohol was being consumed. Ironically, I think it was because we provided the guys in Chicago, and to a lesser extent those in Oakland, with a place to be and something to do that we didn't have any big drug or alcohol scandals there like other clubs of that era.

This brings up the distracting influences of a changing society and the drug culture that today's players have to deal with and that in turn we have to address. In 2007 I was involved in an incident that may make some people question my status as a commentator on these things. Ironically, it was the spring of 2007, and we were still basking in the glow of the 2006 World Championship. That glow was totally snuffed out at about 11:00 P.M. one night when the police in Jupiter, Florida, found me stopped at a red light, napping. Evidently, I'd had too much wine and failed the breath test. The nightmare included being arrested and going through the public process that follows. It was an unforgivable mistake, and any explanation is an excuse. But I admitted my mistake, pled guilty to the DUI, and apologized to everyone who was affected by what I still consider an embarrassing slip in judgment. In my mind, that doesn't mean that I lost all credibility with players when I talked with them about those issues and about how to protect themselves, the club, and their families. In fact, my mistake probably added to my credibility on the subject. To this day, I'm still trying to earn back trust and respect from some family and friends.

That came into play when in January 2010 I had as serious a conversation as I could possibly have with David Freese. David had also been arrested for a DWI. He told me that it would never happen again. I was concerned about him as a person and as a player. We expected him to be a good teammate. I knew that except for that one mistake, he was an exemplary young man. The basis of our team's chemistry is trust, and incidents like that one threatened to erode that trust. We wanted him to be a productive player for us, and we didn't want to see him hurt himself or anyone else, so we were available to do anything we could to help him out. And I tried to explain the consequences. He was grateful for the advice and concern, assuring me that no one in the organization would have a David Freese problem. Sometimes personalizing extends beyond what happens between the baselines.

Wherever I've managed or played, family was always important to us. We felt that family was a way to personalize even more with a player. Having things right with a guy's family can and will give him an edge at the park that helps him to compete. To that end, we did some family things, particularly in spring training, that were outgrowths of what I'd experienced in my early days. Some years we'd have a big family picnic day each season, and after many games we invited the families to come out behind our clubhouse to have some fun. The kids could take cuts at Nerf and Wiffle balls and run around, and it was great fun to see everybody out there.

So, if you're keeping score at home, the negative side of the ledger as I decided whether it was time to retire included dealing with the media, with the players, and with the negative impact on my family life. But there were some positives. I had the same kind of relationship with the coaches in 2011 that I had in 1982 with the coaching staff who wore my good-luck jacket in my absence. Any display of camaraderie like that means a lot to me, and the prospect of not being able to go to work every day with people I respect and like was a strong reason to stay on as a manager.

I had, contrary to the La Russa mystique, great relationships with the great majority of my players, good relationships with the rest, except for the few who were disgruntled with me or my leadership style. More public attention was given to these few than to the rest.

I also really liked the makeup of the 2011 team and the individuals on it, and we were winning more than we were losing. Oddly, though, this last point worked against a decision to stick around past 2011. I talked about this with a lot of other coaches from other sports as well. We all agreed that we didn't get quite as much satisfaction out of doing our jobs as we once did. Even if we were winning, even on the verge of a good season with the playoffs in the picture, we didn't feel that same sense of accomplishment and pride. All the negative elements of the modern professional sports world detracted from the good feelings. Put simply, it wasn't as much fun as it had been. That might sound strange coming from a person with my reputation for intensity and from someone who was often noted for not smiling. I took seriously the responsibility I had, but I *loved* the competition, the winning and losing, and the relationships we built.

It's true that I didn't smile a whole lot during games. I wanted to maintain a competitive demeanor. I wanted to maintain the same exterior whether things were going good or going bad. One reason for that is I wanted to set an example for our players and also to be a constant they could rely on.

Yes, there were lighthearted moments in the dugout, on the field, in the clubhouse, and at many other places, but for the most part, in the middle of the competition, I wanted to be that concentrated center in the middle of the storm. I had to work at that, because on the inside I was a festival of nervous energy, anticipation, excitement, anger, frustration, elation, and just about every other emotion you can name. I know that the anger and frustration sometimes surfaced more readily than my more positive attributes. Whether I should be criticized for that, I can't really say. But I will say this about my intense level of concentration: I have zero regrets about how I went about my business, day in and day out. I might have made plenty of mistakes, but none of them came from a lack of interest or from inattention.

Ultimately, none of this was ever about me; it was always about the players and about winning. Call it "old school" or whatever you like, but the level of seriousness I brought to my job was purposeful and long-standing. Another element that went into my decision was that I couldn't alter who I was essentially as a person to conserve my energy or take shortcuts. If I was going to continue to manage, it would have to be at that same max effort that I'd always put in. I couldn't slow down. It was either do it or don't do it.

As I said, I was raised to be a responsible person. Even when I was in elementary school and I was put in charge of the patrol boys—who helped kids cross the street safely—I took my job as captain seriously. If they weren't on time, if they weren't polite and responsible, then that reflected poorly on me. I only did well if they did well. Take that kid in the 1950s and transport him into the world of professional sports four and five decades later, put him in charge of million-dollar-a-year earners in a billion-dollar industry, and you can see how the pressure to get others to perform and produce gets ratcheted up—way up. Having to attend to that many people and their interests and idiosyncrasies can wear you down over time. The fun factor gets diminished, regardless of how much you smile—or don't smile.

In the end, I saw that all these factors had been present for my entire thirty-three years of managing. Not only had I continued to work in spite of them, but I felt privileged to do so. In 2011, getting a team ready in the spring and competing for a 162-game season to see if we were good enough was as exciting and challenging as ever. As I thought about all of these factors, it wasn't any specific one that made me think it was time to stop. It was just that, sooner or later, all things come to an end.

IMPORTANT AS ALL THESE REASONS WERE, THERE WAS SOMETHING larger influencing me, something related to the intensity of my approach, and in many ways it was indicative of the responsibility I felt to stay focused on the game at all times and on every pitch.

The more I contemplated retirement, the more I found myself thinking about incidents like one that had happened in 1991 when I was managing the A's. In June of that year, we'd gone into Chicago for a series with the White Sox; it hadn't been that long since I left the White Sox, and some of the guys on the team had been there when I was their manager. Among them was Bobby Thigpen, a big right-hander with a strong arm. He'd set the record for saves the previous year with fifty-seven, and he could bring it. I liked Bobby and admired how he'd developed into one of the premier closers in the game. On June 1—and I remember that date because of how much this incident affected me—we were down going into the ninth inning and Thigpen was on the mound. He hit Terry Steinbach, our catcher, in the head with a pitch.

I ran out of the dugout with my heart in my throat after witnessing one of the most frightening scenes in all of sports. If you've never heard the sound of a baseball hitting a helmet and then seen a player drop to the ground like he was a cow being slaughtered with a bolt stunner, then you can't imagine what was in my heart at that moment. My overriding concern was for Terry, but once he was placed on a stretcher, fully conscious yet dazed, my anger turned on Thigpen and the White Sox. I'd watched enough videotape to know that Thigpen's method was to throw inside with the fastball and then paint the outside corner. In our hitters' meeting, we'd gone over that, and I'd told the guys to spit on that inside pitch and then look for the ball away.

As angry as I was at what happened, I was chewing up my own insides because maybe Terry was looking away and when the ball came inside he couldn't get out of there in time. Mostly, though, I wasn't happy that a guy would throw a pitch to that spot knowing that he had such a small window for success, such a small margin for error. I was angry at Thigpen not because of his intent to pitch inside—pitching inside correctly is a prerequisite for getting outs—but because the up-and-in pitch is dangerous, especially with hitters turning into the middle of the pitch instead of away from it. The same inside effect can be accomplished by concentrating the ball at the chest or lower. It's not like pitchers are snipers with scopes and tripods and all that other equipment who can hit a precise target from hundreds of feet away. They can throw to an area, and when they miss, as Thigpen did, the results can be terrifying.

I was scared for Terry. This was my worst dream realized. With so much adrenaline going through me, I was jawing at the Sox, and they were jawing at us, and after Terry was wheeled away both benches cleared, and this could have easily gotten much uglier than it did.

I was so mad that I picked up Terry's bat and flung it onto the backstop. It was either do that and release some of my aggression or do I don't know what. And Dunc, the stand-up guy that he is, led the charge out of the dugout. I knew that Thigpen hadn't hit Terry intentionally; I knew that he was coming inside and it got away from him. But there are consequences to doing that.

After the game, I was required to speak to the press, just like coaches are today. I had calmed down enough that I wanted to do what I was obligated to do so I could get the session over and get to the hospital to be with Terry. The press came into the visiting manager's office, a tiny little closet of a space, and they were all crowded in there with me. I was still steaming but keeping it calm on the outside. At first, all the questions were about Terry and how he was doing, and I was still so pissed that I said, "How do you think he's doing? You saw what happened."

They kept pressing me, and finally I said, "I don't want to talk about it. Whatever you want to ask me about the game, aside from that incident, I'll answer, but I want to get out of here and be with my player."

Everyone let it drop, but one guy wouldn't let the thing go. He was older, and he'd always seemed kind of clueless in the past, so I wasn't sure if he just didn't get it or he was purposely being an ass.

"One of your guys got hit," he said. "What are you going to do about it?"

"I'm not going to talk about it," I reminded him. "My concern is for Terry, and I'm not going to talk about anything like that."

"That's not an answer. Your guy is in the hospital. What are you going to do about it?"

I repeated what I'd said before. Game questions—yes. Terry and the incident questions—no. I gave them one more opportunity.

"That's no answer. Your guy—"

"I'm done," I said, cutting him off before he could finish. "No more questions of any kind. I'm going to the hospital," I said, and as

I was stepping out the door, he replied, "Answer the question. Be a man." I tried to ignore it and repeated that I was done and going to the hospital, when he repeated, louder, that I should "be a man."

I walked up to him, my eyes bulging and my face red, and I gave it to him. "Be a *man*? Be a *man*? There's a *man* in the hospital right now, and that's where I should be instead of talking to you." I shouted a few more things, and Dave Stewart, our pitcher and another stand-up guy, came running in to separate the two of us. And what got shown on the news that night and the next day? A man asking me a question and then me going off on him.

No one showed the lead-up. No one showed me being reasonable and explaining multiple times that I wasn't going to discuss the incident. That reporter was hunting for the bigger story, and I wasn't going to give it to him. Instead, people came gunning for me.

Fortunately, Terry was okay, but I never, never forgot that extreme example of one reporter's terrible behavior and his inability to understand just how much responsibility I felt for what had transpired. I never forgot that sickening feeling as I ran out there to check on my fallen player. Also, I'd learned early on about the media fraternity and how they protected one another.

This story illustrates what was by far the most difficult part of my job, and the number-one factor that influenced my decision to leave managing: I had been taught that of all the things a manager is required to do, the most demanding, and the most exhausting, is to scrutinize every pitch with all the focus and ferocity it takes to judge the possible intent and meaning of pitches that are delivered inside, near, at, or sometimes behind our hitters.

In a way, this task represents everything it means to take on the job of being a manager. It was my duty to protect our players, and with those inside pitches, our hitters' physical safety was on the line. You can't say that you personalize things with the players you spend eight months of your year with, work with all of them to become a family, care about and develop close relationships with them, invest your time and energy in helping them to develop as players and people, and then not be as vigilant as possible about protecting them from great harm. If you don't feel that sense of obligation—or better put, that desire—to protect them, then you're a fraud and everything else you do is sham, just so much window dressing.

For all those years as a manager, pitch by pitch, I had to intensely concentrate to see if our hitters were being abused. That's roughly 25,000 pitches per year (figuring 150 to 160 pitches per game for 162 regular-season games) for 30 years. Conservatively, that's 750,000 regular-season pitches for which my level of concentration had to be a 10 out of 10. I felt this as a personal responsibility, and I also felt it as an obligation to all those who had a stake in us and supported our game.

Just so you understand better what I was doing all the time I was scowling in the dugout, let me tell you what I was looking for when it came to protecting our hitters. If a pitch was inside, I had to determine if that location was intentional. That led to the question of whether or not the opposing pitcher or team was trying to intimidate us. Were they trying to alter our state of mind so that we wouldn't have good at-bats against them? Or were they trying to penalize us for already having good at-bats against them in this particular game or in previous games? Or were they simply being aggressive, trying to "own" the inside part of the plate as a particular pitching style or approach to getting our hitters out?

All of these possibilities, to varying degrees, are legitimate aspects of baseball. When you sign up to play, you know that getting pitched inside or struck by a thrown ball is a possibility. Just because that's a possibility, though, doesn't mean it should happen intentionally or that you should be buzzed inside, have one "flown past the control tower," or whatever euphemism people use to describe and—knowingly or not—diminish the seriousness of an inside pitch.

When I felt like I needed to protect my players, the decision wasn't easy but I had to make it. An incident in spring training that year was still troubling me when I was going over my decision points in early July. We had been playing the Washington Nationals in a preseason game, and Carp had hit Laynce Nix with a pitch on the body. Normally there wouldn't have been anything special about it, but in this case, the year before, Nix had been with the Reds when we'd had the Cueto kicking incident. Dave McKay, our first-base coach, assured Nix that it wasn't intentional, but their bench was convinced that it was payback for the previous year. So then Livan Hernandez hit Ryan Theriot. To my mind, he threw a pitch intentionally that far inside. I barked at their manager, Jim Riggleman, a great guy who I respect and count as a friend. In fact, when I was a player-coach, Riggleman was a teammate and a good one. He knew my philosophy. We would never throw at someone intentionally just because they had a hot bat. We wouldn't use that pitch to try to intimidate or distract a hitter.

We would, however, defend ourselves. In thirty-plus years, I never ordered a pitcher to drill someone because he was hitting well against us. In every stinking case it was a response to our player being thrown at.

I went to Miguel Batista and said to him, "Go after Ian Desmond." Desmond is their shortstop, and in biblical terms an eye for an eye was what I was going to do—shortstop for shortstop.

I hated having to make that call, but it was the right one to make. The difference was that we tell our guys to hit a batter in the back or the butt, the hip area. Nothing high above the shoulders.

Miguel did as instructed.

Angel Hernandez, the first-base umpire tossed Miguel. To his credit, Hernandez told me that he was watching our dugout between innings and saw me talking to Miguel. There was no doubt in his mind what had just happened. Riggleman and Desmond were both pissed off, and much mouthing off between our side and theirs went on.

I agonized over the incident all night. It had involved not only a manager who was a friend but a great ballplayer, Desmond, who I would have loved to have on our club. A few days later, I went up to Jim, and we spoke. Jim was honest with me and said that he didn't order his pitcher to go up and in on Theriot. The guy did it on his own. I told him that we had to protect our players. That was it.

But it really wasn't. As I thought about whether or not this would be my last year, I kept going back to that incident. In some ways, how I felt about it mirrored what I was thinking in terms of this 2011 club. I had everything I wanted in terms of great team chemistry. Still, it wasn't as much fun as it had been. The duty I felt to protect my players had forced my hand, and I'd had to do something against a manager and a player I really liked. That wasn't any fun.

I distinctly remember thinking, *I've had just about enough of this crap.* It was the combination of the accumulation of crap and the constant vigilance that had me close to the edge.

When I added in all the rest—the media nonsense especially—I thought that if I wasn't getting the same enjoyment even under the best of circumstances with this team, then it really was time to get out at the end of the year. I decided that no matter what happened with the club, this season was going to be my last. By not telling anyone, though, I left some wiggle room to change my mind.

Please don't get me wrong. I still loved the game of baseball. Like I told our players many, many times, I wish the game was this simple: Our side. Their side. Nine innings of play. Keep score and see who wins.

But it's not like that, and with all the things I've said here, I don't want this to get lost: I still love the game. I love the unpredictability of it. There's magic in that, but in July 2011, I realized there wasn't enough of it to transform the rest of that lead weight into gold.

I DIDN'T TELL ANYONE OF MY DECISION UNTIL MID-AUGUST, WHEN I first told Elaine, and even then I kept it very quiet. Elaine was surprised, and she would have been more disappointed and upset if she'd thought I was serious. The next time we discussed it, during our September rush, she thought the excitement of the pennant race would have put any thoughts of retirement to rest. When I told her that I was still intent on going through with my plan, she mentioned two things. One, she said it would mean a lot to her and the girls if I passed John McGraw for second on the list of most managerial wins in a career. I could understand their thinking, but I couldn't give in to it, because that was something personal and not professional. Doing it for them, knowing that I shouldn't be there, wasn't something I could do. I hated to disappoint them.

The second thing she said hit me the hardest. She told me that for the last thirty years, she and the girls, whether over the radio, TV, or Internet, at game time would turn on the broadcast, and go about their day while keeping track of our progress. Every day for six months or more, they did that. Our games were so much a part of their lives and had been for so long, that they couldn't imagine going on without them as the sound track for their lives.

Hearing that was the only time I reconsidered my decision. Elaine really made me realize, good and bad, just how intertwined my two families were.

I didn't want 2011 being my last year to be a distraction. We still had the better part of a season to go when I made up my mind. I also didn't tell anyone because I wanted to retain the right to change my mind. There was still plenty of baseball left to be played. I couldn't have predicted that despite all that I was feeling, the fun was going to make a comeback.

CHAPTER EIGHT

Sliding

WE'VE PROBABLY ALL HEARD THE JOKING STATEMENT, "THE sooner you fall behind, the more time you have to catch up." During my life in baseball, I've always gotten a kick out of waking up each day in first place and "not relinquishing the lead." Sal Bando, the team leader on our class AA team, made that statement about our team when we were in the midst of winning the 1966 Southern League Championship. In the last fifteen years, of the 120 big league teams to reach the playoffs, 68 of them had a lead at the halfway point in the season. That means that 57 percent of the time, if you're in the lead at the halfway point, you won the thing. When you're trailing, conventional baseball wisdom tells you that you try to gain a game a week on the leader in the standings. We were well past the halfway point when we made the trade. July 27 marked game 104 out of 162, which meant that we had 58 games to go. We were half a game behind Milwaukee in our division. So we were thinking that our chances of catching them remained pretty good. By the end of July, we'd lost more ground and were two and a half games behind the Brewers.

No reason to panic, obviously—we had fifty-four games left, and with eight and a half weeks remaining in the regular season, we had every reason to believe that no one was going to run away with the division.

That was another reason why, hours before the July 31 nonwaiver trade deadline, we sent a minor league prospect to the Dodgers for their veteran shortstop Rafael Furcal. I've always admired how the Braves' organization did things, and from 2000 to 2005, Furcal had been a part of Atlanta's fourteen consecutive seasons of division winners. He was a slick fielder, and he had lively tools with his arm, bat, and legs. He'd joined the Dodgers as a free agent in 2006 and hadn't had as much success as he had in Atlanta. That meant, with him being in his twelfth year of major league ball, he was seeing a possible finish line ahead and was hungry for another shot at a title. In fact, he joined veterans Dotel and Rhodes in inspiring the team to get to October.

It's probably too much to expect any one trade to have a huge impact immediately on a club. It's rare when a shake-up of personnel sets a team on fire. Of course, we're always kind of hoping that happens, but in the first eleven games following the trade with Toronto, we were 7-4. Not exactly world beaters, but we did see some nice things. Edwin Jackson won his first start for us, beating the Cubs 9–2 on July 29. A few days later, on August 2, we beat the Brewers in eleven innings, with Kyle McClellan back in the bullpen and earning the win, and Octavio Dotel picking up his first save for us. The newly reordered bullpen shut out the Brewers from the sixth through the eleventh. The game was notable for another reason as well.

In the top of the seventh, the Brewers hit Albert with a high and tight pitch. Given Albert's earlier injury, the high risk of injury, and all the other things I talked about earlier in regard to intent, we felt we had to send a message to the Brewers. In the bottom half of the inning, we had Jason Motte hit Ryan Braun, the eventual MVP of the league. He did what we taught and hit Braun square in the back, thereby minimizing any chances of injury. Tempers flared, but I did what I had to do then, we went about it the right way, and I stand by that decision today. Unfortunately, we couldn't follow up that hard-fought victory with another, and we lost to the Brewers the next day to fall three and a half games back.

I was really encouraged by how we went down to Florida and swept the Marlins in four games, but those wins didn't change the fact that we muddled on for the better part of August. From August 9 to August 19, we went 4-5, losing two out of three at home to the Brewers. Carp earned his first win against them since 2009. He also evened his record to 8-8, impressive when you consider that he was 1-7 on June 17.

For their part, the Brewers were getting hot: they would wind up the month of August with a 21-7 record, plus-fourteen, the best in the majors. To keep pace with them, we'd have to win too, only it didn't work quite like that. We followed up the lackluster series against the Brewers by dropping another two out of three to a tough Pirates team; heading into Chicago, our opponent in one of the most intense rivalries in sports, and after losing to Pittsburgh, I expected there to be a huge sense of urgency. I didn't realize that urgency would take on another dimension.

In game 1, we jumped ahead 3–0 in the second and added on in the fourth, before the Cubs beat us in the tenth, 5–4.

Things got much worse after the game. In Chicago you play a lot of day games, so when this game was over, I was able to walk from Wrigley to the lakefront and then to the hotel for a bit of exercise. I walked along reviewing the game in my head, thinking that if we were going to be truly in this thing, then we should have been beating teams like Chicago and Pittsburgh. We'd just lost a series to the Pirates, and now we had lost the first game to the Cubs. What were we going to do? How could we turn this around? I mean, I was just burning up thoughts like these and tossing them into the lake.

I was just past Lincoln Park and the zoo and not quite at the

North Avenue beach when my phone rang. I saw that it was Dunc, so I answered it. I could hear something in his voice immediately.

"I have to go home," he said.

My first thought was, *Absolutely—do what you have to do.* If Dunc needed to leave, then it had to be something serious. Still, just the thought of a couple of games without him was nerve-racking. I managed to ask, "What's wrong?"

"Well, Jeanine," he said, referring to his wife, "has had some issues, and I need to go home and take care of her." We spoke a little longer, and he told me a bit more about a couple of the symptoms that had made her go to the doctor in the first place. Now the doctor wanted to see Dave and Jeanine together Saturday.

"Look," he said, "I'm going to tell Mo, and I'm going to tell you, but I really want to keep it quiet till we find out." We managed to do that, just as Dunc had asked. I credit both the St. Louis media and the club for handling that private matter the way they did.

When we finally got off the phone, I was shaken. I sat on a bench looking across the little indentation that makes up the Gold Coast, thinking about a conversation that Dunc and I had had about the team's strengths as we flew into Chicago for the weekend series. We were searching for reasons and wondered whether we were taking winning for granted. Ironically, we mentioned that it was analogous to personal and family health and taking that for granted. Now, in the context of winning and losing games, what the hell did any of this mean in comparison to what Dunc and his wife were possibly facing? Any thoughts of the Cubs, the Pirates, and all the rest were out the window. I was hurting for my friend, but comforted by the fact that if anyone was capable of taking care of his wife in a tough spot, it was Dunc.

In our lives in baseball together, Dunc and I go almost as far back as it's possible to go. I was signed in '62, and he was signed the next summer. He grew up in Texas, and I'd later learn he grew up hard. We met and were teammates in the A's '63 and '64 Winter Instructional League clubs in Bradenton, Florida, and then the '65 AA team in Birmingham, Alabama. My first impression of Dunc was this: I was a Boy Scout and he was a veteran soldier. It wasn't just the difference in our sizes (I was a physically immature six feet tall, and he was six-four and 220 pounds); our demeanors really set us apart. Dunc was as tough and as coolly calm as a rodeo cowboy, and I was young and trying to figure out a lot of new things.

He was also a talented ballplayer, hitting 46 home runs in '66 in Modesto, where we were both playing. (I was promoted to Mobile for the second half of that season, but we both won championships.) That was a hell of a Modesto team, with Joe Rudi, Rollie Fingers, and some guy who joined the club later in the year by the name of Reggie Jackson. Baseball is a strange game, and despite Dunc being a superior player and a valuable catcher, I was the one who made the '68 major league team. The franchise had moved to Oakland from Kansas City, and I was there opening day in the Oakland Alameda County Coliseum to watch Governor Ronald Reagan throw out the first pitch. Speaking of firsts, I had a couple myself. In 1963 I was the first shortstop in major league history to start a game at age eighteen. In case you're into trivia, here's the answer to a tough question, who are the only three eighteen-year-olds to start a major league game?— two pearls and a turd. The pearls are Robin Yount and Alex Rodriguez. The turd is the one who only had a roster spot because of a bonus rule—yours truly. That first day in Oakland I got sent up as a pinch hitter in the ninth inning with us down 4–1, with the tough Baltimore Orioles lefty Dave McNally on the mound. He'd surrendered a home run to Rick Monday in the seventh to lose his no-hitter and the shutout.

The 100-year-old rules of baseball strategy dictate that when you're losing in the last inning, the hitter should wait to get a strike. McNally knew that, and he'd been cruising through that game taking advantage of us trying to be patient. I got up there, hoping that Bob Kennedy, our manager, would let me swing away. I figured

McNally was going to just try to get one over and jump ahead. Nope. Had to take. Fastball down the middle screaming, "Hit me! Hit me!" I wound up in the hole 0-2 and had to go into defensive mode. In retrospect, that was probably a good thing. I wound up singling off McNally and have gone down forever in Oakland A's history as the first player to get a pinch-hit in the Coliseum. My much less than mediocre major league career can be summed up by an unearned roster spot, a meaningless pinch hit, and scoring the winning run for the Chicago Cubs on opening day in 1973. That run marked my last major league appearance and reads better than it was. I was only on base as a ninth-inning pinch runner for Ron Santo.

Later in '68, Dunc got called up from our AAA team in Vancouver. Who was getting sent down to make room for him? La Russa. Catfish Hunter was a great guy, and he was really feeling for me that I was getting sent down to AAA. "Hey, man, you're an important part of this team. I'm really going to miss you." Well, as it turned out, though I was being sent down, I'd missed the last flight out. So I was able to watch the game that night. Catfish threw a perfect game. Amazing. Afterward, I said to him, "You really were bummed out about me being sent out, weren't you?"

After that, I was yo-yoing between AAA and the big club, and the whole time Dunc was in the bigs. During the brief times I was up, I was able to pick up several very important points and strategies relating to leadership and managing from the A's manager, Dick Williams.

The way he took charge of the A's and made sure his own problem-solving tone prevailed, not the owner Mr. Finley's, became a cornerstone of my own problem-solving style over many years. I also learned from Dick the necessity and value of "playing the game right!" Execution matters and lack of it loses. He really pounded this message into his team's minds. Mike Shannon, a Cardinals legend and a special friend of mine, once uniquely made the point that "baseball is all about execution, and the only ones that disagree are on Death Row."

Finally, it was Dick's advice that led me to the practice of filling my lineup cards with game notes. The very important after-game review revealed many winning nuggets because they were all a part of those cards. You took actual game info, added insight, and came away with "stuff" about your team, your opponents, and what had decided the game just played.

In '72, I was in the minors the entire year while Dunc was with the team, and they won the pennant and were in the World Series against Johnny Bench and the rest of Cincinnati's Big Red Machine. Oakland took the first two on the road at Riverfront Stadium, but split the first two of the three in Oakland to be within one game of winning another championship. Except they couldn't close it out at home, and then they lost Game 6 back at Cincinnati. After the Game 6 loss, Dick Williams told Dunc that he was going to start Game 7 behind the plate. Dunc hadn't caught a game yet to that point in the Series, and Gene Tenace, the A's regular catcher, was having a hell of a Series. But Dick Williams went with Dunc.

Later on, I asked Dunc, "Man, what was that like? It's awesome being in the World Series, but you're sitting there and all of a sudden you're going to catch Game 7? What did you tell him?"

"I'll be ready."

"Weren't you nervous?"

"No."

If anybody else had told me that, I'd have called him on his B.S., but Dunc was like that. That was why people referred to him as "the Quiet Assassin." Being cool under pressure didn't change when he became a coach either. He was a pitching coach with Cleveland in 1981, and Len Barker had a perfect game going. The catcher and Dunc worked together to call the pitches. When it got to be crunch time, the catcher didn't want to take on the responsibility. Dunc said, "Give it to me. I'll take it." Barker got his perfect game. That's the kind of guy you want sitting on the bench with you.

But Dunc isn't all guts. He's a real student of the game: whether he was playing or coaching, his brains and creativity in handling pitchers were just phenomenal. And as much as I think of Dunc as a guy who could be a Navy SEAL or a Green Beret or whatever, he's also a cat lover. The thing to remember is that, even though many men believe that being a cat lover means you're not macho enough, the opposite in fact is true: understanding and admitting our affection for cats is a high form of macho-ness. In any case, Dunc doesn't care, he just appreciates cats' qualities and is into them.

He's a man of high principles as well, so, Dunc being Dunc, he was going to be with Jeanine and help her get through this tough time. I knew not having him around was going to be a real challenge for the rest of us. The pitchers loved and respected the guy as much as I did. The man just exudes confidence, and that's a great quality to have. Nothing cocky about him, just a "we'll get this done," "we'll get this fixed," "things will get better" mentality that served his pitchers well. I knew he was bringing that same attitude to Jeanine's situation, and that was as good and true and necessary a thing as you could ever hope to have.

I was still going to be in touch with him because that's Dunc: even if he wasn't right next to me to bounce ideas off, he was still there in the dugout because of all the things he'd taught me over the years. I can't say for sure what effect Dunc's absence had on the pitching staff at first. Dunc being Dunc, he didn't want to make a big deal about his leaving, but the guys did know what he and Jeanine were going through. I wasn't about to use that as a tool to motivate them. Baseball is baseball and life is life, but if guys were going to take some inspiration, learn some lesson about how to deal with a hard and difficult thing head-on, then they could find no one better to emulate than Dave Duncan.

BY LOSING TWO OF THREE TO THE CUBS, WE FELL EIGHT AND A HALF games back—the largest deficit we'd faced since 2008. With only thirty-six games left and only a little over six weeks remaining in the season, that old adage about picking up a game a week wasn't going to get us there. When I was managing in Oakland in the late 1980s, when we were in first place and that magic number was at 40, I would track it's progress at the bottom of my pitching chart. Setting a goal of reducing the magic number by three in every series not only kept the focus on what was next but was fun and motivating. You can imagine what doing the opposite, counting down to the tragic number, feels like.

There's another marker that we use during a season to gauge our relative position and chances of success: get to ninety wins. We were at 66-60, that same old plus-six we'd been at after the August 20 loss to the Cubs. If we were going to get to ninety wins, we were going to have to win twenty-four out of those remaining thirty-six games, a stretch in which we'd have to win at a .667 clip, or every two out of three.

That was still compatible with a "win the series" approach, but I also felt like that wasn't going to be good enough to catch the Brewers. Unless they really struggled, they'd easily outpace ninety wins. They were already at seventy-five, so they had to win only fifteen out of thirty-six to get there, while we had to win twenty-four. You can't count on that kind of slump happening to a team. Control your mind and your own team. Ninety wins would be great, but considering that we were playing at .524, getting on that .667 pace would be difficult—not impossible, but even if we did, we'd likely still fall short of a division title. We weren't thinking too much about Atlanta at that point, though the irony is that on that same August 20 date, their record was the same as the Brewers'. They were trailing the Phillies, who were pursuing a franchise-best record, but were still playing terrific baseball.

I sat there on the flight from Chicago back to St. Louis turning all of these things over in my mind. My biggest concern, as we looked ahead to a seven-game home stand against the Dodgers and Pirates, was the feeling that the club seemed different. It wasn't that we were backing off our intensity, but something felt slightly off. To date, our team had been so determined to compete the right way, no matter what we'd had to overcome. With all the injuries and setbacks we'd been through, to be six over .500 as of August 20 was an impressive achievement. When the season was in the books, if our 2011 club continued to scratch and claw, then whatever we finished with would be our best. If we were not going to be a playoff team, we'd be disappointed, but we wouldn't have regrets. You can live with disappointments, but regrets will haunt you.

One of the realities of playing the last third of August with the season's end in sight is that you really narrow your focus. The decisions are now all short-term. They are not about confidence-building versus your best chance to win, not about using all the roster to keep players fresh and sharp. They're about staying in contention, and what that meant right now was figuring out the lull in our play and winning the home stand.

Unfortunately, that didn't happen. Despite their ownership issues, led by Don Mattingly, the Dodgers had done a remarkable job of separating their off-field problems from their on-field competing. We lost the opener 2–1. I relieved Carp, who had pitched brilliantly, in the ninth inning, ahead 1–0, after he hit the leadoff batter. As I walked to the mound, the fans were "unhappy." A triple and ground ball later for two runs, the boos were deafening. Twice so far in 2011, both against the Dodgers, I'd relieved Carp in the ninth with a 1–0 lead. Both times we lost. Maybe the next time Carp was ahead 1–0 in the ninth, I should just let Carp finish and not butt in.

In game 2, Lohse was the starter, and we lost 13–2. The sweep was complete when they jumped on Garcia and we lost 9–4. As the game's last innings played out, we were officially in crisis mode. Ten games behind the Brewers and ten and a half behind the Braves. As we gathered ourselves in the dugout, Carp came to me.

"Are you going to talk to the team?" he asked.

"Something has to be said," I replied.

"The veterans want to hold a team meeting after the game."

I thought about that for a minute before replying, "That's not a good idea."

He shot me a confused look, but before he could ask anything, I continued: "If you want to have a meeting, don't do it after the game. Have it before tomorrow's game, and don't let anyone outside of the club know about it. Keep it private. Keep it purposeful."

I've never been a big believer in players-only meetings, and I always thought the team sends out a mixed message when they have one after a game. Of course, the press is going to find out about it, and then that meeting gets perceived as a "cover your ass" move. It's like sending a signal out there that says, "Look. We're trying." Before a night game, the press is allowed into the clubhouse starting at 3:40. I thought they should have the meeting start at 3:00 so no one from the media would know about it. Carp agreed that was a good move.

"Do you have a message I can share with the guys?" he asked. I looked over at him. Carp knew that I would have preferred to be there. Not that I'm such a control freak, but because as a manager and a staff we were all in this thing together. I wasn't going to stop them from having it. In fact, I was impressed that they were stepping forward.

"What do I want to say to them?" I asked Carp. "Tell them that for months scouts, front-office people, players have said things like, 'Man, you guys have hung in there great with everything that you've gone through.' And from what I've seen in the last ten days or so, for the first time all year, we've lost an edge."

I let that all sink in for a moment before continuing. "This is my quote for the team: We're getting ready to mug that respect that we have earned. From the media, fans, everybody. We can mug everything we've earned in the last six weeks. We have done so much to keep the urgency in how we compete that I believe it's a part of us. The lull or difference is because we're discouraged. Milwaukee has gotten very hot and pulled away from us. I think we feel all that gutsy work and the payoff is disappearing.

"We need to regain our intensity. Convince yourself that each of our last thirty-two games is the seventh game of the World Series, the last game of your life."

Obviously, I don't know how that got translated in the meeting since I wasn't there. I also don't know how well received the message was. All I can do is look at the results, and whether the guys did what they did in spite of what we were saying to them or because in some way it motivated them, I know something clicked. I could see in every at-bat and every pitch from that point on that the fire was back. Whether it was what Dunc and Jeanine were dealing with, the message I offered, or what the guys told one another, I can't say with any certainty. All I know is that during that 12-14 sequence following the trade, most of the headlines about the Redbirds had to do with them getting their wings clipped, being grounded, or whatever other bird metaphors you can think of. Most people believed we were done with. I won't go so far as to say that we rose like a phoenix from the ashes, but after that meeting we put together a damn good stretch of baseball, one that made history. We also kept pecking away, doing some of the big and little things it takes to win ball games. A game at a time, a series at a time, we shook off whatever was troubling us and moved forward.

During the off-season, a friend told me about a website called coolstandings.com. I'm not a big Internet surfer, but this caught my attention. The owners of that website use what's called the Bill James Pythagorean theorem to calculate a team's chances of winning a game, their division, or the wild-card playoff position. They claim to run millions of simulations in order to arrive at their conclusions. I once heard George Will say in a speech in San Francisco, "Statistics could be tortured to the point at which they will confess anything." On September 1, 2011, coolstandings.com and its algorithm gave us a 2.6 percent chance of winning the division and a 1.7 percent chance of winning the wild card for a combined 4.3 percent chance of making the postseason. I didn't consult the website back then, and I didn't have any kind of percentages calculated, but as I said earlier, I was more concerned with the basics of maintaining our hard-earned self-respect and respect from others than I was about the playoff possibilities.

I don't think Adam Wainwright was a big follower of coolstandings .com either. The night we lost that last game of the Los Angeles series, he, along with a bunch of players and staff, attended a dinner hosted by the Knights of the Cauliflower Ear. A man named Robert Hannegan founded the group to promote St. Louis as a sports capital. In fact, he was a co-owner of the Cardinals from 1947 until he died in 1949. So this group is very supportive of the Cardinals and the other St. Louis teams.

We ate first and then got to the speeches. Mo got up there first and delivered, without actually coming out and saying it, a "we'll get 'em next year" message. "A lot of the things that we had tried to plan for didn't go right," Mo said that night. Who would blame him? Our prospects were low, and he was being honest.

When it was my turn to speak, I got up and said, "We won't quit."

Then Adam Wainwright, our injured pitcher who had been out for the season, rose to say his piece. He was even more emphatic than I was as he laid out the plan for what would be the miracle comeback, starting with the next week's series in Milwaukee. Adam had been a real presence around the home clubhouse during his rehab, and I commend him for saying what he did, particularly if it reflected the rest of the team's belief. "If we sweep Milwaukee and then beat them three more times at home, all of a sudden we've gained six games in the standings," Wainwright said. "If we do that, all we have to do is make up a couple more games down the stretch. We're still in this thing."

* * *

AFTER THE DINNER, I WENT TO TONY'S RESTAURANT, A PLACE WHERE the family that owns the place treated me like one of them, and sat at a table by myself to think everything through. Dunc is a master of all things as a pitching coach, and sitting down with him and mapping out the rotation with him over the years had been like participating in a graduate school seminar in the art of managing people and situations. Because of him, I was in a good position to look at those final thirty-two games. As I sat there trying to come up with the rotation for those ten series that would close out the season, I worked on a sheet of paper where I had listed the dates and opponents to the last game. I noted that thirteen of the thirty-two games were the toughest of tests. Six versus the Brewers, four against the Phillies, and three head-to-head opportunities with the Braves in St. Louis. I was thinking about who would give us the best chance to stay above .500 and not get caught by the Reds. This was where we were:

67-63
Plus-four
Three games ahead of the Reds
Ten series left to play

By that point in the year, when assessing the pitchers, I was looking at the fatigue factor as much as anything else.

We can see that as the year goes on, pitchers' velocity, the sharpness of their breaking pitches, and the amount of movement on their fastballs vary from start to start. When most or all of these factors are trending downward, we know that they are tired. We can see it in an individual game, and we can see it throughout the course of a season.

The defensive part of the game begins with your starting pitcher. The four starts for the Pittsburgh series were already set—Jackson, Westbrook, Carpenter, and Lohse. The remaining twenty-eight games included three off days, so there was some flexibility in setting the matchups. Throughout the season, an off day meant you could keep everyone in the five-man rotation pitching with an extra day's rest or you could skip a pitcher and keep the others in the rotation. As often as possible, Dunc and I preferred to roll through the rotation without disrupting the flow and providing them all with the extra rest. If a starter was fatigued or sore, then it made sense to bump or skip him. The other reason to adjust could be the career successes or difficulties of a starter against a particular team. By moving a pitcher ahead or holding him back, you add a plus start and subtract a negative one.

At this stage, I thought that three guys were still fresh enough with their regular four days of rest to really be as effective as needed: Carp, Edwin Jackson, and Jake Westbrook. Jaime Garcia and Kyle Lohse had been taking their regular turns all year. In Lohse's case, he'd reached the 200-inning mark—a kind of gold standard for durability in starting pitchers—only twice in his career, in 2003 and 2008. In the two seasons since that last time, he'd gone only 92 and 117 innings, respectively, because of injuries. With Jaime, we didn't have as long a track record to look at. In 2008 he'd pitched only 16 innings, didn't pitch at all in the majors the following season owing to injury, and had pitched 163 innings in 2010. Now, in 2011, he was already at 163 innings.

The way I worked out the rotation was from the last game of the season backward. I knew that I wanted Carp to be on the mound that last day. Call it intuition, call it whatever, but I wanted him out there for that last game, no matter how meaningless or meaningful it was. Then I looked at the thirty-two remaining games and tried to figure out a way to get as many starts from the fresh three as we could. That way, I could let Jaime and Kyle get more rest and be more effective. Carp, Jackson, and Westbrook were all penciled in to get seven starts from August 25 to September 28—that covered twenty-one out of the thirty-two remaining games. With three off days thrown in, the fresh three wouldn't be going with short rest.

When I sat down with Jaime and Kyle, separately, to explain

what I'd devised, their reactions were a bit different. Being a veteran, Kyle was more comfortable expressing his displeasure: he told me he felt strong and wanted the ball. That was exactly the kind of response I had hoped for. Kyle wasn't happy about it, and he let me—and later the press—know that he was willing and able to go out there. I told him that it was a good and productive thing for him to get angry. Be pissed off at me—that's fine. Now take that anger to the mound and be pissed at those opposing hitters.

Jaime's just a quieter guy all around, and it was only his second year in the big leagues, with that arm injury still fresh in his mind. He, too, wasn't happy about the idea of not taking his regular turn in September. But he also said that he wanted to do what was best for the club, and if I felt this was the best thing, then he was okay with it. They both expressed the desire that we make it clear to the rest of the team that this was my decision and not something they had asked for. Understandably, they didn't want the rest of the guys having questions in the back of their minds about their willingness to take the ball when the stakes were high. We told them that of course we'd make that clear to everyone. That was yet another important way to personalize things—to manage their emotions as well as their innings.

In the end, with the extra days of rest, Kyle and Jaime were terrific down the stretch. They both won three out of their last five starts with two of those victories coming on extended rest. Looking back on it now, that move was one of the keys to our comeback. It was based as much on keeping them healthy as it was on winning games.

CHAPTER NINE

The Comeback

THE COMEBACK BEGAN THE DAY OF THE MEETING, AUGUST 25, against the Pirates, the beginning of a four-game series. Up to that point in the year, we were 4-5 against Pittsburgh; unlike in years past, when you could anticipate having some success against them, Clint Hurdle, in his first year with the club, had continued the hard style of play of his predecessors—Jim Tracy, Lloyd McClendon, and John Russell. Clint had motivated the 2011 Pirates with the prospect of completing their first winning season in nineteen years and were tough to play against.

The first pitch of that first game looked bad. Edwin Jackson drilled the leadoff hitter, Jose Tabata, in the back. This was a case of Edwin being overly amped up. He didn't need a meeting to remind him to keep the competitive juices flowing; he was ready to go all the time. Once we shook off that inauspicious start, all the usual ingredients were there—good and bad. Timely hitting, Holliday adding some power with a three-run home run, a defensive lapse on our part allowing a run, our failure to shut down the Pirates after we scored, but a good job by the bullpen with three scoreless innings, including R-zep's contribution and Salas's one-two-three ninth. During the game I noted that of the twelve runs scored between the two teams, eight were scored with two outs. That proves what I had been taught; the hitter has an edge with runners in scoring position and two outs. I was happy about our five RBIs with two outs, less so about their three. Still, if I was looking for an offensive trend that demonstrated we were back on track with our concentration and execution level, this was one.

The next game we fell behind 3–0 in the top of the first as Westbrook got off to a slow start. In the second, we came back when Yadi hit a three-run home run. I have to add that Yadi, like Jackson, was one of those guys who was always ready, always totally into the competition, and that home run was huge for us. So was the fact that the Pirates didn't add on much after that besides one run in the fourth. Again, that failure to add runs to a lead gives the trailing team hope, and we took advantage of their failure with a clutch two-run home run from Berkman in the eighth that made the difference. Having McClellan back in the bullpen also helped a lot, and those additional six innings of shutout ball over two nights from the bullpen was another nice trend. The combination of coming from behind twice and our bullpen shutdown of their offense created an excitement we hadn't felt in a while.

We lost the third game in the series 7–0, with Carp struggling, and I was eager to see how the team would respond with the four-game series on the line the next day. For us to get something going, we had to win the series. A fan checking out our starting lineup would probably have thought we were backing off; after all, we were ten and a half games back. We started the game with three key regulars on the bench. It was a classic "trust your gut, don't cover your butt" decision. Furcal, Molina, and Pujols were running on fumes and needed a day off. When the lineup went up, if the players didn't trust me, they might have thought I was surrendering.

I wasn't. I also wasn't covering my ass by not playing those three starters. The lineup choices I made were very tough ones to make, especially since the meeting had emphasized the need for urgency. I relied on the co-signers to deliver the message to the rest of the team. This was a case of gassed vs. fresh. Playing those three non-starters was our best chance to win a crucial game.

Laird, Theriot, and Craig (the latter two drove in 3 runs combined) proved our outstanding depth by contributing to our 7–4 win. Our ears were full of the sound of the guys chanting, "Win the series," as they came out of the clubhouse and into the dugout. That was good to hear, and they made good on the promise. Winning that game with those three in the starting lineup had an energizing effect. When you get contributions from everyone, the clubhouse vibe intensifies.

If we had lost that game with these regulars on the bench, I would still be trying to explain that longtime manager Gene Mauch's "fresh legs and blood" was our best shot. This would be the first game I added to my list of critical victories.

71-64
Plus-seven
Two and a half games ahead of Cincinnati
Nine series left to play
Series record: 1-0

We had an off day before taking on Milwaukee. Even though we were "facing" Milwaukee in the upcoming series, my eyes were still looking behind us. The numbers above reflect that. In our previous ten games we'd gone 4-6, while the Reds had won seven out of their last ten. Still, the bullpen's performance was hard to ignore— they'd pitched fourteen innings in the Pirates series and allowed only a single meaningless run. Our starters weren't getting much past the fifth, so that was a concern. The off day would help get all the bullpen guys some rest.

*   *   *

OUR CHALLENGE WAS TO BUILD ON OUR MOMENTUM AGAINST THE team with the best home record in the league. Game 1 of the Brewers series proved that you have to take advantage of another team's mistakes in order to be successful in this league. We'd been held to one hit through four innings by a very tough Shaun Marcum. In the fifth, we loaded the bases on two infield errors and a Molina single. Edwin Jackson came to the plate. He'd been in the American League with the White Sox and had batted only four times with them, and he'd gone hitless in interleague play. So what does he do? He singles to drive in a run. Jon Jay followed with a sacrifice fly, and we scored our only runs of the game. They held up in a 2–1 victory. Great performance by Edwin on the mound, and as it turned out, that hit was no fluke. Edwin went 8-for-26, a .308 clip, for us. For its part, the bullpen added two more shutout innings to reach sixteen innings and only one run allowed. All the drills to make one run or to stop one run paid off in the bottom of the ninth inning. With a one-run lead and runners on first and second, we executed the bunt defense, with Albert charging and forcing the lead runner at third base; a first-pitch, game-ending double-play came next. Something was clicking here.

The last game in August saw us win our third in a row and a series clincher with an 8–3 win over the Brewers. Suddenly, Adam Wainwright was looking like a fortune-teller. Jake Westbrook hit a grand slam, and according to someone I overheard on the bench, he had to be held back from running out of the clubhouse to go buy PowerBall tickets with that luck.

Then came a game I consider to be tied for first for the scariest I've ever managed.

I'd made the decision to hold off on starting Carp, even though it was his turn, in the final game of the series. His last outing against the Pirates had been a struggle, and after his five months of pitching, it made sense to me to take advantage of the off day; also, he was usually outstanding against the Reds, who we were playing next. That extra day would really help him through the rest of the rotation into that final game of the season against Houston.

In place of Carp against the Brewers I sent out rookie Brandon Dickson. This was one of the decisions that Jim Leyland and I call "going deep." Over a season there are decisions that require serious deliberations on several levels. This one could have set the mold. Why Dickson and not Garcia or Carp? Garcia would have had seven days' rest, which was good, but then he would have missed the Reds and the Braves. Dickson features a good hard sinker with a developing curve and changeup. I was hoping the unfamiliarity might get him through their very good lineup a few times.

In the end, I figured that the last Brewers game was important, but not as crucial as setting up Carp for the rest of the schedule. I knew it was serving up a juicy topic for anyone interested. I only really concerned myself with one group's opinion: our players. Your players always need to believe you're helping, not hurting, their chances. I felt I could explain it to them if they wanted me to. People assumed that if we had won the first two games, I would switch to Carp to go for the gusto. I was having the opposite thought—we won the series with those two wins, so let's try something unconventional for game 3. If we had lost two, then I might have pitched Carp because we would have been facing elimination with another loss. I'd agonized and agonized over that rotation, and pulling the trigger on this decision was so hard—but flying in the face of conventional wisdom, I strapped on the worry beads, and we all went at it.

One final point about making any really hairy decisions: agony is what it feels like, unless you don't care. If you are aware of the possible consequences, then it's agony. If it works, then it's a good decision. If it fails, then it's a bad decision. You survive by working the process as best you can, which includes remembering that they pay you for using your best judgment. *So use it.*

Top of the first, Furcal leads off with a dinger. A batter later, Albert goes deep. I'm thinking that this is just what the rookie, Brandon Dickson, needs. Go out there with a nice two-run cushion, pressure's off. He gives up a hit, but a double-play ball ends it. Top of the third, Albert hits a grand slam, and we have a 6–0 lead early in the game. I'm realizing that the stakes in this game, already high, have gone through the roof. The risk-reward factor is tremendous.

Mark it down, this is the point where I got scared, but it was "good" scared. Why? Once we took a 6–0 lead, we couldn't lose this game because if Carp had been pitching, we would surely have won it. And a win would make us seven and a half games behind the Brewers. "Good" scared meant that I was "what-if-ing" every possible outcome for the last twenty-one outs, literally pitch to pitch. And I was also concerned because, if we could not protect a six-run lead, the players would be looking at me and would maybe lose enthusiasm that they couldn't recover. If you need proof, check out the bullpen moves. This was the seventh game of the World Series, or the last game of my life.

Dotel, Salas, and Motte finished up. We won 8–4, and that afternoon I was about as happy as I've ever been after a win. As we were going into the clubhouse, Berkman looked at me, and I said, "That's the scariest game I've ever been in."

Berkman's face screwed itself up into a question mark, and then he said, "I thought you'd be pitching Carp. What's up with that?"

As we flew back home for a series with the Reds, I started to think that maybe we could win something this year. I didn't turn my thoughts to the Braves and the wild card, not just yet, but my head was turning maybe forty degrees from looking behind us to my periphery, where I could just make out the Braves and the Brewers in the corner of my eye.

73-64
Plus-nine
Six games ahead of Cincinnati
Seven and a half games behind Milwaukee

Eight and a half games behind Atlanta
Eight series left to play
Series record: 2-0

Thursday night we arrived back in St. Louis. I went to my other favorite restaurant, Dominic's, for more family food and hospitality. Despite experience having cautioned me to stay cool, I was enjoying the Milwaukee sweep and the third-game escape. It was such a close call not to have pitched Carp, but somehow the offense and bullpen led us to a win. I was eating and thinking we were playing with house money heading into the weekend series against the Reds. We had Carp, Jaime, and Edwin ready. Even as careful as I was, I had no clue that four games later we would be close to the edge once more.

* * *

In game 1, we played a very loose game and lost to the Reds 11–8. If you're looking for justice or fairness in sports, you're going to come up empty. The only thing that matters in real-life competition is the score at the end of the game; I got no reward or bonus for the gamble I'd taken with the rotation being manipulated. Except that the extra rest for Carp and Garcia worked out pretty well: Jaime Garcia pitched well for the win in game 2 of the Reds series, and Motte had a clutch five-out save. The series was even, and our favorite challenge, the rubber game, awaited.

In that game on September 4, Edwin Jackson did a more than creditable job for us. He gave up a single and a home run to Edgar Renteria to start the day. We hadn't even settled into our seats, six pitches into the game, and we were already down 2–0. Edwin battled the whole way, giving up six more hits but no more runs. Jay homered and Descalso tripled in our two runs, again showing how much our depth helped us, to tie the game. The Reds scored in the tenth after two outs on a single and a walk that proved huge after another hit, and we lost 3–2.

We had missed several chances in that game, particularly in the ninth when Craig pinch-hit and singled and then did an excellent job of baserunning by reading a ball in the dirt and advancing to second. We had the winning run at second with one out but couldn't get the big hit. Losing two out of three to the Reds at home could have made me poke my still itchy shingles eye out with a sharp stick. But even though it was tough, I realized that we were competing hard. We just got beat.

74-66
Plus-eight
Five games ahead of the Reds
Seven series left to play
Series record: 2-1

Losing the series to the Reds was difficult to accept, but this wasn't baseball on Fantasy Island. We'd played our game and lost. Now we faced the Brewers at home. Westbrook gave us a chance, but Randy Wolf was better. We lost 4–1. Just as we seemed to be getting something started, we lost three out of four. We needed to reverse our fortunes. Games 2 and 3 were going to be pivotal. By my count, this would be our *second* near-elimination time.

Moving on isn't as easy as it sounds, especially at this time of year. Mark McGwire and Mike Aldrete, our hitting coaches, spoke to the guys about Yovani Gallardo and the approach to take against him, but meanwhile I was thinking that we were now really up against it. We were like a tightrope walker—a gust of wind could knock us temporarily off balance, and then we'd either recover or go down.

The next night was a different story. Kyle Lohse, on eight days' rest, pitched six shutout innings against the Brewers. This was a *huge* bounce-back victory for us. Things were teetering on that tipping point again. If we had any hope of winning the series and keeping Cincinnati behind us, we had to win the next one. Lohse came up big for us, and I really believe that additional rest helped his arm and helped his good anger in our 4–2 victory.

The next day Carp sent a message to the team and to the rest of our upcoming opponents when he pitched a masterful four-hit shutout. You know he was masterful because he threw only ninety-seven pitches, had more than one base runner on in only two innings (one because of an intentional walk) and held their Big Two—Fielder and Braun—to a combined 2-for-7. This was the start of his own streak of clutch pitching that carried through to the last game of the regular season and into the playoffs.

We are all familiar with the law of unintended consequences. I wonder if, knowing what he knows now, Nyjer Morgan would have acted up like he did in the ninth inning of that game after Carp struck him out. Carp's words after the game explain it well: "He's a good player. He's a serious talent. He just plays the game a different way. I'm not going to play his game." That is all true, but I have to question a guy who wants to charge the mound after K'ing and has to be restrained by his own teammates. He struck out, took out his dip of tobacco, and tossed it toward the mound. Carp's not going to take crap from anybody, so he said something to Morgan. Albert decided to step in to protect Carp from getting into it and getting tossed and possibly suspended, and then Morgan mouthed off to Albert. Later, in a tweet, he called him "Alberta." Maybe because Morgan had played hockey, he also decided to play the Canada card. Both teams handled it well when the dugouts emptied, with Prince Fielder restraining Morgan and telling him, "C'mon, man, relax, there's nothing here."

You hate to coach aggressiveness out of a player, and Morgan is a talented player who sometimes crosses the line. The year before, when he was with Washington, he was scoring easily on a play and our catcher, Bryan Anderson, was standing out in front of the plate, out of Morgan's way, but not out of reach of his elbow. We went nuts, and the Nationals let us know that they would take care of it.

They didn't play him the next game, which was the right thing to do because we would have had to take care of it ourselves if they had played him.

When you play a team eighteen times during the regular season, there's bound to be some sparks, especially when both clubs have similarly aggressive styles. That's good competitive action, but what Morgan said in that same tweet—that we'd be watching the postseason on television—didn't fit into that category, and neither did his actions in that game. What he did was:

Unwise.

Uncalled for.

Not forgotten.

76-67

Plus-nine

Eight and a half games behind Milwaukee

Six and a half games behind Atlanta

Six series left to play

Series record: 3-1

September 8 was an off day for us, and though I'd have liked to be able to keep the momentum going, having a bit of a breather was important. I've pointed out that we made some good veteran acquisitions, and the presumption might be that the veterans are the guys you want because they bring a certain seriousness to the game that younger players might lack. That's not always the case, and in fact, veterans sometimes bring a looseness to their approach that helps a club relax and enjoy the ride. Arthur Rhodes, Octavio Dotel, and Rafael Furcal are three great veterans we brought in for the stretch run. I can't say enough good things about them. They were so fired up, so enthusiastic about the opportunity to compete.

I don't remember exactly when he began it—it may have been right away—but Rafael Furcal coined the term "happy flight" and started that chant in the clubhouse after we won the final game of the series in Pittsburgh to take two out of three from them. I'll never, ever have another holiday, like a "Happy Thanksgiving," without thinking about that. The chant was a way to remind the guys that the last game of the series, particularly a getaway game when we'd be boarding a plane, was of particular importance. You wanted to leave town on a high note, and the sight of these men, chanting that phrase and acting like a bunch of kids at summer camp, was one of the highlights of the 2011 season for me.

Another fun tradition was the players' annual NFL football fantasy draft. That took place on August 29, just after we'd had the happy flight from St. Louis after beating Pittsburgh. Most of the guys are huge sports fans. So they pair off in teams of two, wear the jerseys of their favorite NFL teams, and, in a meeting room of the hotel we're in, order in food and conduct their draft day. A lot of what they say in response to one another's selections I can't repeat here, but that day is one of the most hilarious of the season. It's mostly hilarious because of how serious the undertaking is and their no-holds-barred approach to decimating one another's ability to judge football talent and assemble a winning fantasy team.

I talk a lot about players and distractions, and while this may seem like one—especially in 2011, when it occurred just before that big series against the Brewers—the proof of its value as a pressure relief valve is evident in the results: we swept the Brewers. That draft not only gave the guys the opportunity to get away from the game for a bit, but also brought them together. The new guys got a chance to bond with their teammates and vice versa. This was a constructive outlet for them, and I hung around the draft room for quite a while just enjoying their company and adding my own critiques to their selections.

The players aren't alone in needing an escape. On September 7, I got out of the clubhouse as quickly as I could after the game to catch a Carlos Santana concert at the Fox Theater in St. Louis. This got some play in the media because I eventually revealed that Carlos, whom I'm fortunate to know through his own and his band's charitable efforts on behalf of ARF, presented me with a medallion necklace he'd worn that night. It had two dragons etched into the surface, and Carlos told me that it would give me good spirit. I wore that thing every day from that point on, through the end of the World Series. Over the years I and sometimes my family have met so many entertainers and athletes of different generations, coaches and people of prominence, that it's impossible to express my appreciation. They have been a very special part of my personal and professional life.

The Braves won both ends of a day–night doubleheader on September 7, which meant we were seven and a half games behind them with nineteen games to go. While I'd been hoping for a Mets sweep, I looked at that development this way: In the first thirteen of the thirty-two games we'd been counting down, we'd gone 9-4 and had moved from ten and a half games behind Atlanta to seven and a half back. That was progress. We needed to make more of it. I can't exaggerate the importance of Carp's clutch pitching in that rubber game against the Brewers and Lohse's win in the second game. They set us up perfectly for the Braves series.

With the benefit of hindsight, I see that late in game 1 we repeated a season-long formula: Edwin Jackson gave up two runs in the top of the first. Some pitchers struggle with the first inning, and that was a pattern we saw developing with him. He went the next five without giving up a run, and that was huge. Again our bullpen was effective, allowing only one run in four innings. We did a good job of responding to their early score with one of our own in the bottom of the first, but we went into the bottom of the ninth trailing 3–1.

Here we were on the edge again, facing the same situation as we had against the Brewers. A loss in game 1 meant that we absolutely had to win the next two to stay alive.

Rookies can be a blessing or a curse, and for the Braves, to that point, their rookie closer Craig Kimbrel had been the former. He'd converted twenty-five straight save chances, and he took the mound against us looking for number twenty-six. Sometimes rookies are good because they are, in the best sense, clueless. Too young and too inexperienced to really feel the pressure. In the bottom of the ninth, Schumaker got things started, as he was supposed to do, with a hit. A fielder's choice put Punto on first with one out. Laird struck out, so we were down to one final chance, down to our last out. Then the curse of being a rookie kicked in. That's too harsh, actually—the unexpected happens to veterans too. Needing one more out to close the deal and put a serious dent in our hopes, Kimbrel walked Furcal on four straight pitches.

Interesting. Tying runs now on base. Can this really be happening?

I looked down the dugout, and the guys were all on the top step, leaning over the railing. My eyes met Wainwright's, and we both shook our heads and smiled. That feeling, that sense that something was about to break our way, sat in the pit of my stomach like a bubble inflating. It's more fun to believe than to doubt.

Theriot stepped in, and it was like Kimbrel suddenly needed a map to find the strike zone. Three more balls. Seven in a row. Theriot took strike one. The next one was wide, and the bases were now loaded with two out. Guys were just going nuts in the dugout, looking at one another wide-eyed and shaking their heads at this sudden turnabout.

Bases loaded, bottom of the ninth, two outs—suddenly, who do we have coming up to bat but Albert Pujols, a .377 bases-loaded hitter with twelve grand slams.

Now, Albert had always been a clutch player for us, but high-pressure situations aren't something that you just wake up born to deal with. For years part of our coaching had been that we taught players to embrace pressure and make it their friend. And the way they'd do that was to confront it. They couldn't hide from it and say, *Hey, whatever happens, happens, so just go out there.* No, they had to step up to make something happen *when* they were expected to make something happen. They had to feel the anxiety, but we had taught them how to handle that anxiety, to use it to become a "go-to" competitor.

How did we teach that? Our first lesson would be never to let them run away. We'd tell the guys to feel it—the more often the better. Over time they'd just get used to it. Just like, if you live near a train and have to listen to signal bells and locomotive sounds all night long, eventually you stop hearing them. It becomes part of your normal state of affairs. That's what would happen once a player acknowledged pressure and anxiety. Some players react by becoming too hyper, and others become too tentative. Experience provides the player with a chance to evaluate his reaction and then make adjustments. The hyper player needs to breathe deeply and slow himself down. The tentative player needs to push himself to be aggressive and let it go.

Regardless of the player's specific reaction, feeling pressure allows it to become his new normal, and by the time he gets to October he has experienced this pressure. That's why you can't play five months with the attitude of whatever happens, happens, then suddenly in September say, *Okay, now I'm going to go out there and make a play or get a hit.* Complacency can destroy your ability to rise to a challenge; the more a player feels pressure, the more he learns how to deal with it.

Over time and through personalizing, I'd recognized that pressure manifests itself in some guys as good fear and in others as bad fear, and I wanted guys to understand the difference between these reactions. Good fear is knowing that you could screw it up if you're not completely dialed in, so you dot all your *i*'s and cross all your *t*'s. You pay closer attention to every small thing. Bad fear makes a player think, *I can't take the pressure. I'll call in sick. I can't make it. I'm going to let people down. I just can't do this.*

Feeling it is the first part of learning to deal with pressure. The second part is preparation. If you've done everything you can in advance to put yourself in the position to succeed, you'll be more relaxed and better able to deal with the pressure that comes with having to perform. That might mean working on your swing, or it might mean knowing the pitcher or hitter you're facing.

Feeling the pressure and preparing for it are vital, but the third part is the golden rule when it comes to high-stress moments, and something that we'd emphasize in all situations, not just pressurized ones: when you're in a position to perform, getting distracted by the possible result creates more pressure than anything else. If you're focused on the result, you feel the anxiety. Instead, concentrate on the process, not the result. *Win through process.*

For example, in the 2006 NLCS game 2 against Billy Wagner, So Taguchi, who had hit two home runs all year, did in the ninth inning to win that game for us at Shea. If we'd lost, we likely wouldn't have won the series in seven like we did. How did Taguchi do it? How did the guy who hit only two out all year do so under such great pressure? As he said later, he knew that Wagner threw hard and up. He just told himself that he had to get on top of the ball. He did and we won. He had been taught pressure was his friend. He controlled his mind, didn't let the distractions get to him, focused on the process, and trusted his preparation against Wagner.

How does all this translate when Albert's got the bases loaded with two outs in the bottom of the ninth against the Braves? Well, for one thing, he doesn't think, *What happens if I fail or succeed?* Or put another way, he doesn't think about the result. His total focus is on the process that defines his best at-bat for the situation. Then, as the pitch is made, it's all about seeing the ball and going after a strike in the zone.

After just seeing the two previous batters walk, Albert got in there and worked the process, figuring he was likely to get a cookie to hit on the first pitch. Sure enough, he got the pitch he was expecting, but he missed it. Still knowing that Kimbrel was not about to fall behind, Albert didn't miss the second one, which he smacked just inside the foul line in right to drive in two runs. Just like that he'd made pressure his friend and the game was tied. Those were the first runs Kimbrel had allowed since June 11, a string of thirty-eight scoreless appearances.

On Albert's clutch hit, we took a chance on scoring Theriot also. That third run would have won it, but he was out when the Braves made two good throws to get him. Jose Oquendo, our excellent third-base coach, correctly gambled over and over. We scored a lot of extra runs because of his sense of the game. Still, we could all breathe again after that one, though I think that I suffered a bit of hearing loss from the eruption of noise from the dugout and the stands. That sensation coming up from the bottom of your feet through the cement floor and into your head as the sound waves vibrate and the roar echoes around in our cave never gets old. It's a primal feeling of satisfaction and vindication, the sense that our side has exerted its will over theirs.

In the bottom of the tenth, two singles set up runners on first and second with no outs. It's a classic sacrifice bunt situation, but also the most difficult to execute because the infield is defending closely. The runner at second is being denied a big lead, and anything less than a good bunt becomes an easy force-out at third base. Too often we hear that bunting is a lost art in the major leagues. But with our season on the line, Descalso, who was pinch-hitting for Freese, bunted perfectly, and Holliday was then the potential winning run at third. Another often-heard lament is that players can no longer drive home the run from third with less than two outs.

In that situation, we teach hitters to stay inside, on top, and through the pitch, thinking right-center to left-center. A Nick Punto sacrifice fly on a great piece of execution hitting brought home the winning run. On that sac, Punto, who'd been nicknamed "the Shredder," got a taste of his own medicine. All year he'd been tearing up teammates' shirts—on flights, in the clubhouse, wherever and whenever. They got him back good. The clubhouse was alive with the sounds of victory, and I walked through it, enjoying the moment, letting them know with a little golf gallery clap of my hands what I thought of their tremendous effort and acceptance of the good fear and how making pressure their friend had paid off for us.

Feeling good about being in it now, we took the second game of the series 4–3. On six days' rest, Jaime Garcia went six strong innings, and Berkman continued a hot streak by reaching base seven straight times over the course of those first two games.

After the game 2 win, Berkman put it well: "If we come out and lay an egg [on Sunday], then the series doesn't mean a whole lot because we really haven't gained that much ground. If we can somehow win the game tomorrow, then it gets really interesting."

And it did.

We took advantage of Tim Hudson's wildness in the third inning when he hit two batters, walked two, and allowed a Pujols RBI single and a huge two-out Yadi double that drove in three of the five two-out runs. Motte closed out the sweep game, a 6–3 victory, by striking out the side, and we sensed that we were looking at a guy who could do a lot for us, taking the baton of the closer relay race.

With that win, we took our fifth game in a row, the longest winning streak we'd have all year. In the process we jumped a high hurdle—not only did we win the series, but the hunger and readiness to play for the sweep was one of our most impressive performances. We could feel it—we were in the playoff race.

79-67
Plus-twelve
Four and a half games behind Atlanta
Five series left to play
Series record: 4-1

Going from the madhouse of playing in front of nearly 41,000 fans in St. Louis to fewer than 14,000 in Pittsburgh was a noticeable change in atmosphere outside the clubhouse and the dugout, but not inside it. The happy flight to Pittsburgh was one of those great ones, and the bus ride to the hotel was a classic. Rhodes took a break from critiquing Dotel's wardrobe and taunted the rookies about their upcoming fashion show. And I have to add here that on flights to away cities, when we know the guys won't be driving themselves anywhere, the team rules allow them to responsibly consume alcohol. And I wouldn't say this if it wasn't true, but the flight attendants on our charters have always made a point of telling the staff that they appreciate how respectful the guys are, that they are among the nicest to deal with of all the teams in the league. We tell the players to respect the opponents, the game, and themselves, and that last one carries over into how they end up treating other people who are a part of taking care of them.

To that point in our thirty-two-game run, we were 12-4 and had knocked off six games of Atlanta's lead. We really felt now like we were in it and that we could do it. One advantage, of the many, to personalizing our leadership style is that usually we are very aware of the team's vibes. It was so clear to us that this group of teammates, after hanging tough all season, was not only playing hard but enjoying the competition and the effort to win. Playing from behind requires a very different mentality.

In 2001 we'd had a similar late-season run from out of contention to tie for the Central Division Championship. That team was a regrouping of many of the players who had been on our exciting 2000 team that started this run of successes, but it also included a key August trade. Woody Williams joined us from the Padres and turned in a 7-1 record with a 2.28 ERA. We were in third place in early August and eight and a half games behind. We went on a couple of winning streaks—eleven straight in August and twelve of thirteen in September. With eleven games to play, we were still five and a half games behind. After eight wins in the last eleven games, we tied for first.

That team had been a bunch of strong character types who refused to accept getting beat. It was more of a veteran club than 2011. Both teams recognized that some seasons you start fast and work hard to maintain your edge and close out the win. Once you get something going, then you're relentless until you close it out.

What we needed to demonstrate in 2011 was relentlessness.

Despite the fact that the Pirates had fallen thirteen games below .500 and were unlikely to end their string of losing seasons, we knew that Clint Hurdle would have them ready for us, and they were. Our 6–5 game 1 loss was another of those close-to-the-edge games that could have knocked us out of contention. Definitely a winnable game. We missed a key crooked-number chance in the third inning, and our bullpen couldn't hold a one-run lead in the eighth. We knew that we didn't have to go undefeated, but also that we couldn't afford many losses like that one.

The next two days demonstrated why this club was so special. A bounce-back victory, with Punto doubling in the top of the ninth (his second game-winning RBI in four games), was the highlight that made *SportsCenter,* but a key play really helped preserve the victory. We were up by two going into the bottom of the ninth. They opened with a pair of singles off Motte. Playing for the tie at home, the Pirates were in a sacrifice bunt situation. We called for our bunt coverage number one to combat it. Furcal bluffed the runner at second back to the bag, shortening his lead. Pujols crashed in from first, but Punto held back at third. The bunt was out in front of the plate, and Yadi pounced on it and rifled a throw to Punto to force the lead runner. If we'd played it conservatively, it's likely the Pirates would have had the tying runs in scoring position. Instead, Motte got a big double play and the game was over, with not many people realizing how big that bunt play was. If you do, then you also understand why I say that "little" play is almost as big as a game-winning home run.

Another small thing turned out to be a bigger deal than you might expect. In the ninth, Matt Holliday was on deck swinging and he hurt his finger. Holliday had to think he was cursed with all that had happened to him during the season. In August he'd lost two games to a back strain while lifting weights, and then later in the month he had to be taken out of a game because a moth flew in his ear. Appendectomy, ear invasion, back strain, quadriceps, tendon in his finger problems. The next day Craig was in the lineup replacing him. You never want to lose one of your bigs to an injury, but especially not when you're dealing with what we were facing in this race. Still, if we had to lose Holliday, it was great to have Craig to fill in. Craig contributed to our 3–2 win and taking the series by doubling in a run with two out. Edwin Jackson turned over the game to the bullpen in the seventh with just those two runs being charged to him. The bullpen was definitely in its groove, with everybody understanding their roles without having names attached to them. R-zep came in to get the last out in the seventh and the first two in the eighth. Dotel finished up that inning, and Motte went one-two-three in the ninth with two strikeouts.

I called Dunc after the game and told him that all the schooling he'd done was really paying off. The pitchers were a confident and prepared bunch. I enjoyed being able to go out to the mound to bring someone else in knowing that they were going to do the job. It's no fun to go out there to take the ball from a pitcher wondering if you're doing the right thing, or having the guy trot off with his head hanging down, while the guy coming in from the bullpen is working his crucifix or whatever token, hoping he gets through it. Prior to the start of the game, Furcal walked through the dugout chanting, "Happy flight!" That continued on the bus ride to the airport after the series win as well as on the flight to Philadelphia.

Now, after that game, I agreed to something that I hadn't allowed since 1996: I let the veterans dress the younger players in women's clothing as part of a hazing ritual that lots of teams engage in. Arthur Rhodes and Chris Carpenter had approached me about resurrecting the practice, which I'd eliminated after the '96 season. I'd banned it then because the guys just weren't being as respectful of the game and themselves as they should have been. I agreed to it in 2011 because of my respect for the guys on this club and the great vibe on the team. We had corrected the blip from 2010 in terms of our competitive spirit at that point in the season, and the guys had earned the right. It meant a lot to them. They knew that other teams around the big leagues had similar rituals and practices. Joe Maddon with the Rays had his team dress for flights based on geography—cowboy hats and western shirts for Texas trips, that kind of thing.

To be honest, seeing the guys in their dresses was different from seeing someone like Ryan Theriot in one of his eye-catching plaid numbers, or one of Arthur Rhodes's violet suits. I got on Arthur all the time about his suits. I'd tell him, "That's too fine for a regular-season trip. That's an October suit."

Arthur would just shake his head and say, "Don't you worry. I've got a closet full of postseason suits. You haven't seen a thing yet."

And Arthur, who has this deep, wonderfully sonorous deejay voice, after nineteen or twenty years in the league, acted like the fashion police. He would get all over Octavio Dotel or anyone else who appeared on his radar screen. At season's end, I regretted having had him as a teammate for only part of one season. But what a partial season it was.

So, with fifteen or so cross-dressers on the bus, we headed to the Pittsburgh airport, and among the hooting and the hollering, I heard some of the guys saying, "We're in it," and, "We got a shot." More important, they were also saying, "Be ready tomorrow, fellas." It wasn't just those words or those gaudy dresses that convinced me the guys were ready. Ever since the road sweep of the Brewers, even when we lost that series to the Reds, you could feel something building. After those two most recent wins, and as I sat there trying to get the image of the rookie Adron Chambers and his red frilly dress and matching red cowboy hat out of my mind, I was thinking: *I'm certain that the guys have achieved the ideal state of mind. They're enjoying and taking pride in competing all out.*

I was glad to hear and see them enjoying the trip to Philadelphia, and when our bus was a few blocks from the hotel, the veterans insisted that the driver drop off the new guys so they could walk the rest of the way. Instead of quickly and quietly getting to the hotel and their rooms, they strutted their stuff on the sidewalk and in the lobby. They may have wobbled uncertainly on their high heels, but they appeared confident and kind of cute in the face of taking on the Phillies, the team with the runaway best record in the league for four crucial games. If nothing else, we were dressed for success.

CHAPTER TEN

The Big Close

I F YOU REALLY WANT TO TEST YOURSELF, YOU PLAY AGAINST THE best. In 2011, during the regular season, the Phillies were setting the standard. When we faced them at their place starting September 16, they had already won ninety-seven games, eighteen more than we had to that point. We were at our season high of plus-thirteen. They were at plus-forty-six. I was really looking forward to taking them on. Eager doesn't begin to describe how I was feeling when we arrived at the ballpark. I was also curious. At some point you have to find out if you're good enough. The answer isn't always the score; it's how you go after it.

The opening game lived up to my early anticipation. We each scored a run in the second, and both pitchers were sharp. Garcia was making the start on his usual rest, but the additional days off he'd had earlier in the month was paying off through his good velocity and sharp control. He left after seven innings, having given up only five hits and one run. In the top of the eighth, Yadi, who in the previous inning had gunned down a runner trying to steal, hit a screamer down the line. We all jumped to the top step, willing the thing to stay fair, and it hit the foul pole for a home run. Albert went 4-for-4 in the game, but Yadi's home run was one of those back-of-the-neck chills that make September so fun.

The bottom of the ninth proved to be equally chilling, but for the wrong reason. We put Corey Patterson in right field to give ourselves a better defensive player out there. For the same reason, Descalso was at third, Theriot was at second, and Shane Robinson was in center. Good glove men all of them. Motte was on the hill for us, and he got the first two outs on a line drive to right and a strikeout. One out away. That out was in the shape of Ryan Howard. He was pinch-hitting despite a leg injury that had kept him from starting. He had always been a dangerous hitter, and the righty-lefty matchup was in his favor. After a first-pitch ball, Motte got two strikes on him. One strike away from a tough 2–1 victory.

As Motte went into his delivery, I could feel my heart in my chest; when the ball launched off the bat, I couldn't feel anything. Howard doubled to deep right and came out for a pinch runner. Okay, now it's Motte versus Carlos Ruiz, a right-handed hitter who had improved at the plate every year. Strike one. Strike two. Again, one strike away.

On an 0-2 pitch, Ruiz was late on a fastball away and hit one down the right-field line. If Craig had been out there, he wouldn't have even gotten to it. Patterson did, but the ball bounced out of his glove, and on a very tough play he got charged with an error. I heard myself say "crap" as I kicked the trash can. So close to a clutch win, and now we were facing extra innings. The advantage in this type of game goes to the home team—every time you don't score in the top of an extra inning, it means you need to get at least six more outs to win. We kept our hopes alive when the Phillies went with a left-handed hitter, Ross Gload. Rhodes punched him out with three straight pitches.

The guys came in, and I could tell they were feeling like one got away from us. They immediately flipped the switch, knowing that the outcome was still up for grabs. After a scoreless tenth, we came up in the eleventh and got our leadoff hitter on base when Furcal doubled.

Now I was faced with a tough decision. Corey Patterson was up, with Albert on deck and the rookie Adron Chambers in the hole. Chambers had pinch-run for Berkman in the ninth. I figured that no matter what, Albert was likely to be walked intentionally. With Furcal on second, I opted to give up an out and advance a base. I wanted that runner on third with one out so that a sacrifice fly, a wild pitch, a balk, or whatever could score him. Patterson did the job. Albert walked. It was an unfair challenge to a rookie, but Chambers had demonstrated he was a fearless competitor. It was first and third and one out when Chambers stepped in. Down 1-2, following another ball, he fouled off two *tough* pitches, then took another ball. Full count. I was sitting there thinking this guy was having a hell of an at-bat whether he was a rookie or not. Working the process, cutting down on his swing with two strikes, just trying to put the ball in play, anything but a strikeout here. The next pitch was on the inside part of the plate, and he pulled it into the hole between second and first for a base hit. 3–2. First hit in his big league career. First RBI. Tyler Greene followed with a huge RBI double, so we got an insurance run. Salas worked around a one-out single in the bottom half, and the game was ours.

No happy flight yet, but a happy clubhouse. Even better, the Braves lost. We were three and a half games back with twelve to play.

None of the small things mattered the next night. We lost 9–2, and the Phillies' Roy Oswalt looked like the Roy Oswalt of old the way he dominated for seven shutout innings.

And the Braves won. We were back to four and a half behind.

Game 3 saw another vintage pitching performance as Carp outdueled Cole Hamels in a 5–0 win. Carp has another gear that he can go to when he needs it, and it wasn't like he cranked it up to ninety-seven or something. In the first four innings, he induced three double-play ground balls to kill potential rallies by throwing pitches with nasty movement down in the zone. Nothing is as demoralizing as seeing a potential scoring opportunity snuffed out by a double play—they don't call them "twin killings" for nothing. Huge uplift for you and a huge deflation for the other side.

Gutty. Clutch. Whatever you want to call it, the guys just narrowed their vision and disciplined their minds to focus on the immediate task at hand and produce great results by not thinking about the results. I'm no Zen master and don't understand the *Tao Te Ching* any better than I do the Dow Jones Industrial Average. I just know that when guys are going balls out and loving the competition, a lot of good things can happen.

Offensively, Albert got us going with a first-inning two-run homer. Then Craig topped him with two homers. Suddenly there was an extra edge to our excitement. Two of our leaders, Carp and Albert, had it going. Scoreboard watching let us see that the Mets rallied late to beat the Braves. We were three and a half back with ten to go.

A note on scoreboard watching. I do it all the time. I tell the guys that if watching how the teams close to you are doing will fire you up, then watch the scoreboard. If it's too much of a distraction and gets you off your process, then don't. We all say the same things after the game, and while it might sound contradictory, it is equally true that we can only control our focus and effort. We can only play one game at a time. But we're human, and we're complicated, and we have the ability to control our minds. Look up. See the score. Return to focus. That's no different from guys having a social conversation on the bench.

Four-game series are tough for a lot of reasons. First, you face the majority of the other team's starters. Second, winning a series means taking three out of four. You can't split a three-game set, but you can a four-gamer. That's obvious in terms of math, but how that affects your approach to the series isn't. Would we have been satisfied with a split against the Phillies, especially considering that we were facing their ace, Roy "Doc" Halladay, in the final game?

Yes, but only if we conceded nothing and gave him and the Phillies our best competitive effort. It was a special challenge for Lohse. You have to pitch well because you know you won't get much to work with. All that contributed to my feeling that this was a critical game. Win today. Win the series. Do that and the answer to the question if we're good enough would be "Hell, yeah."

The key to beating any outstanding starter is to have every hitter go to war from start to finish. Furcal doubled on the first pitch to lead off the game. A passed ball and a groundout plated a run. Albert went after the first two pitches while grounding out. Berkman took a ball and then homered on the second pitch. Have a plan. Execute it.

In the third, Berkman went after the first pitch and singled to drive in a two-out run. Perfect effort. Perfect execution. That was big league hitting, scouting, and the kind of disciplined approach that we stressed. That was why we had hitters' meetings and why our hitters got together with the hitting coaches before each game.

Lohse responded to the Halladay and Phillies challenge with seven and a third innings of outstanding pitching. The ninth proved why the Phillies had so much success. They opened with three hard-hit balls off Motte for two runs and two outs. Rhodes missed the save when Chase Utley singled, but our other veteran, ready-for-anything Dotel, got Hunter Pence for the last out and the save.

The real excitement was yet to come. I was in my office after the game being interviewed. All of a sudden the clubhouse exploded with cheers. I was standing there with a puzzled look on my face when our director of travel, C. J. Cherre, came rushing in.

"Chipper lost a *ground ball* in the lights. Two out and he can't make a play. Infante hits one out off of Kimbrel. It's over!"

The clubhouse was in an uproar. Normally we don't get too car-

ried away, but this was cause for excess. We had just beaten the Phillies on the road, and then Santa Claus made a September visit. I just
stood there, looking incredulous, like someone had just told me that
the earth is flat, the moon landings were a fake, and Budweiser is
really made in Milwaukee. That Braves' loss turned a great victory
into a movie-moment memorable one.

The bus ride to the airport was riotous with ecstatic "Happy
flight!" chants and Motte being good-naturedly skewered for his efforts. "How can you throw when you've got both hands around your
neck?" "You had two pitches working for you tonight—balls and
base hits!" Motte laughed along with them, a good laugh, a winner's
laugh. As per usual, Laird was in the midst of the insults and was
getting more than he was giving. Not a better sound in the world.

We were two and a half back with nine to play. Homeward
bound.

On the flight, I sat there thinking, *The what is how the hell did
we get to this point. The why is too much to put into words.* This road
trip had originally held all kinds of danger for us. When we left for
Pittsburgh, I'd wondered where we'd be when leaving Philadelphia.
A 5-2 record meant that we were squarely in the middle of the type
of comeback that becomes a part of baseball history—if, that is, we
could keep winning. We had to enjoy the reality that two and a half
back with three series left to play, two of which were at home, meant
we had more than a real chance. I just wanted to sit there and soak it
all up, every unpredictable moment of it. That didn't last very long.
We had our scouting reports for our next series against the Mets to go
over, Dunc's book to review, and matchups to think about.

Just how this whole thing had played out to get to that point still
pleasantly nags at me to this day. With just nine games left, three
three-game series, I'd never been more convinced that this was no
fraud on our part. We'd earned this shot, and it was right there in
front of us. I realized how much confidence this team had won from
me and our staff. Ordinarily, getting too high is as dangerous as get-

ting too low. It's best to allow some of each, but not too much. Otherwise, you won't be as ready for what's next. But over and over, this team had enjoyed its successes and suffered its losses without letting their readiness for the next competition be affected, so we let them have their fun.

Back home in St. Louis, I struggled to sleep, but it was the best kind of sleeplessness, because I was so eager to get to the ballpark. If I was churning over any thoughts, it was this: *What should I say to the position players in the pre-series meeting?* I ended up doing something that was somewhat B.S., but also challenged them in a positive way and offered a reward. I told them that we had three series left. If we won each of those, I guaranteed them that we would at least tie the Braves and have a one-game playoff. The guarantee was B.S.—unless I had a crystal ball, I had no clue what would happen—but it seemed to send a positive message. In truth, this was only a slight departure from the "win the series" mantra we always used, and the guarantee wasn't worth the air molecules I disturbed in speaking those words. Didn't matter. I put the prize right in front of them and told them that it was theirs if they just did what we'd been trying perfectly to do the last few weeks.

In game 1 of the series, we trailed the Mets 6–5 going into the seventh, with two outs and no one on base. We then had the kind of rally that reinforced the belief that we had the magic. The middle of our lineup got it started, setting up the bases loaded for pinch-hitter Ryan Theriot. As he had done so many times, he came through to drive in two crucial runs. Up by one with the bases loaded again, Adron Chambers tripled for his second major league hit and three RBIs. Punto singled in the sixth run of our rally. We're magical.

R-zep and Salas closed it out with only a walk in the last two innings, and we'd won eleven out of thirteen and stayed two and a half behind Atlanta, who also won.

Another night, another close one taken. Trailing going into the bottom of the seventh in game 2, we once again found some two-out magic. David Freese, who was really scuffling with only sixteen hits in his last eighty-three at-bats—a .193 average—stepped to the plate with Albert and Berkman aboard and belted a 3-1 pitch into the left-field stands. Another rally started with two outs and no one on. Another comeback sparked by a dugout of teammates for a 6–5 win. Human nature is a powerful force. When it works for you, it helps explain how you get two comeback wins.

The Marlins beat the Braves. We were one and a half games back.

I liked the script for the first two games. I wanted to send the one for the third game back to the writers for a major revision or just to trash it altogether. I would have told them that what they'd penned was too unrealistic. Things like this didn't happen to teams like ours, but on that day they did.

I should have anticipated this nightmare; with so much adversity overcome through positive responses, we were bound to see the other side. Leading 6–2 in the ninth, I decided to go with Motte in a non-save situation. Why not finesse it with some of the others? I figured I'd give them a night off after Jake Westbrook did a terrific job. Like the opening shots in a horror movie, the bottom of the ninth started harmlessly enough with a few hints that something was lurking.

Motte walked the first hitter.

With a four-run lead and three outs to get, we were still in good shape. When Motte got the next hitter to ground one to Furcal's left, we were thinking tailor-made double play, but Furcal made a fundamental mistake: he looked up before he caught it. After that, he fumbled the ball. Instead of two outs and nobody on, it was now two on and nobody out. The rest is best left summarized: walks, bloopers, another error, two big hits, and six runs cross the plate. Final was an 8–6 loss. Where was the magic?

The clubhouse was silent. Morgue-like. Guys were staring vacantly at their lockers. Atlanta was idle, so we'd had a chance to be one game back with six to play. Instead, we were two back. I didn't like what I wasn't hearing and what I was seeing, so I walked in and started talking. I had three main points to make.

First: the kind of shell-shocked, zombie-like frustration they were expressing was how losers went about it. We weren't losers. Instead of just letting this sense of despair suck the life out of them, they needed to be angry. Not with anyone on the team, but with the opposition, with the IRS, with whoever. Just get pissed off and be animated and don't be the walking dead. We needed energy, not doom, to make this happen.

Second: we won the series. We were one-third of the way toward that playoff game guarantee I'd made. We hadn't taken any steps backward in that regard.

Third: let's look at everything we've done to this point to get to a place where we're even thinking about the postseason. Every one of them contributed their talent and their will to win. Why dwell on the ninth inning of this past game? Think about all the fun and the satisfaction we'd enjoyed during this latest run.

When I started on my fourth point, a few guys laughed, realizing that I'd gone beyond my three points. The message was this: nobody said this was going to be easy. The more difficult it'd been, the better we'd performed. We liked challenges. We responded well to them. Enjoy a night away from the game and get ready for the Cubs. We control our minds.

After the meeting, some players and coaches commented that my message had struck the right tone. I was encouraged that they took it as a tough loss but not a crisis. What happened next took on a surreal tone. After going home and reviewing the game, I got a phone call from Albert.

"Skip," he told me, "Rafael is in a bad way right now. He thinks he cost us a shot at the playoffs."

"How bad is bad?"

"He's talking about hanging them up. He's planning to quit."

Albert and I talked for a few minutes, sharing our thoughts about how wrong Rafael was to be blaming himself. He was the "happy flight" man, the guy whose enthusiasm and passion were at the very heart of what we were doing.

I called Rafael and got his voice mail. I left a message asking him to call me back. I didn't hear from him, so I called again and left another message telling him that I wanted to see him as soon as he got to the stadium on Friday. I needed him to talk with me before he made any decisions. My heart went out to the guy. Those kinds of physical errors under the harsh spotlight of a playoff race can be rough. This wasn't a Bill Buckner error, a Bartman foul ball grab, or any of those other legendary mistakes that have taken on mythological proportions over the years. I could have gone through the game and that inning and pointed to any one of a number of plays that could have turned the tide the other way. That's the nature of the game, and people love to play the "would have, could have, should have" all the time.

The final Mets game was an afternoon game, so I had the evening to enjoy dinner and my best friend, a book. Rarely do I allow anything to interrupt my book date, but the loss was a stunner and the consequences too unpredictable. Mostly, I tried to think through how to personalize my conversation with Furcal. Whatever he and I exchanged in our talk, I knew our players and staff would reach out to embrace him.

When I saw Rafael the next afternoon, I closed the door and the two of us sat down in my office. I was struck by the difference in his demeanor. This was like seeing those drama masks, the comedic smiling-faced one now turned into the tragic frowning sad one. Only these weren't masks—this was a real human being just torn up over a mistake.

"Look," I began, "the truth of this is that if it wasn't for you, we wouldn't be anywhere near having this opportunity to compete for a wild-card spot. We just wouldn't. Whether it was what you were doing on the field, in the dugout, the clubhouse, the bus, the planes, whatever, we absolutely would be facing the Cubs in a rivalry game that had no other implications beyond bragging rights. The reason why these games meant so much, the reason why that error, a part of the game, hurt you so much, was because of all you've done to make those games matter."

I let that sink in for a bit before continuing. "We have a good relationship, and I'm counting on you to believe what I said in the meeting before the Mets series. We win three of three sets, and we get a shot at a playoff game. We need your toughness, and there will be plenty of opportunities for you to contribute. I want you to get your mind right, take it easy a bit, so you can come back fresh later in the weekend to really help us out."

I backed our concern for him by giving him the game off. The fact is, the majority of the days off given are prompted by a desire to give a player a mental refresher. This was the classic example. I felt as he walked out that he knew his teammates were behind him and that he'd be ready for game 2.

I couldn't have known when I said them just how true my final words to Rafael were going to prove to be. The guys all knew how miserable he was feeling. Before the game, I saw a number of players go up to him, drape an arm around his shoulder, and tell him, "We'll be fine," or, "Hang in there."

The last of those words had another meaning. For us to hang in there with two series to play, you had to figure for us to win the series we had to win the first game. Except, the first-game was a crushing loss. Carp was outstanding, allowing only one run over seven innings, but the game's hero belonged to the Cubs. Alfonso Soriano's eighth-inning, three-run home run was the difference. Afterward, at dinner with John Grisham and friends, I explained that my postgame Mets meeting wasn't a bestseller but a bomb. The Atlanta win meant we were now three games back with five left to play.

The next afternoon against the Cubs, we were down to our very last out, about to lose 1–0. There is no way to exaggerate the *seriousness* of the situation. We could not afford a loss. If they got the three outs, I thought we'd be done. Our playoff chances would be virtually nil. We then pulled off one of the most improbable and dramatic rallies that any of us had ever seen. As we came to bat, our dugout exploded with enthusiasm and encouragement, an emphatic expression of our will not to lose. I have been around many great dugout moments of support, but never anything like this.

Kyle Lohse was outstanding in giving up just the one run through seven innings, but on the other side, Rodrigo Lopez and his bullpen mates were shutting us out. In the past seventeen innings against the Cubs, we'd scored a total of one run, going into the bottom of the ninth.

Carlos Marmol, the Cubs' closer with electric stuff that moves and darts around like nobody else's, entered the game. We'd seen Marmol a lot, since the Cubs are division opponents, and that worked to our advantage in a less than obvious way. Berkman led off and lined out to center on a well-hit ball that had us all screaming either get down or get over him. Neither happened.

Matt Holliday was back in the lineup for the first time since Pittsburgh. He was having a tough 0-for-3 day, but worked to an advantageous 2-1 count before singling to right-center. Tyler Greene came in to run for him, and we had a little life. When we had a runner at first, the way we'd handle signals was this: the bunt or hit-and-run signs would come from the third-base coach as a relay from the bench. The steal-a-base sign or the green light would come from the first-base coach as a relay from the bench as well. The same with the red light—don't run. The last option was that the run sign would come directly from the bench. Our players are taught to always look at the bench as they return to the bag after a pitch or an attempted pickoff. The sign could come from me, from our bench coach Joe Pettini, or from the trainer. I'm the one who has to make the call.

Now, Marmol is either slow or quick in getting the ball to the plate, and that works to our advantage if we guess right. He also throws balls with so much movement, particularly down, that it makes it tough for the catcher to get a decent pitch to throw on. We also had a huge asset in Greene, who had speed and acceleration.

Our offense had been struggling, so getting the runner to second where one hit could tie it was better than having to wait for multiple hits. On the other hand, if Greene got thrown out, then it would be two out and nobody on and we'd be facing almost certain elimination if we didn't score. I decided the risk was worth it. Our first-base coach, Dave McKay, gave Greene the check-the-bench sign. On the second and third pitches, we gave him the "run if" sign. That means, if he gets a good jump, then go. On neither of those two pitches did he feel like he got that jump. On a 2-1 pitch, he got the good-to-run sign, with an additional gesture to push it, and he took off. I was watching him, watching the pitch, and willing him to second. Not only did he get there safely but the ball hit him and rolled into the outfield. Runner on third and one out. The pitch was a strike. Freese had a 2-2 count.

Just hit something deep and into the air, put it into play somehow. Freese went down swinging. Two out.

One out away from what I felt would be *certain* elimination.

I love this game—not just this game, but *this* game. Yadi and Schumaker both walked. You could feel the "cut it with a knife" tension, but I knew that Marmol's stuff was so hot that command could be a problem. We sent up Theriot, as disciplined a hitter with as great a strike-zone sense as we've got. Childhood fantasy time rolls around. He worked the count to 3-2. Two outs. Bottom of the ninth inning. Bases loaded. For the second time in the rally we were down to our last strike.

I've been in the game thirty-three years, and I don't think I've ever scrutinized a pitch with as much intensity as the one that Marmol delivered next.

A slider high and a little tight. You have to be confident in your ability to judge a pitch in order to lay off, but Theriot does and we are tied. As Theriot trots down to first and Greene touches home, I'm thinking that Marmol could do it again. I see our third-base coach, Jose Oquendo, whispering to Adron Chambers, the speedster and pinch runner for Molina. I know what he's telling him. With a left-handed hitter at bat, the third baseman will be over toward the hole a couple of steps. You can add the steps to your lead in case the pitch is bounced. Get a good walking lead and make sure he has his momentum going toward home as the pitch is delivered. Marmol's movement could lead to something wild. Two pitches later, that reality is a game-winner. Marmol unleashes a wild one, a pitch that nearly kneecaps Furcal before going to the backstop. Adron Chambers comes in with the winning run.

You would have thought we'd won it all. The guys in the dugout sprinted out onto the field, but not before exchanging high-fives, low-tens, hugging, humping, and someone accidentally planting a shot to my jaw from somewhere as wild as Marmol's last pitch. I didn't care. I felt like we'd been struck by lightning, the air in Busch Stadium was so electric. The fans and our dugout cheerleaders had been rewarded by a near-miracle of a comeback as part of our larger comeback. That celebration carried on in the dugout, into the clubhouse, and was heightened when we learned that the Braves had lost. We were two games back with four left to play.

One way to explain how we scored two runs with only one hit that inning was that we willed it to happen. The guys were so into it, so fired up, that they refused to give in. Certainly it was part of the answer, but there is another part to the explanation. Once we activate the will and it generates effort, we need to add winning execution. Holliday's rally-starting single, Greene's base-stealing ability, and three great at-bats were necessary to produce the result. Yadi, Schumaker, and Theriot, with our season on the line, had to balance their aggressive attitude to make something happen with terrific strike-zone discipline.

Rafael was smiling and laughing. Little did he know what the baseball gods had in mind for him the next day.

Clichés are born of truth. You're never out of it until you're out of it. You can't win if you don't try. Put it behind you and live to fight another day. Every bit of that Cubs series was like listening to the most boring speaker in the world go on and on mouthing platitudes, except for one major difference: it was all actually happening right in front of us, and it had you on the edge of your seat instead of nodding off.

Edwin Jackson and Randy Wells both pitched their asses off in the final game of the series. Players on both sides were rising to the occasion. The Cubs broke a 1–1 tie by scoring in the top of the seventh. We trailed 2–1, but Yadi, who was in the midst of a big offensive month, hit one out in response. In the bottom of the eighth, Rafael Furcal, he of the 108 home runs in his twelve-year career, led off with a long bomb to right field at least a dozen rows in that put us up 3–2. Fewer than seventy-two hours before, Furcal had been so devastated that he was considering walking away from the game. Now he'd redeemed himself in the most dramatic way possible, to lead the team to a win, a series win, and, thanks to the Braves losing, a one-game deficit with three games left. All the clichés we mouth about never giving up on yourself, believing in yourself, bouncing back from adversity—they're all true. That was just the most recent example of those truths. Hearing the guys chanting, "Happy flight," in that dugout and seeing Rafael make a quick jump up to the top step of the dugout to acknowledge the fans' request for a curtain call still excites me just thinking about it.

You know, we also often say that life isn't fair, that sometimes it's not meant to be, but sometimes we make it fair for ourselves by taking control of the moment. That's what Rafael did. What we had done was to gut our way back from ten and a half games back to a single game, and all I could do was smile.

* * *

THE GUYS PUT ON THEIR HAWAIIAN SHIRTS FOR A VERY, VERY HAPPY flight to Houston, maybe because Houston is as close to Honolulu as they were going to get. On paper, you had to like our chances versus Houston over Atlanta's against the Phillies. After we'd beaten them, the Philadelphia club had gone into a tailspin, losing seven in a row. They were too proud and talented to accept that struggle. We knew they wanted to get things in order going into the playoffs. Prior to the first game of our series, the Astros had already lost 104 games, while the Phillies were trying to get to 100 wins at least and maybe tie for a club record with 102. We don't make up the schedule, we just play when we're told, where we're told, against who we're told.

In reality, Houston was a dangerous opponent. Brad Mills and his staff had done well not to give in to their struggles. In one sense, they had nothing to play for, so that made them very relaxed. On the other hand, these guys were professionals, and they had great integrity. They owed it to themselves and to the game to play hard. Spoiling another team's chances is as good as it gets at the end of the year when you're out of the running.

All that added up to a 5–4 game 1 loss in ten innings. It seemed we weren't done taking the hard way to the finish line. To that point, we'd been doing all the little things right, but the game has a way of evening things out. Against the Astros, we had plenty of chances but didn't take advantage of them. In the second, with runners on first and second with one out, we didn't score. In the third, we scored a run, but had a runner thrown out at the plate on a close play. In the fifth, bases loaded, no one out—we didn't score. In the seventh, first two runners on, then a sacrifice bunt. Runners on second and third and one out. We didn't score.

In the eighth, we were down 4–2. Once again, Berkman came up with a big two-run double to tie it after we pulled off the double steal with Holliday and Albert, a total surprise move. Following Berkman's double, with no outs, we got a walk, but we didn't score any additional runs.

The Astros beat us on a gutsy call by their manager with a squeeze bunt in the tenth. All we could think about was those wasted opportunities. The clubhouse was quiet. The guys knew that we missed one that night. We took consolation in only one thing—Cliff Lee and the Phillies beat the Braves 4–2. One game still separated us. Unlike the atmosphere following the disaster against the Mets, this kind of quiet was okay. We tipped our hats to the Astros and vowed to even the series the next day.

The way the next game started, I was thinking that we were going to need some magic to pull this one out. Jake Westbrook was having an off day. We were trailing 5–0 going into the top of the fourth in a must-win game. The stakes were suddenly at crisis level. If our backs weren't up against the wall, then our shadows were.

The whole bench was up and saying some variation on just one theme: Let's go! We're not going to get beat! Then they went out and did something about it, with a five-run inning of our own. Mitchell Boggs, R-zep, and Eduardo Sanchez all did a good job letting the Astros tack on only one additional run. We went into the seventh trailing 6–5, and the kind of sustained two-out offense that we next produced was one of the hallmarks of this team. Getting on base and then not trying to be a hero with the long ball paid huge dividends for us. Counting down the outs—seven to go with a one-run deficit—we got a crucial bloop base hit from Berkman. Craig hit one to the wall in right for a double that scored Berkman. 6–6.

Yadi walked. We had Theriot hit in place of Schumaker. The snow-globe-exchanging, plaid-coat-wearing, lost-his-starting-job-but-never-complained Theriot gapped one to the wall in deep right-center and wound up at third. 8–6. The Shredder doubled him home. 9–6.

We added to the lead and we won 13–6, with Dotel and then Edwin Jackson, in a rare relief appearance so that we could keep the rest of the pen fresh for the next day, getting the last six outs. Our team heroics were getting harder and harder to believe; if we hadn't been living them, I don't think any of us would have thought they were possible.

I SAT IN THE CLUBHOUSE AS THE GUYS SHOWERED, THEN GOT OUT OF there and thought through the next day's game. Atlanta had lost, and we were now tied. I needed to repeat that to reassure myself that after thirty-one games, we had chopped off a ten-and-a-half-game deficit. We were actually tied for the wild card with one game to play. I still believed that there would be a playoff with Atlanta. They were too good a team to get swept with so much on the line. And given how much we had at stake, I felt great about the decision I'd made to work backward from the last game of the season to set up Carp as the starting pitcher on the final day.

I had one other secure thought on my mind that night. Dunc was going to be back with us in uniform. About a month before, Jeanine had undergone surgery and come out of it as well as could be expected. Since then, Dunc had been by her side, faithful as ever. His obvious priority was her health, not my decision to retire. Right after I told my family, I would have shared my decision with Dunc about the time I told Bill and Mo. But with so much on their minds, it didn't feel right to add my situation to what Dunc and Jeanine were going through. But now, with only a couple of weeks left in the season and Jeanine handling her challenge so well, I'd finally told Dunc that I was done after this season—win or lose. I'd then carefully explained that no doubt Jeanine was the priority, but if there was a way, I hoped he could be in uniform for my last game in Houston.

A few days later, he let me know that their son Chris and his wife, Amy, would be with Jeanine and he would be in Houston. I wasn't surprised when he expressed reluctance, because we were making this winning push and he didn't want to interfere. I honestly assured him that he was with us. We were working his process as best we could. We were managing to survive, but he was sorely missed. And when the players learned that he would be there for game 162, they were all excited too.

The night of our comeback win, I went out to dinner with Rick Carlisle and Keith Grant of the world champion Dallas Mavericks, and some of our coaches. We were sitting and talking when I got a text message. It was from Dunc. He wasn't coming because he didn't want to be a distraction.

I immediately walked outside and called him. As much as I wanted him to be around for that final regular-season game because of the possibility that it might be my last game, I also wanted him there for Carp and for all the rest of the guys. I know that Dunc didn't want to hear it, but it was the truth. We were all in that position—one game, one win, away from what turned out to be a history-making comeback—with his help. When Derek Lilliquist—who by the way did a good job in Dunc's absence—had sat down with the starting pitcher before a game, he would open Dunc's book and consult all the facts and figures that Dunc had stored there. I don't know if you could call it an encyclopedia of pitching, or what. To me, it was more like the secret formula that could turn lead into gold. But only Dunc could then turn that gold into victories.

We were working his process the whole time he was gone, but we couldn't work his magic, didn't possess the same quiet confidence he had, the command of his craft and of himself that made believers out of nonbelievers. I don't know if I was able to make Dunc understand this, but just as our team had earned the right to be in the position to control its own destiny and get into the playoffs, he'd earned the right to be there that final game. No. Doubt. About. It. I was so pleased when he reluctantly decided once again to join us.

When Dunc walked into the clubhouse the next night, the team all gathered around him, telling him how much they'd been thinking about him, asking how he and Jeanine were doing. Dunc stood there taking it all in—polite and composed as ever. Still, he and I have known each other for too long for me not to be able to spot the subtle differences in his composure. The tendons in Dunc's jaw and neck were pulsing, and not with the usual twang that signaled *Get the hell out of my way, I've got business to take care of* that I've seen in him hundreds of times over the year. He was struggling to hold it together, to keep his calm at the ready.

I've been asked if winning that game turned out to be anticlimactic for us after our first five hitters in the top of the first got on and we scored five runs by the end of that frame. Usually you're a fool to think so. But by the time the late innings rolled around and we were up 8–0, we felt very certain that the Astros would run out of outs before they scored nine runs. It wasn't so much the score that gave us confidence—it was the fact that Carp was so into it, competing as hard as possible on every pitch with complete command of all his weapons.

Only when the last hitter, J. D. Martinez, hit a comebacker to Carp, did I see anything approaching relief spread across the big man's face. Waiting by the dugout to congratulate him and the rest of the guys, I knew that this wouldn't be the last time I'd have that opportunity. The last inning, I was really emotional: we had clinched at least a tie, and there would be at least one more game. The score allowed me the rare luxury of enjoying every one of those last moments.

IN THE END, I WAS ALSO ENORMOUSLY GRATEFUL FOR AN OPPORTUnity to participate in what many people say will go down in history as one of baseball's greatest nights. So much will be written—and already has been—about the events around both leagues that I won't go into it here. Just know that since that night, I've watched and rewatched the highlights of those last games of 2011. A baseball life like mine just thrills to sights and sounds like these. The tension and compelling finishes to the games in Baltimore, Tampa Bay, and Atlanta will be talked about forever. Extra inning games, long rain delays, a team coming back from a 7–0 deficit, the integrity of the competition, especially with teams like Baltimore and the Yankees battling so hard with nothing to gain but pride, are further evidence of just how great this game is and how memorable the 2011 season was.

While the guys were in the clubhouse watching the Atlanta game play out, I was in my office with Rick and Keith. I'd look up every now and then when I heard the guys ooh and ahh over the changing fortunes of that thirteen-inning thriller. I had one eye on the TV screen, but mostly I was going over the lineups and matchups for what I continued to feel certain was going to be the next day's game against the Braves. Visiting teams rarely win extra-inning ball games. There's so much pressure on a bullpen to keep a team from scoring, especially when you know that you don't get another turn at bat if you give up a run. Along with that, the Phillies bullpen, very much like ours early on, was going through some things.

When Hunter Pence, a former Astro, fisted a flare into right field to score the lead run, the clubhouse erupted in noise that echoed off the Arch and back to Houston. At that point, we were all riveted to the screens. The collective moans when the Phillies' David Herndon walked Dan Uggla with one out were soon followed by another ricochet of riotous joy as a double play ended the Braves' chances. Just like that, we were in.

I'd never been so glad to be wrong.

Later, after a celebration that in retrospect outdid the three others in 2011, Rick Carlisle, who had just coached an NBA Championship team and had been on a championship team as a player with the Celtics, said to me, "This was the most exciting moment I've experienced in sports."

This was special because the guys who did it were special. I can't compare the feelings I had to what I'd experienced with the '83 White Sox, with the '88 to '90 Oakland clubs, or with the previous winners in St. Louis. I can only say this: the 2011 team had as good a frame of mind as any club I'd ever been around. Remember that simple formula? Our team. Their team. Competition. Keep score, so try to win. In terms of the purity of the competition, I don't think we could have tried more perfectly than we did in that stretch of games when we went 23-8.

Three hundred wins. Five thousand games managed. All these milestones matter in some very real and important sense. They provide you with one kind of satisfaction. I'm not equating managing with pitching or playing. There is no comparison. Baseball is a player's game for the fans. I'm only making a point about longevity and trying to do what you've learned right. Doing the small things right—that sticks with you too; those small things imprint themselves in your mind and provide another kind of satisfaction. As a coach, your goal is to get a team to where the Cardinals arrived in the late stages of 2011. All the parts working together harmoniously.

That's why we play a team sport instead of an individual one. Seeing us overcome so many obstacles, even that last week. When Rafael was just gutted by his failure to do something, mostly because he felt like he let his teammates down, he rose to the occasion days later because his teammates were behind him. That's why we call it "picking somebody up." Whether you boot a ground ball, drop a fly ball, fail to drive in a run, groove a fastball, or whatever, your first thought is this: *Somebody pick me up*. And your first thought as a teammate should be: *I've got you.*

We exhibited that attitude all year and it got us to the point where we were playing the Phillies in the postseason. That's why it was so important for us to have Dunc back with us—to let him know, even though he committed no error, that we were all engaged in picking him up.

As I've said, ultimately it is the players who accomplish the feat. We just enjoyed watching them enjoying their effort, facing the uncertainty of the final result, and then, thankfully, celebrating the result. For our fans, our organization, and everyone with our team, the most excitement we could experience in professional baseball awaited us—unbelievably, we were actually going to the playoffs.

Late in the season, I knew that our chances of getting in hadn't been good (only later when I was told about coolstandings.com did I know how long those odds were), but numbers tell only part of the story. In the post–*Moneyball* era, numbers (or to use the buzzword *metrics*) have attempted to take on increasing importance. The Cardinals created a metrics department in order to stay ahead of that curve, and I appreciated the enthusiasm and affection for the game the members of that department brought to the task. From providing evaluations for potential draft picks, players to sign and trade for, and useful measurements to hone the development of players in the organization, they can have some use. They also believed that they could aid our efforts to write a better lineup, increase our effectiveness with game strategy, including bunting, stealing, defensive positioning, and utilizing the bullpen.

To a limited extent, they were right. Metrics are useful pre- and post-game analyses. What those numbers don't do as effectively is to successfully predict in-game scenarios and how they will play out. No number can adequately account for human nature and how it affects performance. That's why you need to observe and react, moment by moment, in game after game and series after series, to evaluate the human, as well as environmental, factors.

Doing that helps you to answer this essential question: How does this individual play the game? Preparation and personalizing are my passions, but only the second of those can really help you make the determination about an individual and his capabilities. The best example of that is how tough a player is mentally and physically. There's no metric that can adequately measure the size of a guy's heart.

We had the appropriate ratio of preparation to heart—lots of preparation but tons of heart.

I allowed myself that brief reverie, and then I had a bus to catch. That's the great thing about this game. You don't have to wait too long for your next chance to possibly make some history, to pick somebody up, to get across that finish line together.

PART II

Down 4–0 in the third inning isn't a time to panic, but when your opponent has won more than a hundred games and they have a Cy Young–winning pitcher on the mound, panic certainly feels like the only logical option.

During September we had our backs against the wall so often that I swore you could see lines of brick and mortar imprinted on our skin. One game, one inning, even one pitch meant the difference between heartbreak and hope. That wall could either continue to hold us up or come crashing down on our heads.

After losing the first game of the Division Series in Philadelphia, we gave up three runs in the first inning and another in the second and we were down 4–0 to Cliff Lee and the Phillies. If we lost this game, we would be down two games in a five-game series. Hardly an ideal spot for a team to be in, even one that had overcome so much already.

In reality, every one of the last five games of the regular season was an elimination game.

Our club was coming off the field after the second inning in Game 2 and two things happened that lifted my spirits. The first was that even though we were down 4–0, the guys on the bench were fulfilling their responsibility by creating noise and encouragement as our guys returned to the dugout.

In the postseason when you're on the road, the fans are hyperexcited and very loud. That part of the home-field advantage is easy to combat.

One of the strategies we have used so much in the postseason on the road is that every time we come off the field, nobody in our dugout sits down. Everybody stands up. Everybody. Position players who aren't starting. Every other pitcher on the staff.

Pats on the back, clapping, and encouragement, anything to raise the decibel level in the dugout to drown out the home fans is necessary and effective.

I don't know if it sounds hokey or not, but it works. But you need to do it for every inning.

The second thing I saw that night in Philadelphia was more subtle. Dave Duncan pulled aside Carp, who had been struggling that night as we pitched him on three days' rest for the first time in his career.

I found out later that Dave had told Chris that he was coming out of his delivery and trying to make too much happen. Call it overthrowing. Call it too much adrenaline. Carp's mechanics were off and he wasn't nearly as sharp as we'd seen him in Houston the last day of the regular season. Benefiting from Dunc's advice, Carp then had a perfect third inning, and although he came out of the game in the next inning for a pinch hitter, this conversation between Dunc and Carp would have enormous impact later in the postseason—a little bit in Game 5 of this series and a lot in Game 7 of the World Series.

I was slightly discouraged by our inability to take advantage of early offensive opportunities. Still, down 4–0 in the third, it wasn't time to panic. But with Cliff Lee on the mound, and scoreless innings mounting, that hill we were going to have to climb felt like it was growing taller. When you don't get to a top-notch starter early, it's hard to stop their momentum from building.

Elimination, yet again, is staring us in the face. Between the top and bottom of the fourth inning, I sat there scanning the field as our guys warmed up, wondering which of them, which combination of them, was going to embrace the competition and grind it out like we had for the last month or so. We'd come too far to let this thing get away from us. Our top of the rotation starter was already out of the game. The outcome was in the hands of our bullpen, which through most of the season had been one of our problem areas. What did the baseball gods have in store for us?

CHAPTER ELEVEN

Seeing Things in a New Light

THE DAY AFTER YOU MAKE THE PLAYOFFS, EVERYTHING LOOKS DIF-ferent.

I mean this in the most literal sense: October sunlight has a different look and feel to it. That has nothing to do with optics—playoff baseball makes all the difference. In the years when we didn't qualify for the postseason, I always went to the ballpark the day after the season ended to pack and attend final meetings. As part of that routine, I'd go out on the field. In those years, the field, the stadium, looked sadder to me than they had in April or August. The morning after 2011's game 162, despite the red seats ringing the green and brown diamond, Busch Stadium looked less like a leaf turning colors than like a spring bloom. The Division Series against the Phillies was set to begin on Saturday, giving us Thursday to rest and Friday to travel and work out. Watching the younger guys take their cuts at optional batting practice, hearing the sound of a well-struck ball echoing, I took a few moments to think about what we'd done.

Standing on the field, the stands empty except for a few media and organization types dotting the red here and there, I felt satisfied for the first time in a long time. Anytime you make the playoffs, you've got reason to celebrate, but this was different. This had been so hard, but as a result the satisfaction that went with it was greater. We'd done what all the other clubs in the sport had tried to do. Now we were down from thirty teams to eight. I don't think fans, the media, and even some baseball insiders really appreciate how hard a 162-game grind can be, what an accomplishment it is to qualify for the postseason, and just how competitive those postseason playoff rounds are. If they did, they wouldn't look at being eliminated in the first round as such a disappointment.

Maybe it's in my nature, or maybe because we teach the guys that after a big win or a big loss you have to turn the page, but on that Thursday after we clinched the wild card I finally took advantage of the rest day to think deeply about all that we'd done. After that, come Friday, we'd be hot and heavy, looking ahead to the Phillies. I didn't spend too much time on the 2011 season, though. Instead, I leafed further back through my history with Cardinals baseball and reflected on just how far we'd come as an organization over the past sixteen seasons.

Just like the 2011 Cardinals had faced elimination time and time again, I very nearly didn't get out of my early years with the squad. After parting ways with Oakland in 1995, I had a few opportunities to consider, including returning to Chicago and the White Sox. I'd hoped to sign on with Baltimore; something about that legendary franchise and the great tradition of Earl Weaver really appealed to me. But when I'd interviewed with them, I'd thought the position was already vacant. As it turned out, it wasn't, so when I found that out I immediately called back and said thanks but no thanks.

With sixteen years of experience in the American League, going to the National League wasn't something I considered initially. Several people, including Sparky Anderson, told me that I'd love it, and when the name St. Louis came up, I started to think seriously about it. Other people tried to warn me off St. Louis. Since Whitey Herzog had left in 1990, the sentiment among people outside and within the organization was that the team wasn't playing like it once had. Whitey had left the team saying, "Hey, I just can't coach these guys. They don't listen to me anymore." That's on record. Joe Torre, who'd been the manager in 1995, went to the Yankees after being fired, and you know how well that turned out for him; he was also quoted as saying how much he appreciated going to a team where guys were going about it the right way.

Regardless, I had fond memories of the enthusiasm of the fans, the times in '82, '85, and '87 when I'd attended the Series and seen that amazing sea of red, and I was interested. The negotiations with the Cardinals' brass went well, and I was about to sign when Walt Jock-etty, the St. Louis general manager then, told me that we needed to speak about an urgent matter. I met with him and Busch's Jerry Ritter, and they explained that the team was about to be sold to a group who had promised to keep the team in St. Louis. They wanted to be sure that I knew everything before I signed. I appreciated their full disclosure, and I was committed to joining the Cardinal family. I'd talked things over with Dunc prior to this, and he was excited about the prospect of working with the young Cardinals pitching staff, guys like Matt Morris and Alan Benes. Apparently, Walt had already been working his charm on our pitching coach.

When I signed, I became an employee of Anheuser-Busch, which gave me the chance to have a unique experience: an audience with Mr. Busch. Only it wouldn't be just me. I was asked to meet with him during a corporate meeting, with heads of subsidiaries from all over the Busch empire presenting their annual reports or something like that. Mr. Busch sat at an enormous oval table in a room as big as the one that houses the UN General Assembly.

Now, you have to remember this: the '95 season was inter-rupted by a players' strike. The clubs used replacement players in the spring—scabs in the mind of the players' union, but a viable, and cheaper, alternative in the mind of Mr. Busch and other militant hard-liners against the players. He hadn't been very happy when Joe Torre, then his manager, had said during the season that while he was doing as asked and managing the replacement players, he was hopeful that the regulars would come back. Mr. Busch ultimately ordered Walt to fire Joe. That's why I was there then.

So, Mr. Busch asked me how I felt about using younger ballplayers. The Cards had done fairly well with their youngsters, some late-season promotions from the minors, and he said that he was pleased with their performance. Basically he was saying that he'd rather have the younger (cheaper) guys than the older (expensive) veterans. I told Mr. Busch that young players add a certain spark to a team with their enthusiasm, but I disagreed with him about the conclusion that younger players without veterans could compete. When the young guys had come up the year before, there was no real pressure on them. Expecting them to carry the team throughout the upcoming season, against the returning experienced major leaguers, well, that was a different story.

I thought I heard Walt and Mark Lamping, the club president, each moaning very quietly, expecting the ax to drop.

Instead of asking his executioner to escort me out, Mr. Busch just looked at some papers, shuffled them, and without another word, dismissed us.

Out in the hallway, Walt and Mark seemed to enjoy my candor.

I shrugged. "I had to be honest with him."

By March of the next year, the deal was finalized. The Cardinals were sold. I imagine that the negotiations had long been in the works, but Walt continues to claim, jokingly, that I was the one who drove the family out of the baseball business.

At least I got to keep my job.

After I'd signed, a former player I'd managed who'd gone on to coach there told me, "Hey, you know, you've got your hands full there because that team is not really living up to the Cardinal tradition of team and effort and execution. There are a lot of divisions, and it's just not a cohesive team, and they're not going about it the right way."

I thought, *Oh, crap. This is serious.* He couldn't have pointed to any worse problems—especially given the organization's rich history—than those. And he was right.

All along, Walt Jocketty had told me that I was the right man for the job. I'd been in similarly difficult situations in the past, and I'd also experienced the other side of it, the winning, the great team unity. He said that I'd done it in Chicago and Oakland and that I could do it there in St. Louis.

The Oakland club I inherited was a lot like the one I'd encounter in St. Louis ten years later. The players had grown accustomed to doing things their way. Maybe it was a function of the times. The players and their union were gaining more and more control and earning more and more money. Both in '86 and '96, the "I'm in this for me" vibe was present. I'd taken an honest bull-by-the-horns approach in '86, but I didn't think that would work with the Cardinals. Dave McKay, who has been with me since '86 as a coach, asked me to resurrect what he called "the Gutless Speech."

The '86 A's had a core of quality veterans and talented enigmas— Dave Kingman, Carney Lansford, Dusty Baker, Jose Canseco (who was named Rookie of the Year), and Joaquin Andujar. When I took over the A's in 1986 a few weeks after I had been fired in Chicago, I'd had the advantage of playing against them in the division. They developed the bad habits of making a lot of mental mistakes, getting really discouraged, and establishing some cliques. When things were going wrong, misery loved company, and guys would get together and just complain about it all. Basically, their minds were just blown.

The effort level was down, and that was the piece I singled out in my first meeting with them: we were going to play hard. When a guy doesn't play hard, it's the manager who justifiably gets held responsible. "He can't even manage effort." Then the next level is that if the guys are playing hard but they aren't playing worth a crap, throwing to the wrong base and all that, people say, "He can't teach them to play the game right."

I'd joined the A's midseason. I needed to do something to get their attention focused on priority one—how are we going to fix what's wrong? So I told them, "I've been in this division. I know how talented you guys are. I also know how messed up you guys are. I've played against you guys, and it's not even close to being competitive, the effort level. But I guarantee you in the clubhouse there's a lot of effort. Talking crap. Blaming other people. Blaming the front office. Blaming the manager. This stuff's going to stop. Whatever problems there are, you're going to give the manager or the coach a chance to fix the problem. If we don't know it exists, how can we fix it? I guarantee you there isn't anything, from what I've seen here, that can't be fixed, but you've got to speak up about it to us, okay?"

I stared out at the room and caught my breath. No one said a thing. I continued by taking a page from Dick Williams circa 1971. At his first meeting as manager of the A's after coming over from Boston, he had challenged us to quit relying on Mr. Finley, the team owner, and instead look to him and the coaches to solve all problems. Then he'd dropped the bomb. He'd told us that he was going to provide Mr. Finley's phone number in our lockers. We could call him all day today if we wanted to. But after that if we used that number without giving him and the coaches the chance to fix the problem first, he'd have our asses.

I wasn't about to start handing out the owner's number, but I knew we needed to make sure the phone lines to my office were open.

"Let me just tell you something else. I don't really know you guys well enough yet. I don't really know if anybody's going to come up and tell me anything. So listen to this. If there's somebody in here that's a professional major league player that's got any kind of integrity, any kind of balls, and you know there's a problem and you don't give me or the coaches the chance to fix it, you're a no-good gutless mother———. Furthermore, I know you've got these little cliques here.

So if your little team of guys knows that you're pissing and moaning and you're continuing to complain and you don't come and tell me, then all your little cliquey boyfriends are no good gutless mothers too. Now, is there anybody that's got the balls to tell me right now that they disagree with what I'm saying about a guy who wouldn't give me or a coach a chance to fix a problem?"

In some form or another, just about every year since then, when things aren't quite going right, Dave McKay would ask me to dust off that speech. I've only ended up using it maybe two or three times since '86 as a last resort. Once they got over the shock of the language in the speech, I hope they understood this was a way to hold the guys accountable for what was taking place between the lines and outside them. Despite sometimes having to do a bit of acting to deliver it, I also fully believed what I said to be true. In Oakland, the speech worked immediately—we went from last to third that season. The culture began to change, and we had a great run of success after that, from '88 to '92.

I didn't use "the Gutless Speech" to start out my tenure with the Cardinals in '96. I could have, though—it certainly would have been appropriate. I didn't know the personnel. I hadn't seen that team play as often as I had seen the A's club. I needed to know and see firsthand what the situation really was. Instead, to open spring training that year, I used "the Endless Speech." I'd prepared my remarks carefully, and once I got rolling, I looked down at my watch and saw that twenty-five minutes had gone by and I was only a third of the way through. I'd planned on going for only twenty minutes total. I rushed through the next two-thirds, the most important points, in twenty minutes.

All the Cardinal greats—Red Schoendienst, Stan "the Man" Musial, Lou Brock, and Bob Gibson among them—were there. Afterward, George Kissell, the legendary coach and instructor who spent nearly seven decades in the Cardinal organization, a guy who was around so long Branch Rickey mentioned him in his Little Blue

Book, came up to me and said, "Hey, Tony, next time I'll bring a cot."

Not to be outdone, every year since, Bob Gibson has called me to ask when the first players' meeting will be to open spring training. When I tell him 9:30, he says, "Great. I'll be there at 10:15."

Partly because of my never-ending speech, the year got off to a really tough start. I had my doubts about whether I'd made the right choice and whether I was, as Walt had told me, the right person to take on this challenge. Still, the coaching staff kept pushing our way. The players kept pushing back. Dunc, the best partner you could have in baseball, kept encouraging me: "Tony, stay the course. That's why they brought you here, man. Just don't back off. You're doing the right thing."

Part of the reason why that season was so difficult was that we were in the process of replacing a legendary Cardinal, shortstop Ozzie Smith, who'd undergone surgery the year before. The consensus when I joined the organization was that Ozzie's health was a major issue for the '96 season. Walt Jocketty had brought in Royce Clayton to shore up the position. Ozzie was entering his nineteenth season in the major leagues, and he'd endured a lot of wear and tear. The middle of the infield defense is so crucial to a team's success that we had to be sure that if Ozzie didn't recover adequately, if he went down with another injury, or if we could be better offensively and defensively at the position, we had to do what was best for the club's chances of winning. I spelled this all out to Ozzie at a lunch when it was just the two of us, telling him that there was open competition for the starting job. The guy who plays the best plays the most.

That statement applied to every roster decision we had to make, and while it would have been true in any season, it was especially true during this one. Some people in baseball and fans doubted my ability to make the transition from managing in the American League to managing in the National League. The voices were loud enough that there was only one item on my agenda: manage the team as best

I could to win as many games as possible. That meant utilizing the guys who would do the best to help us win. Period.

In the spring, Ozzie felt that he'd outperformed Clayton, and numerically he had. But there's more to an evaluation than that. For example, Ozzie didn't make an error in spring training. Royce made eight. But errors alone don't account for a player's range, the number of balls he's able to get to, or the types of plays on which those errors are made. We believed we had a better shot at winning with Royce playing the bulk of the games—every two out of three, as it turned out. Royce was a slow starter offensively throughout his career, but sure enough, he came around.

Ozzie didn't like that arrangement. Then he got injured at the end of spring training, with a pulled hamstring, proving our point about the necessity of having someone of high caliber on the squad to play short. Finally, Ozzie's dissatisfaction grew to the point that we needed to do something. Finally, everyone agreed the time seemed right and Ozzie announced his retirement. As you know, I'd later go out of my way to make sure that my retirement wasn't a distraction. Everyone is entitled to do things his own way, and I'm sure that Ozzie had good reasons why he wanted the remainder of the '96 season to be a kind of farewell tour for himself. I don't want to equate the contributions of a player to those of a manager. My point here is not to talk about how each of us chose to announce our leaving, but about how my role in Ozzie's final season has been portrayed.

When it was over, Ozzie said that I hadn't respected him and that he wanted nothing to do with the organization as long as I was there. Over the years, he's done just that. On Ozzie's farewell tour, I went out of my way to make sure that, in the last game of a series and the last time Ozzie would be in that city, he either played that day or took the lineup card out so that he could receive the fans' accolades and often gifts from the opposing team. That treatment is the opposite of disrespectful.

I'd seen firsthand how a player ending his career could do it differently. I have a great deal of respect and affection for Reggie Jackson. First, he helped me personally to develop my concept of how to make pressure your friend. He did this by example and by answering my questions about how he was able to rise to the occasion so many times. Second, in 1987, during his final season, despite being the self-described "Straw That Stirs the Drink," his retirement didn't overshadow the rest of the team. Instead, Reggie remained in the shadows and worked tirelessly as a mentor to some of our young hitters like Jose Canseco and Mark McGwire.

Many times during '96 I told Walt that I thought I'd lost the club. I sensed that a few of the guys on the team just weren't buying into the program or buying into me. So I sought help from a championship situation.

I'd maintained a good relationship with Jerry Reinsdorf, the owner of the White Sox and the Chicago Bulls. At one point when we were in Chicago for a series, I asked Phil Jackson, the Bulls' coach, and Jerry Krause, the Bulls' general manager and a former baseball scout, for a favor: I wanted a few of our guys to see how it was done right. I asked a few veterans and the talented young core to join me on a field trip. We loaded into a limousine and headed off to the Chicago suburbs and the Berto Center, the Chicago Bulls' practice facility.

Now, mind you, this was the Chicago Bulls of the mid-1990s, and the magic of the Michael Jordan era was in full swing. We went to the practice facility to see how probably the greatest practice player of all time, Michael Jordan, went about his business. I'd had the privilege of seeing Michael Jordan work before, but I saw all the Cardinal players standing there wide-eyed and with their jaws dropping as Jordan pushed himself and his teammates through the most intense hour-and-fifteen-minute off-day work session. Michael was constantly at the front of every line with this seemingly insatiable hunger to practice. The discipline was extreme, as was the impact it had on his whole team.

Then something happened that I hadn't planned on, but I was glad that it did. When the practice was over, we got invited to go downstairs into the locker room and weight-training facility to meet a few of the Bulls. First Michael Jordan and then Scottie Pippen— before they showered and got on a plane to go to Miami to take on the Heat in Game 3 of a playoff series—saw me. Each of them came up to me and, because I'd met them before, said, "Hey, Tony, how's it going, man? Good to see you." They gave me good manly hugs and then shook hands all around with our guys.

After that, I thought I saw some of those guys who'd been struggling to buy into our program looking at me differently. Some of them thought, *If Michael is okay with him, maybe there is something to this guy.* A glimmer of respect was in their eyes that hadn't been there before. In the games after that trip to see the Bulls' practice, we started getting more competitive. The division was there. Houston had the better team, but they were struggling some. We got back in contention, and we won a wonderful series, sweeping them in September. Long story short, we got into the playoffs.

Before we clinched, we went on a road trip where our magic number was two or three. I started getting congratulatory calls from some of my coaching friends. I took a couple of those calls from my former players, telling them, "This is really weird. This has been hard. I really feel, the day we clinch it, I'm going to go off on the side with the coaches and congratulate them. I'm going to go to the pitchers—Eckersley, Rick Honeycutt, Todd Stottlemyre, Alan and Andy Benes—and congratulate them. But the position players, I mean, I felt like they were in one place and we were in another. I don't think they'll want a thing to do with me."

It was hard to say, but that was the truth.

The day we clinched it, I had every intention of sticking with my plan, but some of the position players came up to me, their shirts soaked with champagne, and said, "This is so awesome. Hey, man, you were right."

Royce Clayton, Brian Jordan, Tom Pagnozzi, John Mabry, and Ray Lankford were all part of that group that doubted me because they didn't know who the hell I was. They didn't know if they could trust me. They didn't know how to take me. After sixteen American League seasons, I knew I had a lot to prove after I came over to St. Louis. After that game, though, almost everybody surrounded me. I really didn't expect to be part of that celebration, but it meant a lot to me that I was. We won those eighty-eight games and the first round of the playoffs against San Diego. We were within one game of the World Series when we ran into Smoltz, Glavine, Maddux, and the rest of the Braves. The whole experience with that '96 team was one of the most exhausting I'd ever been through, but it was also incredibly rewarding.

And some, just some, of that estrangement I felt all year got chipped away. We worked so hard to change the culture in that clubhouse, and I have to give so much credit to the coaching staff who kept our spirits up. I was also fortunate that Walt Jocketty, even during the toughest of times, never said, "Man, I brought in this manager and this coaching staff to fix things. I did my part. These guys are the ones who need to step up now." He showed me a lot about having faith in your people. Lots of fingers were being pointed, but Walt refused to join in on that. He's a good man, but he's also tough when the situation demands.

I made it through '96 partly because I had the support of both Jack Buck and Mike Shannon, two keepers of the Cardinal tradition. At one point, we were making a road trip to San Diego. On the plane, Mike asked me what I was doing when the plane landed. I told him I had no plans. "Well, big boy, we're going to dinner. I need to figure out who you are." We talked baseball, and I told him about my dad taking me to see the Cardinals' spring training when I was in junior high school in the late '50s. I gave him my take on the Cardinals' three World Series in the '80s and Cardinals' history in general.

Mike didn't shake my hand or give me his formal stamp of approval, but anyone listening to the games could hear that he called it like it was. If I was wrong, he said so. If I was right, he said so. If he had a doubt, he gave me the benefit of it. Over the years, our friendship has grown, and so has our mutual respect.

My other advocate was someone I felt was one of the greatest Cardinals of all time—Jack Buck. In fifty years, he reached more people than anyone. I called him "Legendary Jack," and he was. An amazing man with a wife to match—Carole. The best part of my off-field St. Louis experience—from October '96 to June '02—was having dinner with Jack and Carole and whoever else were his guests. Those dinners began, ironically enough, also in San Diego. We had a travel day during the Division Series, and on the flight, and in that velvety voice of his, he asked me, "Is today your birthday?"

"Yes."

"Is your family in town?"

"No."

"You're going to dinner with Carole and me."

I protested that I didn't want to impose, but he insisted. He also asked Dave and Jeanine Duncan to join us. After that, any time I had another invitation from him, I jumped at the opportunity to spend time with one of the most articulate, knowledgeable, and generous men I'd ever met. He was also one of the most colorful dressers. His son Joe made the mistake once of remarking at a breakfast for the radio and TV affiliates that he thought his dad should have turned on the lights before he got dressed. Everyone laughed. Jack got up and said, as straight-faced as could be, "I thought this before, but now I'm convinced. Joe is a bed-wetter and we should have given him an electric blanket."

Jack didn't take himself too seriously. When he was diagnosed with Parkinson's disease, he later said, "I wish I had Alzheimer's, then I could forget to shake."

Every day, I've missed Jack being around.

* * *

THE NEXT YEAR WE HAD A LOSING SEASON. IN '98 AND '99, WE HAD Mark McGwire doing what he did with all those home runs, but there wasn't much else in the way of success for our club. Then, from 2000 on, we had it. We had a team "it." The lack of postseason appearances since '96 was disappointing, but the coaches and I trusted in our ownership and front office. That confidence was bolstered when Walt acquired pitchers Darryl Kile, Pat Hentgen, and Dave Veres and position players like Jim Edmonds, Edgar Renteria, Fernando Vina, Mike Matheny, and Reggie Sanders. Combining all those acquisitions with the change in culture we'd accomplished and the long-standing history of success in the organization, and I had no reason to want to move on. The pastures were about as green as they could be.

Now, here I was sixteen years later in my last season as manager. We had a team that had endured all of these setbacks to hang in, hang in, and hang in there some more. We got better, we fell behind, we got discouraged, and then we resurrected ourselves and look what we'd accomplished. We'd won the damn wild card. We were in the playoffs. And when we celebrated, it was like the celebrations that we had had in the 2000s. The season wasn't like '96 in any way, shape, or form—except at the very end when we won and celebrated. In 2011 we'd won as a team, a complete team.

This was the last year I was going to have this maximum amount of fun and have a team in the postseason. As much as I didn't want to dwell on it, I walked around the field on that off day, taking it all in and thinking, *Damn. We did it. This is it. You always want a shot at it, and we've got one.* And I thought that this was the Hollywood movie end to the season—to have all those dramatic wins, to get in on the last day of the season, and to be part of that last day of the season with those other great games being played to determine who would get into the playoffs. It was part of a movie that was so hokey that nobody would believe it. Yet there I was out on the field and not in my office packing my bags or sitting in a meeting talking about the next year. Well, for me there wouldn't be that proverbial "get 'em next year." I was going to enjoy every bit of this final run for as long as it lasted.

I've said this after the fact, and some people have a hard time believing it's true, but I genuinely mean this: all my postseason experiences since my first in 1983 got better and better. Not just because the results were better, in some cases, but because I enjoyed them more for being able to appreciate them more. I knew how hard it was to get to the postseason and how heightened the attention and the excitement were. Sure, there's something to be said for an experience being fresh and new, but a bit of naïveté numbs you in a sense. You don't savor it because you think there's always going to be another helping served up. Obviously, that's not the case, and knowing that, and having endured a few lean years when we ended the season with no "banquet," I was all the more aware of just how fleeting those moments are.

Standing there in that October light in the near-empty park, I couldn't help but think of that '83 White Sox team. It was different from the 2011 Cardinals in one respect—we didn't have as many guys with championship experience with different clubs like we did with the White Sox—Carlton Fisk with Boston, Greg Luzinski with the Phillies, Jerry Koosman with the Miracle Mets, Tom Paciorek with the Dodgers. But the two teams did share this trait—they'd built unity and they'd had fun competing.

I also thought about those White Sox for another reason. Like the A's postseason teams, that White Sox team had won ninety-nine games and run away with the West Division, but what made that Chicago team frustratingly different was that we'd just stalled in losing that first round of the playoffs to the Orioles. I was going to have to apply some of the lessons learned from all those previous playoff appearances to keep this incredible momentum going.

The postseason is sometimes referred to as a second season—a much shorter and much more intense season where every play is magnified, every strategic move more freighted with importance. We'd been playing with the urgency of a playoff team for a number of weeks already. In a very real way, we were entering our third season. Our thirty-two-game run was over, but did we really want to turn the page completely? Or were we better off thinking of this as just a continuation of that run? Was it possible for a team to sustain that kind of effort and intensity indefinitely? Would the added distractions of the playoffs—securing tickets for family and friends, the increased demands from the media, and all the rest—extinguish the fire that we had burning?

I knew one thing. This team didn't need to hear "the Gutless Speech."

CHAPTER TWELVE

Turning Pages

AFTER ALLOWING MY MIND TO WANDER A BIT ON THURSDAY, AND with our series with the Phillies scheduled to begin on Saturday, October 1, Friday was a time to focus on our opponent. You've probably heard and read about the meetings that go on prior to a postseason confrontation. You might imagine that like in the NFL, where coaches end up sleeping in their offices after marathon nights of viewing film, noting tendencies, and developing game plans, we must have done something very similar. Good assumption, but a wrong one.

We'd faced the Phillies in that big series just fourteen days earlier, and we'd already played them nine times that season. Not a whole lot had changed between that last meeting and this upcoming one in terms of personnel. We both had to set our rosters, and that was going to require some sound strategic thinking, but that was a matter of elimination mostly, and no new, significant additions to the roster were going to be made. It wasn't as if the Phillies had gone out and gotten Joey Votto or some other stud to add to their lineup. I'm sure they would have liked to, given that Ryan Howard, their star first baseman and terrific run producer, was slowed by a leg injury. When we saw them in mid-September, and then later on as they finished out their run to the division title, we could see that Howard was essentially trying to hit off one leg. But we weren't feeling sorry for the Phillies. They had picked up Hunter Pence from Houston, and he was a valuable midseason addition, making their already strong lineup even tougher.

For our part, we were wondering how effective Matt Holliday would be with his finger injury. We had some questions about whether he'd even be on the roster. All teams are banged up by the end of the year, but if we were looking for an edge in terms of injury and availability, one didn't really exist. A diminished Howard and an injured Holliday essentially canceled each other out. Also, Chase Utley, their All-Star second baseman for so many years, wasn't himself. Placido Polanco, who had been dealing with an abdominal problem all season, wasn't all there either. They were a club that had won more than a hundred games, but they weren't at their peak going into the series.

Postseason history is replete with teams that were banged up, and I believe one of two things happens with these teams. Number one, the team overcomes it, like the Dodgers did against our Oakland team in the 1988 World Series when Kirk Gibson hit that game-winning homer in Game 1 in the only at-bat he had during the Series. Most sports fans have a vivid recollection of him barely able to drag himself around the base paths on his injured legs. The opposite can also happen: the healthier team is gung-ho and going after it, so the team that's hurt loses an edge.

We had no doubt of this: the Phillies weren't feeling sorry for themselves. We had so much respect for the Phillies and what they had done, especially in their last series of the season at Atlanta when they'd won all three games to help keep us alive. They deserved the ultimate respect. As banged up as they were, and with the outcome of the series having no effect on their standing, what they did was historic in terms of preserving the integrity of the competition. In similar situations, I've seen clubs take care of themselves by resting frontline players and not making sure that the competition is as even as possible. The Phillies made a decision to play to the max for those three games, and that was classic. That's what we should all do.

Also, by winning those three games to end the season, they'd given themselves some much-needed momentum. Despite being banged up, Philadelphia appeared to have one potentially decisive edge going in, at least on paper. Their starting pitching staff, with Roy Halladay, Cole Hamels, Cliff Lee, and Roy Oswalt, was outstanding: the first three had combined for fifty regular-season wins. Not many clubs can trot out three top-of-the-rotation guys like the Phillies could. In fact, any one of their top three could be a number-one starter on nearly every major league roster. Add in Roy Oswalt as a number four, and you've got one formidable starting staff. That was one of the reasons why they'd gone to two World Series and been one of the dominant teams in the National League the last few years.

By contrast, Lohse, Carpenter, Jackson, and Garcia, our projected starters, had won forty-three games. That's a bit deceptive, since Jackson had been with us for only half a season; if you add in the wins he had with the White Sox, seven, our five guys had as many wins as their four. Throwing out the numbers completely and just going with the gut, however, you'd have the same initial impression—the Phillies' strength was their starting pitching edge.

From our perspective, it wasn't so much about those wins and losses. We felt like we had some vulnerabilities in Jaime's and Kyle's stamina—the same questions that we'd faced late in the season when we'd decided to give them more rest. Jaime was still young and developing the necessary arm strength, and Kyle was approaching two hundred innings for the first time since 2008.

That meant that we'd have to utilize our bullpen to a greater extent. When it came to the bullpens, we believed we had the edge. Even though we'd had our struggles early on, we'd pulled it together a bit, and based on what we'd seen down the stretch, our bullpen was coming in with a lot of weapons and a lot of confidence. On the other side, we felt like the Phillies were at a disadvantage there. Injuries figured into that. Jose Contreras, who'd been effective in a relief role, was hurt and wouldn't be on the roster. The key, then, to getting to those starters was for our guys to string together tough at-bats every time in every inning, so that one of two things would happen: we would break through and score, or we'd run up their pitch count and tire them. Would that be enough? We'd have to wait to see if their starters and our relievers canceled one another out.

We also had Dunc's book on our side. For years, he'd kept detailed notes on every game and every at-bat an opposing team took against us. What he kept track of evolved over the years. On the front side of the opening page of the book, he had the results of the team's last 100 at-bats against our pitchers. Dunc demanded that the pitching chart Chad Blair assembled from watching the video be as accurate as humanly possible. The next day, Dunc took that chart and transferred data from it into his book. Prior to meeting with the starting pitcher, Dunc reviews the information, considers the stuff our starting pitcher has, what that particular pitcher's temperament allows him to do or not do. Then he meets with the pitcher.

The book is invaluable. In 2009 against the Reds, we had a one-run lead in the ninth, with runners on first and second and one out. Ramon Hernandez, since coming to the National League, had hit us well. Ryan Franklin was on the mound. Dunc made a trip out there to talk to him. Dunc came back in. Franklin threw one pitch and we got a double play and we won the game. I asked Dunc, "What did you tell him?"

"If he throws a breaking ball on the outer half, he'll roll over it and hit a ground ball to short."

That's exactly what happened. That book provides us with all we need to know about how to pitch to and defend the opposition's hitters.

We'd won six out of nine meetings with the Phillies during the regular season, and that was a plus. The Phillies owned home-field advantage, and you'd think that was in their favor. I didn't. At least not entirely. Yes, there is the strategic advantage of being able to bat last, but in most other ways I didn't see us being on the road as a terrible disadvantage. It put certain pressures on us—particularly that idea of scoring early to take the crowd out of the game—but playoff baseball raises the intensity level to a high degree. In my mind, that fact offset whether we played at home, on the road, or even at a neutral site. Playoff baseball is just different. Add to that our emphasis all year long that road games are a lot about projecting the attitude that you think that this is your house, but we actually *own* it. That means that the players' body language and behaviors from the moment they arrive at the ballpark to when they go out to stretch, take batting practice, or fire the ball around the infield after an out should be an expression of our belief in taking control of their own minds and taking the crowd out of the game. Baseball is a sport, but it's also entertainment, and playing on the road gives you a chance to strut your stuff in front of people who normally don't know you and your abilities that well. That may sound cocky, but that's the swagger you need to adopt in a hostile situation.

In 2011 we had identical home and away records of 45-36, demonstrating that we put those thoughts into practice and didn't let away games slip out of our grasp. That toughness edge was one that we prided ourselves on having on our side. We could also fall back on a bit of history. In '06 we opened the playoffs on the road in every series—San Diego, New York, and Detroit—and won that Series. In '02 we started the National League Division Series against Arizona at their place and won. We'd also won three of four from the Phils in September at Citizens Bank Park during the comeback. All those positives gave us a good feeling.

In order not to let this postseason opportunity slip away, we had to get the players to turn the page. We wanted those good things from the comeback to carry over, but we also didn't want to think too much about what was now the past. We needed to feel good about ourselves and what we'd done without getting too caught up in that. Obviously, that's a fine line. You feel like you're "hot" coming in, and you want to build off that, but you can't expect that things are going to pick up right where they left off. You have to make that happen, and the way to do that is to focus.

Our challenge was this. We'd made a historic comeback. If we weren't careful, we could have celebrated the fact that, no matter what we did in the postseason, people would remember us. We needed to acknowledge that we'd made history and then put that in our confidence bucket as a reminder of what we were capable of. Most important, though, we needed to analyze how we'd done it and then put those same practices into play against the Phillies. That's what we did.

I learned this the hard way in '83 when the White Sox were my first playoff team. We'd caught fire from June through the end of the season, and when we wrapped up the division, we kept on going. I don't think I did a good job of leading the guys after that. I should have stressed more the need to forget about the regular season and move on to focusing on the next task at hand—beating the Baltimore Orioles. That '83 club was a tremendous group of guys, a great mix of veterans and newcomers, guys with previous postseason success and others hungry for their first taste of it. Chicago fans had to be convinced that the dreaded June swoon or a late-season collapse wasn't going to break their hearts again, but they came around. We became the toast of the town, and we had a lot of fun. Even Carlton Fisk, who'd seen his share of playoff frenzy with Boston, told me that the most fun he'd had was with that '83 White Sox team. Jerry Koosman and Greg Luzinski both said the same thing. In some ways, we had been like the 2011 Phillies. Our top three starters that year, LaMarr Hoyt, Richard Dotson, and Floyd Bannister, had gone something like a combined 42-5 the second half of that year. They were all young pitchers, fearless and ferocious, and we went into that postseason expecting that things would go our way.

They didn't.

Baltimore, the eventual World Champions, beat us in four games. We could have made a better showing. We failed to put the satisfaction of having achieved so much in the regular season behind us. In every postseason since '83, my staff and I have been vigilant about delivering that message about enjoying the success and celebration and then moving on. We did the same with the 2011 Cardinals.

As I said, no elaborate and lengthy preparations went on as we got ready to play the Phillies. The preparations for how we would hit and pitch against them were very similar to what we'd done during the regular season. We had one team meeting beforehand. We held it on Friday before Saturday's Game 1. I always wanted those meetings, even during the regular season, to be on off days because I needed their full attention. Also, on game day you don't want to interrupt their game preparation with needless confusion or distractions.

I had a three-point agenda. The first two had to do with potential distractions.

I said to the players, "I've only got three things to tell you. Number one, find somebody to help you take care of the tickets. The ticket situation will drive you nuts, and you don't need that."

Depending on where a guy is from and other factors, regular-season free tickets for friends and family can be a royal pain in the ass sometimes. You want to accommodate everyone if you can. Just like the intensity on the field gets ratcheted up during the playoffs, so does the ticket headache. There's so much more interest in those games, and if they let themselves, the players can get so wrapped up in meeting requests, checking with teammates to see who has extras, etc., that they wear themselves out. Message delivered, and I trusted that they would act on that suggestion.

"Number two, at each level you go to, you're going to have more and more media around. The media is a part of it. They want to know about us. They want to know how we got here. You should be cooperative, but don't let them get in the way of your work."

The media have their job to do; they are the conduit for delivering information to the fans. We tell our players to think about interviews as a way to talk to the fans, but also never to let that fact get in the way of doing their job. Major League Baseball rules are fair to both the media and the players. Journalists are allowed access as needed and at scheduled times and locations. All the players have certain requirements they have to meet, but generally how they choose to deal with that element of the game is up to them. I just didn't want them to allow the media to detract from their concentration and performance.

In the postseason the clubhouses are closed to the media before the game. A media room is provided, and the manager and a few key players are required to speak to a pool of reporters after the game. That is both good and bad. The clubhouse is more private, but the television rights–holders and the local media are under more pressure to get something different from what everyone else gets. As a result, they make a lot of requests for so-called private time with players and staff. The networks have paid for the broadcasts, so they have a right to expect access to the players. We want the players to be helpful, but in every playoff series I've been involved in, a player has agreed to do an interview at some time when he was supposed to be in a hitters' meeting, or during team stretching, or when he should have been shagging balls during batting practice. That competition for players' time gets more intense the further you advance.

Those first two issues can take away from your ability to have fun and to compete. They also took far longer to talk about than what was the most important point of all.

After watching the last thirty-two games, the coaches and I agreed that that this club had already been playing like every game was the last game of the World Series or of their lives. That had made us tougher to beat and won us games. All we asked of them now was that they continue to do that. We wanted them to continue to have fun competing in this next series against the Phillies.

For the first- and second-time participants in the playoffs, we took an opportunity to visit with each of them. We wanted to give them a heads-up about the atmosphere surrounding playoff games. I talked to Descalso, Craig, Freese, Chambers, Tyler Greene, Lance Lynn, Jason Motte, Salas, and R-zep. We included guys who weren't even going to be on the roster for the NLDS, guys who'd be on the traveling squad, to help prepare them in case they were needed anywhere down the line this season or any future season.

I walked around the outfield during batting practice, speaking to each player individually. The message was the same: we'd faced the kind of playoff intensity in all the crisis games we'd had in the regular season—we'd experienced that kind of excitement level. Whatever their part was in each game, they had a real edge, because they'd already experienced it. Those thirty-two games were as close as they could get to actual playoff-game experience.

Those face-to-face meetings also gave me a chance to gauge the guys' mind-sets. As with most of those personalized discussions, I wanted to conduct them outside my office. I reserved my office for meetings about more serious matters—disciplinary stuff, that kind of thing. I wanted these exchanges to be more mutual and more open, and my office wasn't the place for that.

I could tell that all the guys were ready. The next question we had to deal with was deciding which of them would be on the squad.

PRIOR TO THE FRIDAY WORKOUT AND THAT BRIEF MEETING, THE staff had gotten together both with and independent of our general manager to determine the roster. Major League Baseball has certain rules about the composition of the postseason roster, and Mo made sure that we understood these before finalizing our choices. If a player is injured during a playoff series, he can be replaced, but only with a pitcher in the case of a pitcher, and only with a position player if another position player goes down. If an injured player is replaced on the roster, he can neither reenter that series to play nor play in the next one. That's a lot of detail about a procedural matter, but it figured in our decision in regard to Matt Holliday and his finger injury.

In the old days, management and uniform staff made all kinds of decisions about a player's status without consulting him. Because of how integral our personal relationships with the players were to our success, though, I couldn't and wouldn't want to make a unilateral decision and then inform the player. That Friday, while Matt was working out with the rest of the club, we were watching him with keen interest. At one point, I walked up to him to chat. You have to remember this about Matt. He was recruited to play both football and baseball at Oklahoma State University in his hometown. He chose to sign with the Colorado Rockies, so he didn't play college football, but he has that football player mentality and toughness.

I said to Matt, "Listen, here's the deal. We can replace your intangibles. We can't replace your tangibles."

Matt nodded, knowing that I meant that we could add someone else to the roster who could do a good job of cheerleading and being a good teammate, but we couldn't replace what he brought in terms of offensive production. We needed to know if he could play full-time. If he could only pinch-hit, we would consider keeping him on the roster, but we weren't sure yet if we'd go that way.

Next, I went through the eligibility and injury rules with him so that he understood fully the consequences of our decision.

"Basically, what I'm telling you is that if you're on the roster, we need you to be able to play and keep playing."

Matt looked me square in the eye and in his good ole boy Cowboy accent said, "I can throw. I can hit. I'm about to take BP, so you can see for yourself."

We watched him take his swings, and he looked good to go. Matt had been with us long enough and done enough that he'd earned our trust and respect. We had to let him know our concerns and the consequences of this mutual decision.

I moved on next to talk with Kyle McClellan. This one was a bit different. I knew what Kyle was going to say. Of course he wanted to be on the roster, and I wanted him there as well. The problem was, as the season went on, and after having begun the year in the starting rotation, we'd seen the effects of those innings on his arm strength and velocity. He'd nearly doubled his previous season high in innings pitched. We'd also seen a general decline in the sharpness of his other pitches. Also, Kyle had been regularly undergoing various treatments for his arm and shoulder. I talked to him during his workout. I could see the concern in his eyes, and this was going to be tough news to deliver to him.

I used the "pat and pop" technique: I told him that he'd been a valuable contributor to our success all year. We'd asked a lot of him, and he had delivered. All very true. I then told him that we'd gotten reports from our team doctor and our trainer. Combine those concerns about the health of his arm with our observations about the decline in his performance, and we felt it was best for the organization, for him, and for his future if he didn't pitch in this series. We would be taking too much of a risk with him and our chances of winning if we did.

Kyle tried to convince me that he was okay, that he wanted the ball. He said all the right things, and I knew this was really painful for him. Finally, I spelled it out the best way that I could.

"Kyle, you know that the Phillies stagger switch-hitters and right and left throughout their lineup. Plus they have rights and lefts coming off the bench. You're our most effective reliever against both righties and lefties. Nobody else can go after both like you can. So if that's the case, can you tell me why we'd make this choice if we didn't feel it was in your best interest as well as giving us the best chance to win?"

My lawyerly, irrefutable logic was fighting with his passion and desire to compete. I wished that we could have kept him on the roster, but the reality was that we couldn't. The thing about personalizing is that even as you get close to the players, you can't ever get so close that you allow your judgment to be clouded. This time the pat on the back was followed by a punch to the gut.

My thinking about the rotation for the Phillies series began in the forty-five minutes following our victory over Houston in game 162. While the guys were agonizing over those final innings between Atlanta and Philly, I was in the office going over some stats and messing around with some ideas about how to get the most Carp for our buck. I knew one thing without a doubt: we had to have Carp pitch in two of those five games. Had to.

I came to that conclusion immediately, even when I was still in Houston before the champagne was uncorked. While we hadn't fully committed to the idea of him starting on three days' rest, I know that I first considered it back then. After we were sure we were in and we were headed back home on the plane, I looked at the rotation again. What we had found over the years about the best-of-five Division Series was that pitching your two best pitchers twice gives you the edge. Ideally, you'd like to have your number one go in games 1 and 4 and your number two in games 2 and 5. We couldn't do that. Carp obviously wouldn't start the first game on Saturday because he had just pitched on Wednesday. That meant that the soonest he could go was the second game on Sunday. If necessary, he could then start the fifth and deciding game, assuming there was one.

The night we clinched the wild card, we were on our way back to St. Louis. The guys were still celebrating, but some of that initial jubilation had quieted. I was still sitting there with a pad and pencil taking notes about the possible rotation for the upcoming series. I got up and walked back a few seats to where Carp was. I held out the paper and tapped the space on the page where I'd penciled in his name.

Carp smiled and nodded. "I'm good to go."

"Not yet. We'll wait and see how you are Friday."

"I'll be ready."

I walked back to my seat. Carp's response was no surprise. Of course he'd want the ball. I already knew that. I just wanted to let him know that we were going to wait a bit before fully committing to see how he felt. I was sure that some people were wondering why I'd kept him in for as long as I had in such a lopsided game. Two reasons. First, whether Carp threw eighty or a hundred pitches really wasn't going to matter in terms of his ability to bounce back and pitch on three days' rest. Second, Carp had been throwing as loose and easy as I'd ever seen him in carving up Houston that night. There's pitches and then there's *pitches*. Particularly toward the end, Carp wasn't throwing high-effort strikes and balls. He was in as stress-free a mode as you can have while still making quality pitches. Why take him out? In each of the last two innings, if he had any hiccup, I would have bagged him for a reliever. That wasn't necessary; he was relentless.

With Carp unable to pitch in the first game, we had a number of points to consider along with a number of pitchers. The first candidate was Kyle Lohse. He'd had success against the Phillies during the regular season. He split a pair of decisions and had a good 1.76 ERA against them. More important, pitching with six days' rest during the comeback, he had beaten Halladay. Kyle would be on six days' rest this time too, and though he didn't like having his turn skipped—and there was a lot said about it—Kyle pitched a lot better down the stretch when he got more rest.

The same was true with Garcia. Jaime's win-loss record against the Phils wasn't great. He'd had no decisions in the two games he started, but in fifteen innings against them he had an 0.60 ERA. Anytime you average less than one run a game in two starts against a club, you know you're doing well. Carp had also been really effective against Philadelphia, going 2-0 with an 0.60 ERA.

It was clear that Carp, Lohse, and Garcia would be three of the four guys to start, but in what order? Based on keeping everybody in the rotation pitching with regular or extended rest, the first option was to go with Lohse in game 1, Garcia in game 2, and then Carpenter in game 3 in St. Louis. Edwin Jackson would go in game 4 if needed.

Option two was to flip-flop Garcia's and Carp's starts. That would mean using Carp on three days' rest in game 2. He'd never done that before, but I didn't really worry about how he'd respond. He'd been so efficient against Houston in game 162 that I didn't think his arm would be that stressed. That option would also put him in line to start game 5 on regular rest.

Another factor in our favor with this choice was that Jaime Garcia pitched much better at home than he did on the road. That third game might also be an elimination game, and it was good to have that edge in mind. I don't know why Garcia pitched better at home—and there are too many factors to consider in order to explain it—but the results spoke for themselves. He was 9-4 at home and 4-3 on the road, with an ERA of 2.55 at Busch Stadium and 4.61 elsewhere.

Along with all that analysis, we also had to check in with Carp on Thursday to see how his arm was responding. He'd iced up after the Houston game, of course, and we wanted to see how he was feeling one day later. I sought him out and said, as I do very frequently when asking guys these kinds of questions, "Put your hand on the baseball bible. How are you feeling?"

"I'm good. Normal tightness. I'll be ready."

"Not yet. We'll check with you tomorrow."

Many times a pitcher does feel good the day after a game and then lousy the next day after that. Maybe it's part of the euphoria that comes from a start, the lingering effects of the adrenaline high that masks some muscle soreness.

On Friday I repeated the process with Carp. He raised his hand and swore on the baseball bible: "I told you, I'm good."

You're in there.

I faced a similar situation in 1990 with the A's. We were in a tight race with the White Sox, and Dave Stewart, a guy who compares favorably to Carp in his attitude and ability, won one Wednesday going eleven innings. He knew that we had a key weekend series against the Angels coming up, and he said to me that he could go on Sunday. We had an off day on Monday, and he would have taken his regular turn on Tuesday but with an extra day of rest.

"Skip, I'm better on three days than I will be on extra rest. I'll be too strong then."

I'd said the same thing to Stew I said to Carp: "We'll see."

Stew swore on the baseball bible that he was ready. We gave him the ball on three days' rest, and he beat the Angels 4–1. With guys like Stew and Carp, you trust them to do what's best for the team and for themselves. You believe that they know enough not to put themselves and their future at risk.

When I'd made up my mind, I called Dunc. He had gone home to Missouri, briefly, to be with Jeanine, but at the insistence of his wife and their sons, Chris and Shelley, he was going to join us for the trip to Philadelphia and stay with us for as long as we kept going. He agreed with my thoughts: Carp was the starter.

In a lot of ways, Dunc and Carp are cut from the same cloth. Carp's a lot more vocal—in fact, as our number-one starter, he takes on a leadership role in the dugout when he's not pitching by being the most vocal guy on the bench—but he's also a very serious guy with a good and cutting sense of humor that jumps up on you like a sneaky fastball. On August 22, just before he came to me to ask about having that players-only meeting, we were up 1–0, and I sent him back out there to start the top of the ninth. He hit the first batter, Juan Rivera, and I decided that was enough. I didn't like the matchup against Andre Ethier. I went to get him.

"You've done a great job," I told him. "I'm bringing in Arthur." With that, I held out my hand for the ball, and he gave it to me. He started to move off the mound, and I said, "Hey, Carp. Wait here with me until Arthur gets here. We'll walk off together."

Without batting an eye and with no hint of malice or sarcasm, Carp turned toward the dugout and said, before taking his first step, "I'll take the applause. You get the boos all to yourself."

The boos got louder after a triple by Aaron Miles and a fielder's choice scored two runs.

It's true that you have to beat the best to become the best. Our road to a championship wasn't going to be easy by any stretch of the imagination. I knew one thing. Our competitive nature had been tempered by the competition we'd gone through all year. We were going to compete hard. We were a long way from 2010, and I was hoping that we'd be remembered for more than just that simple fact of the passage of time. In 2011 we hadn't just turned the page, we'd turned a corner. I liked how we'd come to the park ready to compete. So, while the Philly fans roared and the experts waited for the inevitable to unfold, we stood on the foul line knowing, and eager to prove to everybody else, that we belonged there.

CHAPTER THIRTEEN

Split

YOU GO INTO EVERY GAME WITH A PLAN FOR HOW YOU WANT TO attack a team offensively and defensively. Obviously, sometimes that plan works out as you'd envisioned it and sometimes it doesn't. Anytime you put two individuals or clubs together in a competitive environment, you can't predict what will happen with any great accuracy. That is why, as the expression goes, you play the games.

What did we do, then, to start off the series against their ace, Roy Halladay, in Game 1? We jumped him for three runs in the top of the first. Our style all year long, but especially in the postseason, was that if there's a doubt, be aggressive. It gives the club the feeling of trying to make things happen offensively. As I pointed out before, that meant employing the "get him early" approach. We did exactly that.

On the second pitch of the game, Furcal led off with a single. With the count 1-0, I put on the hit-and-run with Craig batting. Craig got a really tough pitch to hit and swung and missed. The good thing about the pitch being that tough was that their catcher, Carlos Ruiz, had a difficult pitch to throw on, and Furcal stole second.

Craig's job was clear—get the runner to third—but Halladay showed how tough he is by striking out Craig on a nasty 2-2 cut fastball.

With first base open, Halladay pitched around Albert and walked him on four pitches. Here's where our off-season work on the roster paid off. Hitting behind Albert, Berkman was going to get good pitches to hit, and that's exactly what happened. After throwing four straight balls, the last thing Halladay wanted to do was to fall behind in the count. Berkman jumped all over a fastball and drove it deep into the right-field stands for a three-run home run. We teach that no one, with the exception of the starting pitcher, sits on the bench while we're at bat. During the postseason, that's never an issue. When we got a huge home run like Berkman's, with all that adrenaline flowing, we almost needed a rule to keep the guys from running out onto the field as if this were a walk-off homer.

We accomplished exactly what we wanted to do in that first inning. Citizens Bank Park wasn't silent, but all the frenzied pregame energy was diminished a few notches. In that situation you want your pitcher to go out there and shut them down, let them know that they are in for an uphill battle. Kyle set them down in order on five pitches, two more than the absolute minimum. That kind of efficiency was exactly what we'd hoped for and knew that Kyle was capable of. At that point, round one went to us. Of course, in baseball there are no knockouts, no fights waved off after a single round. More important, we liked what we saw—the guys were playing the same way they'd been playing for the last six weeks.

We had an opportunity to add on to our lead in the second inning, when Schumaker led off with a bloop single to right. A groundout to first advanced him to second base with one out, but we didn't score. The obvious truth about adding on runs is the math. The more you score, the more the other team has to score, but what it does for both teams psychologically is potentially even more important. For example, there's a long-standing manager's dictum that when you score a run late in the game it's like scoring two. That's because the opposition now has to score two runs to top your score.

I can't say for certain that our failure to add on there was the "cause" of our eventual loss, but it certainly contributed. Schu's base hit would be the last hit we got off Halladay. After that, the former Cy Young winner retired twenty-one straight hitters. That's impressive pitching. The fact that the first twenty of those outs resulted in the ball not getting out of the infield shows just how dominant he was. Unlike at Busch Stadium, where the dugouts are down the line a bit farther away from home plate, at Citizens Bank Park you feel as if you're there right behind the hitter. We could all see what Halladay was doing to us after the first inning, and it was damn impressive.

Despite their lack of success against him, nothing seemed to discourage the guys. They weren't getting down, no one was pounding his bat in frustration or slamming his helmet. Man after man went up there and came back to the dugout, stating the obvious, "This guy has got it tonight."

When I say that was impressive, I mean that watching a guy at the top of his craft going against a group of guys who are also competing hard is fun—after all, it's what the game's all about. I'm a baseball fan. I loved sitting there watching up close an exhibition of why Major League Baseball is the best in the world.

The Phillies scored one run in the fourth on Shane Victorino's single. Lohse was more than holding his own at that point. He'd allowed just two hits and that lone run. We were past the halfway point of the game, up 3–1. If you had told me before the action started that was going to be the score at that juncture, I would have taken that result. Of course, if you had also told me how Doc Halladay was pitching, I would have been concerned. No lead is ever too great, and despite how I had said that the Phillies had a few players who were banged up, I certainly wasn't feeling sorry for them. Despite hitting off only one leg, Ryan Howard hit a three-run home run in the bottom of the sixth to put them up 4–3.

What we saw Howard do that night, and what we'd seen Berkman do against us in 2010 when he had his bad leg, was impressive. Most power hitters are guys who drive the ball with authority, using their bottom half (hips, butt, legs) as a base. They get their leg drive going and use their front leg as a kind of brace to hold them in position through the swing. We call that hitting against the front side. Even though Howard's legs weren't 100 percent, he was still a very strong young man. While he couldn't really drive forward, he could use his powerful arms and chest to generate enough bat speed to hit that ball out of the yard. I've seen many guys do something like that even when they aren't hurt. They get their weight transferred to the front foot out ahead of a pitch in the zone, but because of their great hand-eye coordination and strength, they can still make hard contact. That's exactly what Kirk Gibson did in that pinch-hit home run in '88. I call that "flipping one," but that doesn't begin to capture how much strength and timing it takes to do that.

Following the home run, we considered getting Lohse. We could see that he had started to leave his pitches up in the zone, and that meant that his usual good movement wasn't there like it had been earlier in the game. Dunc and I had discussed this scenario ahead of time, since we felt that both Lohse and Garcia were vulnerable to tiring. We saw that once they got into the sixty-five- to seventy-pitch-count range, they became more susceptible to arm fatigue and a loss of quality stuff. We didn't want to push it with either of them.

Howard's home run came on Lohse's seventy-fifth pitch. We were down only one at that point, and I elected to let him face Shane Victorino. Unfortunately, he singled and Raul Ibanez homered, making the score 6–3. I replaced Lohse with Octavio Dotel, and the veteran retired the only two men he'd face on strikeouts.

The Phillies added on five more and we rallied for three to make the final score 11–6.

This is Bill Veeck, the legendary owner of the White Sox and the man who gave me my first job. My arm is in a sling from dislocating it in a scuffle during a Brewers game—believe it or not, I was trying to break it up. *(Photo by Tony Inzerillo)*

Spring training with the White Sox in 1980. *(Photo by Tony Inzerillo)*

Where it all began. With my first coaching staff *(left to right):* Ron Schueler, Art Kusnyer, me, Roland Hemond, Loren Babe, Orlando Cepeda, and Bobby Winkl

Here I am being sworn in by Judge Abraham Lincoln Marovitz after passing the bar in 1980. *(Photo by Tony Inzerillo)*

Charley Lau revolutionized hitting by pioneering a full-extension swing in which the top hand leaves the bat. *(Photo by Tony Inzerillo)*

White Sox owners Jerry Reinsdorf *(left)* and Eddie Einhorn *(right)* always demonstrated their commitment to their players and coaching staff with the care and attention paid to every part of the workday. *(Photo by Tony Inzerillo)*

Dave Dombrowski *(left)*, who began his sports leadership career with the White Sox, and Roland Hemond *(right)*, the general manager who taught me the importance of team chemistry. *(Photo by Tony Inzerillo)*

Saluting the crowd after winning the 1983 Western Division Championship. *(Photo by Tony Inzerillo)*

Shaking hands with Baltimore manager Joe Altobelli before Game 3 of the 1983 American League Championship Series. *(Photo by Tony Inzerillo)*

After a tough loss in the World Series the season before, the theme of my spring training opening day address to the '89 Oakland A's was "We're on a mission." (© Michael Zagaris)

love this picture of me with Sparky Anderson (left), one of my most influential mentors, and legendary NFL coach Bill Walsh (center). (Photo by Dennis Geaney)

Pacing in the dugout during the 1989 American League Championship Series against Toronto. *(© Michael Zagaris)*

Signaling to the third-base coach from the dugout. *(© Michael Zagaris)*

Celebrating with my wife and daughters in the clubhouse after winning the '89 American League pennant. *(© Michael Zagaris)*

Almost all of the Rookies of the Year who I've managed *(left to right):* Mark McGwire (1987), Ron Kittle (1983), Walt Weiss (1988), Ozzie Guillén (1985), and Jose Canseco (1986). The only one missing is Albert Pujols (2001). *© Michael Zagaris*

With both the A's and the Cards, having Hall of Fame closer Dennis Eckersley was a huge advantage. *(© Michael Zagaris)*

This shot is from the early years of working with Dave Duncan, a player and pitching coach for whom I have always had immense respect and admiration. *(© Michael Zagaris)*

Our team was ecstatic after winning the '89 World Series.
(© Michael Zagaris)

Another shot with Dave Duncan, this time listening to the national anthem before the start of a Cards game. *(Photo by Scott Rovak)*

Celebrating our Game 4 win against the Padres in the 2006 National League Division Series with Chris Carpenter. *(Photo by Scott Rovak)*

Introducing the teams before Game 3 of the 2006 World Series. *(Photo by Scott Rovak)*

With Bill DeWitt and Walt Jocketty as we are about to be presented with the 2006 World Series trophy. *(Photo by Scott Rovak)*

Jumping into the arms of Albert Pujols after we won Game 5 of the 2006 World Series. *(Photo by Scott Rovak)*

Wearing my now-infamous "Smooch Your Pooch" T-shirt during the 2006 championship rally. *(Photo by Scott Rovak)*

The three wonderful women in my life: my wife, Elaine *(right),* my older daughter, Bianca *(left),* and my younger daughter, Devon *(top). (Courtesy of the author)*

Here comes the man! The legendary Cardinal Stan "the Man" Musial. *(Photo by Scott Rovak)*

Here, Cardinals great and longtime sportscaster Mike Shannon is taping spring training. *(Photo by Scott Rovak)*

Vietnam veteran Lieutenant General Hal Moore *(left)*, the greatest leader I've ever met, and Hall-of-Famer Red Schoendienst *(right)*. *(Photo by Scott Rovak)*

"Sweet Lou" Piniella, another eminent player, manager, and longtime friend of mine. *(Photo by Scott Rovak)*

Observing spring training from the sidelines with *(left to right):* Dave Duncan, Bill Belichick, and John Havlicek. *(Photo by Scott Rovak)*

Our catcher Yadier Molina coming off the field. Yadi was a player I could always count on to play with great skill and intensity. *(Photo by Scott Rovak)*

Chatting with longtime friend Joe Torre in the dugout during the 2009 All-Star Game. *(Photo by Scott Rovak)*

I'd take copious notes during every game and later I'd be able to reconstruct each play using what I'd written. *(Photo by Scott Rovak)*

A typical barrage of media before our morning workout on the first day of spring training, 2011. *(Photo by Scott Rovak)*

My right eye is swollen here from a shingles infection I caught during the 2011 regular season. Between my managing duties and constant travel, recovering during the off season was easier said than done. *(Photo by Scott Rovak)*

Deep in conversation about the dynamics of our team with coach Dave McKay *(right)* and hitting coach and record-setting player Mark McGwire *(left)*. *(Photo by Scott Rovak)*

I had disallowed this ritual in 1996, in which veteran players cross-dress the younger guys, but allowed it again in 2011 because of the great camaraderie the team had that year. *(Courtesy of the author)*

Here, the Cards and Phillies are lined up to be introduced at the beginning of Game 3 of the National League Division Series. Look at that sea of red! *(Photo by Scott Rovak)*

Evening setting in as Rangers manager Ron Washington and I shake hands prior to Game 3 of the 2011 World Series. *(Photo by Scott Rovak)*

Albert Pujols, a great hitter and a team leader, and me watching Game 6 from the dugout. *(Photo by Scott Rovak)*

Freese's game-winning home run in Game 6. *(Photo by Scott Rovak)*

Carp *(right)* was always a fierce competitor and a true leader for our ball club. *(Photo by Scott Rovak)*

Sharing a great championship moment with the rest of the Cardinals coaching staff after our win in Game 5 of the NLDS. *(Photo by Scott Rovak)*

David Freese and me holding the World Series trophy. *(Photo by Scott Rovak)*

Saluting the crowd with my wife, Elaine, two days later at the rally following the championship parade through downtown St. Louis. *(Photo by Scott Rovak)*

I can't say that was a good day at the ballpark, but I hoped that rally in the ninth was a sign of better things to come offensively. If we could get into their bullpen, then we stood a better chance. On the other hand, the tail end of that game presented us with another cause for concern. On Matt Holliday's game-ending strikeout against their closer Ryan Madson, he tweaked his finger again. He told us that he felt some pain, but we'd have to wait to see until the next day just how bad the injury was.

We used Matt in that situation, down by five, as a way to see how that finger would stand up to a game situation. The feedback wasn't what we wanted, but at least we knew instead of having to wonder.

In a five-game series, you'd like to get that first game in your pocket. We knew going in that Halladay versus Lohse was a difficult matchup. Their number one against our number two wasn't ideal, but in game 2 that matchup would be more even. While Lee was number two in their order, he certainly had number-one stuff and stats with a record of 17-8 and an ERA of 2.40. Sometimes those number-one versus number-one matchups work in your favor, as they did in 2006 when we faced San Diego in the NLDS. In that game, Carp outdueled Jake Peavy in a 5–1 win at Petco that propelled us to the series win. While we didn't manage to win that first game on the road as we had in '06, I was hoping that some of that '06 magic still remained.

That year we'd squeaked into the playoffs with only eighty-three wins, the third-lowest total of any playoff team in history. With injuries to several key players, we staggered in, nearly blowing a seven-game lead with twelve to play. We got healthy and turned things around at the right moment, winning three out of four before clinching on the final day, when the Astros lost. Prior to that, we'd lost seven in a row while the Astros had won nine straight. Despite "backing in," we got hot at the right time and eventually won the World Series. Though we weren't a wild-card entry that year, in a lot of ways it felt like we had been. Over the years I'd seen wild-card teams make runs deep into the playoffs. Very often, because of the nature of the wild-card standings—you're competing with teams not just from your division but from the whole league—those races go down to the wire. That means that your club has to develop a lot of mental toughness.

In 2006 we'd essentially been playing playoff-type games for the last week before clinching. That helped to toughen us up. The same was true of the '11 team, only we'd been in the "playoffs" for a lot longer than that. In 2006 we'd also endured injuries to key players: Carp, Mark Mulder, Albert, Jim Edmonds, David Eckstein, and Jason Isringhausen had all gone on the DL at one point or another, particularly in the second half of the season, when we had struggled.

Despite the similarities, 2011 clearly wasn't 2006. Carp pitching on three days' rest was a complete unknown. I suspected that with him on limited rest, we weren't going to see him go deep into the game. That meant that it would become a bullpen game. We were decidedly better than we had been, but our Game 1 performance wasn't outstanding.

I came to the ballpark for Game 2 with some real questions in mind. We were facing what was essentially another number-one starter. If we lost Game 2, we'd head back to St. Louis needing a win to stay alive, and we'd still be facing another number-one starter—Cole Hamels, a guy with a 14-9 record and a 2.79 ERA—and a team that had won 102 regular-season games. Starters with an ERA of under 3.00 are prized possessions. Hell, if you had a guy with an ERA under 4.00 as your third man, you'd be pretty happy. Teams that win a hundred are equally rare and valuable.

Also, in my mind, if we lost, we'd have another game but not really. Coming back from a 0-2 series deficit was mathematically and in every other way the worst it could get. In my mind, that would be as near to an elimination as we could get without our season being officially over.

* * *

As Game 2 got under way, I found myself thinking, as I had since August: *We have to be realistic in our goals, we have to make this a series.* That's all I really had in mind at that point. *Let's make this competitive.* I'd had my share of lopsided playoff series. When you win them, it's great, but when you lose them, especially in a sweep, it's soul-killing. You have failed at your number-one task: having your club do a good job of representing how you prepare them to be competitive.

In 1988 the A's I led lost to the Dodgers 4–1, winning only Game 3 with a walk-off home run from Mark McGwire. Not a competitive World Series.

In 1989 we experienced the flip side of that, beating the Giants 4–0 that tragic year.

In 1990 the Reds swept their way to a World Series title, outscoring us 22 to 8.

Sometimes a team falls short of being truly competitive in a critical game rather than over an entire series. We lost 15–0 to the Braves in the seventh game of the NLCS in 1996. We also lost Game 5 by a score of 14–0. You don't like being on the losing side of series like that or games like that.

I knew going into Game 2 that a kind of tsunami effect could occur if we lost. Going down 0-2 in a five-game series meant that every game after that was a potential elimination game. I'm not saying that we couldn't have climbed back out of that hole, but it would have been a steep, dark, and dangerous climb. Not one I would recommend to anyone. With Carp on the hill, we at least liked our chances to be competitive. When Rafael Furcal, using the same mind-set we'd had against Halladay, tripled on the very first pitch, I knew we weren't going to have any trouble bouncing back from that opening game loss. When we failed to bring him in, I was still confident in our club's ability, but disappointed that we'd failed to capitalize.

The Phillies backed us up further against the wall by taking a 4–0 lead after the second inning. We didn't capitalize and they did, with a crooked number in the first and then by adding on with a single run in the second. Crap. Part of the reason for that early deficit was that Carp wasn't getting ahead of the hitters. He threw a first-pitch strike to only one of the seven hitters he faced, and that one, Shane Victorino, flied out. He fell behind, and then he had to come in with strikes, and a good-hitting team takes advantage of that. He threw thirty-eight pitches in that first inning, a lower total than it might have been only because he got an inning-ending double play. Carp's not one to fall behind so consistently. Something was up. I didn't like the idea that our starter had thrown more than a third of the total number of pitches he might be expected to deliver in the first inning.

I also didn't like what I saw in the second inning, when Molina and Theriot were called out on strikes. From our perspective, Jerry Meals was having a rough day umpiring behind the plate. Cliff Lee seemed to be getting pitches and Carp was not.

Some things were written about this game and the complaints about the umpiring behind the plate. That happens when one pitcher pounds the strike zone and the other is erratic. As a manager, you have to be on the alert for bias. Everyone in the game is a human being. Everyone is biased. So you have to check yourself. Of course you expect every call to go your way. Bias naturally factors into that. You want things to go your way, whether it's a ball/strike call or an out—even with inside pitches, bias will show up. These biases can lead people to have a difference of opinion. Whether or not that difference is the result of a bias is what takes insight and experience to determine.

Umpires, being human, are also subject to anticipating, just like players and coaches. I was aware of that from my earliest days as a manager, and I knew that this was about the hardest part of finessing your relationship with the game's officials. I always had to check myself before calling an umpire, a player, or anyone on their anticipation. *Don't be paranoid*, I told myself time and time again. I tried never to use umpires as an excuse for a loss.

Sitting there watching those first innings of Game 2 unfold, I felt that the home-plate umpire might be biased toward Cliff Lee first of all and the Phillies secondarily. Cliff Lee has a reputation as a strike-throwing machine. Always around the plate. Pitchers like that are going to get what people refer to as "the benefit of the doubt." That's just another way of saying that someone is biased toward believing them, or believing what they've heard about them to be true. Another way to think of this bias is in terms of assumptions or anticipation. I could cite examples of an umpire falling victim to this very human tendency to assume and anticipate. When a fielder bobbles a ball, the umpire may suspect that, because the grounder hasn't been fielded cleanly, the runner has a better shot at beating the throw. This doesn't happen all the time, but enough times. We sometimes use the "ball beat you, you're out" mentality on tag plays. That's another version of anticipation and assumption.

As observant as I'd been my entire managerial career, in my mind, with some bias acknowledged, I believed that Jerry Meals was expecting Lee's borderline pitches to be strikes. Not a lot, but enough.

When Carp struggled again in the bottom of the second, I went out there to talk to him, hoping that Jerry would come out from behind the plate so we could chat. I'd never had a problem before with Jerry, and this wasn't anything personal, but I felt like the strike zone wasn't being applied consistently. That's all we ever ask of umpires. Have whatever zone you want, but just keep it consistent throughout the game and for both sides. We'll adjust.

When I was out there with Carp, Jerry came out to join the discussion, and I said, "Hey, Jerry, we've got a lot of game left."

Based on what I'd said to him, you might think I was delirious. What did the amount of the game remaining have to do with balls and strikes? What I was primarily afraid of was another bias. Umpires know the game. They also read or hear what's being written or said about a series. I've already said that I understood that in most people's minds the Phillies had a decided advantage over us with their pitching and their one-hundred-plus-win ball club. Jerry had seen how Halladay just carved us up. He knew what caliber of pitcher Cliff Lee was. He also saw that we were already down 4–0. His human nature may have been telling him, "Hey, this is the way this game is supposed to go. The Phillies are heavily favored. The Phillies already have a lead. I anticipate that this game is going to wind up the way that it should, based on the experts' opinions and the evidence I have before me." Maybe he wasn't consciously having those thoughts, but what I saw in some of those calls led me to think it was a distinct possibility.

For that reason, I delivered the "There's a lot of game left, Jerry" message. I wasn't being disrespectful of Jerry in that situation. I was doing what I needed to do to protect our club and our chances of winning the game.

Later on, I explained during a between-innings interview on the national broadcast what I was thinking. I didn't explain myself as fully as I have here. Maybe saying anything on television like that wasn't the wisest move on my part, but I was asked a question and I answered it as honestly as I could. I admitted that I was upset. We were on the verge of elimination. I was doing my job by protecting my players. As I said, and as Carp said afterward, he wasn't going to say anything. He's a player. I'm a manager. I have to have my players' backs, and I believed we had a legitimate gripe. As it turned out, a few of the Phillies weren't happy either.

After two innings, with Philadelphia tacking on another in that frame to go up 4–0, we were even unhappier.

Fortunately for us, Dunc was on the bench. The two of them sat there between innings, and I knew that Dunc was talking with Carp about more than mechanics. As a pitching coach, you have to be part physiologist and physicist to understand how the body works and the ball moves through the air and part psychologist to understand how the pitcher's mind works. Dunc is the best at both, and I knew that he was helping Carp figure out a way to keep the Phillies right there, to block out whatever other distractions there might have been about the strike zone, the high pitch count, and the fact that he was going on three days' rest.

Just hold them right there.

He did just that in the third, throwing only eight pitches, including a three-pitch strikeout of Victorino to end the inning.

After the game, we learned from Carp that when he'd warmed up for the game he hadn't felt particularly strong, so he went out there in the first couple of innings and tried to put extra effort behind every pitch. He was out of sorts mechanically. When the game was over, Carp also told us this: if he ever got a chance to pitch with three days' rest again, he'd learned a lot from this first experience. He wouldn't try to force it. *He would "pitch with what he had" and not try to add to it.*

With Carp appearing to settle down, two other things had to happen if we were going to get back in the game. One was that we had to hold their offense down with our bullpen. Carp was at sixty-four pitches after three innings, and it was clear there would be no complete game for him that night. This was turning into a bullpen game, and we'd have to do better than we had the night before. And two, we were going to have to find a way to score at least five runs in order to be ahead. Talk about a tough situation.

We responded in the top of the fourth. With our dugout making lots of noise, Berkman walked. One out later, we got a single by Molina. Theriot hit a huge double to drive in a run. Jay singled to drive in Yadi and took second on the throw home. I pinch-hit Punto for Carpenter, but he struck out. That was a big miss, but then Furcal picked him up by singling with two out to drive home Theriot. Jay was out at the plate trying to score from second, but that was a good move by Jose Oquendo. It took a great throw to get him, and you always want to put pressure on the defense in that situation and stay aggressive.

4–3.

The bullpen then took over. Salas was the most rested reliever we had, with four days off, so he was the guy who should come in to pitch multiple innings. He gave us two shutout innings. That was a big lift for the club. By keeping it a one-run game, we knew that we were only a pop away from being tied—we could manufacture a run and still square the game going into the last few innings. Knowing that you just have to chip away a run at a time makes a big difference.

We did just that in the top of the sixth after we had two outs and nobody on.

Theriot doubled, and Jay singled to score him and went to second. Schumaker, pinch-hitting for Salas, got an infield hit. He dove into first base to beat the throw, as he had done so many times in his career. That's an aggressive but not particularly smart move. It's both dangerous and inefficient. If you run through the bag, you will get there quicker than when you dive. I think he made it only twice in his major league career, both last year. Furcal hit into a force-out, and the inning ended at 4–4.

We'd been excited in the dugout all game, and the energy level was high as the guys trotted out to take their positions in the bottom of the sixth. My anxiety level was equally high. We'd scored to tie it, and momentum was on our side. If we let the Phillies get ahead, all that we'd done to climb out of that 4–0 hole could be lost.

We decided to start the inning with Octavio Dotel, the veteran who was very good for us after we got him from Toronto in July. At thirty-seven, Dotel, out of the Dominican Republic, was a veteran who'd seen it all since coming up to the big leagues in 1999. His first two years in the league, he'd started a total of thirty games, but he'd been pitching in relief ever since. He had been with twelve different clubs, including us, during his thirteen years. We liked him as the setup man, the eighth-inning guy, to get to our closer. He'd been a closer himself, so he had the tools and the mind-set we liked— someone who could go out there at the start of an inning and shut them down.

He also had postseason experience, and you can't underestimate the importance of that.

So, even though it was only the bottom of the sixth, we went with Dotel as our specialist to give us the best shot at them not scoring after we'd tied.

He set down the Phillies in order in the home sixth.

Our seventh began with Craig hitting a triple and Albert singling him home to give us a 5–4 lead.

We had runners at first and third with nobody out after Berkman singled. This brought up Freese, facing Brad Lidge. Freese hit a ball to Lidge, and Albert did a heckuva job baserunning, avoiding the double play and staying in a run-down long enough to allow Berkman to wind up at third and Freese at second.

The Phillies walked Yadi intentionally, bringing up Theriot, who had just had two clutch doubles. But on the first pitch, he hit into a double play. We were ahead 5–4, but we'd missed an enormous chance to possibly break the game open.

But part of toughness and character is continuing to play when everything is not falling into place.

We sent Dotel out for the seventh, and he got an out. They pinch-hit Ross Gload, a left-handed hitter, for Lidge. To counter that we brought in the left-hander Rzepczynski. Dotel had thrown nineteen pitches to get us four outs, but we couldn't push him further than that because he'd pitched the day before, even if he'd only thrown seven pitches.

The Phillies switched off Gload for Ben Francisco, a right-handed hitter, and R-zep induced a fly-out.

This out was big because of what had happened to him the night before when they got three hits—bing, bing, bing—against him. He didn't faint. You like to see guys bounce back, and he did. He also has another dimension to his game that proved helpful. After Jimmy Rollins singled, we used our running game defense effectively. Knowing the Phillies wanted to get that lead run into scoring position with two outs, we executed the pickoff perfectly, one of those little things we talked so much about, with R-zep getting the ball to Albert, who then threw down to second and Furcal. Just like you practice it in spring training.

But then came the eighth, no doubt the hairiest inning in this near-elimination game. The whole time we were playing the top of the eighth, I was running through the Phillie hitters due up in the bottom half of the inning, looking at all the various scenarios and trying to figure out who we needed to pitch.

Rzepczynski hit Utley with a pitch to start the inning. The next two batters were Pence and Howard. A difficulty we faced in taking on the Phillies was bullpen matchups. They had two switch-hitters in Rollins and Victorino, and they had left-handed hitters in Utley, Howard, and Raul Ibanez, who could all hang in there and hit well against left-handers. As if that weren't tough enough, another right-handed hitter, Pence, was hitting .317 against left-handers. If Rzepczynski had retired Utley, we would have liked to have him face Howard in a lefty-lefty confrontation. But now, could we risk him pitching to Pence?

Our "what-if" actually came down to three "what-ifs": Do you leave R-zep in to face Howard and maybe get him out? Do you go to your closer Motte to get five or six outs? No. I dismissed that one right away because Howard and Victorino would come up after Pence. Lefties were hitting .270, a pretty good number, against Motte, and righties were hitting .162. That wasn't really a fair challenge.

The last "what-if" parlay was to go to the right-hander Boggs to get the right-handed-hitting Pence, and then Arthur Rhodes, our veteran left-hander in the bullpen, to go after the lefties Howard and Victorino.

In addition to those lefty/righty percentages, I had to factor in a few more things. For one thing, Boggs had had a bad game the day before, and in our late-season push, Rzepczynski had been outstanding. But when R-zep hit Utley, I suddenly had a tough call to make. The day before R-zep had given up three hits. Now, in Game 2, he'd gotten an out in the seventh and then allowed a base hit to Rollins, who he then picked off. Of the first six men he'd faced in the postseason, five had reached base. Now he was about to pitch to a hitter who batted .317 against left-handers.

Talented as R-zep was, this was his first postseason, and you've got to read the human being. I chose Boggs. He got a grounder from Pence to force out Utley at second.

In going to Boggs, I'd already committed to bringing in a left-hander to face Howard. After that Game 1 home run, we weren't feeling too sorry for the guy with the bad leg. I called Arthur Rhodes from the bullpen, and he struck out Howard. Two outs.

Now what did we do?

Victorino was really good from both sides of the plate, but we wanted to turn him around to hit left-handed, because he was a .270 hitter versus right-handers as opposed to .308 batting right-handed against left-handed pitchers.

We had a lot to think about before using Motte in that situation to get four outs. He had pitched two and a third innings against the Phillies in four games in the regular season. In those appearances, he'd allowed five hits and six runs, five of them earned. That's an ERA of 11.32 and a batting average against of .348. Further, over a three-year period against them, he had an ERA of 11.88 and an opponents' batting average of .368. But we brought him in, believing that turning around Victorino was that important, and he'd be facing an improved Motte.

Jason got two quick strikes and then retired Victorino on a fly ball to end that inning; it seemed almost too easy.

In the ninth, Motte struck out Ibanez, got a fly ball out from Polanco, and a groundout from Carlos Ruiz. Motte recorded four outs on nine pitches, clearly showing that he was a better pitcher against the Phillies than some of those previous bad numbers would indicate. Though the stats told us one thing, we went away from those percentages in favor of our gut. And it worked.

From trailing early to tension with the umpire, a late rally, and our bullpen going six innings without giving up a run, this had been a draining game. You wouldn't have known that from the reaction in the clubhouse. Their "happy flight" chants were echoing down the hallway.

That game really said something about us. I had put so much emphasis on Carp being able to start that game on short rest, and he'd gone only three innings. Who would have thought that our bullpen, so inconsistent in the beginning of the year and in a state of flux throughout the rest of the season, was going to play such a crucial role in what I saw as a near-elimination game? The guys had picked one another up offensively and on the mound. We'd told them that they needed to continue to do the things well that had gotten them into the playoffs, and they'd responded.

It was now down to two out of three games, and the Cardinals were heading home.

Even though it didn't happen exactly the way I'd envisioned it, at the postgame press conference I said that winning this game made it a series. In the final analysis, the bullpen's performance in Game 2 created the template for the postseason. If they were good enough, we were good enough. If they weren't, we weren't. And then I added, "I hope it comes down to Halladay and Carpenter in Game 5. I mean, that would be an experience of a lifetime for any of us. That would be more than worth the price of admission."

And I meant that. You've got to plant seeds.

CHAPTER FOURTEEN

Hanging in There

E VEN IF WE'D LOST GAMES 1 AND 2, WE WOULD HAVE RECEIVED almost the same reception from our intensely loyal fans.

In a city with slightly more than 350,000 residents and about 800,000 in the metro area, it's remarkable that the Cardinals routinely draw more than 3 million people year after year. We were one of nine clubs to draw that many fans during the 2011 regular season, with only Milwaukee and Minnesota joining us as a small-market club with that kind of attendance. In fact, of all the teams that drew more than 3 million, we had the lowest population. St. Louis ranked fifty-second in terms of population in the country, but you would have thought that all 350,000 St. Louis citizens were at the ballpark on October 4 for Game 3. Just short of 47,000 fans were in Busch Stadium that Tuesday late afternoon, and it seemed as if every one of them was either wearing red, red in the face from shouting, or red-palmed from clapping—in most cases all three.

Some clamor got stirred up after the game about the start time. With the sun angling lower in October and the shadows lengthening across the mound and home plate, the hitters' vision is affected.

The stadium lights help some but not much until far later in the game. Albert, Matt, and Lance were some of the most vocal critics of the start time, and they should have been. As three of the team's co-signers, they took on that responsibility knowing that in some corners they were going to be seen as complainers. But as Albert himself said, we couldn't do anything about it in the long run. With the Yankees playing Detroit, the Bronx Bombers' far larger market was irresistible to the networks, so they got to play in prime time. That's the nature of things today. Besides, the environmental conditions are the same for both teams.

Not to take anything away from Cole Hamels and Jaime Garcia, but the fact that no runs were scored until the seventh inning, when the shadows were gone and the lights had taken better effect, speaks to the impact of the start time on hitters. We try to tell the players to focus on the things that are under their control, but these guys are only human.

I'm not naive enough—and I'm too much of a pragmatist—to call for a return to the old days when postseason baseball was played almost exclusively during the day. We all have fond memories of some of that black-and-white footage of Bill Mazeroski's home run in 1960 to win the Series or even Bucky Dent's drive to win the playoff game against the Red Sox at Fenway in 1978. Playing in the same division as the Chicago Cubs, the last holdout to finally install lights in their ballpark, I have mixed feelings about daytime baseball. In the summer heat, it can be incredibly taxing to play in the afternoon. I understand that television frequently dictates scheduling in the postseason, and all you can hope for then is that the start time doesn't have an effect on the quality of the competition.

While I understood what those guys were saying about the conditions, we'd talked about this issue before. I'd told them that they couldn't have it both ways. Television revenues are enormous, and the networks pay their money, so they get to set the schedule. The players want to earn as much as they can, and a lot of the money that's available to today's players comes from those TV dollars. So the players can either take the money that television affords them and all that goes with it that they view as a negative, or they can forgo the higher income that TV money has provided and eliminate those dissatisfactions.

By any standard, the competition rose above the difficulties of a late-afternoon start and the fact that this wasn't an elimination game. The two clubs fought as hard as they could possibly fight. We had multiple chances to score, particularly in the late innings, some clutch hits led to runs, and some great pitching produced key outs—all the ingredients you could want in any game, but especially one that was pivotal in the series. Whoever won Game 3 would have the elimination-game edge on the other.

Our plan was to continue to crank out tough at-bats, hoping to get to Cole Hamels right away. Though he had won just fourteen games in the regular season, Hamels had an outstanding ERA of 2.79. He's a tough left-hander with good command of four different pitches. He walked only 44 in 216 innings, while striking out 194. Those are outstanding numbers, and he was even tougher in the postseason in 2008, when he won four games. For his part, Jaime Garcia was making his first postseason appearance. Based solely on experience, you had to say that Hamels had the edge, but through the first six innings neither pitcher gave an inch.

In the first inning, we'd tried to put our aggressiveness to work. After Albert doubled with two outs and Berkman was hit by a pitch, we successfully executed a double steal to get both men into scoring position. It was obviously a risk, but one worth taking. If nothing else, it sent a message to the opposing side—we are going to make something happen. Though the double steal ended up not paying off when Freese struck out, we'd planted the seed.

By the top of the seventh, you could say that both pitchers were in command, but that wouldn't be entirely accurate. To that point, Hamels hadn't retired us in order in any inning, but he kept making the big pitch when it mattered. I'm sure that fans were thinking that opportunity after opportunity had slipped through our fingers, but you also have to credit Hamels, who was competing hard all night. It was both frustrating and fascinating to watch. Garcia, on the other hand, had allowed only three hits through six innings.

Our fatigue concern was still lingering, and we started looking for signs of struggle as Garcia went deeper into the game. Through six, he'd thrown seventy-eight pitches, including four intentional balls. He hadn't started for seven days, so he was as fresh as he could possibly be. Despite that, I debated lifting him for a pinch hitter in the bottom of the sixth when we had runners on first and second, thanks to a hit and a semi-intentional walk to get to Jaime's spot in the order. I had Holliday available to pinch-hit. I opted instead to let Garcia go to the plate: the main reason was that to that point Garcia hadn't surrendered a run. His pitch count was okay, and he'd showed no sign of tiring in the fifth or the sixth. This was as tough a decision—stay with an effective starter or switch to the bench?—as I would have to make during the entire postseason run.

In a close game, you have to consider how many more chances you're going to have to score. Bringing in Holliday to pinch-hit in that position, a prime RBI spot, was a good option. However, we were the home team and had that last at-bat in our favor, so I let that factor influence me. That's how fine those distinctions become. We wanted to get Hamels out of there so that we could get to the Phillies' vulnerable bullpen, but we also suspected that if we sent a pinch hitter up there to get the percentages in our favor, Hamels would have remained anyway. I decided to go against sending Holliday up there, despite what we'd been feeling late season about Garcia's stamina. I knew that this was one that I'd end up taking a very close look at after the game regardless of the outcome—especially since this was a crucial decision in a crucial Game 3.

Garcia struck out to end the mini-threat, and we sent him out there to start the seventh, as confident as you could be in a guy who to that point was throwing shutout ball. Jaime had been aggressive in the strike zone most of the night, but he fell behind 3-0 on Shane Victorino. The first thought I had was that, despite being good to go physically, Garcia had been distracted by the decision the previous half-inning, and he'd been wondering if he was going to stay in the game. Add to that he'd been disappointed by his strikeout, and he was a different pitcher to start the seventh. He eventually allowed a single to their leadoff hitter. Garcia retired the next two hitters, working around a passed ball to get to two outs with a runner on second base. At that point I felt confident that my read of how good his stuff was had been accurate.

Still, it was key decision time. Ruiz was the next scheduled hitter, batting in the eight hole ahead of Hamels. We wanted Hamels out of the game at that point. With first base open, I signaled Yadi to have Garcia issue four intentional balls to Ruiz.

Now, year in and year out, Hall of Fame–type managers like Sparky Anderson and Bobby Cox had some of the highest intentional walk totals in the league. I had a higher total in 2011 than average, but as a rule, my total was on the lower side. There were two reasons for that. Unless there was a huge advantage, I rarely would issue an intentional walk to load the bases because that really added to the pluses on the hitters' side and took away from the pitcher's advantages. I also believed that unless you had a significant advantage, telling the hitter on deck that "we can get you out but not the guy ahead of you" would give the hitter a psychological edge that our pitcher would then have to overcome.

Therefore, one of the strategies we employed a lot was the "un-intentional" intentional walk, and it was particularly effective in the National League, where the pitcher hits. Often the eighth-place hitter comes up with two outs, a runner in scoring position, and the pitcher on deck. If you walk the eighth-place hitter and the pitcher makes an out, then the leadoff man comes up to start the next inning. We'd rather try to use an eighth-place hitter's aggressiveness against him, hoping that he'll swing at a borderline pitch and get himself out.

We had a sign for it, from the dugout to the catcher, and from the catcher to the pitcher. You're telling the pitcher that he's going to pitch at the edge (of the strike zone) or off the edge and that the catcher is going to help by centering his receiving position either at the edge or off the edge. What you have going for you is that the hitter, since there's an RBI situation, wants to get that bat going. And he may be more apt to chase a pitch out of the strike zone. Sometimes you may get a call from the umpire on one of these "edge" pitches, which changes the count.

In my sixteen National League years, I would be hard-pressed to find a strategy more effective than that one to help us win games and prevent runs from being scored. But sometimes pitchers aren't on board with this strategy. They think they can get anybody out, and we encourage that thinking—to a point. One time in spring training in 2004, when we were going over this as one of our fundamentals, Woody Williams, one of our veteran pitchers, spoke up and said he didn't like it, and then Matt Morris chimed in and said, "I've got to go after the hitter. That's how I compete."

"That's great," I responded. "But it's not smart." In the back of the room, the legendary Bob Gibson was sitting on a stool. He was listening to all this, but not saying a word. I took a shot and said, "Bob, everybody knows that you were one of the game's great competitors. Did you ever pitch around a guy to go after the next guy?"

"Are you kidding?" Bob said. "All the time. When Henry Aaron was hitting and [former Milwaukee first baseman] Joe Adcock was behind him, Aaron had no chance to get anything unless he stepped into the other side of the batter's box to swing at it. I knew I could get Joe Adcock out."

But you've really got to explain this strategy to your pitchers and pick your spots to use it. You don't want to use it just to get to the next hitter who might be just as good. In our case, Charlie Manuel sent up Ben Francisco to hit for the pitcher. Francisco was a reserve outfielder who'd hit .244 during the regular season. He had a bit of pop in his bat, homering six times in 250 at-bats. To that point in his career, he was 1-for-9 with no RBIs against Jaime. After that at-bat, he was 2-for-10 with three RBIs after he drove Garcia's pitch deep into left-center for a three-run homer. In the end, the decision to walk Ruiz was easy, but now we'd made things more difficult for ourselves by coming into the dugout down 3–0.

I'd had multiple opportunities in the span of an inning to get Garcia out of the game, but I hadn't. The thing about baseball is that it's the most open and obvious of professional sports, which means that virtually everybody who's watching, whether they have a little or a lot of baseball know-how, is going to have an opinion on what the strategy should be. It doesn't work to the same degree in basketball, football, and hockey because many of the things that happen in a game aren't quite as obvious to the casual fan. With all that scrutiny, if you don't make the "right" decision, you get nailed. If you do, you get hailed. There's a lot of pressure to put the blame for a loss on somebody or somebodies.

Some coaches and managers get very defensive when they're asked about their strategy; right away, they assume they're being criticized and they take it personally. The better attitude to take is that people are paying attention and you should be ready to explain the thinking behind your choices. As a decision-maker, I always viewed the questioning as an opportunity to explain what my process was. Then, if those asking the questions were being fair-minded, they could at least say, "Yeah, I can see where he was coming from," even if they didn't agree.

I picked this up when I was a young manager in Chicago and our general manager, Roland Hemond, told me that if the questioning came from someone in the media, see it as an opportunity to explain what you were thinking and not as a challenge. Your response might or might not impress the questioner, but if you didn't know the answer, or if you acted like the questions bothered you, or if you gave an answer that was pure B.S., then you didn't belong on the bench managing the team. The only times I've really balked at this have been when I felt somebody had an agenda, wasn't intending to be fair, or was trying to create some controversy.

Going into the bottom of the seventh, it would have been easy for the guys to just roll over, but they didn't. Craig worked a one-out walk off Vance Worley, who'd come in to replace Hamels. Albert singled to put runners on first and second with one out. Berkman hit a grounder to second and hustled down the line to prevent a double play. David Freese, who was struggling that night at the plate with three strikeouts in his previous at-bats, then got a two-out hit for us to drive in a run. We couldn't get another big two-out hit, but at least we'd broken through. I can't say enough about Freese picking us up. Here's a guy who had struck out in six of his last seven at-bats in his first postseason, but he kept grinding and got that clutch hit.

In the bottom of the eighth, Theriot singled, and so did Holliday in a pinch-hitting role. We had runners on first and second with only one out and the top of the order coming up. The stadium was rocking, and the guys were on the top step, leaning wide-eyed over the rail, straining hard to will another base hit and another late-inning rally. Furcal got the hit we needed, but it was struck so hard to left that we couldn't get Theriot home from second. The bases were now loaded with still only one out. The collective moan from the stands could probably have been heard all the way across the river in East St. Louis when we caught a tough break. Craig hit a bullet to the second baseman, who turned it for an easy double play.

Gut-shot as we were by that lost opportunity, we had our chance again in the bottom of the ninth. Albert doubled to lead off, and then two outs later Yadi stepped up against Ryan Madson, the Phillies' closer who had saved thirty-two games in thirty-four opportunities during the regular season. Yadi, even with us down to our last out, stayed aggressive and jumped on the first pitch and singled, bringing us within a run. This was nervous leg-bouncing time, and I'm sure that many among the Cardinal fans had their hands clenched in prayer. Ryan Theriot competed hard against Madson, fouling off three pitches before grounding out to second.

We'd lost, but we'd engaged in one helluva struggle. This was one of those "tip your cap to your opponent" games—they'd made the most of their opportunities and we hadn't. Every time you play this game you see something different, something nearly inexplicable. How could we have lost when he had such a good offensive night in one sense (we had twelve hits and four walks, we were never retired in order, and we had two players—Pujols and Theriot—who each got four hits) and such a lousy one in another (we left fourteen men on base, while the other team scored three times on seven hits)? You frequently hear a team say, "We had our chances," but how many can say that in the last three innings they sent the potential tying run to the plate eleven times?

And how do you explain this? In his previous thirty-four innings spanning five starts against the Phillies, Garcia had given up only three runs. And the guy who hit the home run hadn't knocked one out of the park in nearly five months.

That's why we compete. That's why the game is so endlessly fascinating—not to mention heartbreaking. That's also why, in reviewing the game afterward, in really dissecting it, I came to this conclusion: irrespective of the outcome, the fact that we wound up losing the game, I believed that I should have made the move to Holliday in the sixth to potentially break open the game. Please note what I said about ignoring the outcome. You can always look at the results of a choice and determine if it was right or wrong or good or bad. As a manager, you have to do a lot of reviewing after the game in order to learn, but if you keep looking at it in terms of results, you won't learn as much as you would if you just consider whether or not you did the right thing to give your club the best chance to win.

In this case, I hadn't done that, and I would have come to that same conclusion even if Francisco hadn't hit his home run. We'd have had the best chance to win if I'd pinch-hit with Holliday. Holliday was our most dangerous option coming off the bench. The question was: when do we pull the trigger? I didn't in the sixth because the rule of thumb says that you should hold on to that weapon until the last third of the game—the seventh, eighth, or ninth innings. I went by the book, and despite this being an *ideal* pinch-hitting situation—there were two runners on base and Holliday would have been facing a left-hander. Add to that, we would have turned the game over to our bullpen who'd demonstrated their capability already in Game 2 and throughout September. On the other side of the scale, I had a pitcher doing well against a team he dominated and Holliday as a bullet still in the chamber I could fire later. I saw the latter as the tipping point, made my decision, and we lost.

I'd scrutinized the hell out of the decision during the game, and in spite of that, I didn't make the right call. That's no excuse, just a way to make this point. I spend a lot of time before and during games anticipating what might happen next and how I will likely respond. I "what-if" like a madman all the time. So I was prepared for that choice of Jaime versus Holliday. If people say I'm intense and never smile or whatever, I guess that's because I can't do that and grind at the same time. Mostly, it's because while the game is being played, you have to remain on alert for all the twists and turns that you have to anticipate.

No one could ignore the fact that Game 4 was an elimination game. As much as I wanted to keep the focus on the club and the opposition, I couldn't ignore another reality: if we lost, my managerial career was over. How we were going to handle my retirement was an organizational issue, and as much as I would have liked to continue to keep things quiet and just deal with the current club and staff, that wasn't possible. It also wouldn't have been fair to the people whose task it was to find a replacement for me. Mo came into the clubhouse to talk to me about our plan: I would inform the players and staff, asking that no one say anything about my ending my career as an on-field manager, and we'd schedule a formal, public announcement for the next day.

I knew all this was necessary, but I wanted to keep as much of my attention as possible on what really mattered—beating Roy Oswalt and the Philadelphia Phillies. Even though I was retiring, I didn't put any extra emphasis on this game. Don't get me wrong—I wanted to win this one as badly as any other game, maybe a bit more so, since winning meant we could continue playing. But to win didn't require any kind of grand gesture or pulling something out of my managerial motivation bag of tricks. I knew that the guys were ready to play. The clubhouse atmosphere wasn't tense, and the guys weren't gathering in a circle and jumping up and down pounding on one another, like you sometimes see football players doing. They were just going through their routine to prepare for game 166, which was exactly what I hoped would happen.

As an organization, we've had good success in the playoffs. In the sixteen years since I'd arrived, we'd been to the postseason nine times. A lot has been said about our failure to win the NLCS or the World Series. I get that. It's disappointing to lose anytime, but especially in the playoffs. Almost everyone I've spoken with inside baseball, though, has a slightly different take on that, and it's one that I share: there's more pressure in the five games in the Division Series than in the games in the later series. That's not because the series is short, but because the Division Series is like a college entrance exam that determines completely whether or not you get in. Pass it, and you're on to the next phase and hopefully beyond. Each of those phases is more fun and more rewarding. But lose the Division Series and you fail. You don't have your second-choice school to get into. You're done. You barely qualified, other teams with better records didn't.

You really didn't belong here, and now here's the proof. Lose in the later rounds and it's, hey, good season, you showed everyone you belonged, great learning experience that you can use down the line. Lose in the first round and suddenly the season is written off—you're crap and the season is crap. As such, guys really don't want to lose in the first round.

I've heard people say that my intense style works in the regular season but not in the postseason. Well, I formulated my approach from a lot of different places, but one of the most notable was from Sal Bando, the great third baseman out of Arizona State who won all those championships in the 1970s with the A's. He helped articulate the necessary approach to winning championships. I know because I was in that organization and I asked him point-blank: How'd you win those three titles in a row?

Sal's answer was that you have to believe that every pitch of every inning of every game matters in terms of winning and losing and affects whether you advance into the playoffs and then through them. If you think that way and you play that way, then you'll be successful. That's what we've always taught and emphasized. So why haven't we always succeeded? How is it that we've fallen short so many times? Is it a case of being too intense, too wound up, too tight to perform under pressure?

My answer is no. Of the nine times we made it to the postseason, we won seven out of nine first-round playoff series, the ones that the players themselves say are the most pressure-packed. We didn't lose after that point because we couldn't handle the pressure or because our approach was wrong. We lost because the other team was better on those particular game days.

In some ways, we were fortunate that in Game 4 against the Phillies we were facing a familiar opponent. Roy Oswalt had spent the first ten-plus years of his career in Houston. As a divisional opponent, we'd faced him regularly. In his thirty starts against us, he was only 10-9 with a more-than-respectable ERA of 3.19. More recently, in 2011, he'd been 1-1 in his three starts against us, posting a 3.21 ERA. That included the seven shutout innings he'd thrown on September 17, when he'd pitched in the game that clinched the division for the Phillies.

The mark of a great versus a good pitcher is his ability to raise the level of his game when it really matters—namely the postseason. Going into Game 4, Oswalt was 5-1 in his postseason starts. We remembered him well from 2005, when he won an elimination game in the NLCS, beating us 5–1 and surrendering just three hits and that lone run in seven innings. That was the last time we had faced Roy Oswalt in a postseason game in St. Louis. Most impressive, he'd done that after we'd beaten the Astros with a great comeback capped by a home run from Albert. By closing us out, Oswalt also closed out the old Busch Stadium. He had some extra incentive in that game. The Astros' owner, Drayton McLane, knowing that our stadium was due to be torn down to make way for the new ballpark as soon as our season ended, had promised Oswalt a $200,000 bulldozer if he won that game.

I don't know if ending my managerial career was worth a bulldozer or not—maybe a shovel or two—but I also knew this: the two guys remaining in our starting lineup from that 2005 game, Yadi and Albert, had had good success against Oswalt. In his career, Yadi was 12-for-33, a .364 average, while Albert, in ninety-five at-bats, had hit seven home runs and driven in seventeen. Going in, then, you'd expect that two of our bigger bats would contribute offensively.

You also might expect that Edwin Jackson, in his first postseason start and with so much on the line, would have some trouble keeping his emotions in check in the first inning. That's exactly what happened. Five pitches into the game, we were down 0–2. I could hear that bulldozer idling in the distance. Fortunately, Yadi made a hell of a throw to nail Pence on a steal attempt, and Jackson settled down to retire the next two hitters.

For a lot of pitchers, the first inning is the toughest. Very often, on the first trip through the lineup, a pitcher might be limited as to what he wants to show you, so if the hitter is alert, he can have an advantage. Also, it's universally true that, when pitchers warm up, no matter how they feel, they're not 100 percent sure when they get out there what they will have working for them. That's happened so much it's scary. For instance, a pitcher might even find that the mound on the field is different from the one in the bullpen. I've heard guys say after pitching a no-hitter or even a perfect game that when they went out there, they weren't sure what they were going to have. Their bullpen warm-up session hadn't been good. The opposite is also true—great in the bullpen before, lousy in the game.

If we were going to stay alive in the series, we needed another comeback. Of course, it was still very early, and the whole "whoever scores first usually wins" number came into play, but at this point we were well practiced in the art of urgency, and we responded accordingly in the bottom of the first. Skip Schumaker's single and Berkman's double off his former teammate, against whom he was 3-for-5 going in, narrowed their lead to 2–1. We used that first-inning shakiness to our advantage, as had the Phillies, and the aggressiveness on both sides paid off.

Jackson settled down after the first. He began to use his full repertoire and allowed only two additional hits through the sixth. By that point, we were ahead 3–2, thanks to a big double from David Freese. Oswalt, who had been on the disabled list twice during the regular season with back troubles, wasn't as sharp as we'd seen him. Whether that injury was affecting him, I couldn't say for sure, but he walked Lance and hit Holliday to start the fourth. Freese stepped in there with runners on first and third (Berkman advanced on a fly-out), and you could feel the collective anticipation of the crowd rooting for their hometown guy.

David had struggled early in the series, but that big hit in Game 3 did something for his confidence. We didn't add on, but Edwin did a great job of shutting the Phillies down after a leadoff single in the fifth, retiring the next three in order. In the sixth, he was helped out by Albert on a great heads-up defensive play.

Albert's more than just a great hitter. His baseball IQ is high. He's a good, if adventurous, base runner, and I don't think he gets enough credit for his defensive abilities. In this case, it was his anticipation reading a situation and responding that made all the difference. Utley led off the inning with a walk. When Hunter Pence bounced one deep into the hole at short, Utley, who'd gotten a great jump, had the play in front of him. Furcal had no play at second, and as he released the ball toward first, Utley rounded the bag and headed for third. He would have made it if Albert, seeing Utley motoring for third, hadn't come off the bag at first early and then made a great throw to Freese to nail Utley. Potential rally snuffed out.

We kept the momentum going in the bottom of the sixth and added on to our lead. Holliday, whose finger was holding up okay, singled, and then David Freese homered. We were now up 5–2 with nine outs left to get. Being up by three instead of one really changed the complexion of the game. The Phils were more restricted in how they might attack us, and we responded with a different defensive strategy, playing our outfielders not as deep as normal to keep runners off base.

We also decided to turn the game over to the bullpen, beginning to play each defensive out individually. Arthur Rhodes started the inning to face the left-handed-hitting Raul Ibanez. Vintage Arthur— he struck him out on four pitches. We brought in Dotel to face the right-handed-hitting Placido Polanco. Nothing calm about this veteran hitter, but Octavio induced a ground ball. Next was another right-hander, Ruiz, and Dotel got him on a fly ball. Vintage Dotel.

I know that some fans wonder how guys in the bullpen can earn millions of dollars a year for coming into games and throwing just a few pitches, sometimes facing just one hitter, but I can't stress enough how tough that job is. For a starting pitcher, you look at his body of work during the course of a game, sometimes as many as 120 pitches.

You expect he's going to have his ups and downs in the course of a game. Situational relievers live and die with every pitch. Fans, bloggers, the so-called experts, have just a couple of pitches to look at to make their judgments about good job or lousy job, whether that relief pitcher's effort hurt or helped. As much as we stress the importance of focusing on the effort and not the result, with situational relievers and closers, guys who are generally in a game when the outcome is still tantalizingly in front of them, the ability to block out all kinds of distractions is unique to their position. A starter can make a mistake and then pitch through it. A reliever's margin for error is very slim. That's another kind of pressure altogether. In some ways, they are like kickers in football. You don't think much about them until they're lining up a potential game-winner with seconds left on the clock. It takes a certain mentality to get used to that kind of job.

In Game 4, our bullpen came through for us. Fernando Salas allowed a run in the eighth, and it was one of those ugly ones. A single, a balk, a groundout advancing a runner to third, and then a wild pitch pulled the Phillies to within two. We brought in R-zep to face Ryan Howard with a runner on, and R-zep threw three pitches past him to end the inning. Here's an example of that kind of big bounce-back from a rough outing that is so crucial to a reliever's success. Imagine if your boss came to you after you'd lost a sale the previous day and told you that you had to make one call in the next five minutes to sign up a new account or else. Would you feel like you deserved a decent salary if that was what your work life was like every day?

That Philly run meant that in the ninth, with Jason Motte on the mound, any runner on would bring the potential tying run to the plate. Jason had my heart rate climbing when he threw three straight balls to the leadoff hitter, Victorino—a guy with great speed by the way—but he came back to retire him and the next two hitters to earn the save.

The old line about living to fight another day refers to a strategic retreat or withdrawal. We were going to fight another day, but there was no retreating now or ever. The sense of relief and satisfaction at having survived an elimination game was palpable.

We had an off day to get ready, but as was true throughout this postseason—no long speeches, no long meetings. I knew if nothing else that we were ready to go out there and have some fun, October baseball style. I'd gotten what I'd asked for: Roy Halladay and Chris Carpenter, two former teammates, two good friends, were about to go at it head to head. I couldn't wait to get to Philadelphia, the City of Brotherly Love, to see two brothers in arms compete. My anticipation at being involved in a do-or-die game was intense. Those games are the kind you fantasize about as a kid, the stuff of heroic dreams.

Who doesn't love an elimination game, whether it's a game 5 or a game 7? I've talked to many managers and coaches, in baseball and in other sports, and they all agree—nothing is better. Even casual sports fans and people who don't follow sports at all will tune in to a decisive game, a do-or-die, a win-or-go-home, a winner-take-all battle. These games are the ultimate, and early in my Cardinal career I had only been in a few of them, and to be honest, they'd been a bit of a letdown.

Against Atlanta in '96, we had a Game 7 in the NLCS, went into the seventh game eager, and came out with our heads handed to us in a 15–0 blowout. No fun. In 2001 we won ninety-three games, then played Arizona in some really tight NLDS ball games, including a 2–1 loss in the deciding Game 5 when Curt Schilling beat us. We competed really hard. That was fun, but still, losing in the first round was a bitter pill to swallow. No joy there.

Getting to elimination games is one thing, winning them is another. We got that bitter taste of 2001 out of our mouths in 2004 and 2006. We beat Roger Clemens and Houston in a thrilling Game 7. Two years later, we downed the Mets in another great elimination game. Those would be hard to top for excitement, but just having the opportunity to experience the joy or devastation of a deciding Game 5 was enough.

CHAPTER FIFTEEN

Brothers in Arms

WHEN, AFTER GAME 2 OF THE SERIES, I TALKED ABOUT HOW much I wanted to see a matchup between Carp and Roy Halladay, I wasn't kidding. As a fan, and as the soon-to-be-outgoing manager of the St. Louis Cardinals, I wanted to see those two great competitors go at it. The word *great* may get overused. I have some very specific criteria I use when talking about pitchers who have earned that description. In my mind, you have to become great. It's something you work at turning yourself into. It involves doing the things necessary to improve yourself in all facets. You have to work at your craft. You have to work at your demeanor. You have to work on your competitive instincts and refine them. You have to work at becoming an invaluable teammate and leader.

Similarly, for a game to be considered a classic, other criteria have to be met. To me that means that the game has to have serious stakes. The competition between the two teams has to be both fierce and equal. The performances of individual players have to be of extremely high caliber. The outcome should be in jeopardy until the final moments. The action has to arrest your attention because of the brilliant, the surprising, or the unique nature of the performances or the personalities.

Game 5 of our National League Division Series against the Phila-delphia Phillies in 2011 saw an overlap between individual greatness and a classic baseball game. I may have planted the seed about my desire to see that confrontation between our club and theirs, between their ace and ours, but I had very little, if anything, to do with shap-ing the forces that produced the result on the night of October 7, 2011.

One unique feature that made this game a classic is that Roy Halladay and Chris Carpenter share a lot of similarities, beginning with the superficial: they are both right-handed pitchers, they're both listed as being the same height and weight, and it's interesting that they both began their careers as first-round draft picks (Carp the fif-teenth and Halladay the seventeenth in 1993 and 1995, respectively) by the Toronto Blue Jays. Each had made his major league debut and spent the formative years of his career with that team. Halladay had only been with Philadelphia since 2010, while Carp had been with us since 2003.

As I said, greatness is developed. I don't think it's any accident that Carp and Halladay were molded into the top-of-the-rotation starters and serious competitors that they are today while inside the Toronto organization. Carp's first two years and Doc's first year in the big leagues coincided with the two years that Roger Clemens and Pat Hentgen spent in Toronto. All other issues aside regarding Roger, he was a legendarily hard worker, an intense competitor, a power pitcher, and a fierce presence on the mound. Whether by word or example or both, Carp and Doc benefited from being exposed to Roger Clemens in his prime.

Of course, the moment Carp arrived in the big leagues everyone was talking about him. You can't be six feet, six inches tall and weigh 230 pounds, throw serious heat, and have great command of your pitches without attracting some attention, but Carp didn't set the league on fire during his time in Toronto. He was a combined 49-50 with a 4.83 ERA in those first six years. In 2002 he was injured and went only 4-5 with a 5.28 ERA in thirteen games. He was going to be a free agent at the end of that injury-shortened season and didn't pitch in the majors in all of 2003 after having more surgery.

Carp and Doc had also benefited from being around Blue Jay pitcher Pat Hentgen during those crucial first few years in the big leagues. Like Roger, Pat was a former Cy Young Award winner, having earned it in 1996. We were fortunate that we'd signed Pat in 2000. He'd come over as a free agent and won fifteen games for us that year. We were also fortunate that Pat's agent, Bob LaMonte, represented a few ballplayers, such as Toronto's Dave Stieb as well as Carp. When Carp was rehabbing, and a free agent, Pat mentioned to Bob that he thought that the Cardinals would be a good fit for Carp. Pat had had a positive experience working with Dunc, he knew our training staff and facilities would help Carp with his rehab, and he felt that St. Louis was a great place to play.

The first time I saw Carp pitch up close and in person, I had the rain to thank for it. Despite Carp not being able to pitch for us in 2003, owing to the surgery he needed to repair his torn labrum, we signed him as a free agent. Actually, we hoped that he'd be ready by midseason, but a part of Carp's competitive nature got the best of him. In June 2003, we were down in Florida to play the Marlins. Carp was there rehabbing, and one afternoon Dunc and I were scheduled to watch him throw off the mound. Unfortunately, the rain forced us inside. Fortunately, the rain forced us inside. Because of how the indoor cage was configured—a long rectangular net with the pitcher at one end and the hitter at the other—we were able to sit several feet behind the plate.

What we saw had our jaws dropping. A four-seam fastball that, when up in the zone, rose. A two-seam fastball that he could run to either the third-base or cut to the first-base side of the plate. He also threw a good curveball with fine downward action and could change speeds effectively with a deceptive changeup. Dunc and I looked at each other with raised eyebrows. Dunc nodded his head and said, "He can pitch. He has a lot of weapons." For Dunc, that was a ringing endorsement shouted off the rooftops. But as I said, Carp's competitive nature got the better of him. He was so eager to show his new manager and pitching coach that the gamble on signing an injured starting pitcher was worth it. He wound up tweaking his shoulder again, had to rehab longer, and missed the entire 2003 season.

In 2004 he won fifteen and lost five. In 2005 he won twenty-one, lost five, and won the Cy Young Award as the National League's top pitcher. How's that for a pitcher who was one game under .500 for his career? All I can say is, that was a whole bunch of a fully healthy Carp and a strong dose of Dunc. In 2006 Carp went 15-8, but was derailed by injury the next two seasons, after hurting himself on opening day. Again, he bounced back from adversity and went 17-4 and 16-9 the next two years. So, counting his 11-9 season in 2011, he was a combined 95-42 with a 3.06 ERA. Again, those numbers speak volumes about Carp and Dunc's influence. They also tell you that the man worked his rear end off to come back from those injuries, to win two Comeback Player of the Year Awards, to transform himself from a sub-.500 pitcher into the staff ace and an incredible leader.

It's not easy to endure those years when you're sidelined and not contributing on the field. You have so many ups and downs, you have your patience tested at every turn, and on top of that, you've got to endure the pain and be smart enough to know when you might be taking too big of a risk too soon. Carp learned the hard way, based on that throwing session he did for us, that he couldn't rush it. That takes real character to make a mistake and learn from it. He broke down, but he came back stronger. That's a mark of greatness and toughness. Some of the latter I think he developed as a result of his background as a hockey player. Hockey players are renowned for their ability to play through pain—witness the high cost of their dental plans—and that mentality served him well, though it had to be harnessed. The working at his demeanor part of greatness came into play here, in particular as it related to reinjuring himself. The best expression of that hockey-player attitude in Carp comes out in what a hard-nosed kind of guy he is.

What you see is what you get with Carp. He has a lot of integrity and a take-no-crap approach. He won't be shown up by an opposing hitter. This may be one of the hidden parts of the game, but the great pitchers can't stand it when a hitter, after popping up, grounding out, or striking out, acts as if he's somehow been denied his rightful place on base owing to some act of God, unfair trickery, or his own failure to exert his will and talent over the pitcher. It's never that he was *gotten* out; he *made* the out. A subtle but important distinction. It's fine for a hitter to think any of the above, but to display that lack of respect for a pitcher's ability rankles some, and it rankles Carp a whole lot.

I can't tell you the number of times Carp has told a hitter to shut his mouth—or words to that effect—when he went down the line or back to the dugout grumbling and acting out. That's not a smart thing to do. You do not want to rile up a Carp. Hitters have made the mistake of doing that and felt the wrath of his vengeance.

The other part about Carp's personality that I admire is that he's a great family man. His wife, Alyson, and their children are a frequent presence on road trips, and his son Sam is a lot of fun around the clubhouse. But when it's time to shut the door and escort the family out, Carp goes into game mode—whether he's pitching that night or not.

One of the other things he has done as a leader is to institute the practice of having all the starters, with the exception of whoever is on the mound that night, watch the others do their side work in the bullpen. Those little pitching clinics, the give-and-take among the guys that Carp would lead, set the example and sent the important message that every time you step on the mound and deliver a pitch it has a purpose that figures into a larger plan. That leadership from Carp was a huge part of being a number-one starter.

His leadership extends off the field as well. Carp was one of the co-signers, and he took that responsibility seriously. We didn't arbitrarily set the number of co-signers, and different guys handle the role in their own way. When there's an issue that affects the whole club—a matter of team policy, for example—the whole group would weigh in. Carp was one of the guys who would help out when issues were percolating—in other words, when something not fully and regularly visible was cropping up. A number of times he came to me and said, "Hey, Tony, I think that something's up with so-and-so. He just doesn't seem himself."

That's big, because as much as we pride ourselves on personalizing, as a staff we don't see the guys in all the circumstances their teammates do. It would be easy to hide something, easy to just lead us to believe that all is well when it isn't. Carp and a few others would do this kind of thing, exhibiting great discretion and knowing when it was time to alert us or time to handle things among themselves. As I said, I hadn't had to use "the Gutless Speech" in a while, and one of the reasons for that was how personalizing, the co-signers, and our open communication channels had all worked in sync.

All that makes Carp one of the great ones.

I don't know Doc Halladay nearly as well, but I imagine, and based on what I've heard, he's played a similar role to the one Carp plays. Also, if it's true that you can judge a man by the company he keeps, then Roy Halladay must be a good guy. He and Carp have maintained their friendship over the years. That fact added another interesting dimension to the confrontation in Game 5.

What I do know very well is what kind of pitcher Doc Halladay is. He and Carp aren't clones, but they do have very similar stuff. What makes them both so difficult to face is that they have a number of quality pitches and have command of them—they can throw them to different spots effectively. That's a deadly combination. Great starting pitchers have the ability to throw enough differ-ent pitches that they can give you a different look each time through the lineup in a game, in a season, and over the years. Carp and Hal-laday both do that.

One difference is that Halladay's change-of-speed pitch has more downward action and is more like a forkball than Carp's, and he throws that pitch more often than Carp does. Halladay, like Carp, also throws two versions of his curveball. The first is what we call a "get me over" pitch. He uses it early in the count; it doesn't have the same sharp darting action as the other curveball, and it starts out of the strike zone and then finishes in it. The variant on that curveball, the "put away" pitch, is one that starts in the strike zone and breaks out of it, a pitch that he hopes hitters will chase.

It's funny that guys like Carp and Halladay hardly ever have easy games. That's because their game is at such a high level that hitters gear themselves up to face them. The best hitters want the challenge; others know they're overmatched but go at it hard, and a few just want to avoid being embarrassed.

As we stressed with our hitters in facing dominating pitchers like Carp and Halladay, you have to pick your poison. There are sev-eral components to that. First, some pitchers are naturally better at throwing to one side of the plate. Some left-handed pitchers work that outside corner and struggle to come inside on right-handed hitters or away on left-handed hitters. When that's the case, as a hitter, you can look for a ball in that zone that is more comfortable for the pitcher. However, with Carp and Halladay, that's not as easy to do because they are equally effective at throwing to either side of the plate. They can also elevate the ball and keep it low in the strike zone, changing a hitter's eye level. As a hitter, you can't protect both the outside and the inside corner or up and down. Pitching is messing with a hitter's balance by moving the ball in and out. It's also about messing with his timing by changing speeds. By pitching inside, the pitcher hopes to speed up the hitter's bat. Then the pitcher goes soft. If he wants to slow the guy's bat down, he reverses that pattern.

The other dimension of picking your poison is this: guys like Halladay and Carp love to get ahead in the count. If you're not up there ready to swing, then he gets ahead 0-1 and that opens up the opportunity for him to work the corners. The problem is, if you're up there being too aggressive, you may immediately swing at pitches at the edge of the strike zone, which are more difficult to hit hard. So you could end up being behind anyway or having made a quick out.

We also let our hitters in on a bit of pitcher's methodology. As a hitter, you have to think a bit like the pitcher. What does the pitcher want to do if he has a runner on first base? Get a double-play grounder. What's the most effective way for him to do that? To throw a pitch down and in to a righty and down and away to a lefty, hoping that the hitter will try to pull it but instead roll over the top and beat it into the ground. If the pitcher's trying to keep the ball in the ballpark and not give up a home run, he's going to pitch away. That's the traditional way to go about it, but today a lot of hitters will look away to extend their arms. If the pitcher or catcher sees a hitter trying to do that, the pitcher has to come back inside. That's why having the ability to work both sides of the plate is so important.

Guys like Carp and Halladay aren't afraid to come inside. I'm not talking about moving a guy off the plate, although they have no hesitancy about doing that either. A timid pitcher doesn't want to go inside because, if he misses, he tends to miss out over the plate. Great pitchers—top-of-the-rotation starters—have to own the inside corner. So there's the trouble. If you're looking outside and cheating out there a bit, a great pitcher can bust you in on the hands.

My daughters are both dancers, and they might object to this analogy, but the game within a game that goes on between a pitcher and hitter is a lot like what I think a tango is. A push and a pull, inside and out, come here, no get away. That bit of intrigue, combined with two pitchers performing at the top of their game, is sure to produce a classic.

Carp and Doc didn't disappoint.

I CAME TO THE BALLPARK FEELING THE LEAST NERVOUS I'D EVER been for a big game. I can't think of a better tribute to Doc and Carp. I knew going in—and I imagine that Charlie Manuel did too—that we weren't going to have to get involved in the game early with pitching decisions. For most of the year, and in the first four games of the series, I'd had to do that.

This was different.

When you send your number-one starter out there in an elimination game, you're sending out your horse, and you expect to ride him as long as you possibly can. There'd be no quick hooks.

Not being nervous was a strange feeling for me. Mostly I was calm because of the pitching equation, but I also knew this was likely to be a game in which we'd have few chances to score, so there probably wouldn't be a lot to do offensively. That said, I'd have to really grind hard on the decisions that did need to be made, just as the players would in their at-bats. I also felt this: if one or the other of these two great starters struggled, the game would essentially be over.

Since you don't have a quick hook with your number-one starter, if they struggle, it can mean a couple of crooked numbers go up on the board against you before you get him out of there. It doesn't happen often, but you hope for the best and prepare for the worst. In that case, either well ahead or well behind, the pressure wouldn't impose itself. Of course, in any game it could happen that both starters struggle, and if that happened here, I'd have to "what-if" the hell out of the situation to figure out what to do, but the likelihood of both these guys blowing up was slim at best.

Of course, I also knew that the deeper we got into the game, my little "vacation" was going to come to an end.

Carp was going on his usual four days' rest, so we had no concerns about that. He didn't have a history of starting slow and giving up runs in the first inning, but what he'd said to us about the lessons he learned from Game 2 was encouraging. Whether he'd be able to put them into practice was another matter. Although he learned the lesson while going on short rest, it made sense to apply it anytime he felt he didn't have his best stuff.

Our hitters did what they were supposed to do immediately. Rafael Furcal tripled to deep right-center to start off the ball game. He was ahead in the count 2-1, and as he later said, he was looking for a pitch to drive in that situation, knowing that Doc didn't want to fall behind 3-1. He got what he wanted and executed perfectly, stroking the ball into right-center field. When you try perfectly, you often get good results. Next, Skip Schumaker put up one of the great at-bats of the series. We'd come to expect that from one of our best "gamers." Halladay, realizing that he needed a strikeout or a pop-up to keep the runner at third, went after Schu hard and aggressive early in the count. Down 0-2, Skip fought off two pitches. Halladay was grinding, coming after him with four straight strikes before he threw one off the edge that Schu took for ball one.

As a hitter, down in the count like that and with the runner on third and no outs, you want to make contact. Early in the count, ahead in the count, you're looking to get a ball you can hit hard. Down 0-2, it's all about survival and making contact. Another foul, a ball, and another two tough pitches that Schu spoiled, and the count was 2-2 in what was to that point a nine-pitch at-bat. You could almost hear the sound of Schu's grinding of that at-bat over the crowd's roar. I watched him, steely-eyed and locked in, level the bat over the plate, waiting.

I'm convinced that the longer an at-bat goes, the more the hitter has an advantage. Pitchers have to show you more of their stuff early, and they get frustrated when a hitter barely makes contact to foul off a tough pitch. The more time the hitter spends in the box, the more comfortable he gets with his looks.

Halladay kicked and fired, and Schu's bat lashed out and drove it into right field for a double. Furcal trotted home, and the hand claps and back thumps drummed in my ears. Not what Doc had ordered, but certainly what we needed. We wanted more.

We weren't going to get it.

The Phillies made a nice defensive play on Albert. With Schu on second, Albert played to the situation and, trying to move the runner to third, hit a ground ball to second. Instead of taking the sure out at first, Utley gambled and nailed Schu at third just as he had been nailed in a previous game. Now, instead of a runner at third and one out, another prime scoring opportunity, we had a runner at first and still one away. A wild pitch and then catcher's interference put runners on first and second with one out. That's when Doc did what the great ones do. He elevated his game and retired the side on a foul-out and a groundout. Still, for an inning in which only one run was scored, a lot of stuff went on out there. We were encouraged by the fact that we'd forced Doc to throw thirty-three pitches that inning. We wanted into their bullpen.

In comparison to Doc's struggles in the top half, Carp was on his game from the get-go. He got ahead of the first two hitters 0-2 and retired them. A first-pitch strike to Hunter Pence and then a ground ball ended the inning. Eleven pitches. What a great start. The guys in the dugout were all on the top step waiting for Carp. We'd been excited about scoring the first run, and now about shutting them down so convincingly. Carp sent another message in that first inning, to himself, to us, and to the Phils: this was not the same Chris Carpenter on the hill that night who'd labored so mightily in Game 2. This was Carp, the great Carp, the top-of-the-rotation guy at the top of his game. Would he be able to sustain that? I knew the intensity would be there, but what about his stuff? He'd thrown 237 innings in the regular season, the most since he won the Cy Young Award in 2005, when he threw 241 in winning twenty-one and losing only five. For his part, Halladay's 233 innings was far below his career high of the astounding 266 he threw in 2003, when he won twenty-two ball games (with a career-high nine complete games) and the Cy Young.

In the opening game, we'd seen Halladay struggle in the first and then be lights-out after that. We weren't sure if he could do that again. After Freese struck out, Punto hit a bullet to the third baseman, and Carp grounded out. Carp making the last out wasn't the worst thing—he didn't have to run the bases and we'd have the top of the lineup batting in the third and getting their second look at Doc.

We were gathering evidence to answer our question about whether Doc would get on a roll like he had in Game 2. He retired us in order in the third, with Schu's line drive to center the only hard-hit ball. Even with two really good at-bats against Doc, Schu's evening was over. He left with an oblique injury and was replaced by Jon Jay.

In the bottom of the fourth, the Phillies had a mini-rally going. Carp hit Chase Utley on an 0-2 pitch when he was trying to establish the inside against him. How the Phillies responded reinforces what I said about the great pitchers—you have to pick your poison, and sometimes it can end up hurting you. After Utley was hit, both Pence and Ryan Howard went after first pitches and made outs. That aggressive approach works when you get hits, but leads to low pitch totals when you don't. On the other hand, if you wait and hold back, you may find yourself in a hole and have to battle back. Not much fun either way. Then, with two outs, Victorino singled, putting runners on first and third. Carp rose to the challenge. In a tough at-bat with Ibanez protecting, Carp finally got him to fly out to right. This was a classic example of Tom Seaver's "special" outs theory even though we were only in the fourth inning.

Carp and Halladay swapped scoreless innings in the fifth, and at the midway point we still held a 1–0 lead with Carp at a very efficient sixty-eight pitches. We liked what we were seeing: on the one hand, a few more runs would have been nice, but on the other, because the game was so close, Carp had no room to relax at all. Not that he needed that added incentive to maintain focus, but 1–0 games do keep everyone sharp, since all the players know that any play, any potential misplay, could spell the end of that lead.

Of course, pitchers don't do what Carp and Halladay were doing by themselves. Obviously, they need those infielders to stay alert, and low pitch counts and getting ahead of hitters make it easier for position players to maintain their concentration out on the diamond. The other important element you need as a pitcher is the one player in front of you—your catcher.

Most baseball people will acknowledge that in the National League, Yadier Molina and Carlos Ruiz are the two best receivers. Just as Carp and Doc are strikingly similar, so are Yadi and Chooch. Both guys came into the league admitting that they were primarily focused on their defensive play. They both threw well, blocked pitches well, and took the time to learn their pitchers and develop into great game-callers. Once they established that part of their game as real strengths, they both worked on their offensive game. As I sit here today in 2012, Carlos Ruiz is third in the league in hitting at .354, while Yadi is sixth at .326. That's just one metric, but both catchers have steadily improved their offensive production throughout their careers.

What a lot of people don't seem to understand is that, in my estimation, Yadi could always hit. In 2002 he hit .280 in almost 400 at-bats at Class A Peoria. The next year, 2003, he hit .275 in Knoxville, our AA affiliate. He split time between AAA Memphis and the big league club in 2004, hitting .300 in 129 at-bats in the minors and .267 in 135 at-bats with us after being called up when Mike Matheny was hurt. When Matheny signed as a free agent with San Francisco, Yadi took over. We hated to see Mike go, but we'd watched Yadi during his time with the big club and were convinced he could do the job at that level.

Maybe the questions about his offensive ability stem from the slow start he got off to in 2005. I recall a game early that year when we were down a couple of runs late, and I left Yadi in the lineup to hit in an RBI situation. He made an out. We lost the game. Afterward, at the press conference, I was asked if I had considered at all taking out Yadi for a pinch hitter. I said this, "He's so good defensively, he could go hitless for the season and he'd still be our catcher." It was only a slight exaggeration; our staff knew he would hit enough. That label might have stuck with him, even though he wound up the year hitting .252.

What's most impressive, though, is that Yadi has the ability to raise his game in the postseason and in RBI situations. I have had several managers tell me over the span of time I had the pleasure of putting Yadi's name on the scorecard that they believe that he is as respected as a really tough out as any of the other big guns we've had in our lineup—guys like Rolen, Edmonds, and Pujols. The statistics bear that out. In his career in the big leagues—including the start of '12, when he's been tearing it up—he's a .277 hitter in the regular season. In the eleven playoff series he's appeared in, he has a .309 average and has driven in twenty-three runs. And the higher the stakes get, the better he gets. He's hit over .300 in the NLCS and the World Series.

You have to know Yadi and all the intangibles he brings to the ball club to understand why he's the best. You can't help but like him. Maybe it's his electric smile, but guys just gravitate toward him. Though he's grown more confident in his English over the years, he's a bit self-conscious sometimes, but his effervescent nature helps make him a great teammate. It's only natural that the Latin ballplayers spend a lot of time together. There's a group, Yadi among them, who play dominoes before games pretty regularly. It's not like they segregate themselves, and a lot of times one of the other guys will play along with them. Of course, a lot of ball-busting goes on, in both languages, and being bilingual myself always helped me a lot. I might not smile and laugh and let on that I'd heard what had been said about who, but I got a good daily dose of private chuckles out of their banter.

Behind that great smile is the heart of a lion. In 2006 Yadi hit a two-run home run in the ninth against the Mets in the seventh game of the NLCS. That and his catching Wainwright helped break a lot of Mets fans' hearts. Ever since, if I told him that I was thinking of giving him a day off in New York, he'd look at me like I was crazy and say, "No. No. Before or after New York. I like to hear them boo me." Mets fans took full advantage of the opportunities Yadi provided them to vocalize their displeasure.

But when it's time to prepare for a game, Yadi, like Albert, is a regular visitor in "the Dungeon"—to prepare himself offensively and defensively. He's gotten so good at evaluating the opposition's strengths and weaknesses. When you add in how he processes Dunc's input, Yadi's game-calling has gotten so precise that several pitchers have told me they shake Yadi off only as a way to mess with the hitter's mind. He puts the fingers down, and they go with what he thinks. That does so much to instill confidence in everybody and speeds up the game as well—a big consideration when you have a 162-game season.

Catchers have to do a whole lot for your ball club, and in the sixth inning Yadi showed his stuff. With one out, Utley singled to right field. On the first pitch, he broke for second. Yadi came out of the chute firing and hung a clothesline from home plate to second base that had us all just gasping in awe and shaking our heads. That kind of throw will make a manager think twice about flashing the steal sign again. What made that play so impressive was that Utley chose the right pitch to run on—a seventy-three-mile-an-hour curveball. Utley was fifty for fifty-two in stolen bases over the last three years. Yadi's throw was great, but another defensive play also helped. Punto got the tag down in a hurry, another subtlety of good defensive play that often goes unnoticed. In 1–0 games, there are few if any bigs—it's all the smalls that add up to a win.

Carp got Pence on a groundout to end the inning, but the guys all went to Yadi between innings, knowing how big that play was. Not only does Yadi have a strong arm, he has a quick release with incredible accuracy. Because his arm is so good, he's fearless with it. How many other catchers would try to pick a runner off first when the winning run is standing on second base and an errant throw will bring that winning run home? Yadi would.

Any catcher has to be tough. I've seen Yadi get plowed into, to the point where he could barely even stand, and he was saying he's okay and wants to stay in the game. You might have to question his intelligence based on that, but Yadi is the smartest catcher, the best signal caller, and the possessor of an amazing ability to connect with pitchers. More than anything else, it's Yadi's baseball intelligence that separates him from the pack.

In Game 7 of the 2006 NLCS, we went into the ninth inning tied 1–1. After Scott Rolen singled, Yadi hit a home run to put us up 3–1. In the bottom of the ninth, I brought in Adam Wainwright to close it out. He gave up a couple of hits, got two outs, then walked Paul Lo Duca. The bases were loaded, there were two outs, and Carlos Beltran, our Cardinals nemesis, was coming to the plate. With the series on the line, I turned to Dunc and said, "Don't you think we need to make a trip? Make sure we're thinking right?"

Dunc nudged me and said, "Yadi's got it."

I looked out on the field to see Yadi trotting out to the mound.

We sat there. I can't stress enough what that means. Yadi was in his second year, and the NLCS was on the line. Sitting there and watching Yadi take care of it was a huge, and well-deserved, vote of confidence. Normally, the manager or the pitching coach would have been out there. We trusted Yadi completely.

Yadi went out to the mound and told Adam that he thought a first-pitch sinker outside was the way to go. On the way back to the plate, though, he had a change of mind. Since strike one was a priority, he was worried about what he'd originally said to Adam, because while Adam had a good running fastball to the third-base side of the plate, it wasn't a true sinker. He was concerned that the pitch would be up too much and right into Beltran's wheelhouse. Great thinking on his part.

Since Yadi couldn't go back out to the mound, in his crouch, he sent the "follow me" sign to his pitcher. Basically, that sign was telling Adam to ignore what they'd just talked about and go with whatever sign Yadi next flashed.

Yadi called for a first-pitch changeup. That's unorthodox and goes against what a lot of baseball people believe. The point of a changeup is that it is off-speed, but if you haven't thrown any other pitches before it—and this was Adam's first time facing Beltran—there is no contrast between fast and slower. Gutsy call—it also worked.

Beltran was knocked off balance and took strike one looking.

I sat there and said to Dunc, "What the hell was that?"

"Changeup."

"He can't call that."

"Just did."

Beltran fouled off the next pitch, and then stood there frozen as a curveball came in. The pitch was head high, and every hitter in the world would have given up on it. Except this one dropped right in the zone. That pitch is tied for first as the best one to ever end a championship series. Game over. Series over. On to the World Series. Brilliant pitch selection by Yadi. Brilliant execution by Adam.

If it isn't clear yet, let me say this: in my fifty years in the game, thirty-four of which I spent intensely observing it, Yadi is the best catcher I've ever seen. When you have a meeting on the mound with Dunc and Yadi, you have the best pitching coach and the best catcher in the game out there together. Beyond brilliant.

* * *

BY THE TIME THE SEVENTH-INNING STRETCH WAS OVER, THE "WHAT-ifs" were in high gear. What happens if Carp has an issue? Who's coming up? Who's the best option to come in? You're counting down the outs, looking at the lineup card, scrambling your brain trying to figure out who is going to get those last outs. What you don't know is how all of this is going to play out, what all the factors might be. You get ready for as many of them as you can conceive.

I liked our chances with Carp, and I really wanted him to go the distance, since that would mean he was continuing to pitch effectively. In a 1–0 game, the tipping point is so clearly visible, and each pitch and each play have magnified importance. The stress level also goes up a couple of points. Carp showed his competitive nature, and I'm sure he gave his good friend Doc a lot of grief about it in the off-season, when he singled to center to lead off the eighth. We got a break when Furcal bunted and Ruiz's throw to second was off-line and both guys were safe. We were in a good position to score a so-called insurance run, especially after Jon Jay laid down a perfect sacrifice bunt to advance the runners to second and third. The Phillies did the wise thing and intentionally walked Albert to load the bases and set up a potential double play at second and a force-out anywhere. Their strategy paid off when we stranded both runners with a strikeout and fly-out. Some people didn't realize that there was a big "what-if" in that inning. Carp having to run the bases added to my questions about his ability to get through the eighth inning. How had his not being able to rest on the bench affected him?

Then, in the bottom half, Rafael Furcal, the guy who was so heartbroken about a regular-season error that he wanted to quit the game, robbed Carlos Ruiz of a base hit. Yadi set up on the outside corner, but Carp's fastball tailed in on the right-handed-hitting Ruiz. Ruiz hit the ball hard and down up the middle. Rafael saw the inside-out stroke and was leaning that way, took two short steps to his left, and then laid himself out in a dive. He gloved it, got up, spun, and threw a seed to first to barely retire Ruiz. Incredible.

That play in the eighth was a good example of those points about anticipating and knowing how someone is going to be pitched. Admittedly, we were a slightly better-than-average ball club defensively throughout most of the season, but when we got rolling, the defense picked up considerably. That's the thing about defense. If you're a decent athlete and you're willing to work at it, you can transform yourself into an above-average fielder. When Matt Holliday came over in the trade, and then later when he got a big contract with us, he felt like he had to prove his worth. He worked hard on his offense, but he also put in the time in 2010 to turn himself into a very good defensive outfielder. I've heard basketball coaches say that playing defense is all about hustle and you can't ever let yourself have an off night with desire. Your shooting may be off, but intensity and focus on the defensive end aren't about skill as much as about desire. Baseball defense takes some skill, but it's not like hitting or pitching. Guys who excel defensively do so because they make it a priority.

As the bottom of the eighth continued, the Yadi-Ruiz comparison took a bad turn when, with two outs, Carp struck out the pinch hitter Ross Gload on a nasty pitch in the dirt for a dropped third strike. Gload took off for first, but Yadi's throw was wide of the mark for an error. That brought up Jimmy Rollins, who hit a bullet up the middle. Carp's hockey days paid off, though, when his deflection of the ball sent it toward Nick Punto, who was charging hard from second base. Punto's quick release got the ball over to first in time. I felt a bit like we'd dodged a bullet—a low-caliber one that was likely to go wide of the mark, but still one to make your heart skip a beat.

As befitting the classic nature of this game, Carp's challenge in the ninth inning was to retire the heart of the Phillies' lineup. Utley, Pence, and Howard compare favorably to any 2-3-4 in baseball. Few experiences in our sport measure up to seeing your pitcher on the mound in the ninth with the score 1–0 in a playoff game. Carp was three outs away, and seeing him out there, I felt privileged to be a part of such a classic game. Those thoughts didn't last long. We needed three more outs.

He retired Utley on a first-pitch fly-out to the warning track on which Jon Jay made a fine running catch. Believe me, our hearts were in our throats on that one. Jay is a major leaguer. Of Cuban extraction, he was born in Miami, and he loves to play the game. He runs well and gets to a lot of balls hit his way, but the thing about that play in the ninth is this: he's a young guy who wasn't intimidated one bit by the high-stakes setting of this game. He had positioned himself properly—deep, to prevent a double, given the score—and he got a great jump on a ball that could have easily gotten over his head.

Next, Carp got Hunter Pence to ground out on the second pitch. He then did something I can't recall ever seeing him do on the mound. He smiled. Most great pitchers like to keep that poised and deadly assassin look on their faces at all times—*This is deadly serious business, and I'm a deadly serious guy.* That's why some of them don't shave and in the past have grown badass mustaches and beards or whatever to make themselves look even fiercer. Goose Gossage used to come in and close games looking like we'd just dragged him away from working a bar brawl as a bouncer.

But there was Carp smiling. And this was even before he retired Ryan Howard on a curveball by getting him to ground out to second. Sadly, Howard lay on the ground in pain after snapping his Achilles tendon. That's a part of the heartache of a classic game. One team is out there jumping up and down, and Carp is out there no longer smiling but just beaming and shouting, and another man's writhing in pain. I hated to see Howard get injured, but I loved seeing Carp do something he'd never done before in his career. Under the most pressure-packed conditions, in the 340th start of his career, he'd pitched his first 1–0 complete-game win ever.

I'm not the fastest learner, so after those previous two times relieving Carp in the ninth in a one-run game, the coaches had tied my arms and legs to the bench.

I'll never forget the look of elation on his face after that last out—that look of complete and unbounded joy captured our club's feeling perfectly. We'd been the wild-card team that just squeaked into the playoffs, and we'd defeated the team with the best record in the league.

In baseball history, in a winner-take-all game, just two other pitchers, Jack Morris of the Twins in 1991 and Ralph Terry of the Yankees in 1962, had pitched complete-game shutouts in which their team scored a single run. People still talk about those games, and I have no doubt that they will keep talking about our victory over the Phillies.

What seemed like hours later, in the clamor of the clubhouse, I sought out Carp. We'd done our congratulating of each other earlier. I said to him, "What the hell were you smiling about out there in the ninth?"

Carp gave me a puzzled look and an even bigger smile. "What else was I supposed to do? I was having fun out there."

PART III

Sometimes adding on isn't enough. After Lance Berkman drove in Rafael Furcal in the top of the fifth inning to put us up 5–2, I felt good about how we were doing offensively. We'd scored in three of the first five innings. We'd also responded in the fourth with three runs, and now that single run after the Brewers had scored twice in the bottom of the first to erase our early advantage was on the board. Jaime Garcia had settled in after the first, allowing just a hit and a walk through the fourth.

We would have loved to have taken the first game of the series at Miller Park. Though we'd come back from losing the first game against the Phillies, we felt that the Brewers were a different club in this regard. For the most part, they were healthy. They'd been on a roll the second half of the season.

Their team was an offensive juggernaut. Their big RBI guys—Braun, Fielder, Hart, and Lucroy—contributed equally and heavily, combining to drive in nearly half of their runs in the NLDS. A quick glance at the lineup card had told me that they were coming up in the fifth, as well as Jerry Hairston Jr., who'd also had a very good first-round series. I sat there scanning my matchup cards, hoping for the best but preparing for the worst.

Four batters and four runs later, with a battered but still battling Garcia on the mound, I made the walk from the dugout to get him. That 5–2 lead had evaporated. No one was out, and the playoff-thirsty (and apparently bloodthirsty, since as I stepped onto the field I heard someone bellow, "I hope you get shingles again!") Brewers fans were going nuts. Jaime handed me the ball. I could see that he was disappointed he hadn't been able to give us a better outing and preserve that early lead. We had known that because of the dominance of right-handed hitters in their lineup, it was going to be tough for the left-handers.

Octavio Dotel came in, and though we didn't need to remind him, Yadi and I both told him, "Hold 'em right here." Octavio nodded as he tugged at the bill of his cap.

Seemingly before I could get back to the dugout, a Dotel error and a Yuniesky Betancourt home run led to their fifth and sixth runs of the inning. Still nobody was out. A double following an out put another runner in scoring position. Six runs and six hits and an error.

The Brewers tacked on another, as did we.

9–6. The game was over.

Down again in another series, this one at least was seven games, but we certainly didn't want to go down 0–2 after the next one and then face another crisis game. After that sublime effort from Carp in Game 5 of the Division Series, we were back in the real world. How were we going to patch together our tired starters and our newly revived bullpen into a unit that could get us twenty-seven outs? I sat there long into the night, poring over the scouting reports, looking at the number of innings our guys had worked, wondering how we could keep their potent offense in check. Job one was to stop the Brewers from scoring. Job two was to score ourselves.

CHAPTER SIXTEEN

Hold 'Em Right Here

I NEVER LIKE LOSING, BUT I ESPECIALLY DON'T LIKE LOSING THE first game of a series. We'd started to make a habit of it, doing so in four straight, going all the way back to the end of the regular season. We'd come back to win them all, but this Brewers team was going to be difficult to contend with.

As much offensive power as they'd shown in their division series win, they'd actually been outscored overall: the Diamondbacks had scored twenty-five runs to the Brewers' twenty-three. We thought our staffs matched up well. Still, the Brewers were playing really well at home; they were a league best 57-24, and if it came to that, Games 6 and 7 would be at their place.

As we prepared for the first game in Milwaukee, it wasn't lost on me just how much time had passed since my first experience as a manager in a league championship series. Everything had been so new to me then, in '83, and given our brief trip, it seemed to be over before I knew what hit us. It was like a first at-bat in a game—I was just trying to get a feel for what kind of stuff these playoff series and league championship games specifically had. I was 0-for-1. In a sense,

I was able to go back to the dugout and check out some things in the video room to prepare for the next at-bat I hoped to get. Of course, I had no idea I wouldn't see that at-bat for another five years.

When I moved on to Oakland, the players were better prepared for postseason play and I had a few more clues than I'd had in '83. From 1988 to 1990, we won three American League pennants, with a World Series title sandwiched in there. Suddenly my average was looking a lot better, having gone 3-for-4 in league championship opportunities. More important than the wins, though, was what I learned during that period about how the intensity level rises when you're one step away from the World Series.

Like any hot streak, mine had to end. It began in '92 with the A's and continued through my first several NLCS appearances with St. Louis. Losing in '92, '96, '00, and '02 was tough. That's one reason why I say that finally winning the NL pennant in '04 was so meaningful and was among my biggest thrills in managing in the National League. When you're accused of not being able to help your club win the big one, you feel a different sense of satisfaction when you finally break through. Coming back to beat Roger Clemens with three runs in the sixth on big hits from Albert and Rolen and then watching Jason Isringhausen sew it up with a one-two-three ninth was immensely gratifying.

I don't buy that there was a monkey on my back—or as some would have it, an entire zoo—because of our early failures to get to the World Series. I was glad that, at least for that year, I wasn't going to have to endure more comments to that effect. Like I said before, if you're going to play, then keep score. "Fired up" just barely describes the kind of heat—not pressure but desire—I had going into our matchup against the Brewers.

Even is a great word to use to describe the series between Milwaukee and us. During the regular season, we'd split our eighteen games. Looking not just at our records but at how we matched lineups and pitching staffs, we thought we were pretty even there as well. Seeing a team that many times during the regular season gives the hitters and coaches a lot to work with. Our hitting coaches, Mark McGwire and Mike Aldrete, had a large sample to draw from to formulate a plan for attacking their pitchers, Zack Greinke, Shaun Marcum, Randy Wolf, and Yovani Gallardo. We would be prepared to make adjustments based on what we'd seen, especially against their starters. Being able to do that was one of our strengths. Our coaches' analysis, the use of video, and our hitters' proficiency, all contributed to that. If there was any edge at all to be had, we saw that as it.

Heading in, the media and the fans were all abuzz about the rivalry that had developed between us. Our competitiveness had increased to a heightened state in 2011. The old "if it bleeds it leads" syndrome took over because of the bad blood the media and the fans perceived as existing between us. I've already said my piece about the Nyjer Morgan incident, and the less said about him the better. To Ron Roenicke's credit, and to their general manager Doug Melvin's credit, there was no sign of any kind of retaliation. I pointed out before that my respect for Prince Fielder had deepened. I had similar opinions about Ryan Braun. We'd seen them come into the league and develop into as potent a pair of hitters around. Prince had become a real leader with the Brewers, and even when things got hot between the two clubs in the regular season, Fielder was a voice of reason and calm. So I wasn't surprised that when Jaime, who really had little command in the first inning, hit Prince with a pitch, he simply tossed his bat aside and trotted down to first base. Clearly there was no intent, Fielder knew it, and we got on with the business of playing the game.

That's not always easy, and it seemed like, for several reasons, that had grown increasingly harder to do against the Brewers throughout 2011. Earlier in the year, some of our guys had complained to me about the lights being brighter at Miller Park in Milwaukee when the

Brewers were hitting and darker when we were hitting. After I had Dunc check it out for four innings, he agreed that there were differences, but who knew if they were deliberate.

I brought it to the umpires' attention, and the Milwaukee fans thought I was whining. But if I think there's any credibility to an issue brought up by a player, I'm going to back the player and then take heat for it. When it comes down to a doubt about an issue, you're honor-bound to take the side of your team, your family. The way Sparky Anderson and Dick Williams mentored me is that you play the game between the white lines and don't give in to the bull. I detest the bull. I've angered Dunc several times by not complaining about things like this. There was a flurry of corked bats with a certain American League team in the 1990s. Dunc wanted me to ask the umpires to inspect the bats. I told him, "I don't want to stir up anything. Let's just play ball."

Dunc isn't a whiner, far from it, but he has a fairness streak as wide as Texas. I have the same ethical sense as he does, though. We both hate having to deal with the stuff that goes on between and outside the lines when the rules are sometimes stretched and other times blatantly broken. It's always a tough call to make in deciding how to resolve those issues. Let it go and you're hurting your club's chances of winning. Vocalize your suspicions too loudly or too publicly and you become a whiner in the eyes of some.

The second game of the 2006 World Series presented precisely this kind of situation. We could see that Detroit left-hander Kenny Rogers seemed to have stuff on his left hand when he was pitching. I had no doubt he had it. I knew that if I had gone out that inning and had him undressed by the umpires, they would have found it and he would have been suspended for the rest of the Series.

When we received confirmation from our video people upstairs that they had seen it as well, I used our at-bat in the inning deciding what to do. I probably had three or four minutes to think about this, and I was fretting over it. Looking back, this was the toughest game decision I've *ever* had to make. The consequences, no matter how I handled the situation, were significant. But right or wrong, I felt that making a big deal went against the game being decided by whoever played the best.

I also knew that when it's cold like it was, pitchers frequently use a bit of pine tar to improve their grip. Most hitters would generally be okay with that, since they don't want to see pitchers out there with no clue where the ball is going to end up once it leaves their hand. Granted, Rogers used it to excess, and the rules clearly state that applying a foreign substance to the ball is forbidden.

Mostly, though, I was thinking about the incident involving Roger Clemens and Mike Piazza. In the 2000 World Series, Clemens played for the Yankees and Piazza was with the Mets. Clemens picked up part of Piazza's broken bat and threw it at the Mets catcher as he ran down the baseline. After that, every time the Yankees and the Mets played each other, the teams were forgotten. It was all about the drama and controversy between these two guys. If I went out there to raise the issue about Rogers, would the same kind of thing happen? Would that detract from the Series?

I finally decided to go with what I was taught—that the game should be decided by who plays the best—and not stir things up. If I had formally lodged a complaint about it, to this day 2006 would have been remembered as "the Pine Tar Series." If we had won, our victory would have been tainted because I protested. And if we had lost, I might have been ridden out of town on a pine-tar-gunked-up rail.

Rather than make a big show of it, I went to Randy Marsh, the crew chief, and said, "The guy's got some stuff on his hands. I don't want to stir it up. Just tell him to get it off and let's play ball."

Randy did that, and Rogers still went out there and shut us down without it.

When I got back to the hotel, my wife, Elaine, asked me, "Do you have any idea what's going on? You're getting beaten to death by the commentators."

"Elaine, I just didn't want to compete that way," I said. It turned out that was the only game we lost in the Series. We won the next three to claim the championship.

When you have a job like this with as much exposure and attention as there is, then philosophically, you'd better have a place where you can go to make some of the tough calls, somewhere you can look at yourself in the mirror and live with it. I felt like I'd done that in '06, and I was hopeful I wouldn't have to deal with anything remotely like that again versus the Brewers. Good rivalries are great for the game.

With the Oakland A's, from 1987 to 1992, we had terrific battles with the Minnesota Twins, who had great players like Gary Gaetti, Kent Hrbek, and Kirby Puckett, who were managed expertly by Tom Kelly. Guys slid hard. Guys swung hard. Guys pitched inside, but there were no cheap shots. It was a pleasure to be part of that competition because it was just both teams trying as hard as they could. If you lose, you tip your cap. If you win, you feel good about it without embarrassing the other side.

In the late 1990s and into the 2000s, the competition was the same between the Cardinals and the Houston Astros. It was a pleasure to play against Craig Biggio, Jeff Bagwell, and Lance Berkman, hard-nosed guys who laid it all out on the line. It would be the same in the NLCS: two teams playing as hard as they could and as well as they could without any of the bull going on to detract from the games.

Familiarity may breed contempt, but it also makes preparation easier. We'd faced the Brewers in two series as part of our last thirty games of the regular season, and before the start of the first of those they'd beaten us eight out of twelve times. Winning five out of six, including that crucial sweep in their ballpark, had pulled us even, not to mention increased our confidence level against them.

With a lineup as potent as the Brewers', we knew it would be of primary importance to limit their scoring—that meant focusing on pitching and defense. We started with their one-two punch, Ryan

Braun and Prince Fielder. During the regular season, we'd had pretty good success against them. Braun was just 16-for-71 (.225) against us, and Fielder went 14-for-60 (.233). They had combined for five homers and eighteen RBIs. Obviously, Dunc had devised a good plan against those two, and being well prepared, Yadi and our pitchers executed that plan effectively.

When the staff checked with the guys, our read was that the players were willing and eager to compete—no one seemed content to coast by on what we'd accomplished in the NLDS. We detected no fatigue or complacency or oversatisfaction. Still, it's always hard to predict how such a dramatic series will impact a team. I would have liked to have had more time between our emotional victory over Halladay and the Phils, but we had just one day to travel and work out before the first game.

On workout day, I met with all the players. I reinforced my message about distractions, emphasizing that now that we were in the next round, ticket and media demands would increase. I didn't want to belabor the next point, so I was brief. I thought that the media and the fans had blown all out of proportion the things that had gone on between the two teams apart from the games themselves. We were two very similar teams, both aggressive and both wanting to win badly. Whatever minor flare-ups there had been occurred earlier in the season. We'd just played good hard baseball in defeating them those five out of six times at the end.

All I told the guys was this: I believed the Brewers just wanted to go out there and play. That's what we wanted. Don't get baited into anything or read too much into anything that happens. Don't start anything. Don't respond to anything. Don't give in to anything.

Then we went out and played.

THE SCORE IN GAME 1 WAS MISLEADING. BECAUSE WE'D SCORED FIVE runs through the first five innings—a helluva accomplishment—we liked how each hitter was approaching his at-bat. Garcia had recovered from a shaky first inning and was pitching effectively before things went *boom* in the fifth and their potent offense took advantage of their opportunities to the tune of six runs, handing them the lead and the eventual victory.

In scrutinizing Game 1, it became clear that our position players had been ready to play. Our offense put together a bunch of quality at-bats, we were alert on defense, we got good jumps, and our body language demonstrated life. The Brewers confirmed what we already knew—they were a dangerous club. They now had an important advantage by winning Game 1. We had a big challenge ahead of us. We couldn't lose the first two games. Twenty-one out of twenty-four times the loser of the first two games on the road has lost the league championship since it went to a seven-game format in 1985. You don't want your team to be defined by numbers, and you want to believe you can make it twenty-one out of twenty-five, but the decisive nature of that trend drove home just how important winning Game 2 was.

I then started to look ahead and think about how we were going to beat the Brewers. Shaun Marcum, another pitcher who began his career in the Toronto organization, was going to start Game 2 for them. Lifetime he was 50-32, which translates into an impressive .610 winning percentage. Marcum is not a guy who's going to overpower you—his fastball tops out at about ninety—but he's got an excellent changeup, a couple of breaking balls, command of all those pitches, and a real feel for changing speeds. He was 1-1 against us in the regular season, winning 4–3 and losing 2–1 with a no-decision added in there.

Of all their starters, our staff thought we had the best read on how to make adjustments to beat Marcum. We also felt that there was some question about his health that would affect his stuff and his command. Based on how frequently and how well he changed speed, we told the guys to look either soft or hard. We knew we'd be less effective looking for both his eighty-mile-an-hour stuff and his ninety-mile-an-hour stuff. Another example of picking your poison. We told the guys that his ball down in the zone had good movement, and we were going to try to get him to get the ball up more.

In Game 1, Albert, by his own admission, had had a rough night. A key strikeout and a double-play ground ball had him in a less than upbeat mood following that loss. He told the media afterward that he was going to make some adjustments, and like the great player that he is, he raised his game to match the situation.

In the second game, Albert came up huge for us. That wasn't a surprise, not just because Albert had done that before, but because we noticed that Albert had that look about him all day. Nick Punto noted it during batting practice, and I saw that look of quiet determination myself—Albert's Carp-like assassin demeanor had been turned up another notch overnight. During batting practice, I observed that instead of releasing his frustration and anger by trying to drive every pitch out of the park, he was fine-tuning his stroke, making those small adjustments he'd talked about. Albert's a proud man, and that was part of his intensity that day, but he also took exception to some of the bull that was going on with tweets and comments and all the rest of that. He also took some grief for saying of the pitch on which he hit a double-play ball that seven times out of ten he'd hit it out of the park. That's a bold statement, but Albert can back it up. That's what the great ones do. If you're going to talk the talk, then you better be able to hit the hits. Like I tell the guys all the time, if listening to what other people say fires you up, then pay attention to it. If not, then ignore it. All that Game 1 scrutiny didn't make Albert lose his focus.

You couldn't ignore Albert on this night. You couldn't ignore the modifications he'd made. In the first inning, he pounded a ball into the second deck in left field for a two-run homer to put us up 2–0. Next at-bat, he doubled to deep center. Third time up, another double, this one into the gap in right-center. For an encore, he sliced a double down the right-field line. You hear that good hitters use all parts of the ballpark? Well, in one night, in successive at-bats, Albert showed how that's done. I'm not saying that he went out there with the idea that he was going to hit the balls to those exact locations, but what he did do was not try to do too much, take advantage of what was given to him, and drive in five of our twelve runs on the night. If I can talk about Carp and Halladay carving hitters up with surgical precision, the same thing can be said about Albert's handiwork with a thirty-five-inch, thirty-three-ounce piece of wood.

I don't want Albert's performance to overshadow what the rest of the club did. We had seventeen hits and scored those twelve runs, and with the exception of a Prince Fielder solo home run in the eighth, our bullpen shut them down from the fifth through the ninth. Taking out Edwin Jackson in the fifth inning with us up 7–2 and runners on second and third was a mark of how much respect we had for the Brewers' offense, not any indication of my lack of faith in him. It was an unorthodox move, but the urgency of the moment demanded it be made. We still had fourteen outs to get. I sat there calculating how we were going to get them and who would be best able to do that, given the situation.

In the regular season especially, you want to give your starter a chance to earn the W. Given the urgency of the situation and our desire to do anything not to fall behind in the series 0-2, we had to do what was best for the team. Taking Edwin out in those circumstances was something you'd do only in the playoffs or toward the end of the season in a critical game.

As a general rule, the starting pitchers get the benefit of the doubt. Paul Richards told me this: "Don't be afraid to lose a game if you win more games later by having given a guy a chance to stay in the game." But if you're preaching to your position players to feel the urgency every inning, to play defense and approach every at-bat as though it's the most important inning or at-bat of their life, and you don't send a corresponding message to your team that you're managing with that kind of urgency, then you're going to lose credibility. And you're going to lose an edge.

We found ourselves in this position several times in the post-season. As a means of personalizing, I went to each of the guys affected—Jackson, Garcia, Lohse—and said that, yeah, I was concerned about what I was seeing, but who was it we selected to start the game? We had the confidence to start them in the first place, and that says more about our faith in them than anything else. In Edwin's case specifically, I reminded him that when I made out that chart for the pitching rotation for the last thirty-two games of the season, his name was second behind Carp's. We wouldn't have been on our way back to St. Louis having this discussion if it wasn't for that fact.

Still the reality that our starters were struggling was hard to ignore. Albert's impressive performance helped us to the win, and taking one of two at their place gave us a lot of confidence, but we still had a long way to go. For me, it was less of a happy flight and more of a relieved flight. Funny how that word *relieved* kept cropping up, and would throughout the rest of the series.

CHAPTER SEVENTEEN

The Right Kind of Bull

Heading back to St. Louis with the series tied at one game each, we were grateful for an off day before Game 3. In the two games, our starters had gone a total of 8.1 innings and our bullpen 8.2. We used eight different relief pitchers in them, including Kyle McClellan, who'd been added to the roster along with Lance Lynn. Skip Schumaker had strained a muscle in Game 5 of the NLDS, and rather than add another position player, we opted to go with another pitcher. Kyle McClellan took Jake Westbrook's place. That was a tough call. If one of our starters couldn't go, Jake would step in. The best way to condition him was off the roster.

I've learned a few things in my years as a manager. I handled the Jake situation very carefully. Because of how well respected Jake is, keeping him out of the rotation and off the roster against the Brewers could have upset the team's makeup. I didn't want to do that. In 1987 with the Oakland A's, we'd made the mistake of taking Mike Gallego, the hard-nosed utility infielder for those championship clubs, off the August 31 eligible-for-playoff roster. That upset his teammates because Gallego was such an important ingredient in that team's chemistry. Ultimately, we failed to make the playoffs. Now, those A's were a bit more temperamental than this edition of the Cards, but still, I didn't want to make a move that would cause any kind of rift. So, before I even spoke to Jake, I consulted the co-signers. They simply said that they understood. They felt the same way about Jake as we did, but if the staff thought it best to hold him out of the NLCS, then that's what we had to do.

Jake demonstrated why he was such a positive influence in the clubhouse and on the bench with how he handled it when I told him he wasn't going to be on the roster. On the off day, I found him and started launching into my list of reasons for making the move. About a minute into it, Jake gave me the stop sign. "Skip, thanks for this, but you don't need to go on. I get it. I want to do whatever it takes."

I could have hugged him; instead, I told him that his role was to continue to work out as if he was going to be back in that spot starter role in the next round—the World Series—or replacing someone who might get injured in this one. We felt he couldn't do that and work out of the bullpen effectively. For that reason, we held him out of the league championship series.

Despite the tough starts we'd gotten in Games 1 and 2, Game 3 was Carp, and coming off his huge win in Philadelphia, we liked our chances in his matchup against Yovani Gallardo. Despite carrying a no-hitter into the eighth inning against us in May, we'd had success against Gallardo overall. He had a 1-7 career record versus the Cardinals, with a 5.66 ERA, more than two runs per game higher than his total regular-season ERA. We beat him twice in early September, but he was having a strong postseason, putting up a 1.29 ERA in fourteen innings to that point. His career numbers against us indicated that he had some confidence issues in facing the Cardinals. We didn't possess some magical capability to hit him. He struggled early in his career against us, and the numbers could tell only part of that story.

For his part, Carp had beaten the Brewers twice late in the season, allowing just two runs in seventeen innings. His win over Halladay and the Phils had boosted his career postseason record to 6-2 with a 2.94 ERA. All signs pointed to a low-scoring game, but all those numbers could suggest only a probability. I had other numbers to think about.

The bullpen was very much on my mind that off day. Because we weren't playing, that meant that all the guys in the pen would be more or less fresh. In thinking about who we might use in relief, we had to consider not just the righty/lefty matchups and the relative strengths, weaknesses, and tendencies of the hitters and pitchers, but also how many innings they'd gone during the regular season and in the postseason, and how many times they might have gotten up to throw but not come into the game. All that, along with the game situation itself, would go into deciding who got the call.

When I first entered pro ball in 1962, and throughout my playing career, who received the call from the bullpen seemed a relatively simple matter. Most clubs had their starters and then a few starter wannabes, generally young kids or washed-up starters who didn't have the stamina to go nine innings. They also had a select few who functioned in the bullpen to finish up games. They also may have had a guy who pitched just long enough to get to the closer. To be honest, I don't even know when the terms *closer, setup man,* and *specialist* came into baseball's lingo. If somehow today a 1950s manager or player could be rescued from a deserted island, after those fifty or so years in isolation he'd think everyone using those words was maybe talking about the Mafia, not modern-day baseball.

Back in the very early days of the game, starters were about the only type of pitcher used. If a manager wanted to replace the starting pitcher, he generally put in another man from the rotation who wasn't pitching to either close out a game that was close or mop up one that wasn't. For those who know and love baseball's rich history, the names Chief Bender, Eddie Cicotte (he of the infamous Black Sox), Mordecai "Three Finger" Brown, Walter Johnson, and Rube Marquard should be familiar names, known for their prowess as starting pitchers. However, if we were to use the rules instituted in 1969 to establish the "save" as a statistic, each of those guys earned a fair number of them in their careers during the so-called dead-ball era. For example, Walter Johnson would have been credited, according to William McNeil in his fascinating book *The Evolution of Pitching in Major League Baseball,* with thirty-five saves in his career, while Brown would have had forty-nine. That's in addition to the number of wins they had while starting. Like many other starting pitchers of the era, they served as temporary relievers.

The great Grover Cleveland Alexander pitched from 1911 to 1930. In 1916 he threw an astounding 389 innings. That's eleven innings shy of doubling what we consider today the mark of a work-horse starter. For his career, Alexander won 373 and lost 208. As a temporary relief pitcher, he appeared 96 times, with a record of 23-17. To have had 581 decisions (wins and losses) in his career is practically unfathomable today. That meant he had very few no-decisions; in fact, of his 600 starts, he completed exactly 437. You could also say his managers had 437 no-decision games.

I'm not sure I would have liked to have had such limited involvement in the pitching side of the game back then. I was around in the early 1970s and saw a manager, Vern Rapp, at Indianapolis of the American Association do things very differently from the rest of the teams in that league and elsewhere in baseball. I discussed this a bit with Buzz Bissinger when he was working on his book *Three Nights in August.* There's more to that story.

When I was playing in the minors and my career was about over, I was in the American Association and paying a different kind of attention to the game than I'd brought to playing every day. In 1977, the last year I was going to play, I went back to Florida State University. I was two quarters short of my law degree, and I was going to graduate in March.

I don't think anybody knows this, but I graduated with honors from law school. That wasn't because I was a brilliant student, but because I was competitive. I had gone to law school with a couple of friends who started with better grades than me. So, mostly to win the "grade games" competition, I studied harder. A professor told me I should try to get a clerk's job with the Fifth Circuit Court of Appeals in New Orleans because that would look good on my résumé. He told me he had a friend there and they could work it out. I was with the White Sox organization at the time, but they called the Cardinals, who had just moved their minor league franchise to New Orleans, and I became a player-coach that year with New Orleans. That 1977 spring training was the first time I met George Kissell.

New Orleans's manager, Lance Nichols, had to undergo treatment for lung cancer, and I was asked to take over the club for two weeks. Years before in the American Association, I got to see Vern Rapp and how he handled his staff. Rapp had some nasty relievers, and he would turn the game over to them in the seventh, eighth, and ninth innings, and it was hard to get a doggone hit. I swore I would never forget that.

Over time Rapp had figured out that the more times a hitter gets to face a pitcher, the better the looks he gets. Part of that may be the starting pitcher's fatigue, but also, the more you face a pitcher, the better you see the ball coming out of his hand and the easier it is to gauge the movement, the velocity, etc. I don't think Rapp was the first to figure that out, but he used the fact to full advantage. He realized that a fresh reliever being seen by a hitter for the first time, even if that reliever didn't have stuff as good as the starter's, was a better alternative in the later innings. That reliever had to have at least one nasty "put away" pitch; whereas a starter couldn't rely solely on his best pitch, a relief pitcher could.

I don't necessarily agree with that premise, but if you look through baseball history, some of the early dominant closers—Bruce Sutter, for example, with his split-fingered fastball, which, when he threw it, was kind of a novelty pitch—had great success. Wilbur Wood, a knuckleballing left-hander, had fifty-six saves from 1967 to 1970 before being converted to a starter. His managers, Al Lopez, Don Gutteridge, and Eddie Stanky, must have had nerves of steel to send out a guy in a save situation with a fluttering off-speed pitch that often baffled the catcher as much as the hitter.

Of course, Mariano Rivera, perhaps the most dominant closer of all time, relied almost exclusively on his one outstanding pitch, a cutter. Tug McGraw had his screwball, and Trevor Hoffman later in his career featured his changeup, but I think of those guys as exceptions. They were pitchers who had such incredible command of an explosive pitch that they didn't need to mix it up. Most pitchers don't have that kind of one-pitch dominance. As a result, they have to rely on other pitches as well. The essential truth of Rapp's statement remains in place. Compared to a starting pitcher, a relief pitcher, particularly a closer who will face hitters just once a game, can be more one-dimensional in his approach.

There's enough difference of opinion about gas versus guile to take up an entire book. Simply put, speed kills, but not all the time. If that plus fastball is the only thing you have, you better locate it on the corners. That might work for a season, but over time you need to develop a second pitch to put into the hitter's thinking. Big league hitters will eventually catch up to any fastball, and the longer you go in the count throwing that same fastball, at the same relative speed, with the same relative location, and with similar movement, the more time you're giving them to gauge it. Jason Motte was learning the harsh reality of that in 2011. All things considered, for just about any pitcher, the real estate mantra about "location, location, location" applies here.

Most important was the question of whether or not any guy could make those pitches, fastballs or whatever, in the ninth inning. Baseball history is filled with guys like Ron Davis, who was a great setup man but couldn't keep his emotions in check to restrain his closer's stuff in the ninth.

When I began managing full-time in the big leagues, most pitchers detested being in the bullpen. Much of that bias about relief pitchers being "wannabe" starters still existed. Dennis Eckersley is one of the best cases to this point. He also became one of the best relievers to play the game, and he became a Hall of Famer doing so.

In 1987 the A's had five starters, all with potential injury problems. We were looking for protection for our rotation, and the best guy we could find was Eck. We had beaten him up all spring when he was with the Cubs, but we still traded for him. Eck and I had a little history. When he was with Boston and I was with the White Sox, he had drilled a couple of our guys and I'd yelled at him a couple of times. The most recent time was in spring training, right before we got him from the Cubs, when we were knocking him around pretty good. Jose Canseco hit a ball off the wall and then stole third base. Eck looked at Canseco and said, "What are you trying to do? It's spring training, and I'm just trying to get my work in."

Canseco pointed at me in the dugout, and I yelled at Eck, "Yeah, I told him to do that." I was still upset that he'd treated a number of our players badly.

We barked back and forth a bit. All of that in a spring training game.

When Dennis arrived, I told him why we'd traded for him.

He told me he still wanted to start. That fit with our plan because he was brought in as insurance in case one of our other starters got hurt. However, in his first relief appearances, Dunc and I told him that he was looking so good in the bullpen that we were going to keep him there. He'd go out there and try to prove his point. All that did was show us what he was capable of as a reliever. Yet Eck was always complaining to the press, "I'm a starter. I'm a starter. I'm a starter."

Then, when the media really pressed him, he said, "Relievers are guys that aren't good enough to start. I'm good enough to start."

So I called him in and explained to him, "Dennis, that used to be true, like twenty years ago. You look around—more and more clubs are giving as much attention to their bullpen as their starting rotation." Both quality starters and relievers get treated as stars.

But Eck still wasn't convinced.

We were in Boston for a Thursday game in July 1987, and we were battling Minnesota for the division lead in the American League West. Eck pitched 2.2 innings for a save—something unheard of today. He came off the field, and he was all excited. We were all excited.

Of course, the writers knew we had this thing with him wanting to be a starter. So they came in to me and said, "Dennis is out there saying he still wants to be a starter."

I said, "What?"

I told the clubhouse man that I wanted to see Eck. I shut the door after he came in and said, in so many words, "We had a great win. We should be able to enjoy it, but instead we've got to deal with your complaints. That's enough. I'm sick and tired of hearing that, and I don't want to hear that anymore."

He still talks today about having to go to the principal's office to have his ass chewed out. Like a punk, with an attitude I had to admire, he went back out and told the writers, "I'm not allowed to say I want to be a starter."

But as he had more and more success in the relief role, he said, "You know what? There's a rush when you go out there in the ninth inning. You just have to air it out, and if you get three outs, guys come over and shake your hand."

At the end of the season, when everybody was packing up to go home, he came by to shake my hand. He said, "I know we've already been through this. You've explained about the bullpen. I get it. I like some things about it. All I ask is for you to keep an open mind about me being in the rotation the next year."

I said, "Dennis, we'll keep an open mind." But at the winter meetings our general manager, Sandy Alderson, as part of his great off-season moves, made a trade, sending Jay Howell, our closer, and

Alfredo Griffin to the Dodgers, and we got Bob Welch as a starter. I called Eck that night, and he said, "I know. I know. I'm a reliever."

And the rest is history. But the funny thing was that that winter, since Eck had never been a closer from the beginning of the season to the end, we were actively trying to get left-hander Dave Righetti and put the two of them together. And then Righetti signed with the Giants. That meant that Eck got the ball all the time. He wound up saving forty-five games in 1988, when we won our first pennant at Oakland. If we had gotten Righetti, who knows if it would have worked out as well.

After Eck got into the Hall of Fame, he said, "I didn't know I was going to be good at closing. If I had known, I would have shut up and done it."

SETTING UP YOUR BULLPEN REVOLVES AROUND FINDING A QUALITY closer, and then you work backward from there, into the sixth inning, but today figuring out that strategy takes a lot more than just getting guys to accept their role. It took me a while to refine all my thinking and test my theories, but in the end the time spent and the heartaches and frustrations endured proved to be worth it.

Dunc and I were among the first to use the closer, like Eck, only in the final inning. Dunc came to me early in 1988 and asked what I thought of our club. I told him I thought we had a really good team. Sandy Alderson had a huge off-season adding key people to fill out our roster.

"How many guys do you think we have as good as Eck who can pitch in the ninth inning?"

"None."

"Then doesn't it make sense that the more games Eck is available to pitch just in the ninth when we're ahead, the more wins we'll hang on to?"

"Yes."

Dunc was the guy who came up with the idea. I just agreed with him.

Dunc's idea would work only if two conditions were met. You had to have quality setup guys to get you to the ninth with the lead intact. If you didn't, then holding your closer for the ninth wouldn't produce the wins you were after. The lead would be gone by the time you got to the "space" you'd reserved for him.

Also, if you didn't have a really good team, one that would have a lead going into the ninth more than two or three times a week, the same idea applied: if you're behind often, you shouldn't hold on to your closer till the ninth, because your closer is going to just sit there. This is the "don't leave a bullet in the chamber" idea.

Similarly, we also believed that the game could be decided well ahead of that, so we started using relievers not just as bridges to the closer but as quasi-stoppers. Putting an end to a potential threat or limiting the damage already done is part and parcel of a reliever's duty.

I actually learned a lot about how a bullpen should function from a hitting coach, Charley Lau. I had first met Charley when I was eighteen and with the Kansas City A's in 1963 and Charley was the backup catcher. Twenty years later, Charley was a hitting coach for us when I was a young manager with the White Sox. To me, he's the greatest hitting coach of all time. He revolutionized our game. I even asked Charley for advice when he was the hitting coach for the Kansas City Royals in the late 1970s and I was with the White Sox. Whitey Herzog, who was managing the Royals then, did not take too kindly to that and didn't want Charley giving tips to an opponent. Charley felt like he was a teacher and if someone asked him a question, especially someone like me who'd known him for a while, he was going to answer.

And Charley also knew a lot about pitching, or more specifically, what pitchers can do to hitters. He told me that what worried him most as a hitting coach was when a manager on the other side had a bullpen and he used his bullpen to make it as hard as possible to score in any inning they were playing. That's why when managers like that got into the seventh or eighth inning, sometimes they matched up two or three pitchers in an inning. Then, in the ninth, they'd let the legitimate closer face whoever came up, even if the matchup didn't thrill them. If the closer wasn't available for any reason, they applied that seventh- and eighth-inning philosophy to the ninth. I filed all this away for later use.

I have to credit two other men for helping to shape my early thinking on the subject of bullpens: the White Sox farm director, Paul Richards, a pitching-oriented guy, and Ken Silvestri, the organizational pitching coach for the White Sox. The way they had set up the first team I managed, the AA Knoxville Sox, was with excellent young starters—Richard Dotson, Steve Trout, and Britt Burns—and with veteran relievers.

A veteran bullpen is the formula we've continued to use over the years—except, ironically, in our last two World Championships, both of which we won with predominantly young relievers.

In September 2006, Jason Isringhausen had gotten hurt, so our closer was Adam Wainwright—a rookie. Along with Adam, our other main right-handers in the pen were Josh Kinney, another rookie we had called up, Braden Looper, and Josh Hancock. Our two left-handers were Tyler Johnson, another rookie, and Randy Flores. We opened the playoffs in San Diego, and we started Carp, but toward the end of the season Carp had been showing some wear. In Game 1 against San Diego, I relieved him in the seventh, even though he'd given up only one run. We won that game with Johnson and Wainwright for the last two and two-thirds innings.

The next day we started Jeff Weaver, who'd had problems against left-handed hitters all season. But Dunc, in his genius, told him, "Throw your curveball." And he curveballed them to death, mixing in a few fastball and changeups. He held them to two hits and no runs over five. But when he was getting ready to go through the lineup for the third time, I yanked him. Again, we went to our young bullpen—Johnson, Flores, Kinney, Wainwright. We won that game, 2–0.

Looking back on those two games in San Diego, I pulled Carp, our stud pitcher, for young pitchers. I pulled Weaver with a two-hit shutout for the same young guys. That trend of going to the young guys didn't end in the NLDS. The point is that we won the whole thing with a young bullpen.

The similarities were there in 2011. Sure, we'd added Dotel and Arthur, both veterans, as was McClellan, but look at the guys who were pitching most of the innings in relief—Boggs, Salas, Lynn, Motte, Rzepczynski. They were all young guys, all making their play. That should certainly put to rest the myth that Tony and Dunc don't like young pitchers or players.

As a result of all the left-right thinking we have to do, we spend a lot of time evaluating the strengths and vulnerabilities of all our pitchers.

Rick Honeycutt, who pitched in Oakland and in St. Louis for Dunc and me, was kind of a template for the ideal left-handed reliever. He ranks up there with the premier setup men of our time. Not only that, he could also pitch the ninth inning, facing lefts and rights, like he did in 1989 when Eck was hurt. To get right-handers out, a lefty has to be able to pitch to both sides of the plate, with either a sinker or a cut fastball. He also has to have a quality breaking ball and changeup. Honeycutt had those pitches and could do all that. He also had guts and a really good pickoff move to first base.

Even though you want the opposition to pinch-hit so that you can get a particular hitter out of the lineup, the best hitters aren't going to be lifted. As a result, left-handed relievers face top-quality left-handed hitters. They're generally not as easy to get out. Almost without exception, a left-handed hitter is good because he looks for a ball out over the plate and he doesn't give in. For a left-hander to retire a good left-handed hitter, he's got to be able to do two things.

He's got to be able to command a pitch he would throw inside on the edge of the plate, so he can pitch to what's called a "wide plate." Then he's got to be able to command the breaking ball on the outside edge of the plate. If a left-hander misses over the plate with either his breaking ball or his fastball, that pitch gets mashed.

There really is no "last" guy on the staff. But he might be the third left-hander in the bullpen, which is a real luxury because most times you can't find two. And if that third left-hander also can be an "innings" guy, then that could be the best-case scenario. Most of the time, though, that seventh guy in your bullpen is a right-handed pitcher because you definitely need more right-handers than left-handers. There are simply more right-handed hitters than left-handed hitters. For years, the National League Central was a right-handed-hitting division. You could pitch in our division for many years with only one left-hander on your staff.

During the off-season and into the beginning of 2011, our bullpen was built around that idea of having veterans and youngsters. Early on we caught lightning in a bottle with our young right-handed relievers, Salas and Sanchez particularly. We started to use Motte as our inherited-runner guy—he was the best at coming in with runners on. He also worked in the eighth as a setup man, while Salas closed for us. Boggs has a power arm but was a bit erratic. After our midseason trades got McClellan back into the bullpen and added R-zep, along with the two veterans, Dotel and Rhodes, suddenly we were able to establish balance with the young right-handers. When Salas suffered from wear and tear, he switched roles with Motte. We had to nurse him along a bit in that role, but he improved as the season went on and into the postseason.

Injuries are a serious obstacle to overcome, so throughout the year two of the major questions become: How do we keep pitchers healthy? And how often do we pitch them? We would tell our pitchers that Dunc and I would never risk a pitcher's arm to win a game, no matter how important the game. But we'd impress on them the critical importance of them being honest with us. You might think you're really being heroic by staying in the game and taking a beating, but all you're doing is risking your career and your effectiveness. The way we gauged that was to emphasize the importance of going into the training room to get treatment for any pain—stiffness, soreness, or anything more severe. We also wanted them to do their conditioning and stretching work, which, along with the treatments, ice, massage, and electrical stimulation, serve as preventative maintenance. As much as you want guys to be honest and seek treatment and maintenance, sometimes, because of the competitive nature and desire, fear, or whatever, some guys just won't go in there and won't tell you in all honesty how they are feeling.

Between the daily reports from the trainers and the observations of our pitching coach, the bullpen coach, and the bullpen catcher, you formulate a daily "who's available?" list. Because not every guy will be 100 percent honest—most of them generally believe they're okay even when they're not—those observations by the staff are critical. Generally, before every game, the relievers are on the field throwing, just to play catch. They're checking to see how their arm feels, and they report back—honestly, you hope. A lot of pairs of eyes are on them as well to provide a safety check.

Ultimately, you never know for sure how guys are feeling until they're in the middle of it all. That's the thing about the bullpen—you do everything you can to plan around it, to manage it carefully, to use it as a resource, but you just never know exactly how it's going to all play out on the field, especially when you've been asking a lot of them. That was exactly what we'd done in Games 1 and 2 against the Brewers.

FOR THE FIFTH POSTSEASON GAME IN A ROW, WE SCORED IN THE first inning to start Game 3, this time putting up four runs against a somewhat erratic Gallardo. After Carp worked around a one-out walk and a hit batsman and retired the side, Rafael Furcal set the tone in the bottom of the inning, as he did so often, by singling. I can't say enough about how important that is. The pitcher goes out there, and all of a sudden he's throwing from the stretch instead of the windup. Sure, pitchers work from the windup and the stretch in the bullpen beforehand, but there's enough of a time gap, especially when you're the visiting team, that throwing off the game mound feels a bit different. Those eight warm-up pitches—most of which, if not all of which, they throw between innings out of the windup—may not let you establish any feeling of comfort out there. Add throwing out of the stretch to that lengthy time between bullpen and field, and that leadoff hit, and a lot of pitchers struggle in the first.

A wild pitch and a Jon Jay double brought home a run, and we added on nicely after that, despite a Yadi double-play grounder. Three walks in the inning, one intentional, and big hits from Albert and Freese put us up 4–0. Anytime your pitcher makes the last out in the first, you know you've done some damage.

Little did we know that was all the damage we were going to do against the Brewers' pitching staff that day. Our inability to add on was frustrating. By the fifth inning, the Brewers had pulled within a run. Carp wasn't his outstanding self. Dunc and I talked about it, and we didn't like what we were seeing. Pitch count factored in a bit, but we could see that his velocity and movement had nudged downward on the scale and his breaking balls weren't as sharp. More important, though, was that he wasn't getting ahead of the hitters. He had thrown first-pitch strikes to only twelve out of the twenty-three hitters he'd faced to that point. We'd have liked to see the percentage closer to 70 or 80 and not just barely above 50.

Also, Carp had gotten only six called strikes without contact. That's a double-edged sword. With certain pitchers, you want them to pitch to contact—make the hitters get the ball in play. That usually leads to a low pitch count, but in this game Carp wasn't getting that. Several of the Brewers hitters seemed to be "on" him, seeing his pitches well. Fifteen balls fouled off added to Carp's total. Also, Carp had already faced their one-through-five hitters three times, and we were only roughly halfway through the game. That old adage about making hitters see someone new proved important.

With all that in mind, I told Carp that he was done. I went with Fernando Salas to start the sixth. Salas had pitched well in his one inning of work in Game 2. The righty matchup worked in his favor, and he retired Hairston, Betancourt, and Lucroy in order. We had in mind from the beginning that Salas would work just one inning. We liked the idea of bringing in Lance Lynn to start an inning rather than enter with runners on base. Many times younger guys feel a little less pressure when starting an inning. Lynn also worked a perfect frame. We were down to the final six outs, still hoping we'd add on, but thinking about and prepared to stop them from scoring.

Our plan was to get those outs one at a time in the top of the eighth, and that worked out perfectly for us. Lynn retired the right-handed-hitting Braun. Four men faced, four outs for Lynn. Just what we needed. I called on the lefty R-zep to pitch to the left-handed-hitting Fielder. R-zep had seemed to be growing in his confidence as the postseason progressed. He'd appeared in both Games 1 and 2, pitching 1.2 innings, and he hadn't allowed a hit. Remember what I said about demeanor, competitiveness, and greatness? I can't go so far as to say that R-zep is a great relief pitcher yet, but we could just see how his body language had changed. When he came out of the bullpen, in how he warmed up, and in the way he attacked hitters, we could see that he believed he could get these guys out. It seemed like he stood taller or something. Watching him strike out their slugger Fielder and registering that great reaction—not showing a guy up, but expressing both his pride and his sense that he'd done just what he'd thought he could do—was great to see.

I brought in our closer Jason Motte for a four-out save. I stated earlier that we were one of the first teams to go to a ninth-inning closer the majority of the time. All of the things I've said before about some pitchers being better with runners on base, some being better at starting an inning, and some being better at getting up again after sitting between innings, all played a part in our thinking. In this case, I simply believed that Motte gave us the best chance against Rickie Weeks. My choices were to use up one of our other right-handers, Boggs, McClellan, or Dotel, for one hitter or go to Motte. He was used to that role of coming on in the middle of an inning, so we went with him. Also, the bottom of the order was coming up in the ninth.

Motte was at his best that night, retiring four hitters without allowing a hit. For the game, our bullpen faced twelve hitters and retired everyone. You can't do any better than that. I had sat in my office for hours on the off day, churning through dozens of "what-if" scenarios throughout the game, and then those guys went out there and did, by far, the harder thing. It would be nearly impossible to exaggerate the impact of their performance on the psyche of the club. It was like watching a replay of how we'd won during our stirring comeback. After the first inning, we hadn't added on, making us so vulnerable, and all too often those games come back to haunt you. We needed our bullpen to be perfect, and they were.

Seeing these kinds of performances on a regular basis helped solidify our belief that we had a legitimate shot at going all the way, but more than that, it was impressive how the rigors of the regular season and Mo's trade deadline moves had transformed one of our early weaknesses into a second-half and postseason strength. From July 28 until the end of the season, we had the third-best bullpen ERA (2.86) in all of Major League Baseball. It's hard to believe, based on our postseason performance, that this was the bullpen that had the second-highest blown save total in the National League and surrendered the third-highest total number of home runs.

After the game, Carp was asked about his confidence level in leaving the game in the hands of the bullpen. He also commented on the influence of the veterans, Arthur and Octavio, on the younger guys. Arthur had a different perspective. He said that what the two of them brought was a sense of fun—they'd blare loud music and mess with each other. I think what I saw out of those guys, not just when they came in after getting the job done but even out on the mound, was what Arthur was talking about. Coming out on top in a competition is fun.

We were now ahead in the series 2-1, but as we looked ahead to Game 4, we were careful not to become complacent. Complacency wasn't the problem; Randy Wolf was. He kept us off balance all game in a 4–2 loss.

And just like that we saw that our one-game lead was gone. We were even again—tied two-all in the series and 11-11 for the year. If there was give in either team, I don't think anyone could see it.

CHAPTER EIGHTEEN

Making It Happen

GAME 5 MARKED ANOTHER REVOLUTION OF THE STARTING PITCH-ing rotation in the series: both starters for Game 1 were back on the mound. The fact that both pitchers had been hit hard offset any advantage we had from having just seen Zack Greinke.

In situations like this, though, having Dunc on our side was an edge. If anybody can help a pitcher figure out what went wrong, what he can do differently this time around without veering too violently off course, it's Dunc. Anytime you try to get a pitcher to fix things between outings, you risk taking him out of his comfort zone, but Dunc was the master at making improvements without the negative side effects. In Garcia's case, we felt good that he would give us a different ball game in Game 5, but we also trusted our bullpen more with each passing day.

One trend that we hoped would continue in Game 5 was our bats waking up. Part of that was a testament to Mark McGwire; our hitting coach since 2010, Mark had been instrumental in helping guys at the plate. For much of his time with the team, I'd felt like Mark's contributions to our offense hadn't really been recognized. This was especially true because he does coaching the right way—staying in the background, helping out when needed, and recognizing that this is the player's time. Granted, we'd always been a good-hitting club. In the last ten years, the only time we slipped out of the top-five rankings was in 2007 when we fell to sixth. Hal McRae, our hitting coach from 2005 to 2009, was an important part of that success. It was also a result of how we teach players the sound basics of hitting, something Mark had been helpful with throughout the 2011 season.

The first time I saw Mark was in 1984 when the U.S. Olympic team he was playing for came through Chicago. That Olympic team was loaded with future major league stars, but the player who got as much attention as anyone was Mark. He had a bit of Charley Lau in him—great timing and an easy swing, but could hit the ball a long way.

Then the next time I saw him was in 1986 when I joined the A's and Mark came up as a September call-up. I'd been hearing about him for a while and I knew he was a key part of the talent developing in the farm system. I never interviewed for a job in my life. After I got fired by the White Sox, Oakland flew in all their front-office guys to Chicago's O'Hare airport, where I met them. They told me, "This is not an interview. We're here to convince you to take the job." Part of how they tried to convince me was to trumpet the talent they had in their system. Mark's name came up, putting him on my radar once again. I'd need that radar later to track the flight of some of his prodigious home runs.

When Mark came to our A's spring training camp in 1987, his timing and power were still special—so much so that Mark made the club as a kind of utility man. He was swinging the bat with such promise that we decided to take him north and find a place in the field for him. After two or three weeks, we made him the regular first baseman, and he set a rookie record that still stands by hitting forty-nine home runs. And that wasn't all that easy because the ball didn't carry in Oakland at night. He might have had fifty, but his wife was going to deliver a baby the last day of the season, so he left the club to be with her.

At that time we had two great young hitters in Jose Canseco and Mark. One was signed out of high school, Canseco, and the other went to college at USC. One was really scientific about hitting and the other wasn't, but it was just the opposite of what you would think. Canseco was the scientific one.

Mark said, "I just want to see it and hit it." But his stroke had a hole in it. If the pitcher threw the ball up, he couldn't get to it. He did well enough for a few years, but over time pitchers figured out how to get to him. Then in 1991, when he was hitting .201, I sat him for the last game of the season so he wouldn't drop under .200. That winter we hired Doug Rader as our hitting coach, and Doug got Mark back to where he had been, hitting .268 with 42 home runs and 104 driven in. But it was about the same time that he started having all the heel injuries that would mar his career.

Over the next couple of years, Mark was on the disabled list a lot, playing only seventy-four games total in 1993 and 1994; as a result, he had time to watch a lot of games in the clubhouse with our video man, Chad Blair. Through these sessions, Mark started to appreciate things like how the pitcher and the catcher worked together to execute a game plan to get hitters out. Then he started thinking about his batting stroke. Like most things in sports, your foundation is your bottom half. Mark's feet were injured, but they were also the key to his reformation as a hitter.

From the outset, Mark's stance was a bit awkward. He was pigeon-toed—his knees were cocked toward each other. He had his hands out in front of him, and he'd tilt the bat toward the pitcher. Hardly a textbook swing. He got on top of a lot of balls, but since that naturally put top spin on them, they didn't carry as far as they might have.

As a golfer, Mark understood the importance of a solid foundation. He started opening his toes, pointing the back foot more toward the catcher and the front foot more toward the shortstop side of second base. By doing that, he could get rotation with his hips. With this total reconstruction of his stroke and his thinking, he could hit the high fastball, whether it was thrown by Randy Johnson, Billy Wagner, Mariano Rivera, or whoever. He also learned the art of making adjustments.

Then he took the knowledge that he had accrued and, as he got deeper and deeper into his career, added the power of his mind and his concentration. Over time he developed a deep appreciation for the subtleties of the game, not to mention the discipline to tune everything out. He began his career as a player with great natural ability, but he evolved into someone with a thinking man's approach. It seemed like the more he learned about the game, the more he enjoyed it. That was especially true of hitting.

During the home run chase in 1998, the elements of his personality that would later make him such a valuable coach became even clearer. In the midst of all the hype, all the media, he was the consummate teammate, one who didn't enjoy having the spotlight shone on him. This sense of team came in part from being around those great Oakland A's clubs. It's true that there were some strong egos on those clubs, but the majority of the guys were really into being a part of a team. Mark saw that and later became a mentor to young hitters like Jason Giambi, just as Reggie Jackson had helped him. Mark believed that the team came first and kept his home run chase in the proper perspective. Some media people interpreted that as Mark being surly or unable to deal with all the pressures. That wasn't the case.

Mark had to retire prematurely, in 2002, because of his back. Since then, his integrity over the issue of performance-enhancing drugs (PED) has been widely discussed, but rarely does anyone mention that he walked away from the benefits of a long-term contract that owed him $30 million. His strong character wouldn't let him take money he didn't feel he deserved. Some guys might have hung around, spent a lot of time on the disabled list or whatever, just to collect a paycheck. Not Mark. He had his contract torn up because he didn't think he could perform to the level he wanted.

After he left the game, I kept inviting him to spring training. He turned me down a few times, but I eventually found out from his wife, Stephanie, that about four o'clock every afternoon, once he had picked the boys up from school, he came in and watched games on TV. He started with the East Coast games. He'd watch a double-header every night, and he really was into analyzing the hitters. I'd talk to him every once in a while, and he always would tell me what he thought hitters, including our guys, were doing right or wrong, pointing out things like how well Manny Ramirez, Alex Rodriguez, and Albert Pujols were getting on top of the ball and getting through it, getting that great underspin that helped the ball carry.

He's still got a passion for the game, I thought. The more I heard him speak, the more I felt that everything about his approach would make him an outstanding candidate for our staff. In November 2009, I decided that I wanted to make an offer to him for the job as our hitting coach the next season. Before making the offer, however, Mo, Bill, Mark, and I all spoke about this possibility, and everyone— most of all Mark—agreed that he needed to address the issue of performance-enhancing drugs that was still hanging over him. Several years earlier, Mark had declined to testify in front of Congress about PEDs, and since he had retired, he hadn't addressed the issue at all. We didn't know what he was going to say, just that he had to say something.

Based on my observations of his deserved reputation for integrity, I knew he would tell the truth, but I didn't know specifically what he was going to say. In January 2010, Mark admitted to using steroids, and on the morning the announcement was made he called to tell me what was about to be all over the news.

Since the first accusations were made, I'd always defended him. I did that because during our time in Oakland and St. Louis, I'd seen Mark work so hard in the gym. The key to my defense of Mark was that our Oakland weight-training program was overseen by Dave McKay. I knew that Dave would have zero tolerance for any illegal activities in our program. Zero tolerance. When questions were being asked, Dave assured me that at no time was there anything going on to enhance the workouts. Dave's integrity is impeccable. Also, Dave was one of the most knowledgeable baseball men about the use of weights in our sport. Baseball didn't always accept the idea that weights were an effective training tool. I'd experienced their benefits in my playing career. They aided me in my recovery from injuries, so when I saw what Dave was doing in those early years in Oakland, I bought into his program immediately.

It's easy in hindsight to point fingers and assign blame. The truth is that a lot of factors made it difficult to assess what was going on. Only when some players came forward and admitted to their use of PEDs did a lot of people say that what was going on was obvious.

The issue got even murkier when the supplement creatine, protein powders, and other legal substances came into vogue. Additionally, guys started to eat better, drink wine instead of hard liquor, and generally do a greater amount and variety of workouts to gain strength and flexibility. Working out became a part of nearly everyone's routine. Guys liked the way they looked and played as a result of their efforts. At some point, creatine fell out of favor because of its dehydrating effects. Even though that substance had stopped being used, we noticed that guys were still getting bigger and stronger. That's the natural progression—the longer you work out, the bigger you'd get. Guys who'd been working out for years wouldn't raise any suspicion if they came into spring camp looking more muscled than they had the year before.

We were suspicious of some players who seemed to get bigger faster than you'd suspect, even if they were working out. A smaller group of players got bigger but didn't work out. That raised our eyebrows. Something was up, but whatever it was wasn't on display.

Also, in most cases, what was visible to us—weight training and improved nutrition primarily—provided an explanation for the increases in muscle mass we were seeing. Mark fell into the category of guys whom we had no reason to be suspicious of.

As a staff we did have questions about what we were seeing in regard to guys who weren't known for working out religiously, or at all, and were still making big gains. We didn't have all the information, and neither did Major League Baseball or the players' association. All of us wanted to do whatever we could to protect the game and the players. The union was going to protect the players by using the collective bargaining agreement and the right to privacy as it pertained to testing. What could we, as a staff, do in the face of all this uncertainty and legal wrangling?

We don't police our guys away from the ballpark. My defense of Mark was based on what I could observe and my knowledge of the type of program we ran. The other point I knew was when he had his heel injuries, they'd gotten to the point that they threatened to end his career. Later on when he admitted to using human growth hormone (HGH), that jibed with what I knew about Mark. At the time, HGH could be prescribed legally by doctors, and Mark had in fact received a prescription for it to treat his serious injury.

That day in January when he called, Mark was very emotional. We'd known each other for nearly twenty-five years. I was especially close with Mark, as I was with many players over the years. How he chose to deal with his revelation confirmed what I'd known about him from early on—he's a guy with a lot of integrity. I was just relieved to finally have it out there, finally have it addressed, so that Mark could move forward with his career in the game and begin his next chapter.

After Mark was hired and made his statement, both publicly and privately, the media focused on my motives for hiring him. Some commentators may have wanted to compliment me, and others to criticize me, for presumably hiring a friend out of loyalty and helping him rehabilitate his career. Regardless of intent, I was insulted by those assumptions. I take my responsibility to my employers, fans, teammates, and the game itself too seriously ever to engage in that kind of nepotistic behavior. Mark was hired based on his merits.

Period.

The only question I had about him at the beginning was whether or not he could translate what he knew about hitting into words the players could understand. Sometimes when you know something inside out, you think that other people do too and you take for granted that the words and concepts you've been using inside your head will have meaning to someone else. By the time we got out of spring training in 2010, he had simplified what he was saying, and communication was never an issue again.

Throughout his two years with the team, we could see how our hitters responded to him. He had the unique ability, common to only the most successful of coaches, to connect with everyone from the biggest established stars to the youngest players and everyone else all up and down the roster, regardless of role. Holliday, Craig, and Descalso—three guys at different stages in their careers—all had strong working relationships with Mark. Each of them at various times went to him, asking him questions about their swing and their approach. In 2010 Mark felt that a lot of the guys needed to reexamine the value of the time they spent in the video room. It can be a productive tool, a waste of time, or something that detracts from your performance. He and Mike Aldrete led a number of sessions in there watching video with the guys, breaking it down, and clearly demonstrating how they could take what they were seeing on the screen and put it to use in the cage and then on the field.

Mark's approach wasn't just technical, though. He also put personalizing into motion, first establishing relationships with guys, then helping them. This became a particularly important element of Mark's success that we witnessed during the postseason in 2011. David Freese, who'd struggled through a period of six strikeouts in seven at-bats, really benefited from Mark talking to him and revising his approach just a bit. The results were impressive and immediate—as the playoffs continued, you could see David adding more and more confidence to what Mark had put in place with this thinking and mechanics. Not every coach can do that.

I can't stress enough how important our coaches are to our success. The longer I was in the game, the more teaching we had to do at the big league level. Having great coaches made that task easier. Years ago, before we had instructional leagues, players worked their way through Classes D, C, B, A, AA, and AAA before getting to the show. Also, young players didn't have guaranteed contracts like they do now, and free agency didn't exist until the 1970s. As a result, clubs didn't have to promote guys except for two reasons: need and merit. Also, in the pre-expansion days, there were far fewer jobs at the major league level. Clubs could stockpile guys who otherwise might have played at a higher level but who just couldn't break into the top of the depth chart. In those days, guys coming up to the big leagues had really been schooled. It wasn't uncommon for a guy to get his first taste of big league action after having already pitched 1,000 innings or had 1,000 at-bats in the minors.

With that kind of experience and that kind of exposure to instruction, unless you're a rock, you're bound to pick up some ideas about how the game should be played. Today that part of baseball is different as well. With the economics of the game, the collective bargaining agreement, and the talent pool being spread across so many different teams, if you're young and talented you've got a good chance of getting to the major leagues more quickly. But that means we have to coach young players nearly as much as the minor league staff does—sometimes more. That's a far cry from the way it used to be.

Coaching isn't just about putting on the uniform and working the strategic elements of the game. If you don't have the passion that someone like Mark McGwire has and can't communicate well and really be a teacher, then you're not going to last long in the business. With both hitters and pitchers, we have a team philosophy, but we take a highly individualized approach. We're not looking to clone anybody; we want players to know and employ basic fundamentals, but the rest we tailor to the individual. That's probably the greatest challenge teachers of baseball face. We build a curriculum, establish certain requirements, but how you get your pupils to perform well is determined mostly by how well you understand the needs and abilities of your widely varied pupils. That's why, in our organization, we looked for people like Mark who could demonstrate the ability to personalize, develop, and nurture their relationships with the players. After all, the players are the ones who have to go out and execute and perform. That said, if your coaching staff—and that includes the manager—are all paying attention to every game all year, you never know when that attention or expertise might save a run, create a run, or give you an edge. Proper coaching is like a guy coming off the bench to get a hit or a reliever coming in to get a double play— it's that tangible and legitimate.

As we fought our way through the series with the Brewers, I thought about how rewarding this was for all of us. The entire coaching staff had contributed, including third-base coach Jose Oquendo and Dave McKay at first, Derek Lilliquist and Jeff Murphy down in the bullpen, Joe Pettini on the bench, and Mike Aldrete working with the hitters along with Mark. The coaches were in uniform, but our staff contributions included everyone who was in regular contact with our team.

Of course, the coaches with the most responsibility on the staff are the pitching coach and hitting coach. I've been on a staff with the greatest pitching coach and the greatest hitting coach in history in Dave Duncan and Charley Lau, but I think it's harder to be an outstanding hitting coach than an outstanding pitching coach. Why do I say that? A starter pitches every five days and works in the bullpen once between starts, so he works two times every five days. You have relievers who are limited as far as what they can work on before games, depending on how much they've been used. And by and large, pitchers are more coachable than hitters. They're more willing to experiment. I think you can find more qualified pitching coaches—I'm not talking about great pitching coaches—than you can find qualified hitting coaches. That may have to do with the fact that many former pitchers become pitching coaches. They've spent a big part of their lives watching, discussing, and dissecting their craft.

The hitting coach, on most clubs, works with every hitter every day, whether it's in the batting cage outside or the batting cage inside. That's time-consuming. When you factor in all the video analysis required, the commitment is even greater. Now, because of the multitude of hitting coach duties and the tremendous impact of access to technology on the job description, some clubs have an assistant hitting coach. It hasn't gotten to the point of being like the pro golf tour, where each player has his or her own swing coach.

All that is a tall order for anyone, and yet in a couple of short years Mark had handled it with skill. He wasn't overwhelmed by the workload—he was fired up by it. It was an attitude that we needed our coaches to have, and an attitude that would continue to show itself at the plate in Games 5 and 6 against the Brewers.

OUR BATS CONTINUED TO PRODUCE IN GAME 5, AND AS WE'D DONE throughout most of the playoffs, we gave our starter an early cushion, with three runs in the second inning. Garcia took that lead and ran with it, pitching two more scoreless innings, and in the bottom of the fourth, when we were ahead 3–0, we got the first two men on base with no outs.

Using some unusual strategy, I had a position player, Nick Punto, try to move the runners over with a bunt, with Garcia on deck. Normally you wouldn't do that with the pitcher coming up next, since most pitchers can't handle the bat as well as a position player. But I knew that Nick was an excellent bunter and that Jaime had a really good idea at the plate. In a way, I flip-flopped the usual roles of the eighth and ninth hitters. Punto got the bunt down and moved the runners to second and third.

The thought behind this was that we needed to score in that inning, even if it was only one run. With just one run, we'd add to our lead and gain momentum. I thought Garcia could get the bat on the ball. I put the contact play on with Freese at third. That meant that when the hitter made contact with the pitch, Freese would head for home, forcing the drawn-in infielders to make a play. Even if he was out, we still would have another runner in scoring position.

With Garcia hitting left-handed, the third baseman, although he was playing in for a possible squeeze bunt, was over toward the short-stop hole. Depending on how far away the third baseman is from the bag, the runner off third can get two, three, four, five extra steps. That's a really critical edge, especially with the contact play on, that you don't have with a right-handed hitter. Garcia hit a ground ball to the shortstop, and Freese, with a good break, scored the all-important add-on run.

Once again, the little things—bunting the runners over, making contact, getting a good jump—had produced a run. Some call it "small ball," but the runs we manufactured were big. In the National League you face one side or the other of this equation in a lot of games: *How to make one run. How to prevent one run.* Those two ideas are all-encompassing. The spring drills, the in-game strategy, and your postgame reflections are about how one run was made or how one run was stopped by both sides.

What we did in that inning was a perfect example of playing for one run, and it was the kind of play we'd practiced hard during spring training. In the American League, where the designated hitter rule makes conditions ripe for offense, teams tend not to emphasize those kinds of one-run plays. The potential for the crooked number, with another big bat in the lineup, dictates the strategy in the American League.

Milwaukee scored its first run in the fifth on a two-out single by Corey Hart. Hairston then singled, and Braun came to the plate representing the tying run. Garcia hadn't thrown that many pitches, sixty-eight, but we did have that issue in the first game of the series when Braun, who'd already hit a home run, then doubled off Jaime in a later at-bat. By getting Braun out, we'd have a three-run lead with four innings to play. I wasn't going to take the chance of a repeat. I brought in Dotel to face Braun. In eleven career at-bats against Dotel, Braun had struck out nine times. Not only did Dotel strike out Braun again to extricate us from that jam, but he gave us a flawless sixth too.

This move to Dotel highlighted how Dunc and I had shifted our approach: when in doubt, go with the bullpen. For us, doubt meant that we'd seen something different in the starter's demeanor, delivery, or pitches. At this stage in the year, the benefit of the doubt went to the reliever. That's how far the bullpen had come from the beginning of the season.

We had one additional tense moment, but Lynn pitched out of it in the seventh with a double-play ball to end the inning. We had scored another run off Greinke after two outs and nobody on in the sixth when Albert singled in Furcal to make the score 5–1. On the other side of the ball, we kept making good pitches when we really needed them. Lance gave up a couple of hits before retiring Braun, and then it was up to R-zep to take on Fielder. A three-run homer would make the score 5–4—instead, R-zep struck him out again.

In the eighth, we added on yet again, getting two insurance runs when Holliday doubled with two out. The offense was relentless, especially with two outs. Motte didn't need much else to sew things up. The bullpen allowed just two hits over the last four and a third innings to bring us one win away from the World Series.

With the way the Brewers had played in Miller Park, none of us thought that win would come easy. We didn't want to go to a seventh game. In spite of what I've said about how dramatic they can be and how fun they can be, a good old boring win to earn a trip to the

World Series would have been just fine with us. The off-day thought was that we wanted to impress upon everyone the urgency that we felt here. We knew that we had Carp if the NLCS went to seven games, but we also knew that having Carp go in Game 1 of the World Series would be a huge edge for us. During the workout, we made sure to remind the players of how good we'd feel if we were starting the World Series with Carp instead of him winning Game 7 of the NLCS. A lot of them probably recognized that without being reminded, but I've learned never to take anything for granted.

Our series clincher against the Brewers was the polar opposite of how we beat the Phillies to advance. Instead of a taut 1–0 pitchers' duel, the two teams combined for eighteen runs and six home runs. I made five pitching changes. That pushed the total for the series to twenty-eight. I didn't get shingles, as that Milwaukee fan hoped, but I did have sore legs from all the trips to the mound. The good thing was that, on my way out there, I always knew what was on the other side of it—I knew that I could trust the people who were waiting. Obviously, when neither team's starter lasts past the second inning, you're in a bullpen game.

In the top of the third, I pinch-hit Craig for Jackson, even though we were already up 7–4. Two runners were in scoring position, and with Jackson already on a short leash and the heart of their lineup due in their half, I thought it best to go with a better hitter and a fresh pitcher. Craig's pinch-hit single put the score at 9–4. I yelled, "Happy f——ingness." The boys laughed and I folded my arms and reset my scowl. We got twenty-one outs from our bullpen, with Salas going two innings, R-zep 2⅓, and Dotel, Lynn, and Motte going the rest of the way. Moves like that, and bullpen performances like that, show just how much the game has changed over the years.

Back in '83 with Chicago, Doug Rader, who was managing the Rangers at the time, commented on the fact that my club somehow found a way to win. We didn't always do it elegantly, or by the book, or by doing something that wound up on the highlight reels, but we won. Doug inadvertently gave that team its motto and Chicago embraced it: winning ugly.

I can honestly say that we didn't win Game 6 of the NLCS ugly. Just because you go to the bullpen a lot and your team's starters have a 7.03 ERA for the series doesn't mean that the games were awful to watch or that the performances were horrid. (That had a lot to do with the quality of the Brewers' hitters.) We won with everybody, and for a manager, that's a beautiful thing. We got contributions from so many different players, and I honestly believe that's the best way to do it. Maybe because I was such a borderline major league player myself, I like it when all twenty-five men on the roster do their part. The bullpen certainly deserves credit for contributing in a big way to our success against the Brewers. They went 3-0 with a 1.88 ERA in one out shy of twenty-nine innings. The bats may have put the runs on the board, but the bullpen made sure those runs were enough to win.

We got more outs from our relief corps than we did the rotation. After the series was over, someone told me that the Elias Sports Bureau had done some digging and learned that we were only the second team to do that in a six- or seven-game series. The first was the '79 Pirates against the Baltimore Orioles. And what was that Pirates team's signature line? Sister Sledge's "We Are Family." Funny that those Pirates were led by a slugging first baseman, and future Hall of Famer, Willie Stargell. We were also the first team to win a postseason series without a starter lasting past the fifth inning.

With the exception of Nick Punto, all the starting position players had at least one hit. The NLCS MVP was David Freese, who capped off a great series by going 3-for-4 with three RBIs and a home run in Game 6. For the series, those numbers added to his .545 average and total of nine RBIs and three home runs. He also had a ten-game postseason hitting streak going. Mark's work with David to get his front foot down sooner, so he could lever off it, had paid off. Mark had the insight; David had the ability. He demonstrated the quality that all high-average hitters and great run producers have. He got on a roll and he stayed hungry.

The Hall of Famer who was famous among his teammates for displaying this trait was the great Henry Aaron. When the A's traded me to the Braves in 1971—they needed Mudcat Grant more than me—I was the recipient of one of those great gifts that have marked my career. I got to be Henry Aaron's teammate. In one of my first weeks there, I was on the bench and heard someone say, "It's starting."

I asked what that meant.

"Hammer's getting hot."

They started making bets on the bench about how many line drives in a row Hank would get in consecutive at-bats.

I was asked to set the bar, being the new guy and all.

I did some quick calculations. I figured three games he could keep that up, so I said, "Eight."

They pelted me with sunflower seeds. They then made their calls, all of them in double digits.

I sat there thinking, *No way*.

The Aaron way.

This particular hot streak had him reach fifteen. That was fifteen consecutive plate appearances where he centered a ball flush on the barrel head.

I'm not saying that David Freese is Hank Aaron, but he's got a similar mentality.

The other thing about Hank was how humble he was and the degree to which he shared credit for his success with his teammates. David exhibited both in our NLCS celebration. On the podium, while accepting the award for being the Most Valuable Player in that series, he said, "I thought this should have gone to the bullpen."

That was a high-class and genuine statement. Sharing the spotlight like that made it clear to me that David would never win a "Dig Me Like I Dig Myself" award.

A bit of history here about the "Dig Me." A number of times

when athletes reach the highest level in professional sports, they can fall victim to all the compliments and special treatment many of them have received their whole athletic lives. We teach them to engage their ego but not to be egotistical as a way to be a key part of our club's success. Sometimes they cross the line and become arrogant and/or selfish. As a coaching staff, we've had to fight through that—get the guys back to ego but not egotistical. You can do it in ways that are subtle, direct, aggressive, or comical.

My comical choice for years has been to tell a player, usually within earshot of his teammates, about my "Dig Me" T-shirt. I tell them that it hangs in my locker and it says "Dig Me" on the front. Then I tell them that on the back it says "Like I Dig Myself."

So, whenever I see that arrogance, any hint of it, the "Dig Me" story comes out. Now that I'm retired, I can finally tell the truth. The "Dig Me" T-shirt doesn't really exist, though over the years guys have brought me various incarnations of it.

Albert was Albert, and his .478 average and nine RBIs and two home runs would have earned him MVP honors in most other series. Despite his finger issues, Matt Holliday wasn't far behind, hitting .435, with five RBIs and one home run. Up and down the lineup, the offense kept the pressure on. We'd talked before the series opener about making adjustments offensively, and we'd done just that. Of our big guns, Yadi and Albert had tied for the team lead against the Brewers during the regular season with seventeen hits in the eighteen games. In six NLCS games, Albert had eleven hits, Freese had twelve, and Holliday had ten. Freese hadn't hit a home run against them in the regular season and had driven in only two runs. A lot of credit has to go to Mark and to Mike Aldrete for giving the guys good intel, and even more credit has to go to the players for taking that information and making the necessary adjustments. Nothing is more satisfying to a staff than doing the review work, devising a workable plan, and seeing the guys executing on the field.

I wasn't going to tell them this next bit, mostly because we'd already talked about it so often. I wanted them to feel the significance of the moment, but have a plan for dealing with it. With the bat in your hand, think about how you're going to make something happen. Make it happen. Make it happen. Make it happen. I can't tell you how many times in my career, both as a player and as a manager, those words rang in my head. For years I had written those words, and others, on my lineup cards. Those little aphorisms, daily affirmations, or whatever you want to call them might seem hokey or over-romanticized in what is just, after all, a game.

That night in Milwaukee, as I waited my turn to take the podium for the postgame press conference, these words reverberated in my head: *We made it happen. We made it happen.*

As the guys celebrated and the champagne soaked us, I thought of that '83 Sox team again. Knowing that that was my first playoff experience, Greg "The Bull" Luzinski had said to me, "Skipper, you won't believe how fast this goes."

I planned to tell the guys that, but for now I wanted them to just let loose.

PART IV

In the eighth inning of Game 5, with the game and the Series tied at 2–2, right-hander Octavio Dotel took the mound. Texas had three right-handed hitters coming up in Michael Young, Adrian Beltre, and Nelson Cruz, then a left-handed hitter in David Murphy, then a right-hander in Mike Napoli and another left-hander in Mitch Moreland.

If Dotel could get three outs in a span of four hitters, that would be good.

I'd already worked out the "what-if" sequence an inning or so before. We had Rzepczynski, a left-hander, available to face the Texas left-handed batters. We also had Motte, our closer, who was very much rested at that point.

After Young doubled to lead off the inning, we had to get somebody up. They might get the runner to third base with Murphy coming up. I called to the bullpen, and I knew we had a problem, but it wasn't unexpected. When the hometown fans are excited, it gets loud and the bullpen phone is hard to hear. We had dealt with the same problem during the Philadelphia and Milwaukee series because the fans in those two stadiums are over and around the bullpen. In Arlington, the problem was more acute. The pen is set up vertically, with the mound nearest the field. That's from where the players and coaches watch the game. The problem is that the phone is back by the bullpen home plate and closer to the stands, making it hard to hear the ring and harder to hear the voice on the other end of it.

The phone rang and rang. Eventually our bullpen coach, Derek Lil-liquist, answered, and I told him, "Get R-zep up." I hesitated for a second and then said, "Get Motte going easy." In bullpen lingo that meant: get R-zep started and close to being ready to go in the game, but have Motte just loose enough so that when they got the next call he could really start to warm up in preparation to come in.

Dotel struck out Beltre. Cruz, who had just set a playoff record for home runs in the previous series, was next. I decided to walk him inten-tionally and bring in my lefty, Rzepczynski. As I walked to the mound, I pointed to my left arm and considered the next "what-if": would Murphy or a pinch hitter face R-zep? At the mound, Yadi and I talked about it, and it was clear that Murphy was staying in the game. I said, "You know, if we can get an out with this lefty, we can pitch around Napoli, who's been killing us, and force them to make a move with Moreland."

All the while, I was thinking Motte was up and playing catch.

R-zep got Murphy to hit a ground ball that looked like an inning-ending double play, but it deflected off R-zep's glove for an infield hit. It was one of those unique baseball plays reminding us that just a few scant inches can determine a good or bad result. In this case, bad for us—Texas had the bases full.

"Dunc. Tell Motte to get ready. We can stall."

Dunc reported back to me after his quick call. "Motte's not even throwing."

"What do you mean he's not throwing?"

"Nobody's up."

What the hell had happened? Could the crowd noise have been that loud? I knew that talking to Lilliquist had been like trying to talk through bad cell-phone reception. Was this going to cost us?

I thought we still were all right with R-zep against Napoli. Yadi knew what the drill was. We wanted the ball down in the strike zone with movement from either his sinker or his slider. The idea was to take advantage of Napoli's aggressiveness. I was a little hot at this point. We'd just missed a double play, and Motte wasn't ready, but I kept trying to churn out "what-ifs."

So I got back on the phone and said, "Get Motte going."

R-zep hung a slider, and Napoli doubled to drive in two runs. 4–2. I let R-zep pitch to Moreland, and he struck him out.

With Ian Kinsler coming up, I headed to the mound to replace R-zep. I waved to the bullpen for the right-hander, still kicking myself over the miscommunication but hopeful that Motte would put an end to this thing. I was talking with Yadi, trying to explain that I wasn't sure why Motte hadn't been throwing, but "he's in now," I said. "Let's get the third out." In thirty-two-plus seasons, I managed more than 5,000 major league games. I probably changed pitchers 15,000 times. But on 14,999 of those occasions I knew when I went out there who I was taking out and who I was bringing in.

When I looked up, Lance Lynn was standing there waiting for me to hand him the ball. The same Lance Lynn who'd thrown forty-seven pitches in Game 3 and who was only to be used in an emergency.

I looked at him and asked, "What are you doing here?"

"What?" he answered with a puzzled look.

Immediately, I started my mind scramble. There was only one thing to do. I couldn't risk an injury to Lynn. I hesitated for a moment before handing the ball to Lance. According to the rules, Lance had to face one hitter. So I told him to take his warm-up pitches and then intentionally walk Kinsler. He responded with the same puzzled look and the same one word—"What?"

I couldn't decide whether to stay pissed or laugh. I almost went with the punch line when you're asked a number of "whats"—"What, hell, I'm no lightbulb." I passed on the humor, thinking, if we started laughing on the mound, it would confirm the belief of all those who insisted that the only explanation for these bullpen moves had to be the gamblers getting to me. Instead, I explained to him that this was not an emergency and I wasn't going to risk him stressing his arm needlessly.

I walked to the dugout wondering if the so-called Father of the Modern Bullpen had just cost us a game and possibly the Series. Would I go down in history being remembered among fans and my peers sarcastically as the guy who created the intentional walk specialist for the nonwalk situation?

As soon as I got to the dugout, I told Motte (I hoped) to get ready. The intentional walk seemed like a strange strategy to many, but my trip to remove Lynn and bring in Motte was by far the weirdest and most awkward moment of my career. The walk back to the dugout was even worse. All I could hope was that my teammates would pick me up in the ninth inning. Surely, there were no more surprises left.

CHAPTER NINETEEN

Back Again

THERE'S NOTHING QUITE LIKE GOING TO YOUR FIRST WORLD Series—this is true whether that first trip is as a manager or simply as a fan. My first trip was spent watching from the stands.

In 1979, the year I had managed all of fifty-four games as an in-season replacement and had won exactly half of them, Roland Hemond asked me to attend the Series with him. Roland had a policy of sportsmanship that we had to make an appearance at the World Series to congratulate the league champions. By that point, Bill Veeck felt that I'd shown enough to be hired for the next season. Going to the World Series was both a reward and a kind of graduate school seminar on baseball.

Thinking back on that first trip, it was ironic that in 2011 our bullpen had just tied a record held by the '79 Pittsburgh Pirates, since they had played the Orioles in that World Series. Obviously, we weren't the only baseball people at the games. Major League Baseball hosted executives, scouts, and managers from all the teams, put us up in the same hotel, and provided us with transportation to and from the games. That was nice, but it was also in some senses horrifying for a newbie like me. I sat there among baseball men with hundreds of years of experience between them and listened as the game and the managerial decisions of two legends, Chuck Tanner of the Pirates and Earl Weaver of the Orioles, were discussed. Actually, it wasn't like a grad school seminar—it was more like a cross between analyzing a law school mock trial and observing an operation while sitting above an operating room theater in medical school.

These guys debated, cross-examined, laid out their exhibits from A to Z, and called in expert witnesses (mostly themselves) in looking at every nuance of the choices the two clubs' leaders were making. They also incised, resected, and grafted while performing a playectomy on every pitch. I sat there mute, wondering, *Holy crap—could I ever survive this kind of scrutiny?* It was only after I finally made it to my first postseason in '83 and we lost to the Orioles in the ALCS that I got my answer. That year we lost in four games, though our elimination game became a classic: we went 0–0 through nine innings, only to lose in the tenth. Despite the disappointment, I learned several things in that series, but perhaps most important, I realized that concentrating totally on what the job requires is the only way any manager can ever handle the pressure of his peers' intense evaluation.

I knew that, as a young manager, I lacked expertise and experience. I had been a position player, and despite how closely I observed games and asked questions about pitchers and pitching, my knowledge of that area was still a deficit for me. The only thing that would make up for that was more experience, more observing, and more questioning. The same is true with a pitcher-turned-manager—that kind of manager is going to be less comfortable making offensive decisions. Fortunately, you don't have to have extensive experience in all phases of the game. That's why you have other coaches on your staff.

As much as all of them contributed, I knew from the earliest days of my career that I was the one who had to make the decisions—all of them and all of the time. That's what I was paid to do, and if my ass and my job were going to be on the line based on those decisions, then I wasn't going to turn them over to anyone else. That's just the reality of being a manager in the big leagues. That's the ideal "take charge" attitude that fits your responsibility as a major league manager. If at first you're not ready, then learn as fast as you can.

Besides expertise and experience, another thing you need in order to make decisions and manage is the courage of your conviction. To be honest, I don't know where I got that from. In 1980, when I was thirty-five years old and had still less than a season's worth of experience under my belt, the Baltimore Orioles came into town fresh off that crushing loss in the '79 Series. Earl Weaver, who was twelve years into his initial fourteen-year run as the Orioles' skipper, after eleven and a half seasons managing in the minors, was well known for his baseball acumen and his temper. Before the first game of the series, the Orioles were scheduled to take their batting practice at 5:15 P.M. Roger Bossard, Chicago's legend of a groundskeeper, came to me before that and said that we should bag batting practice. The field was too wet from the rain that had been moving through. We informed the Orioles through the proper channels, and I thought that was that—no BP for either team. At about 5:20, one of our coaches told me that Earl Weaver had confronted a member of the grounds crew, saying that since the rain had stopped, he wanted the tarp off the field and the batting cage rolled out. Earl made it clear that it had to be done.

What could they do in the face of that except do what Weaver demanded and then inform me? I stomped out of my office, feeling like my head was going to explode. I charged out onto the field, where the Orioles were already hitting, and yelled at their batting practice pitcher to stop. When he didn't, I ran out to the protective screen in front of the pitcher waving my arms. There I was, standing between the hitter and the pitcher, going off on them while their BP pitcher gave it right back to me. Now I was really pissed. I told them if we couldn't take batting practice, then neither could they. No batting practice meant no batting practice.

I told the grounds crew to roll the cage back out behind the center-field fence. I stood right where I had been, my fists thrust into my back pockets, my temples throbbing, and my jaw clenched. As the Orioles walked off the field, some thought I was nuts, and a few guys said something to the effect that Earl was going to have my ass for this one. I didn't care.

What they'd done was push several of my buttons. First, they violated my sense of fairness. If *we* couldn't hit before the game, *they* shouldn't hit before the game. They'd also taken a shot at our status—we're *the* Orioles, and you're the White Sox. Forget that shit. More than anything else, though, I knew this: I was responsible for everything that went on as it related to the playing of the game on that day. They tried to take advantage of the members of our family, the grounds crew, and that wasn't going to fly even if they were Orioles. Sitting here today, thinking about my reaction that day, I can see that they were right. I was nuts. But I understand why I acted as I did.

Over the years I was involved in a bunch of situations like this one—some of them this confrontational, others less so. They had several common denominators: *taking the responsibility I was entrusted with seriously; reducing the issue as best I could to what was right versus what was wrong; and mostly, knowing there was always a score at the end of the game and we were trying to have more runs than the other side.*

WE'D DONE MORE THAN OKAY SINCE THEN, AND WITH THE OPENING game of the World Series set to begin two days after we'd eliminated the Brewers, we had some work to do. While we hadn't had to do extra preparation work for the Phillies and Brewers, because we'd played them so much during the season and not long before the playoffs began, there was a big difference in preparing for the Texas Rangers in the World Series, because we hadn't played them in years.

Two days wasn't a lot of time for either club to prepare, but the thrill of being in the Series offset any fatigue we might have experienced.

Since the Rangers were not a familiar opponent, we really went after any video of their hitters and pitchers we could look at. For several years, we had been relying on Chad Blair's video analysis for our regular-season opponents. We had another important advantage—Dunc's pitching and defense charts. All the information that Dunc supplied from his meticulously kept charts and sophisticated categories fit well with the current look we were taking from the videos.

Although we refrained from contacting any American League friends—to avoid any conflicts of interest—we did have advance scouting reports. Mo had assigned Matt Slater to set up a number of scouting pairs for the various playoff teams and contenders. Mike Juhl and Bill Gayton handled the Rangers for us.

Dunc took charge of formulating our plan to face the Ranger hitters. He identified the most dangerous area to stay out of with each hitter and other vulnerabilities. On game days, we would share this information with the starter in person, then give the relievers an oral report in a separate meeting. We'd all heard so much about Elvis Andrus, Michael Young, Ian Kinsler, Josh Hamilton, Adrian Beltre, and Mike Napoli, but it was Nelson Cruz who'd had a breakout performance against the Tigers in the ALCS. He'd gone 1-for-15 in the first round, but then hit .364 with six home runs, driving in thirteen. He was hot coming in obviously, so we had a look to see his at-bats against the Tigers. David Murphy, another lesser-known Ranger, had gotten seven hits in seventeen at-bats. These Rangers were a potent offensive club.

Up and down the lineup, they really took healthy swings. If our pitchers kept their deliveries on the edges of the plate, changed speeds with those pitches, and mixed location, up and especially down and in and out, the Rangers' hitters would react like any other good hitters. It would be tough for them to center balls if our pitcher messed with their balance and timing. That would be important against a club that had hit just slightly over .300 with runners in scoring position against Detroit.

We also had the advantage of having watched the Rangers and Detroit play on television. Their games often played on our days off or at different game times from ours. Even though the last game of that series was very one-sided—Texas won 15–5—we felt we got an unintentional assist from the Tigers in being able to watch them pitch against Texas. Detroit pitched a lot of that series very effectively against a very dangerous lineup.

Our hitters had access to the scouts' written report on the Rangers' pitching staff to complement the meetings led by Mark McGwire and Mike Aldrete. During the regular season, the hitters could study all their own at-bats against a particular team's starters or relievers. We didn't do that with the Rangers because we didn't have guys with a whole lot of at-bats against any of their pitchers. Before each game, the hitters got a more detailed review of the Rangers' staff.

Generally, their starters—C. J. Wilson, Colby Lewis, Matt Harrison, and Derek Holland—had live arms but had combined for an 0-2 record in the ALCS. Their bullpen had a good right-hand and left-hand mix. Their two right-handers (Scott Feldman and Mark Lowe) and two left-handers (Darren Oliver and Mike Gonzalez) fit well with their three late-inning specialists—Mike Adams, Alexi Ogando, and Neftali Feliz, the closer. Like our previous playoff series, their bullpen got a fair amount of work and did well. The starters went 28.2 innings, while the bullpen went 26.1 innings. Matt Harrison was the only starter who got out of the Tigers series with an ERA below 4.0. Just as we looked for vulnerabilities and tendencies in their hitters, we did the same with the pitchers, and so we looked closely at those numbers.

Although the numbers said that this was likely to be a high-scoring series, they didn't—and couldn't—take into account a couple of things. First, lack of familiarity works in the pitcher's favor.

Second, this was the World Series, and how guys would perform with so much on the line wasn't something that any metric could predict. That was the human equation—and it was what made the games worth playing.

Today you can get a lot of information from different statistical services. This is helpful in all phases, including the running game. But you have to be careful with raw numbers: the total number of stolen bases, for instance, doesn't accurately account for how the bases were stolen. Sometimes a team might have put on the hit-and-run, and other times it might have been a straight steal. Those differences won't show up on the stats.

More than anything else, the intelligence you tried to gather on the running game was the situation and counts when they were likely to put a runner in motion. Kinsler and Andrus, the two hitters at the top of their order, were more likely to straight steal. The Rangers didn't hit-and-run much, not with Josh Hamilton and the rest of their bashers to follow.

We felt we had a good to very good defense against the running game. We had Molina's great throwing arm, and we had a bunch of pitchers who had good moves to first base and were capable of improving their release times to the plate. We felt it would be important to neutralize their running game, because stolen bases were not featured in our offense. An added deterrent was that three of their four starters were left-handed, and they generally do a better job of holding runners close. However, our run-manufacturing game stressed hit-and-runs and good baserunning. We were above-average in these areas in 2011. Their catcher, Mike Napoli, was a plus offensively with thirty home runs, but didn't possess as strong an arm as Yadi's.

Another edge we had was home-field advantage—thanks to Prince Fielder of Milwaukee, who homered in the All-Star Game to give the National League the victory. *If* necessary, Games 6 and 7 would be at our place. We had our rotation set through the first four games while remaining flexible and able to adjust as the Series continued. Carp would open Game 1, followed by Garcia, Lohse, and Jackson.

Our immediate concern, obviously, was the opening game of the Series. Despite our success in bouncing back from game 1 losses, we didn't want to put ourselves in that hole. Even if we didn't know recent history—the winner of Game 1 had gone on to win the World Series seven of the last eight times, twelve of the previous fourteen, and nineteen of the last twenty-three—we wanted to establish ourselves early in the game and early in the Series, especially at home.

The magic number for official team meetings is six—three during the season and one before each playoff series. You only get to six if you reach the World Series. Interestingly, since our first meeting before opening day, this meeting before the World Series was only our second meeting at home.

As we usually did, we held the off-day meeting in the clubhouse dining room. I liked the idea of being in a smaller setting where we were surrounded by team photos of winning celebrations—graphic proof that the real fun of competing was winning. Surrounded by photos of Ozzie Smith hitting a playoff-game-winning home run against the Dodgers (the picture was so vivid I could almost hear echoes of Jack Buck's call, "Go crazy, folks. Go crazy. The Cardinals have won on a home run by the Wizard!"); David Eckstein about to be mobbed by his teammates after a 2005 grand slam; the guys in the clubhouse after the 2006 World Series win; Bob Gibson delivering a pitch in gaining his seventh straight Series win. Seeing those images made you want to add even more to that stirring Cardinal tradition.

As was the case before the NLDS and the NLCS, our staff felt that asking this club to push harder, dig deeper, and care more was the wrong message. We all agreed that this team remained focused on playing as hard and as well as they could and possessed a confidence that was hard to beat. The meeting would be brief and would include only a handful of points.

Since I had been taught to speak carefully, I had always taken time to think through and prepare my comments. I'd tried to keep them in the ten-minute range. Once I'd made my remarks, we'd move on, and I wouldn't give it too much more thought going forward. But sometimes I would remember the effect my words had. Sometimes those words did what I'd hoped, and sometimes they didn't. One case of each sprang to mind.

In any season, game, or in life, I'd rather start bad and end better than vice versa; unfortunately, in the 1990 postseason with the A's, the good speech came before the ALCS against the Red Sox. I set a proper tone by referencing what the Red Sox had been saying about us, that they had more competitive heart than we did. That was an easy chip to place on our shoulders because we had gone through a lot to win 103 games.

The bad speech came before we played the Reds in the World Series after sweeping the Red Sox for our third straight AL pennant. On the day before Game 1, I spoke before our workout and did not feel a response from the players. We walked onto the field as defending World Champions who were more interested in "digging ourselves." Lou Piniella's Reds were much hungrier than we were. Later, after much soul-searching, I realized that I hadn't lit a fire under the guys—we played with little passion. I totally mugged the message that would have made us more competitive. I should have challenged them. We had a chance to make history by repeating as World Champions. History would have trumpeted their egos. I had the example to follow with Vince Lombardi challenging his Green Bay Packers to win their historic third straight championship.

I could have thrown down the gauntlet; instead Lou's "Nasty Boys" bullpen and the rest of their talented squad swept us.

Our 1988 and 1990 World Series losses haunt me more from a manager's perspective than from any other. That '88 squad resisted, during the week off between winning the pennant and starting the World Series, our attempts to keep their intensity level up in the mid-week workouts. I didn't push them and we wound up losing our timing edge—pitches that would have been hammered were being fouled off. We lost the championship. We weren't about to lose that edge again in '89 by making that same mistake. Our pre-Series workouts included some intense intra-squad games prior to taking on the Giants. For the last one, Eck was scheduled to pitch the very last inning, and in it he drilled Canseco. That brought an end to the workout, but the mystery of Eck's intent still goes on.

It's always good to feel better as you approach the end. I can't remember feeling better about a postgame meeting than after the 2006 NLCS Game 6 loss to the Mets with Carp starting. With our Game 5 win in St. Louis, we set ourselves up to win the NL behind Carp and avoid Game 7. The atmosphere in the clubhouse was funereal. I had to say something. It just clicked as I walked into the clubhouse. Rather than brood on the Game 6 loss, I started describing the exciting experience of playing a sudden-death Game 7 for the National League championship and a World Series ticket. We had all dreamed about playing in, starring in, and winning that game. That was an opportunity to treasure forever. That would only be possible if each of us did all we could to prepare and then compete with no regrets afterward. I asked several veterans who'd previously won a Game 7 to speak—Rolen, Pujols, Scott Spiezio, and Eckstein. I closed with this advice: Do whatever you need to do to get ready. If that means stay out all night in the City That Never Sleeps, then go for it.

Given all that history, what an ironic end to my career list of official meetings that the 2011 speech before Game 1 went, maybe, five minutes. I repeated the tickets and media cautions. Then I added one piece: I asked all first-time World Series participants to stand. We had a bunch. My advice to them and to everyone else was that each of us could 100 percent compete at our highest level and still pause for a moment from time to time to take in the incredible World Series scene. I encouraged them to consciously take a mental break to understand why the Fall Classic is like playing on Fantasy Island forever. Then we could go back to the first game of their lives—and the last game of my life—as Game 7 players.

Game 1 was played under fairly ideal conditions for mid-October. A twenty-mile-an-hour wind that swirled around the park made it important for the position players to keep checking the flags. After the ceremonial first pitches were thrown out by Bob Gibson, Bruce Sutter, and Adam Wainwright—the pitchers who recorded the final out in the Cardinals' four most recent World Series wins—it was time to have at it.

CHAPTER TWENTY

Run Not Hide

TEAMS WANT TO SET THE TONE EARLY IN A BALL GAME. WINNING a game often means being ready to play the first three innings, and while people usually think of this as applying to the offensive side of the game, it actually works both ways. Defensive readiness is just as important. The efforts in the top of the first inning by Yadi and Carp were as important to the eventual outcome as any other play in the game.

Game 1 began with Carp falling behind the Rangers' leadoff hitter, Ian Kinsler, 2-0. Early in the game, you might be tempted to take a strike or work a walk, but Kinsler, just like we would have tried to do, remained aggressive. It paid off for him on an infield hit after he really hustled down the line. The Rangers got even more aggressive when, with the count 1-0, Kinsler broke for second on a hit-and-run. Andrus swung through a tough pitch to hit, a cutter down and away, and Yadi made a great transition to throwing and nailed Kinsler. We'd countered their aggressive move with a great defensive play. Then, with nobody on, Andrus grounded a ball to Albert Pujols behind first, and Albert fed Carp at the bag. But Carp had to reach for the throw and ended up diving face-first, glove-first, into the bag for the out. If there was a signature defensive play in the World Series, that was it.

Not the way you usually think of setting the tone, but that depends on what kind of song you want to play. The lyrics to this particular refrain were: "You want it. We want it. Who's going to get it?"

On that attempted hit-and-run, I hadn't pitched out. Carp is quick to the plate and doesn't need a slide step. This was just pure outstanding execution by two top-tier players. Much was made in the first game about the chess match between Ron Washington and me, but that analogy falls far short. In chess the pieces are restricted in the movements they can make. They have no minds, no will, no capabilities of their own. Sure, as managers we make moves, but then we have to sit back and watch the players determine the outcome. If I was enjoying a good run as a manager into and through the postseason, that was because of what the players did. I frequently rolled the dice, and the guys came up with the 7 or the 11 that made us winners.

Thanks to Yadi, Carp got out of the inning, despite falling behind each of the first three hitters he faced. In the second, he worked carefully around the white-hot Nelson Cruz to issue a walk and then retired the next seven in a row to get us to our half of the fourth in a scoreless game. That inning, we caught a couple of breaks. Albert got hit on the foot on a C. J. Wilson breaking ball to lead off the inning. Matt Holliday went the other way and doubled to right field. Berkman punched a fastball away that snuck past Michael Young at first, and we were up 2–0.

Taking the mound after taking the lead, Carp is usually outstanding at executing one of the basics of winning pitching—the shutdown inning right after your team scores. The teaching key is to concentrate completely on getting that leadoff hitter. This time, though, the credit went to the Rangers. In the top of the fifth, they also got their leadoff man on, and after Carp struck out Cruz, Mike

Napoli hit a fastball up and out over the plate deep to right. The score was tied.

I can't say for certain that Yadi's throw in the top of the first or Carp's quick delivery times to the plate influenced the Rangers' strategy, but in their half of the sixth, with the score still tied, Kinsler was on first again with nobody out. They elected to lay down a sacrifice bunt rather than try the straight steal or the hit-and-run. The sacrifice worked to get Kinsler to second base, and with Hamilton coming up, we knew this was going to be a crucial test.

If you're looking for a classic example of Tom Seaver's belief that not all outs are the same and that a few in each game are more crucial than the rest, then Carp facing Hamilton and Young with the go-ahead run on second base is one of the better ones. First, Carp retired Hamilton on a fly-out, and then he stranded Kinsler at third to preserve the tie. Albert's diving play to snare Michael Young's sharp grounder with two outs once again proved why he is such a fine athlete. When the ball left the bat, you could feel the atmosphere change in our dugout, with all the guys thinking the tie was broken. Seeing Albert laid out in full extension had me thinking of his wrist, but I knew he wasn't thinking about his health at all—just getting the out. Having taken away one of their chances made us even more eager to push one across ourselves and grab momentum by the throat. By retiring their number three and four hitters, Carp had put himself in a position to earn the win, as long as we could hold on.

As they had for weeks, our players found a way to make something good happen at the plate. With one out, David Freese continued his hot streak, doubling off the wall in deep right-center to extend his postseason hitting streak to eleven games. During Yadi's at-bat, Freese advanced to third on a wild pitch; after Yadi's strikeout, Nick Punto, our eighth-place hitter, stepped to the plate. We had Carp take his place in the on-deck circle. The inning before, I'd done my "what-ifs" and decided that if we had runners on, I'd pinch-hit with Craig when Carp's spot came up. Allen is a very patient and smart hitter, and against the left-hander Wilson, he was one of several righties we had available coming off the bench. As he had proven in the deciding NLCS game against the Brewers, Allen is also a good pinch hitter, especially in an RBI situation—equally dangerous against pitchers throwing from either side. Craig executed the two-strikes-against approach very well.

Of course, in that situation you're not going to give your opposition a "tell" by sending a pinch hitter out there to the on-deck circle. Ron Washington was prepared for the possibility of us hitting for Carp. He had Alexi Ogando, their fireballing starter-turned-reliever, up and ready. Possibly they hoped to force Carp out of the game because Wilson seemed to unintentionally intentionally walk Punto. Four straight were well wide of the plate, including a couple of curveballs that bounced and came dangerously close to getting away and bringing home the lead run. If that was one of those kinds of walks, then they were treading a fine line.

In any case, when Craig was announced as the pinch hitter, Ron Washington went out to get Wilson and to bring in his right-hander with the live arm who'd been sensational in their series against Detroit and Tampa Bay. In those two series combined, Ogando had pitched 10.1 innings and given up only one run on four hits. He's one of those guys with explosive stuff. With him in the game, we could have gone with a left-handed hitter off the bench, Descalso or Schumaker, but I believed Craig was the right man in the right spot. As hard as Ogando throws, and with the kind of movement he has, there's not as much of a "percentage" advantage in having a left-hander up there as there is with a guy who might come after you with breaking balls or change-of-speed pitches. Besides, Allen was our guy; we were going to stick with him and ignore the book. He'd hit .315 in the regular season with a .555 slugging percentage. In the postseason, he was only 4-for-18 (.222), but numbers don't tell the whole story.

Allen, anticipating that he might be used, had gone into the batting cage inside Busch to take swings. Mike Aldrete was preparing him for his potential at-bat. He was already thinking along with us, getting himself prepared. That's what a professional hitter does. While he was certainly cheerleading on the bench, he wasn't just sitting there getting caught up in what was happening in the moment. He was thinking about how he could make something happen.

And then he went out and did.

He fell behind 1-2 and switched to his two-strike approach. He got his lead foot down sooner, shortened his stroke, and took a ninety-eight-mile-an-hour fastball into right field, just in front of Nelson Cruz, for a base hit. Allen's fist pumps at first were trumped by the buzz in the dugout. Later we'd learn that this was the first game-winning RBI pinch-hit in the World Series since Gibson's home run against the A's in 1988. It was also Allen's second consecutive run-producing pinch-hit. But who cared about history right then? We still had nine outs to get.

Since we were young in the bullpen, with the exception of the veterans Dotel, Rhodes, and Westbrook, I was hoping our first bullpen challenge would have included a lead of several runs and just a few outs to get. This being the World Series, I wanted them to get an introductory appearance before the real pressure began. I should have known better. All year long the pressure had been unrelenting—just because we were at the end didn't mean that would stop. And so our bullpen was tasked with protecting a one-run lead through the final three innings.

I chose Salas to start the seventh with two right-handers in Beltre and Cruz coming up. He got Beltre, but the still-sizzling Cruz singled, and after a walk to Napoli, Salas was done. Time for "Scrabble," as the alphabetically complex Rzepczynski was sometimes referred to. This was an easy one. R-zep wasn't likely to face Murphy, their left-handed-hitting outfielder, who I figured they'd pinch-hit for. That was okay with me. As I've pointed out before, that's the plus-value of R-zep. He can get the righties out just as effectively. They countered with Craig Gentry, with runners on first and second. R-zep struck him out.

Esteban German, who'd seen limited action with only eleven at-bats in the regular season, came up to hit for Ogando. We had faced him in Kansas City and knew he had a good base-hit stroke to all fields. R-zep put him away on three quality pitches down and in and out of the zone.

Six outs to go. Six very tough outs. Dotel faced the top of the lineup and retired Kinsler and Andrus; then Rhodes came in to get Hamilton to end the eighth inning. The ninth belonged to Motte, who technically still hadn't been named our closer, though he'd been playing that role for quite a while. The way Dunc and I figured it, Motte was in a groove and distracting him by asking him or compli-menting him about that pivotal role was taking an unnecessary risk. At this point, it was academic. Having a one-run lead and needing three outs to close out your team's win is a distraction no matter what the job title. Motte joined his bullpen mates and worked a hit-less inning. We were up 1–0 in the World Series. What better early-Series message could we send than this: our bullpen was going to be a weapon again.

We couldn't have known it then, but a tone was in the process of being set. Good pitching will get out good hitting. We'd seen an excellent example of that in the first game, one that solidified the im-pression that despite how talented the two clubs were offensively, we might be in for a low-scoring series if the pitchers were sharp.

The trend continued the next night when Jaime Garcia returned to his early-season form in a precision performance, going seven in-nings and allowing only three hits and one walk while striking out seven. The only problem was that, up until the bottom of the sev-enth, Colby Lewis was matching him pitch for pitch. I was thrilled to see Jaime enjoying that kind of success. I knew that it had been hard on him to get the early hook and not perform up to his level of expectation.

In the lead-up to the game, I'd sought him out a couple of times, just to check in with him to see how he was doing. Jaime's from Reynosa, Mexico, but grew up in Texas. As we talked, we slipped into and out of Spanish and English. I'm not completely calculating when I do this, it just comes naturally to someone who's bilingual. Having these shared languages helps with personalizing—it establishes another point of commonality with some of the players, just as anyone would look for in getting to know another person. I knew Jaime was disappointed in himself at times and feeling like he was disappointing the club. But he also knew that we would not have gotten there without him.

I'd seen that a television crew from Mexico had been interviewing him, focusing on the fact that he was the first Mexican-born pitcher to start a World Series game since Fernando Valenzuela had done that for the Dodgers. In fact, I'd been able to speak Spanish to Mexican radio and TV to praise Jaime's first two years. All the attention on him was especially stressful because he had a country full of fans pulling for him and watching intently. In today's public climate, any player with a story is subject to excessive praise or criticism, and that makes our emphasis on embracing pressure and focusing on process particularly important ways of dealing with the extra attention. Everyone has to tune out fans, country, family, and friends. No one is immune. Work the process—that's the key to coping.

In Game 2, Jaime was firmly planted back in the place he'd been at the beginning of the year. A walk and a hit in the fourth were the first runners he allowed, after two were out (a case of a pitcher maybe relaxing a bit after cruising through several innings and getting one out away from being back in the dugout). This was the only real trouble he'd been in all night.

As Yogi Berra once famously said, it was déjà vu all over again in our half of the seventh. With one out, Freese singled, and after another out, Punto came to bat and also singled. I went with Craig again in place of Garcia, knowing that we couldn't wait for another scoring opportunity. In came Ogando for Colby Lewis. Craig was on Ogando's first fastball, but fouled it off. Ogando rushed another one up there, and same as before, Craig got that foot down early, went with a fastball low and on the outside corner, and lined it into right-center field.

The score was 1–0 as we went into the eighth. Salas and R-zep did their thing in the top of the inning, each striking out one and R-zep getting a ground ball out. To that point, we'd had some outstanding pitching in the game. The bottom of the eighth brought the other element of the low-scoring pitchers' game into focus. With one out, Albert smoked a Mike Adams pitch into deep right field. Nelson Cruz made a fine running catch with his back against the wall to prevent an extra-base hit.

That catch was just one of several nice defensive plays the Rangers made that night. In the bottom of the fifth, we'd had a two-out rally going after Punto singled to right and Jaime walked. Furcal came up in that spot and did his job, hitting a screamer up the middle that bounced once and was actually going past a diving Elvis Andrus, who caught the ball behind him. He then flipped the ball out of his glove to Kinsler, covering second, to end the inning. It was a tremendous play, one that I reviewed after the game as I looked at a few of the things the Rangers had done earlier in the game to stop us from scoring.

None of that would have mattered if we'd done our job perfectly in the ninth. That's the thing about 1–0 games—you have no margin for error. Ian Kinsler, down 0-2, hit a Motte pitch that was down but tailed back over the plate too much, off the end of the bat, blooping one just barely out of the reach of Furcal and the outfielders. Then, with Andrus at the plate and the count 1-1, Kinsler stole second base. Yadi delivered a laser right on the bag, but Kinsler was in there by a microsecond. I use that measurement intentionally.

Both our side and theirs had Jason Motte on the clock to measure the time it took him to get the ball to home plate—from the time he went into his delivery after having set to the moment when the ball reached Yadi's glove. A delivery time of 1.3 seconds is usually fast enough to prevent a steal. Motte has two deliveries from the stretch. One is a tick slower than acceptable at 1.4 seconds. He uses that delivery when he needs more stuff and command. He also has a 1.2 time that is excellent; combined with his excellent quick pickoff move, it makes him hard to run on. On the first pitch he delivered to Andrus, a high fastball, he was at 1.4. Andrus was bunting, but took ball one.

We knew that Texas had to put on some kind of play. Hit-and-run. Bunt. Bunt-and-run. Straight steal. If the guy's going to bunt, you want the ball up in the zone. Great bunters will always get the bat above the ball and kind of catch it with the bat, not jabbing at it but bringing the bat back toward the catcher. That's harder to do on a high pitch, and you can get a lot of popped-up bunts, bunts fouled off, or bunts missed because of a high pitch. That's also a great pitch for a catcher to throw on. More frequently, that poor bunt attempt occurs when the pitch is out of the zone. The other danger is that some umpires won't give you the high strike, so anything up might result in the pitch being called a ball.

With a 1.4 delivery time, though, you're in the "stealable" range. The Rangers knew it, and we knew it. To counter their advantage, we had two options: throw over to first or pitch out. For the throw-over, we have a sign for one of two options: the normal throw-over, and the best shot. That move is always followed by a quicker delivery home—about 1.2 seconds. Motte has a very good best-shot move. He's got quick feet and a quick release. I didn't want him to show Kinsler that one yet. Picking him off would be great, but we really wanted to shorten his lead or decrease his jump.

I gave Motte the normal throw-over sign.

In this case, you hope to accomplish something else. Often, upon seeing any movement from the pitcher, a hitter who is supposed to bunt will "show" the bunt. He'll start to square around and bring the bat into bunting position early. Andrus showed, just as he'd done with the first pitch.

On the next pitch, I didn't flash any sign, and Motte came to the plate. Andrus showed bunt again and fouled off the pitch. The time was 1.4 again.

I had a dilemma.

At this point, Kinsler had seen only the normal throw-over move after the 1-0 pitch. If we had come back with that really good snap throw, there's no doubt in my mind that that would have shortened Kinsler's lead. It might even have picked him off—who knows?

The problem with having Motte do that, though, was that I would be telling him, in essence, that he needed to speed up his delivery to the plate. A common bad side effect of the pitcher speeding up his delivery to the plate is that he leaves the ball up in the strike zone. Again, the possibility of that pitch being called a ball comes into play.

So I was thinking to myself, *Do I want Motte to speed up his delivery to the plate if they're trying to give us an out by sacrificing with Andrus? What if the next pitch is a ball, moving the count to 2-1, which is often the best hit-and-run count? Then, if Motte speeds up his delivery to make the count 3-1, he could be in danger of walking Andrus to put two runners on with nobody out.*

We had thrown out Kinsler trying to steal in the first inning of the first game, but that was with a release time better than 1.4 seconds. Also, I didn't think they were going to try to steal second with Kinsler on a 1-1 count. A bunt seemed more likely.

I decided that they wouldn't risk a steal, so I didn't flash the sign for Motte's best-shot pickoff move. I weighed preventing the steal against throwing a strike and taking the out the Rangers were trying to give us. I was wrong.

Kinsler stole second on the next pitch, and now the tying run was in scoring position with nobody out. I don't know how the inning would have played out if I'd defended that steal better. I do know that I didn't and it directly impacted the outcome.

At least the pitch was a strike that put Motte ahead 1-2, but he wasn't able to put Andrus away. He singled to right-center. I was thinking that they would end up with runners on the corners, but Kinsler went to third and came around the bag. He appeared trapped there for an instant, but the throw back in from the outfield ticked off the glove of Pujols, who was in cutoff position, and not only did Kinsler get back to third, but Andrus got to second with nobody out. Our execution on the outfield relay was faulty, and it set them up for the tying and go-ahead runs if they executed.

Now we were in it pretty deep. No one out, runners on second and third. What I said about legitimate closers being your go-to guys in any situation doesn't apply here. This is no knock on Jason Motte. He'd been closing for us for only a short time. He had all the tools to become that kind of go-to pitcher, but to get there he needed more experience. In the World Series, you can't use the philosophy of "lose a game now if it will give you the opportunity to win more later." This is one of those catch-22s we all face in life. How are you going to get experience in these kinds of situations if no one gives you the opportunity? The thing is, Jason did get that experience in Game 1 when he was given another one-run lead to protect.

What I also had to consider was that Josh Hamilton, a left-hander, was coming up next. All things regarding Motte and his experience were trumped by this. I liked the matchup of the lefty Rhodes against the lefty Hamilton. Hamilton handles the fastball well, and that's Motte's out pitch. What I was hoping we could do was get an out without that runner on second getting to third. I'd take our chances having a tied game, believing we could score in the ninth.

Things didn't work out for us, but they worked out exactly right for the Rangers. Hamilton not only hit a sac fly but hit it deep enough into right field that Andrus got to third. Michael Young executed well and drove another fly ball deep enough off Lynn to score Andrus.

It ended 2–1.

Motte and I talked afterward. He needed to hear from me that nothing had changed. The next ninth-inning save situation would be his. The way the inning played out, I felt Rhodes was a better bet to pitch to Hamilton. I just repeated that closing is a tough job. Look around every day and you'll see that some closers struggle. In the end you need to be tough to handle coming into a situation and dealing with the ups and downs. I had no doubt Motte was tough enough.

In the final analysis, the Rangers executed better than we did a couple of times. Tip your cowboy hat to them. With the Series even, we were headed to Texas.

CHAPTER TWENTY-ONE

The Middle on the Road

Y FAMILY AND I ALL LOVE MUSIC. LIVE IF WE CAN GET IT, RE-corded if we can't. In fact, as I sit here reviewing this material on another searing hot day in Northern California, I've taken my break from working a couple of times to talk to the manager of the band Nickelback. Elaine loves rock, and she's hoping I can get some tickets for her. My efforts got my mind on music, and I started to think about the 2011 World Series in its entirety. In a way, it was like an album. For those of us old enough to remember, you used to buy songs all packaged onto a piece of vinyl, a cassette tape, or a CD. You could actually put your hands on it, look at the artwork on the cover, read the liner notes, and put the thing on display someplace that told people you were a music lover.

Just as albums are constructed carefully, the Series turned out to be well crafted for its audience, though we weren't aware of trying to do that. We had those first two games decided by a single run. They were swift and precise and focused encounters, with great hooks that grabbed your attention and made you want to stay tuned. The middle three games, like in any album, were a bit more scattered—

they made you look at them a little while longer to see their appeal. Finally, the last two games really put on display the kind of virtuosity, the emotional wallop, and the big finish that would have you replaying them over and over again for years to come.

Obviously, I don't want to dismiss either the quality or importance of those three games in Texas. With the two-three-two home and away game arrangement of the Series, we now faced the possibility that, even though we'd been three outs away from a huge 2-0 lead, we could be swept on the road and the Series would be over.

Of more immediate concern was Game 3. In thirteen of the last eighteen World Series, the winner of Game 3 went on to win. That translates into 72 percent of the time. As I've said before, numbers and percentages aren't certainties, but you still have to acknowledge the trend. It's not that we needed any kind of extra incentive, but just as we did with pressure, acknowledging the presence of the crucial nature of Game 3 was important to our approach. We'd been a good road club during the regular season, and to that point in the playoffs we were 4-2 in away games. That is the mark of a resilient, focused, and well-balanced team. Unlike in the regular season when you go in with the mind-set of winning a three-game series, the truism of "take them one at a time" really applied here.

Still, before we could turn our attention fully to Game 3, I had some thinking to do about that ninth inning of Game 2 and how we'd defended the run. That night, when things had settled down and I was alone in my office, I started replaying that inning. I kept returning to this thought: if we had defended that potential stolen base attempt better, they wouldn't have stolen that base. What naturally followed that thought was this: If they hadn't stolen a base, they wouldn't have scored. If they hadn't scored, we'd have won and we'd now be up two games to none. That "if" was a tough one to digest. Even so, I still believed that how we'd handled it had been the correct way. I didn't regret the choice I'd made and still thought it was the right call.

Just to be thorough and do my due diligence to find out if maybe I was missing something, I turned to a good friend and managing peer, Jim Leyland. I always count on him to give me an honest answer. I ran the situation by him. Jim agreed: we had played it right. If Motte had tried to be quicker to the plate, it would have been hard for him to get the ball down in the strike zone. And if he'd walked Andrus, Jim said, "you know they're going to score." I appreciated hearing Jim's confirmation. With that one put away, I turned to the next phase. What could we do better in our defending-the-run game?

The running game often doesn't get a lot of attention, but, like I'd seen that first time in '79, everything in the World Series gets scrutinized to a far greater degree. When you hear someone talking about how things are magnified, I'm not sure they understand that term in the same way that I do. In any case, to prove my point about the World Series microscope, both the Rangers' manager, Ron Washington, and Kinsler were asked about that stolen base. In so many words, they both said the same thing: "We believe we can run on Motte." Kinsler also stated that the play was just that close, that microsecond I talked about. That was encouraging news. And in our message to our pitchers, the solution to the "problem" was obvious.

The next day at our press conference on the off day in Texas, I said that with Motte in the game, we could prevent the stolen base. I said what I did as a reminder to our pitching staff. We were going to defend the run with our best move on possible pickoffs and by being quicker getting the ball to the plate. They all knew that with Yadi's release and his arm, we could get valuable outs that way. Anytime a team gets a runner out without the ball being put in play by the hitter—on a pickoff play, an outfield assist, a caught stealing—the pitcher is grateful to his teammates for picking him up.

We had talked to the guys before the Series about the potential distraction of the media, and that became real after Game 2. There were a number of reports and critical judgments about our players that had nothing to do with what was going on between the lines.

If you believed all that was being written and said, you would have thought that another kind of running game was going on. Albert was one of the many guys on the team who didn't talk to the media after Game 2. All kinds of speculation flew about what was going on, and Albert took a lot of heat for it. What was troubling was that Albert was accused of ducking the media. If you had all the facts, you wouldn't have made that accusation.

Given how Game 2 had gone, with all the pitching changes and other things, it had been a long night. Because of how the fortunes in that game ebbed and flowed, and also because the outcome wasn't clear until the ninth, the writers' story lines probably changed a bit. They had to do some work to finalize their pieces. That took more time. A half hour after the game ended, a large group of guys went home. The media wanted to speak to them, but that was after they'd already left.

Some writers got on Albert's case, saying that he was a veteran, the face of the franchise, and he should have understood the circumstances and why there was a delay in them coming to talk to him. Albert's point—and my point—was that it should cut both ways. This was Game 2 of two at home. We were flying out early the next morning to get to Arlington. We had to be at the ballpark to take the buses to the airport at 9:30. We'd scheduled an earlier than normal, and longer than normal, workout at their place so the guys could adjust to the unfamiliar ballpark. We wanted them to check all the angles to see how balls came off the fences, see how hard the infield dirt was, see how quick the grass was.

So the players needed to get home, finish packing, get their families squared away—since this was the World Series, the guys wanted to have wife, kids, moms, dads, and whoever else with them in Texas—get some sleep, get up early, and haul everyone and their luggage to Busch. These writers and other media people should have known and respected that. No one was ducking anyone. The guys were just trying to do their jobs, keep their focus, and win the Series.

Like most disagreements, this was a case of "he said, she said" and crossed wires that blew something all out of proportion. That's what the intensity of the media produces.

Albert's a proud guy and generally one of the most in-demand players for interviews. He believed he was being unfairly singled out and that an unfair representation of what had happened was being presented as the truth.

Again, the slow news day phenomenon may have contributed to this. We had the off-day workout, and Albert made himself available to the media. Several media people asked him about his "absence" the night before, and he responded, "To try to rip somebody's reputation for something like this I don't think is fair."

Some people might think that this was another case of Albert finding something to motivate himself, but I doubt it. He doesn't need to take on the media to get fired up to win a ball game. It's true that Albert had some things go against him in Game 2, and to that point in the Series, by Albert's standards, he was not performing up to par. He was 0-for-6 in the first two games. Albert unfairly caught hell for what amounted to nothing but a story line. What nobody could know then was that Albert was about to be an even bigger part of everyone's story the next day with his hitting display.

Before the Series began, most people felt that both teams had potentially explosive offenses and that the games might be high-scoring. So far, that hadn't been the case. I sensed, based on how the hitters reacted to being in the warmer, dryer fall air in Texas and out of the damp and humid air in St. Louis, that those initial predictions might come true. Guys came out of the cage after taking their cuts in BP remarking on how well the ball carried. Some parks get referred to as "launching pads." Another Texas ballpark, the one in Houston, has that reputation.

I can't take credit for this line, but it's become a part of baseball lore. In 2005, when we lost to the Astros and they went off to the World Series, Albert rocketed one out of Minute Maid Park off Brad

Lidge. Berkman, who was playing for the Astros then, and the rest of their club were flying out that night to St. Louis. Berkman got a few guys' attention and said, pointing out his window, "Hey, look, there's Albert's home run ball." Berkman made a very quiet flight to St. Louis into a fun ride that helped the team turn the page. They wound up beating us the next game.

I sensed our guys needed a similar approach to help us get over the Game 2 loss. We'd been told before the Series started that our workout time would have to end anytime before 4:00 P.M. That's when the Rangers had the field. We made our arrangements to leave St. Louis with enough time to get a good workout in to acclimate to a foreign ballpark. After we arrived, Katy Feeney of the Major League Baseball offices let us know that the Rangers had changed their minds and moved up their workout to 3:30. I was in the clubhouse when that call came in, so a few guys were milling around and could overhear me. I said to Katie, "That's unacceptable. We already moved our flight up to earlier this morning because of what we'd been told. Tell them no way."

I then paused to consider my next comment. "And tell Nolan Ryan that I'm not Robin Ventura either." I was, of course, making reference to the White Sox player (and now manager of the club) who had charged Nolan after being hit by a pitch, slipped while going after him, and found himself in a headlock and punched on the top of the skull a few times.

I heard a few guys laughing, and before I knew it the story had spread among them. They added on by saying either to me or within earshot of me, "Hey, let's go watch Nolan kick Tony's ass." A few of them even suggested they'd form a circle around me schoolyard style and shove me back into the center to let Nolan keep whaling on me.

Never underestimate the power of humor, especially when you offer yourself up as a target for a joke, or a punch for that matter.

The guys were the ones who really came out swinging; Allen Craig's solo home run in the first inning eventually got lost in the postgame hullabaloo, but not in my mind. With two pinch-hits to drive in big runs already under his belt, he stepped up as our right-fielder against Matt Harrison and hit a home run to left. Three at-bats in the World Series, three hits, three RBIs, and now a home run. Even though to this point in the Series he wasn't playing full-time, he was having a big impact. To win, you need those kinds of contributions from guys other than your middle-of-the-lineup offensive threats. Getting that first run was key.

Kyle Lohse struck out the first two men he faced and held them scoreless through three.

Albert got his first hit of the Series to start off the fourth inning. I wasn't surprised. Mac had come to me after batting practice and said that Albert had felt locked in, and Mac had seen it himself. He said this was just like what he'd seen that day in Milwaukee. Albert liked his stroke, and Mac had seen how he was centering the ball really nicely. As much as you need contributions from Craig and others up and down the lineup, the club feels more comfortable when the big guns are active. They feed off that, and the fourth inning was a good example of Albert setting the tone. After Holliday hit into a fielder's choice (as evidence of how well the Series was being pitched, to that point he was 1-for-6), Lance Berkman, who coming into the game was 3-for-8, got another hit. David Freese doubled to drive in the first run. We stayed aggressive, and on a Jon Jay fielder's choice both Berkman and Freese scored on a throwing error by their catcher-turned-first-baseman Mike Napoli.

We caught a break there, and Theriot capitalized on it when he singled to drive home Yadi. We put pressure on the defense, and anytime you can score a run without a hit you take that chance. We'd added on four to go up 5–0.

The first time through the order, Kyle Lohse had his usual arm action that produced good velocity and movement as well as deception on his off-speed stuff, but in the span of six pitches in the bottom of the fourth he gave up three runs. We could see that he wasn't the same pitcher we'd seen those first three innings, and when he gave up another hit, this time to Napoli, it was time for Salas. This was an unorthodox way to try to get a win, but this was the World Series and our evaluation was based on who had the most quality pitches to give. I didn't worry about what would be said about it, or if I hadn't made the move. That's the immunity I talked about—just do what you think is best—if it doesn't work out you're going to get hammered either way. We'd used our former closer early in games before to good effect, and with the help of a great throw by Matt Holliday on a potential sacrifice fly that nailed Mike Napoli at the plate, an unconventional inning-ending double play bailed us out of trouble. After we each scored three times in the fifth, given how productive both offenses were being, this was shaping up to be one of those games about which people say that the last team to bat was going to win. I don't give in to that kind of thinking. We were still thinking about how we could score and how we could stop them inning by inning. That said, in a ballpark that rewards hard contact, and with two talented offenses getting hot, it would have been difficult for any pitcher to hold them down.

In the top of the sixth, after singling in his last two plate appearances, Albert stepped in with one out and runners on first and second. His home run to left off Ogando was one of those shots that you know was hit just about as well as a ball could be struck—not perfectly, but close. In that at-bat, Albert demonstrated that point about velocity not being enough. Ogando was trying to go low and away, but the ball tailed back over the plate above the belt. Barely keeping it fair, Albert had incredible bat speed on that shot. Yadi added a sacrifice fly to make it 12–6. After that, our bullpen settled in, with Lance Lynn allowing the Rangers' last run in the seventh.

Albert added a two-run shot in the seventh and another homer to left in the ninth, having himself a pretty decent day at the plate. Actually, it was a historic day at the plate. For the night, he was 5-for-6, scored four runs, drove in six, and had fourteen total bases. The first three of those feats tied major league records, and the last set one. With those three home runs, Albert joined Babe Ruth and Reggie Jackson at the top of the heap. Damn good company.

I thought that on each of those home runs his swing went from near-perfect to perfect. Mac looked at me after the last one and confirmed what I was thinking: *That's exactly what is taught.* I'd add today that those swings were videotaped from the first-base side, and anyone would benefit from the hitting clinic that tape provides— going back to go forward, hitting off the firm front side, the head still, the swing coming through from top to bottom, the full extension, the top hand coming off the bat.

That 16–7 score looked like a blowout, but it certainly wasn't. We worked our tails off throughout the game. Scoring in every inning after the third was something, but I was never able to fully relax.

In thinking about what had happened to Lohse, how he could have experienced such a drastic turnaround, I considered another possibility. The other club just put really good swings on decent pitches. That happens. Equally inexplicable to some people is how a team can score sixteen runs on fifteen hits one night and score no runs on just two hits the next. That's what happened to us in Game 4. There is an answer to how that marked a difference in offensive production in consecutive games could exist.

Derek Holland pitched a helluva game against us. The home-plate umpire established a consistent and aggressive strike zone, and Holland exploited it well. We didn't have a hitters' hangover, we hadn't used up all the hits in our bats, the guys weren't overconfident. A good professional pitcher threw what may have been the game of his life on the biggest stage against our potent offense. It happens.

Edwin didn't have the same command as Holland, so he didn't take advantage of the home-plate umpire's aggressive strike zone. He wound up walking seven in five and a third innings but gave up only three hits and three runs, which told us something. He struggled with his command, but he was working his ass off out there, making quality pitches in situations when the game might have gotten completely out of hand. The fact that Edwin threw four shutout innings after giving up a lone run in the first was a positive. Relieving Edwin in the sixth, Mitchell Boggs overthrew a sinker in a double-play situation and surrendered that three-run bomb to Napoli on a ball up in the zone, making Jackson's pitching line look worse than it actually was.

The Series was tied at 2–2, and visions of that Kinsler steal of second base in Game 2 still popped into my head at odd moments. If I was Yadi, I would have snagged those thoughts and with a rifle arm delivery thrown them out. But I'm not, and I kept thinking and thinking about how we might have been up three games to one except for that one play.

As I pointed out before, I was okay with my decision involving Motte and our defense of the running game that second night in St. Louis. Anytime you lose it's disappointing. Manage as many games as I have, lose as many as I have, and you start to figure out some trends in how those disappointments break down. Let's start with the premise above. All losses are disappointing. You go into every game expecting to win. When you don't, you're, well, disappointed.

Sometimes you lose and feel less disappointed than at other times. For example, if your team plays hard and loses, that stings. If your team doesn't show up and compete the way you know they can, that *hurts*.

What I've always done is assess not just the team but myself. That's why I devised this three-point scheme for categorizing losses. Remember that opening premise: losses = disappointment.

Loss number one is the least disappointing on the managerial scale of self-assessment. None of the moves you made, none of the strategic decisions, had a meaningful impact on the outcome of the game. Some nights, what you do is ineffectual in the strictest sense. They have no direct effect on the outcome of the game. I can't say those kinds of losses are rare, mostly because, as my self-assessment scale works, I really analyze my actions with precision. Game 4, when Holland shut us down, is a case in point here. I made moves, but in the end they didn't matter in terms of outcome.

Loss number two is different from loss number one in this regard: I experience the same level of disappointment, but my decisions did matter, and after analyzing them, I can conclude that the key decisions that directly affected the outcome were the right ones to make. That was Game 2 as it pertains to what we've already gone over—run defense with Motte.

Loss number three differs from the others both in degree and in kind. These losses are monumentally disappointing to me. Why? Because the outcome-producing decisions I made were the wrong ones. In this case, I beat myself up. I feel like I would if I had struck out with the bases loaded, or given up the walk-off hit.

If you think that you screwed up something and contributed to a loss, you're ticked off and you can't sleep. Those times, you're better off hitting the streets to try to walk it off. If you are really ticked off, then you just hope somebody tries to mug you. That sounds very dramatic, but it's the truth. If you're in your room on the road or at home and you're that angry with yourself, you've got to do something. It didn't happen very often, but it did happen, like Game 2 of the NLDS when I didn't pinch-hit Holliday.

The reason it didn't happen more often is that I knew how anguished or ticked off I was going to be if I messed up, so I worked my butt off not to be put in that position.

That is one helluva motivator.

More than just being a motivator, examining losses like I do is a way to hold myself accountable all the time and in every way. Doing that, of course I'm going to take losses personally. That's why they always disappointed me and sometimes hurt like hell.

One type-three loss that always comes to mind is when the White

Sox were playing the Tigers in Detroit in 1981. With a one-run lead, I pitched to Rusty Staub with runners at second and third and two out instead of walking him. Ed Farmer left a ball up in the zone, and Rusty, a great pinch hitter, hit one up the middle for a two-run single, and we lost the game. I should have never pitched to him. The left-right percentage was in his favor, and he was a great hitter. Bad decision. Bad outcome. Bad Tony. I pummeled myself over that one.

I'VE ALREADY MENTIONED THE CRUCIAL NATURE OF GAME 3 IN A seven-game series. The percentage of teams that win Game 5 and go on to win the series is 55 percent, a considerable drop from 72 percent for Game 3. Obviously, lots of variables play into this. The one variable that we focused on in Game 5 in Arlington was the rematch of Carp and Wilson. Both sides were getting their second opportunity to see the starting pitcher. We thought that would prove interesting. "Interesting" didn't begin to describe some of the strange things, such as our bullpen confusion with Lynn, that took place.

In the thirteen postseason games Carp had pitched in his Cardinal career, we'd won eleven of them. This time, we fell short of getting that twelfth win, and it seemed to me that a dozen oddities, quirks, and missed opportunities in the game got in the way of achieving it. As I've said many times, baseball is endlessly fascinating and those seemingly inexplicable turns of fortune I talked about before are just one part of what makes this almost daily game so amazing. You never know what you might find lying in the middle of the road to World Series Championship.

As much as the game involved odd turns, it began the way so many of our postseason games had—we scored first. Game 4 had been the lone exception to that trend, and we quickly reversed it in the second inning in this one. After a leadoff walk to Holliday and a wild pitch advancing him, Berkman also walked. One out later,

Yadi singled to drive in Holliday. Berk got all the way around to third when Murphy couldn't field it cleanly. We took advantage of the miscue and got another run on Schumaker's groundout.

The top of the third saw something new emerge. With a runner on third and one out, the Rangers chose to intentionally walk Albert to get to Matt Holliday. He couldn't make them pay for that, and his double-play grounder ended the inning. A Moreland home run and then a pair of two-out hits put the tying run on second, but Carp got out of it. The number of times our staff limited the damage contributed so much to our wins.

This was an opportunity denied.

There are a few ways to make note of what Carp did. Our pitchers' success in limiting the damage isn't an official statistic, but in keeping track of runners in scoring position, two-out RBIs, and other metrics, we're basically providing numbers for that effort. The opposite of opportunity denied is opportunity missed. Much was made after the game about the odd nature of the events with the bullpen, but that emphasis masked what we saw as the essential truth of the game: who took advantage of opportunities and who didn't.

Carp got the first two outs of the sixth, then Beltre homered to tie it. I knew Carp was upset with himself. He threw a big breaking curveball. It was down in the zone, but Beltre went down on one knee to get it and golfed it out of the yard. Tie game at two apiece.

During the top of the seventh, another play that people would later label "odd" occurred. With one out, Craig walked. Albert has earned the right to put the hit-and-run on, based on his demonstrated insight into the game, and he chose to do it. He signaled to Craig, but when the pitch came in high, he didn't swing. Craig was thrown out easily. All I thought at that point was, *Damn. That didn't work.*

A bit of context is needed here. Albert doesn't play the game to the beat of his own drummer. Any accusations to that effect, any suggestions that Albert was being selfish or doing anything but trying to do what he thought would best increase our chances of winning, are way off base. Any local observer who follows our club closely, views the game objectively, and isn't interested in knocking Albert off a pedestal that they falsely perceive to be there would see the truth of that statement demonstrated time and time again. Any national observer who makes the same assumption just doesn't have enough facts to go on.

Why did I let Albert make that call? Because that's what you do with a few select players whose level of understanding of the game allows you to trust their judgment—you let them exercise it. Carlton Fisk, Mike Matheny, and Yadier Molina were all catchers who had the green light to call for pitchouts independent of the bench. Same with guys who not only can run but know how to pick their spots. If, over time, you demonstrate that you can steal bases at a high rate of success, we give you the freedom to run.

Another point: Albert is a great hit-and-run man. With really productive hitters, you sometimes hesitate to pull the trigger to call this play because you are, in effect, taking the bat out of their hands. You're forcing them to swing. And sometimes it's a really close call. You decide on the side of trusting a productive hitter to do something special. But when you have one of those hairy times when one of your top guys is willing to do it on his own, sacrifice his at-bat for the team, it's a winning gesture by that teammate.

Like I said, from his first years in the club, we'd hit-and-run with Albert a lot, mostly when he was the second hitter in the inning. We won a number of games, and he got a lot of hits, with the hit-and-run play. A lot of times he would come up to me before the start of an inning and say, "Hey, I'm thinking about doing the hit-and-run here. What do you think?"

I'd generally say of his thinking process, "That's really good." Or a few times, "That's not a good time."

One of those times I would have said no to the idea was in the situation that arose in the seventh inning of Game 5. If he had come to me before the inning and said he was thinking about the hit-and-run,

I would have said, "I wouldn't do it. This guy's wild, and they're not pitching to you. You're not going to get anything you can handle."

In the ninth inning we were down 4–2 with one out. Neftali Feliz hit Craig with a pitch. Albert then went to a 3-2 count. Now, Albert's a good contact hitter, but he also hits a lot of hard ground balls, and he helped us set the National League record for double plays grounded into last year. So we started Craig off first.

Feliz made a great pitch and struck out Albert, and Craig was gunned down at second base. Two outs. No one on. We lose 4–2. One of the worst situations to be in is having to explain failed strategy because quite often you come off sounding defensive. I don't like being defensive, and I don't like losing when that tough loss/tough call thing comes into play. That's probably when people see me get surly or prickly.

A LOT WAS MADE OF THAT PHONE MIX-UP AND LYNN'S INTENTIONAL walk. Motte came in immediately after that and struck out Andrus to end the inning. But hey, I understand that baseball's an entertainment as well as a competition. We took our lumps, but our undoing came from Murphy's infield single and Napoli's double, not from any drowned-out, noisy communications. We'll never know what might have happened if Motte had faced Napoli. I did know that this club had shown it was special by its response to adversity all year, through the comeback and the playoff run. Although they were bummed after this loss, they took my idea of "special" to another level. Everyone wanted to take responsibility for the loss. Our hitters said that they should have added runs, our starting pitcher said that two runs should have been enough, our bullpen coach and relievers said the miscommunication was their fault. That willingness to share responsibility over a loss that put us on the brink of elimination again, down 3–2 in the Series, placed a star next to the 2011 club indicating just how much this was an "us" and not "me" club. I told them that whatever happened with calls to the bullpen and whoever came in or didn't was entirely my responsibility. And it was.

What really hurt us was that from the third through the eighth innings, five out of the six times we had runners in scoring position we didn't score. We definitely had our chances but didn't come through. Leaving nine men on base left us vulnerable to their comeback.

We'd put ourselves in jeopardy. I had to come up with something quickly to say to the guys before we headed back home.

We had a meeting in the clubhouse afterward, and my words were "We're not going to allow anybody who's not in this clubhouse to dictate our attitude and determination to compete in Game 6 and Game 7. We control our minds.

"You know how hard this season's been. We've been here before. We lost the first game in the Division Series to the Phillies and then got four runs down in the second game. And then we lost Game 3 of that series. Elimination game and we won. I don't need to remind you all of how many times a loss could have done us in. And it didn't. We're still here."

To finish up, I did something I'd done during the comeback by planting that seed in their minds, getting them to anticipate a positive just a bit.

"I don't want to get too far ahead, but if we get to Game 7, Dave and I have a really great way to pitch that game. After we win Game 6, we'll share it with you. I think you'll agree how likely it is that we'll win that Game 7."

I then chose to refer to another great comeback in sports. "This is going to sound like Ben Crenshaw at the Ryder Cup, but I've got a really good feeling about us going back to St. Louis and winning the next two games."

CHAPTER TWENTY-TWO

You Had to See It for Yourself

A THLETES ARE OFTEN CRITICIZED BY SOME FOR RELYING SO HEAV-ily on clichés to talk about the games they play. To some extent that's true. We do get asked a lot of questions, and sometimes, whether because we've been asked the same one so many times, because they speak the truth, or because we're speaking guardedly to protect ourselves, a teammate, or our club, we resort to the tried and true—just like this one.

Every now and then something happens that's so special, so unique to our own experience, that often, when we're asked to speak before what's gone on has had a chance to register in our brains, we reach into the box of clichés that sits right alongside the David's sunflower seeds and the Gatorade on the dugout bench, hoping to find one that fits the situation. On the night of October 27, 2011, the media, the fans, the players, and the coaching staffs all resorted to one cliché or another, none of us really capable of putting into words what we'd all just been through for four hours and thirty-three minutes and how it was going to figure in our lives after being a part of it.

It was worth the wait, to get through both the 4:33 and the two days off between Games 5 and 6. The first of those was a travel day, the second a cancellation due to rain. We were just going to adjust and be ready. The rhythm of the Series was thrown off, but I can't say that accounted for the somewhat erratic action that took place on the field in the first six or seven innings.

As early as noon I had gotten a couple of calls from C.J., our director of travel, telling me that the commissioner's office had called with the news that the forecast was anywhere from bad to really bad. They were putting us on notice that the game might be canceled. Rain had played havoc with a Rangers-Tigers ALCS game, and they didn't want the same thing to happen in Game 6. The fact that it was rained out had a plus and a minus. The extra day off with no game stories to tell meant that the media went after us about the Game 5 loss. That was more than made up for by the fact that Carp might be available if we got to Game 7.

Thanks to Rick Carlisle, I was able to handle the media better than I would have otherwise. He'd been at the game, and on the scheduled day off he and I got together. Obviously, as head coach of the Dallas Mavericks, he's had a lot of experience in dealing with tough questions. He knew the situation I was in, so he suggested that he play the role of the questioner. He came after me intensely. That dress rehearsal really helped with my control when I faced the media for real later in the day.

Unfortunately, I also had experience with an interrupted World Series. The Loma Prieta earthquake of 1989 in California was an enormous tragedy. The fact that the Series that year was between two Bay Area teams magnified the impact for the immediate area as well as the rest of the country. Understandably, our hearts and minds were elsewhere in the immediate aftermath. We all had friends and family in the city of San Francisco to be concerned about, and our personal lives had been seriously disrupted. Like anyone else, we wanted our lives to get back to as close to normal as possible, as soon as possible. We were a professional baseball organization, and we needed to play—if for no other reason than to bring some relief from the stresses of dealing with a natural disaster and to send a signal that the Bay Area was going to be okay.

Once we got word that the original five-day delay would be extended another five, our thoughts returned to the Series. Naturally, I was concerned about how we would get everyone to refocus after such a calamity. We'd won the first two games, and we had a great club that was peaking. How was an eleven-day layoff from game competition going to affect them? Naturally, I checked in with the guys—Dave Stewart, Eck, Carney Lansford, and others—and asked them how they were feeling.

Carney, "Captain Intensity," said, "Tony, we could play the games next spring and still go after them."

I was glad to hear those remarks, but I also wanted to be prepared. I'd read Pat Riley's book *Showtime*, about his years with his championship-winning clubs in L.A. In it, he talked about how he'd organized a three-day camp kind of getaway when the playoffs were about to begin and his team was taking on the task of repeating. Instead of just having workouts, they'd travel someplace where the guys would all live and practice together and not go home to family and their regular lives. During the day, they'd go over their scouting reports, game plans, and practice. At night they'd get together as a team and talk, reaffirm their goals, and bond as a team.

I thought that was cool and wondered if that was something we might be able to do.

On Tuesday, October 24, I learned that the Series was going to resume that coming Friday. The Bay Area forecast was for a chance of rain, so we might not be able to do what we intended there. I called the GM, Sandy Alderson, and told him about my plan. He got in touch with our owner, Mr. Haas, and that Wednesday we were all on a charter flight to Phoenix, our spring training home, for workouts. I felt like the guys needed to get away from the area. There was lots of talk in some circles that the Series should just be canceled entirely.

Hearing all that could have cast a pall on the whole season for the guys. You want a World Series title to be a celebration, not an afterthought or, worse, what some people would think of as a black eye for the sport. I could understand that lives were lost and people were upset. But if we were going to play—and I fully supported the idea that we should—then the cloud of negativity hanging over the Series was one we had to get out from under.

Some people said baseball was just a game, and that puzzled me. If it was just a game, then why were pro football and college football games being played and no one was objecting? If baseball was just an entertainment, then why weren't people complaining about movie theaters staying open or television shows still being broadcast? The guys were human, and they had to be feeling down. I had told them that we were going to Phoenix to work out, to have dinner together as a team, to talk about all the things that had begun right there in spring training, and we were going to put a nice finishing cap on that by winning the Series.

Something happened that I couldn't have predicted or planned on. As we approached the airport, the pilot came on the intercom and told us that if we looked off to our right, we could see the A's spring training complex. Traffic was backed up all around Municipal Stadium. The pilot added, "You guys are going to have some kind of crowd for your workout."

We did. The place was mobbed, and when we went out there to practice, we got an amazing reception. That squad had a bunch of personalities on it—Dave Parker was the DH, Don Baylor the hitter off the bench—and they just basked in that attention. The life was back in them.

We went out to dinner that night. As coaches, we talked to the guys about getting our minds back right, but mostly we all just laughed a lot and enjoyed ourselves. Dave Parker, who is as quick-witted as any player I'd ever met, took control of the evening's entertainment. For two years he had filled our off time with barbs directed at one teammate or another. I told Dave he should have hosted his own late-night talk show. To this day I'm sure when Eck hears "Parkway's" name, he cringes. The next day we went out and had a bit of fun with the coaches and the players. We later learned that more than 10,000 people had come out to watch us, that kids got to skip school. The whole thing was a real feel-good.

We regained our edge and took Games 3 and 4 to sweep the Giants. Their pitching was hurting that postseason, and we got it done.

No one could say how that extra day off would impact this 2011 Series, but one thing we knew coming in was that this was an "all ready" game for the bullpen—with two days off, each of them had had enough rest that they'd be fresh. What the extra day off was going to do to Jaime's preparation was something we talked about with him. He was pitching with six days' rest. We'd given him extended rest throughout the comeback, and we told him that he'd done well in those starts when he didn't get his normal four days. To tell him that this was just another game and to treat it that way would have been B.S. Besides, we never say things like that, and he'd have seen right through that attempt to "relax" him. Tell him that he was working with the kind of time off between starts that he'd had a number of times before and had success with it and you're being honest. Draw on your past success. Do the things we tell you about embracing pressure, acknowledging it, and doing the job you've done before.

When I looked in Jaime's eyes, he was excited, and I was glad to see that. This was the perfect example of what we coach. If you're going to win a championship, you're going to face these kinds of moments, so you prepare for them by getting well acquainted with pressure. By doing that, you understand that this is the edge you've worked at gaining all year. Go out there and be the guy.

Whatever the case, from the outset of Game 6, Jaime didn't look like the Jaime of Game 2. A leadoff walk and two singles scored the dreaded first run, but then, fortunately, Jaime settled down and got two strikeouts and a ground ball to limit the damage—exactly what we needed him to do in that situation. As the guys came into the dugout, the starters and the bench guys—especially Carp, Wainwright, Laird—all said, "We need to answer."

They were right, and we did.

With two outs and a runner on in our half of the first, Lance Berkman got a ball out over the plate and drove it into the left-center-field bleachers to put us up 2–1. As soon as they scored, one of our key guys made a real statement, and that let them know that we were going to do whatever it took. In retrospect, even with all the late-game heroics, Lance's home run was almost as important as what Freese later did.

Jaime walked Napoli to lead off the second. I looked at Dunc and said, as I had in the first, "Something doesn't look right." A Craig Gentry single put runners on first and second, and here we caught a National League break: their pitcher had to hit. Of course, their pitchers had been taking batting practice for a while through the playoff run in anticipation of getting to the World Series. But that's not the same as live pitching. I was also "what-if-ing" about how we could keep them from scoring, paying particular attention to our bunt defense options. We went with our number-four play, and Jaime made a nice pitch. We executed it perfectly. David Freese was charging hard, as was Albert. Furcal drifted toward the hole, while Theriot held the runner close near the bag. They held their ground for a bit before breaking for the corner bags. Seeing them move, Jaime delivered the pitch. David fielded a bunt hit hard and at him, and with Yadi yelling, "Three!" at the top of his lungs, we turned a neat 5-6-4 double play. That slight risk in putting on an aggressive defensive play paid off.

We were one out away from slamming the door on their good opportunity and giving Jaime a nice confidence boost. Unfortunately, Ian Kinsler, who'd gotten one of the three hits off Jaime in Game 2 and had walked two other times against him, which told us he was getting good looks, went deep into the count again before doubling to deep center on a 3-2 pitch to drive in a run. Again, Jaime didn't let them score another run in that inning. As important as that was, we could still tell that something wasn't quite right with him. We couldn't see anything obviously flawed with his delivery, but his stuff didn't have its usual life.

In the top of the third, Jaime worked around a one-out single with the help of a double-play ball off the bat of Adrian Beltre. We got out of the inning, but I decided that was enough. The rainout and our pen being fresh influenced that decision, as did their being a strong right-handed club. Also, as had happened in the last part of the season during the comeback and into the playoffs, those lingering questions about Jaime's stamina were still there.

The main factor was this: we were in an elimination game, and we couldn't let things get away from us early. I went up to Jaime and said, "That's enough. I'm going to make a change."

The dugout isn't the place to start any kind of debate or to let your teammates know that you disagree. At this point, because we'd been stressing urgency for so long, the starters had been through the so-called quick hook enough times to understand the decision. As Jaime nodded, I could tell he was disappointed, in himself as much as in the decision. I then added the clincher: "We don't want to get you hurt." Dunc and I were legitimately concerned that if Jaime continued to struggle and his competitive nature took over, he might try to do too much and hurt his arm again.

I went with Fernando Salas, sticking with a pattern that we'd used to succeed before. I have to give Fernando a lot of credit. He'd been our saves leader for the season, but he adjusted well to his new role and never complained. Matt Holliday dropped a Nelson Cruz fly ball, and Salas wasn't able to pick him up. He allowed Napoli's single to right, and the Rangers took the lead. At that point, it seemed like Napoli was building a case to be the Series MVP. I didn't think that single run would hold up as the game- and Series-winning RBI for him, but he was having a helluva Series against us. He wound up hitting .350 and driving in ten runs.

The slack play continued when, on a bunt back to him, Salas tried to get the runner at second and threw wide of the bag into center field. Fortunately, Salas didn't let that affect him, and he retired the next two men.

At the end of every inning, I worked through an analysis of what had just transpired. So far, in four innings, we had done a good job three times of limiting the potential damage of their offense. In any game, you never know how important those stops are going to be.

Another error on a leadoff at-bat, this time committed by their first baseman, Michael Young, led to a run. Berkman was the beneficiary of that mistake. A Holliday walk, a fielder's choice, and a groundout produced the run. This was all about taking advantage of a break. To score that run, we didn't have a single hit. In fact, if it weren't for the error, the ball would have never left the infield.

When Josh Hamilton reached on David Freese's error on a pop-up to start the fifth, that was the third time in a row a half-inning had begun with a defensive miscue. I stood there wondering, *Is this a full moon game?* All kinds of stuff that shouldn't have been happening was going on. It seemed like each error was more inexplicable than the one before it. These were routine plays, and the guys making the errors normally didn't slip up like that. Sometimes defensive lapses can become contagious. I had to push that thought aside and keep a positive frame of mind. We'd fix those problems later. Dwelling on a negative would be counterproductive.

Each time, when the guys came in, I said to them, "Keep playing." Physical errors like the ones we made were going to happen. As long as they weren't mental errors, a lack of effort or a lapse in concentration, I was okay with them.

The Rangers capitalized again when Young drove one into the left-center-field gap to put them up for the third time in five innings. I wasn't going to let Napoli pad his possible MVP credentials later in the inning, preferring to walk him to face David Murphy. That put runners on first and second. Salas then walked the bases loaded with an unintentional intentional walk to get to the pitcher. This was nervous time. Following his double, Young had advanced to third on a fly-out. By walking Napoli, we'd purposely put another runner in scoring position, something you wouldn't normally do unless the pitcher's slot was coming up. Colby Lewis was an American League pitcher, but if he somehow managed to get a hit or another defensive lapse occurred, it could mean two more runs. Salas didn't keep me on tenterhooks for long. Three straight strikes and Lewis was out of there.

As the guys came back in, the bench was up and chirping, "Hey, we're in this game," "We dodged a bullet," and "They're not getting crooked numbers." Everybody recognized that the Rangers' missed opportunities were working in our favor.

During the top of the fifth, I'd already had Lance Lynn up in the bullpen and Jon Jay in the batting cage loosening up to pinch-hit for Salas. I wanted a leadoff-type hitter there since Salas's spot was coming up first. It didn't matter. We went three up and three down, with Schumaker making the last out.

As a result, I used the double switch and put the pitcher in that spot to buy two places in the order and to save a player. I also went with Lynn out of the bullpen because I was hoping to get two innings from him. Even though Lynn had thrown forty-seven pitches in Game 3, by having him throw those four intentional balls in Game 5 instead of live pitches, I'd effectively gotten him four days' rest. Luckily, we didn't have to deal with the communication problems with the bullpen like we had in Arlington. At Busch, we can see the relievers from our dugout and our bullpen phone is tucked far enough beneath the stands that the noise doesn't interfere as much.

In the visitors' sixth, Lynn gave up a two-out single before Michael Young lined out to right. Michael Young made eight errors in 160 games as the Rangers' first baseman. He'd made one in the fourth inning of this game, and then, with Lance Berkman at first on a slow roller to third, Young made his second error of the night on a bad throw trying to get Berkman at second base on a Holliday grounder. We wound up scoring a run when Lewis walked Freese, loading the bases, and Ogando came into the game and promptly walked Yadi. The score was tied, and for the second time we'd scored a run without a batted ball leaving the infield. I wasn't sure if the baseball gods were laughing or crying.

With Nick Punto up and still only one out, we were looking to break this thing open. Ogando threw a first-pitch strike, and then, on the second pitch, Matt Holliday got caught taking too aggressive a walking lead off third and was picked off. Not only that, to literally add injury to insult, he hurt his wrist. Matt's overaggressiveness cost him and us. We weren't going to put on the squeeze play in that situation, so there was no need for him to take that kind of lead. Ogando's stuff had too much life and his command was just erratic enough to make him tough to bunt on. Worse, Matt was out of the game and, as it turned out, the Series.

An Ogando wild pitch advanced the runners to second and third. Punto wound up walking to reload the bases, and Ron Washington, demonstrating that he wanted to end the Series right here in Game 6, brought in his starter, Derek Holland, who'd pitched so effectively against us in Game 4, in relief. The plan worked. Jon Jay grounded one right back to Holland.

Between innings, as I did my analysis, I had two options. I could think of these two instances of getting a run without the benefit of a hit, and not getting even more runs with a clutch hit, as a reflection of our offense not really producing. Or I could recognize the positive in the team having tied the score going into the last three innings of a home game. I took the latter view, telling those other thoughts to get the hell out of there before they'd even had a chance to settle in. I did the same when I briefly thought that if we were to lose, this would be the worst possible way, because we were not playing well to that point.

Those runs we'd gotten—or maybe the Rangers handed us—were important. Just as the times when we'd limited them to a single run were important. Don't do something to lose the game when on defense. Do something to win the game on offense. Do that nine times and you win. Of course, at this point, I couldn't have foreseen what shape those somethings to win and to lose would take.

I also had to think about our less than perfect efforts.

Holliday had made a fundamental baserunning mistake, we had committed three defensive errors, and yet we were still right in there. Three times earlier in the game we'd given them more outs, but our pitchers weren't caving in. That was impressive—if the pitchers had caved, whatever offensive heroics were looming later in the game wouldn't have mattered. We were able to come back from two-run deficits, but could we have dug ourselves out from a three-run, four-run, or five-or-more-run hole?

I was unhappy about our not playing a clean game, but I kept the positive self-talk going. I'd learned a long time ago that if I gave the guys any suggestion that I was upset, that I was giving in to the negative or acting at all like this wasn't our night, they'd pick up on that and feed off my negative energy.

Six pitches later, I needed to maintain that same positivity when we were down 6–4. Beltre and Cruz both homered. Our scouting report had told us that if we got balls up in the zone a bit and over too much of the plate, these two were going to launch them. That's exactly what happened. Busch Stadium was so quiet I could have yelled to Lilliquist in the bullpen to see how Dotel and R-zep were doing as they warmed up.

After the home runs and after striking out the dangerous Napoli, Lynn gave up a bloop single to Murphy and then made a nice play to retire him at second on a poor bunt by Holland. It was time to get

Lynn—he'd been out there awhile. I told him, "Hey, you got us five outs. These guys can hit. You did well." I meant every word.

Whatever good vibes Carlos Santana had passed on to me with that necklace back in September seemed to have worn off. Dotel wild-pitched Holland to second, and Kinsler twisted the knife a bit by singling him in. We were now down by three runs with nine outs left to play. Not impossible by any stretch of the imagination. A run an inning could get us there. The bench guys continued their late season refrain, "We can't lose!"

Holland made that task more difficult by retiring the side in order in the bottom of the seventh. Once again we didn't get the ball out of the infield. Six outs in the game, possibly the season. I recognized that with their closing bullpen staff and that deficit, things weren't going to be easy. The situation was desperate, but not hopeless. I remembered what I'd written on my cards earlier that day: "keep on believing," "be good enough," "be tough enough."

In professional sports, toughness is more important than talent. We had both. And I still believed.

R-zep was the logical choice to replace Dotel, with Hamilton, Moreland, and Beltre due up. He neutralized the left-right trap very nicely with three very quick ground-ball outs. Given all the late-inning heroics, I don't want R-zep's inning of work there to go unremarked on. We were still down three, but if they had added on again, or if we'd had a really protracted inning with a number of pitching changes, we could have started to feel sorry for ourselves and begun thinking that it had been a nice ride, but it was time to step off it. That possibility, given the makeup of this group, was unlikely, but R-zep's energized and efficient disposal of three tough hitters was more than just a glimmer of light.

We were still in this.

Allen Craig, who replaced Holliday in left in the top of the seventh, was due to face Holland, who'd retired all five men he'd faced to that point. I was just returning to my usual spot in the dugout after having said, "Great job," to R-zep before letting him know that that was it for him. Out of the corner of my eye, I saw Allen's bat lash ferociously around in his follow-through. He hit Holland's slider right over the image of number 45 Bob Gibson. Down by two with five outs to go. Even though we didn't score again in the inning, we had three hits. Instead of bemoaning a lost opportunity, the fact that we kept battling like that was another of those flashes of light, like R-zep's performance.

Needing to hold them right there, I called on Jason Motte in the ninth. Like R-zep, he gave us a lift, working quickly and around a one-out walk to send us back to the dugout.

I walked to the far end of the dugout as the guys were coming off the field to say to the guys on the bench, "This is when we need you."

The bench responded, "Let's get something started."

I felt good hearing all that support coming from everyone.

THAT AFTERNOON, BEFORE THE GAME HAD STARTED, MO HAD COME to my office. He'd told me that our owner, Mr. DeWitt, wanted to be sure that if we lost the game, the players took a few minutes to go out on the field, even while the other team was celebrating, to thank the fans. The official presentation of the trophy would take about ten minutes to set up, so we wouldn't be doing anything to detract from a Rangers celebration. Of course, that was the right thing to do, both the salute to the fans and Mo's coming to mention it to me. I appreciated the reminder, and went back to my business.

As their closer, Neftali Feliz, took his warm-up tosses, I got on the phone to remind Lilliquist to give the guys left in the bullpen the heads-up about thanking the fans. I told him not to say anything until there were two outs and it looked like we were going to get beat, and then tell the relievers who were left to come down to the dugout to join their teammates. I went around to tell the guys in the dugout who either had played in the game or were not eligible to play in the Series. I said, "We've got a real shot here, but we need to corral the guys and step out for a minute to salute the fans."

They were already on the top step, and as I walked along I saw a row of Cardinal red hoods and hats. When they heard me they turned, and I caught a glimpse of their faces before they turned back around, nodding, some of them pivoting their gaze from one of the outfield scoreboards to the infield and back. Were they wondering if somehow one glance would reveal something different from the previous one?

I settled in. The sound of one of Feliz's explosive fastballs was audible over the crowd's expectant and nervous thrum. I took a deep breath, and as I had done probably more than 45,000 times before, I watched my team come to bat in their half-inning.

Feliz was well rested, and it showed. His fastball had the kind of jump to it that the best hard throwers have. Theriot went down swinging.

Two outs to go.

Albert stepped into the home-plate circle. He was hitless in three at-bats. I couldn't ignore all the flashbulbs going off or the appreciative roar of the fans. Everyone was thinking that this might be it for Albert. With his free agency being one of the hot topics of conversation around the major leagues, what else could you think at that point? But Albert clearly wasn't thinking about it. On Feliz's first pitch, a fastball out on the edge, Albert reached out and stroked it into left-center field for a double. He pointed to the sky. I was looking at Feliz, hoping I could read something in his demeanor, but I couldn't see his expression. The four straight balls to Berkman told me something. There was no way they wanted to put the tying run on base. I was hoping that maybe the moment had gotten to Feliz. His strikeout of Craig said otherwise.

In a fitting bit of irony, David Freese, who'd rooted for the Cardinals as a kid, who we'd received in a trade from San Diego for his favorite Cardinal, Jim Edmonds, came to the plate as potentially the last hope for Cardinals Nation.

One out to go.

A ball.

A strike looking.

A swinging strike.

One strike left in the season.

I hoped that David would get his front foot set sooner. On the swinging strike he hadn't.

David Freese then did what many people don't think is possible. He made me smile.

I watched as Feliz stood at the back of the mound, gazing into the outfield. They were one strike away from winning the World Series—what better moment to take it all in?

What better moment to take it all away?

When Freese extended his hands and stepped slightly toward the outside corner, setting that front foot, he hit Feliz's fastball on a line drive. The sound of the contact was so pure, but as the ball reached its peak and then started into its downward flight, like everyone else in Busch Stadium I would assume, I wondered if what I'd thought at first might be a walk-off home run was going to turn into an out. Cruz went back on it hard, but the ball went back even more quickly. If he gloved it, he was a World Series hero for the ages. If he didn't, we were still in this thing.

Hitting hard off the wall, the ball caromed back far enough that if Cruz hadn't had the presence of mind to get back after it hard, we might have seen another first: an inside-the-park walk-off home run. I stood there clapping my hands, smiling and marveling at the determination in this whole scene. Here again, I felt a bit of an advantage. I didn't think the Rangers had a good read on Freese's opposite-field power and how his ball would carry that way. If they had, Cruz might have been positioned deeper. If Cruz had recognized it, he might have broken back more quickly. Whether human nature factored into this at all, them being one strike away, I can't say.

As excited as we all were, we still had a runner on third and two out. Yadi jumped all over the first pitch and nearly ended the game right there. His line drive to right was hit hard, but directly at Cruz. Believe me, the thought of not being too greedy and just being grateful for what we had didn't cross my mind. I wanted that game over, and Yadi nearly made that desire come true.

We all had so much adrenaline pumping through our bodies and were enjoying the moment, but everybody immediately changed gears after Yadi made the out. As we'd been doing for so long, we weren't going away. We knew the reality. The score was tied, and we had more game to play. Let's go play defense.

Kinsler popping up on the first pitch I thought was going to be huge for us. Jason Motte was in his second inning of work, something he'd done nine times already that year. Kinsler certainly helped by going after that first pitch, and I think it was a sound strategy to go right after Motte, hoping that he'd leave a good one to hit out over the plate. He didn't, and when, after a first-pitch ball, Andrus blooped one into center on the very next pitch, it felt like the inning was being played at an accelerated pace.

We knew that Hamilton would go up there swinging. We'd talked to the pitchers about not getting too much of the plate on the first pitch. Jason missed. Hamilton didn't. With one swing, we were right back where we'd been going into the ninth inning—down by two. To his credit, Jason got the final two outs. The dugout had quieted for a bit after the home runs, but as the defense came in, the noise level jumped up again. I heard a lot of talk about there being no way that we were going to get beat.

Once again, I had to make that call to Lilliquist to remind him about management's request: remember to thank the fans. I'm not sure, but I think I set a World Series record for thank-you reminders that night. I don't know if Lilliquist ever told anybody. It didn't matter, the guys had another plan in mind as a way to thank the fans for coming out to the ballpark.

Darren Oliver, who'd just turned forty-one earlier that month, and who'd pitched for the Cardinals back in '98 and '99, was their choice to face us in the tenth. He was their Arthur Rhodes, a veteran left-hander who'd been around for a lot of years, eighteen seasons, and was likely to be unfazed by the situation. He was going to face our youngsters, Daniel Descalso and Jon Jay. Descalso had entered the game in the eighth and had singled in his only at-bat. The classic matchup of youth versus experience was on. I watched, knowing that these young guys understood the moment. They weren't so young that the "ignorance is bliss" factor was coming into play. Daniel had very little experience at shortstop, but there he was in a game destined to become as memorable as any World Series game, and he was unflappable.

He went up there and really got into his competition with Oliver, fouling off three near-put-away pitches before singling to right. Were we going to have to trot Yogi back out and have him say "déjà vu all over again"? After taking a strike, Jay, who was 1-for-3 since coming into the game in the fifth, singled to shallow left, one of those break-your-heart jobs that pitchers hate. The pitcher's spot was next, but I'd gone through every position player at this point, so the only option was to use another pitcher—a starter because they had more at-bats than anyone else among the staff—to go up to bunt the runners over. When I'd looked at the cards the previous inning, I'd already laid out my plan. Edwin Jackson was in the on-deck circle. If Jay made an out, Edwin was going to hit. Among the pitchers available to hit, he had the most pop in his bat. If we had one on and one out, he was the man I hoped could step into one and get a base hit to help us.

I was pointing at the umpire, indicating that I was sending up Jackson as a pinch hitter. Then I quickly reconsidered. This was a bunt situation, and Kyle Lohse, the better bunter, was going to go up there. I had made a mistake and wasted Jackson. The thought crossed my mind that if we tied I'd have wasted a valuable player. I'm sure people thought we were running around like Cardinals with our heads cut off. That meant that Lohse was now pinch-hitting for the pinch hitter.

I stood there shaking my head as I scratched Jackson off my card, mumbling, "You've got to be kidding me."

Lohse bunted the ball past the pitcher and third baseman, so the shortstop had to field it, and the runners advanced.

Runners, and speedy ones at that, were on second and third with one out. Scott Feldman, a right-hander, was called in to face Theriot and Albert, the next two hitters and both right-handers. Feldman got Theriot on a ground ball to third, but Descalso was able to score because the infielders were playing back. They had traded an out for a run.

Being down one instead of two was huge. Though Jay wasn't able to advance, with his speed, any ball into the outfield would give him a great chance of scoring to tie the game. The Rangers weren't going to let Albert beat them. They intentionally walked him, the potential tying run, to face Berk. He was 2-for-4 and had walked once, driven in two runs, and scored three. Berk was 3-for-9 against Feldman. Also, Berk had been clutch for us all year, he was having a productive year as a run producer, and he'd been seeing the ball well all night.

As bad as I felt about wasting Jackson, I at least had the presence of mind, earlier in the inning, to call down to the bullpen, telling them to get Jake Westbrook up. I'd seen dozens of extra-inning games like this—lots of back and forth and then a long stretch when neither team is able to score. The ebb and flow takes on that cadence of in and out. I also knew that we'd gone through a lot of pitchers, so if the game did evolve into a marathon, I wanted the guy who could go that distance in there for us.

I was hoping Jake would be needed.

Berk went up there attacking and fouled off the first pitch. After a ball, he fouled off the next one. We were down to our last strike for the second time in the game. We'd been in the same spot in the ninth. Two thoughts competed in my mind. Whenever you're behind and end up losing but don't go quietly, you feel good about how you competed. A spirited rally means something. We were fortunate that the lineup had turned so that, if we had to be in this position, either Albert or Lance would be in there. Also, a brief image of Adron Chambers sprinting home to score the winning run in that game in Chicago briefly flashed through my mind. I was still hopeful.

Feldman threw a fastball in, but missed just slightly, and Berk lined it, not a bullet but solidly, into center field. We were tied at 9–9. Berk was so cool in that situation, even when he got to the bag at first. He just calmly took off his batting gloves, looked out into the outfield, most likely watching the replay as if he were at home. Later on, he was asked how he handled big-game pressure. He said that he prayed for calmness and to be able to compete. He was indeed calm, and he did compete. He also answered a lot of Cardinal fans' prayers. When asked what he was thinking during that at-bat, he said, "Nothing." I loved that. No thinking, just doing.

I sensed in the ninth when we'd tied it that people were going to talk about this game for a long time. When we did it again in the tenth, I knew that people were going to talk about this game forever.

When Albert made it to third, I'm sure a lot more prayers were launched. Craig grounded out to the third baseman to end the inning.

We'd added Jake to the roster because his approach seemed the most similar to how we'd seen the Tigers' pitchers working against the Rangers' right-handers. After retiring Nelson Cruz, Jake gave up a single to Mike Napoli. That guy just impressed me. He'd tweaked his ankle, and there was some doubt about whether he could play, but he was on base five out of six times, with three of those coming on walks. Jake retired the next two, and for the first time since the ninth, we entered an inning not having to score in order to stay in the World Series.

David Freese led off for us against Mark Lowe, who mixed a

mid-nineties fastball with a very sharp breaking slider. By the time Lowe threw the third of three straight balls, I was already "what-if-ing" the straight bunt or the show-and-bring-back bunt, then switch to the hit-and-run with Yadi. I watched Lowe intently, looking to see if he was around the plate, trying to figure out if the hit-and-run would be a good option. Descalso was in the hole, and he was our best chance to drive in a run if we got the man to second. Yadi liked the hit-and-run, and so that worked in the favor of hit-and-run. After Descalso was Jay and Westbrook. If it came down to it.

Three pitches later, David Freese did a solo version of the hit-and-run. He was soon joined by every one of his teammates in doing that. He hit a fastball on the inner half and crushed it to straightaway center field onto the grass of the hitters' backdrop.

In situations like that, it's almost as if the ball has some gravitational pull on you. As it climbs, it lifts you up, body and spirit. The guys at the rail rose up on their feet, craned their necks, and raised their arms above their heads. They were uplifted and exultant, as was I, experiencing what I imagine weightlessness must be like.

As much as I wanted to charge out there and join the guys clustered around the plate, waiting to tear the jersey off Freese's back and leaving the Hall of Fame to ask for shreds if they wanted them, I hugged Dunc instead, and then the rest of the coaches and I all gathered in the dugout. Shaking hands and shaking our heads, marveling at the wonder of it all.

Later on, as the postgame press conferences went on and on with so many stories to tell and so many questions to be asked, I heard Lance Berkman say of his big hit in the tenth, "I actually felt pretty good because I figured I was in a no-lose situation. If you don't come through right there, it's only one at-bat and it's over with, and they might talk about it for a couple days, but it's not that big a deal. If you come through, it's the greatest, and plus you've built a little bank account of being able to come through, so that if I don't come through tomorrow I can be like, 'Well, I came through in Game 6, what do you want from me?'"

What we want from our players most often is that they do the routine things. When they do the spectacular, as so many of them did during the course of the season, and then again in this one game, all those failures to do the routine just recede into the background—at least for a little while. There was analysis to be done, but that could wait for another time. The only analysis we had room for at this point were the numbers:

1. We were down to our final strike twice.
2. We were the first team ever in playoff history to score in the eighth, ninth, tenth, and eleventh innings.
3. We were the first team in playoff history to trail five times and come back to win.
4. We were the first team in playoff history to be behind in the ninth and in extra innings to win.

This was going to be another of those sleepless nights, the rare few, the pleasurable few, when you can't shut down because you're so wired from the great and classic things that went on that day that resting feels like erasing and you don't want to let those images go just yet.

Elaine and I went to Shannon's restaurant after the game with Rick Carlisle and Howard Schultz, the chairman of Starbucks, and friends. We stayed until about 3:30 in the morning.

It was fun to relive that sixth game, but about the middle of the dinner I started to get distracted, turning my attention to Game 7. Dunc and I had decided that Carp was going to start. But just to make sure, I called Dunc later that morning and said, "Let's discuss the alternatives."

He said, "Carp's pitching." And then he hung up on me.

One analysis down, plenty more to go.

CHAPTER TWENTY-THREE

We're History

MAYBE BECAUSE MY THOUGHTS HAD BEEN ON CARP AS WE SAT there into the early-morning hours, a great moment in hockey history came to mind. I remembered that Herb Brooks and his 1980 Olympic hockey team had beaten the Soviet Union in one of the greatest upsets in sports. That group of amateurs and collegians took on and defeated a hockey juggernaut, a team that had won every gold medal since 1964. In "the Miracle on Ice," they beat the Soviets in the medal round, advancing to the championship game against Finland. That last part is what some people may forget. The Miracle on Ice was an inspirational victory, but it wasn't for the gold medal.

Those guys had to put that victory behind them in order to better focus on the next one. That was our job as well. I did what I usually do and contacted the co-signers, one of whom was Albert. I hadn't bothered to look at the clock before calling, but his sleep-tinged voice set off alarms in my head. I forget sometimes that not everyone is a night owl like I am. Albert said that he was up, it was just that his voice was hoarse from all the shouting he'd done. Once I'd gotten home, I'd watched the highlights, and seeing those guys form that scrum waiting to attack Freese as he approached home plate and then just pound on him had me feeling that electric buzz all over again. The joyous look on the guys' faces was worth every bit of the struggle they'd gone through—in the game and in the season—to get to that point. I wanted to do everything in my power to ensure that they got to experience that same elation again.

I told Albert the obvious. What they'd done was great. What they'd done was beautiful. It was special. They'd carry those memories and accomplishments with them for the rest of their lives. I thought about meeting one of the stars of that great Olympic hockey team, their captain, Mike Eruzione, when he came to spring training a few years before. He talked about the experience and the inspirational words Coach Brooks had delivered. If they didn't beat Finland to win the gold medal, they'd regret it for the rest of their lives. If they lost the game, they'd be haunted by it for the rest of their lives.

If we wanted to carry Coach Herb Brooks's message to his players to its conclusion, then we had to be ready to try to win Game 7. Also, if we didn't win that game, then what we'd done in Game 6 would lose some of its importance.

Now they had to do something else.

"Put your Game 6 memories in a box. Tell the guys to put them in a box, set that box aside. It's all about Game 7."

I didn't say this to Albert, but what they were experiencing was like being a kid at Christmas. You open one present, and it's a car racing set that you've always wanted and think is the coolest thing ever. But don't go running from the room to set it up and start playing with it just yet. There's another box to open, and that present contains something even better, something that will make the first gift even cooler, something that will make you treasure all of them even more.

I'd seen it happen too many times not to make those calls. You would win a dramatic game and the next day the fans, the media, and even the players think that it's going to carry over and the other team is going to be down. More often than not what happens is that the celebrating team (us) is still celebrating and the other team (Texas) has got a slight edge and you get beat.

Once we were all at the park, I also had the coaches contact a certain number of players each to deliver that message to the squad. Good or bad, we all tell our players to put it behind them and move on, but on rare occasions like this one, the message is subtly different. "Put it behind you" is generally followed by "And forget about it," but what we'd done in Game 6 wasn't anything we ever wanted to forget about.

Asking guys to compartmentalize like that is not always easy. When something good or bad happens, it's incredibly difficult not to let it seep onto the field, and in some cases, you're better off not even trying to prevent it. I'd seen that firsthand in the aftermath of Darryl Kile's passing on June 22, 2002.

That 2002 club endured the hardest challenge any team could face. They had to learn to go on even in the face of something so terrible that they could never put it behind them even if they wanted to. That's life, though. You go on. I don't claim to have any special insight into how you go about it. I lost both my mother and my father and don't live close to my sister Eva and my brother-in-law Vic or any extended blood family on Elaine's side in Virginia and Tennessee as well. But because I'm away from Elaine and the girls so much, we've created, with the blessing of the Cardinals organization, a family-friendly environment in the club. By doing that, we hope to alleviate what those families are going through.

What I can say about that 2002 season was that the coaches and I reached out to the team in a way that was more emotional than ever before or since. We engaged with guys on a deeper level, trying to understand the different ways that his death was affecting them all. No two people deal with loss in the same way, and such was the case with our team. With something like a death of a teammate everyone loses the focus to compete to some degree; it's only human. Guys start questioning the fact that they spend so much time away from their families. Everyone finds it hard to dive back in with the same intensity when you've been thinking about how you've got a team-mate that just isn't coming back. In many ways, the ordeal, traumatic as it was, became one of the most important I've experienced. If ever there were a season that showed me just how important it was to be connected to our players both professionally and personally, it was 2002. We might not have won the World Series that year, but we achieved a victory unlike any other.

In the years since, as an organization, we'd done some things to keep Darryl's presence with us. When we were at home, every time I made a call to the bullpen—and as you know, I make a lot of them—and I was pointing out there to bring a reliever in, I was also pointing to Darryl. There's a small sign hanging in that bullpen. It's simple and direct, just like Darryl: "DK 57." It was there in the old stadium, and it's there now in the new one, and knowing how the Cardinal family feels about Darryl, and about tradition, I imagine that it'll be there wherever the Cardinals call home in the future.

Darryl's impact and influence go beyond the Cardinals—he was so highly regarded that two other teams, the Astros and the Rockies, have similar signs in their bullpens. I think Darryl would appreciate that when we go to those away games, we like knowing that a little bit of home and Darryl is there with us. Believe me, during that last series of the regular season when we won and got into the playoffs, the number 57 and the initials DK were on my mind. Now that I'm no longer traveling with the club, I still have Darryl's practice jersey, a photo, and one of his gloves.

Both the Astros and the St. Louis Baseball Writers established the Darryl Kile Good Guy Award. It goes to the player who best demonstrates the qualities that Darryl had as a "good teammate, a great friend, a fine father, and humble man." Mike Matheny was the first Cardinal to receive the award, and now that he leads the club, Darryl's traits and his legacy are sure to go on.

I don't know, maybe I'm old-fashioned enough to still believe that sports teach us a thing or two about how we should live our lives. I know that we demand that our players represent the organization in the best way possible. I can't possibly compare what the 2011 Cardinals endured to what the 2002 Cardinals went through in losing a beloved teammate. I will say this about them, though: like that squad, they kept going.

And now here we were on the verge of going on to the very top. When we got there, Darryl would be there too—maybe not the way he was in '02, with Albert carrying his jersey onto the field, but there nonetheless. About the highest compliment I can pay this club is to say that Darryl would have loved playing alongside them.

CARP HAD MISSED BY ONE SEASON THE OPPORTUNITY TO PLAY WITH Darryl. He was another in the long line of quality guys we've had anchor our rotation and make significant contributions to our success. Matt Morris, Andy and Alan Benes, Todd Stottlemyre, and Woody Williams are others I'd put in that category. Now that baton is in the process of being passed on to Adam Wainwright. I have no regrets about how I managed all these years, but I do wish that guys like Alan Benes, a real prince of a human being and a great competitor, had been able to enjoy longer careers. He was really ravaged by injuries and never got to fully achieve what he was capable of. Rick Ankiel is another guy I have tremendous admiration, respect, and affection for. To endure what Rick did, to suffer through that bout of wildness from the mound and then come back and have a career as a big league outfielder, takes guts. He never blamed anybody for his struggle. If you've seen a guy go through something like that—seen a guy be torn up by his failure to do something that once came so natural and easy as breathing and then bounce back—well, then, you'll never judge anybody ever again. You'd heap benefits of the doubt on any other struggling player until he proved you wrong. Rick never did blame anyone, and I'd say the same thing about Big Mac and anybody else who's had a rough go of it.

I understand that the fans and the media don't have the privilege that I do to get to know these talented athletes as human beings. That's why I'll never assume anything or paint with a broad brush. The old line about walking a mile in a man's shoes applies whether they've got spikes on the bottom or not.

There was another reason why I was thinking of Darryl and Todd Stottlemyre. Like we were doing with Carp, they'd both pitched in the postseason for us with three days' rest. In Game 5 of the 1996 National League Championship Series, we'd tried to wrap it up in St. Louis, but Atlanta scored seven runs off Todd. That was the game we lost 14–0, and we went on to lose the next two games in Atlanta too. Darryl Kile was asked to pitch on three days' rest in Game 4 of the NLCS in New York in 2000. He made it only three innings, giving up seven runs.

I did have some experience with postseason success and three days' rest, however. That was all thanks to the remarkable efforts of Dave Stewart. With the A's, we had Dave work on three days' rest in the postseason. Each time he was pitching a Game 4, and in two of those he wrapped up best-of-five league championship series for us—by beating Boston in 1988 and in 1990. In 1988 Stew pitched seven innings of a 4–1 A's win. In 1990 he pitched eight innings in a 4–1 win.

I probably should have thrown Dave out of the mix in looking for precedents to base my decision on. Stew was an amazing physical specimen. Combine that with an absolutely unshakeable belief in himself and his ability to do anything he willed his mind to do, and you have someone who could accomplish what few can. His ferociously competitive nature made that a winning trifecta. Possessing those attributes, Dave was our horse and the closest thing possible to an undefeated Triple Crown winner.

I didn't want to rely solely on my memory, though, so before

Carp's first three days' rest assignment in the NLDS, I asked some of the club's media relations people to help out. According to them and according to baseball-reference.com, between 2000 and 2010 there were forty-three starts made in the postseason by pitchers who were on three days' rest. Those pitchers combined for a poor 11-20 record and a high 5.05 ERA.

Some notable exceptions in clinching games did exist. The Florida Marlins' Josh Beckett worked on three days' rest in New York to blank the Yankees, 2–0, in the decisive Game 6 of the 2003 World Series. Marlins manager Jack McKeon didn't want to risk trying to win a Game 7 before a rabid crowd in Yankee Stadium.

And then, in what is considered one of the best-pitched games in World Series history, Minnesota's Jack Morris, operating on three days' rest, worked ten innings to beat Atlanta, 1–0, in Game 7 of the 1991 Series at the Metrodome. John Smoltz, also working on three days' rest, had pitched the first nine innings in scoreless fashion for the Braves.

So it could be done.

Because Carp had that one prior go at it, and he assured us that he was feeling good, and he believed that he'd learned a valuable lesson to just pitch with what he had and not try to add, he was our man. We'd worked our bullpen pretty good in Game 6, so using Westbrook meant that the only pitcher we needed to be careful with was Salas—we'd used him a lot to that point. We kept to our routine of asking guys if they were okay, but this was the seventh game of the World Series after all. Everyone said that they could go if needed, including the rest of the starters and Jake. We did our usual observation, and I sketched out a plan ahead of time.

If Carp had warmed up poorly, or if he couldn't go because he felt sore, we weren't going to do anything to jeopardize his career and we'd go with the plan I'd hinted at: Westbrook would have gone. Lohse and Jackson were both available for extended innings. Westbrook matched up well against the Rangers. In the seventh through the ninth, we'd go with our regular cast. Even though all hands were available, we'd try to avoid using a starter in an unfamiliar relief role unless we had to.

We knew that the Rangers were a resilient club. The World Series stage is different, but they were a team that hadn't lost back-to-back games since August 23 to 25, when the Red Sox beat them three straight. That covered thirty regular-season games plus an additional sixteen in the playoffs. That just shows how good a club they were. One concern we had was Holliday's health. He'd sprained his wrist and was done for the Series. The effect of not having his big bat in the lineup was factored into my "what-ifs."

We had the luxury of being able to put Allen Craig into left and batting second, while Berk moved into the cleanup slot. Matt's absence would be felt, but being able to give Craig another start along with Jon Jay, an upgrade in defense in center, made this roster move easier to deal with. We added Adron Chambers, who gave us speed and defense, but not the bat Holliday has.

I knew that the co-signers and the coaches had made sure everybody got the "put away Game 6" message. I'd get a good indication of whether that message had taken hold in the pregame workout. If I didn't get a good feel, like I had before the first game of the '90 World Series, I'd have to intervene. That night during batting practice, as the guys stretched and threw to loosen up, we detected no Game 6 hangover. Based on how the guys were taking their swings and going about the drills, I saw that they'd done what we'd asked of them and were fixating on Game 7. I didn't know what was going to happen, but we were ready to play.

There was no team pregame speech. Instead, the staff all circulated through the roster during the workout beforehand to do the pat-and-pop. We've done a great job. We've got a shot. Let's go get them.

* * *

So much for the theory that the Rangers might be disappointed for having failed to win the championship in Game 6. Kinsler singled on the first strike from Carp. They stayed aggressive, and Carp's delivery home was below 1.2. Kinsler stumbled, and Yadi came up throwing and fired to first to pick him off. Still not settled in, Carp walked Andrus. In short order, Hamilton and Young both doubled to right field, and we were down 2–0.

This was also the third time in four innings we had trailed by two. If we were going to win, we needed another comeback. We'd been down this road so many times that there was almost—and I stress *almost*—a confidence factor. The three days' rest question sat like a buzzard in a tree, waiting to be answered. Carp had fallen behind on the first four hitters. They produced three hits, a walk, and two runs. Then he got first-pitch strikes against Beltre and Cruz and retired them both. That was huge. To retire two of the other team's hottest hitters in a situation where they were capable of putting us in a huge hole was vintage Carp.

I didn't detect that Carp was rushing, as he had against the Phillies on short rest. Hopefully, he'd made some adjustments. He came in looking grumpy, and I took that as a good sign.

An even better sign was us tying the score in the bottom of the inning after two were out. The Rangers appeared to be taking a "don't let their big guy beat us" approach by walking Albert on four straight. I don't think they were pitching around Berkman, and maybe Harrison was just trying to be too careful, but he threw four more out of the zone, and we had runners on first and second. One of the previous night's heroes, David Freese, stepped in, getting a huge ovation from his hometown crowd. While watching the highlights of that game, I'd seen some of the interviews the guys did, and I got a kick out of seeing Berk and Freese up there together, taking turns, and on one Berk chimed in on a David question and the two of them were struggling to keep a straight face. Now, with a full count on him and the two previous hitters having walked, Freese did his thing: noting that they were trying to pound him inside, David looked for and got a pitch on the inner half to the edge and with a nice compact stroke doubled into the left-center-field alley. We were tied.

Freese's success didn't come as a surprise to either the staff or his teammates. Matt Holliday had moved to the St. Louis area in the off-season, and the two of them worked out together all winter. Matt was one of his biggest supporters. Matt would tell me and Mac that he thought David could be a solid twenty to thirty (home runs) and eighty to ninety (RBIs) guy. "He's been through a lot. That toughened him up," he'd say. David has had more than his share of injuries, and when you're seldom healthy, it's hard to get into any kind of groove. Everybody in spring training had sensed that this was a more committed and determined David Freese.

It all came together in the playoffs for him.

We threw the ball around a little bit in the top of the second to put a runner on third with two out, but Carp got Andrus on an easy comebacker to keep the Rangers from taking the lead. Carp was still struggling with his location, but after a visit from Dunc, he seemed to settle in.

In the bottom of the third, Allen Craig homered with one out, his third in six-plus games. Twenty-six of his sixty-three hits were for extra bases in the regular season, and three of his five hits in the World Series were home runs. Not bad for a kid who played his college ball at UC Berkeley as a shortstop and was an eighth-round draft pick. I kidded him that if he'd worked harder in college, he could have helped out his alma mater more. The school was in the news in 2010 for having to cut its baseball program because of the state of California's budget crunch. People rallied around the team, including Allen, to help finance and support it, and the program remains alive today.

Since he comes from such a renowned institution, you'd expect Allen to be a bright guy, and he is. He's so articulate that he can sometimes come across as much older than he is, and he carries himself with a veteran's presence on the field. He and his wife, Marie, are animal lovers, and that endears them to me. Their pet tortoise, Torty, though lacking an imaginative name, became a semiofficial mascot thanks to his Twitter account. Has any team ever had an odder pair of mascots than Torty and the Rally Squirrel?

One of the things that's always fascinated me about baseball is how on any given night a different facet of your team can either emerge or recede. If we'd lost Game 6, I'm sure there would have been more than a couple stories about our loose defensive play. Albert's second-inning throwing error aside, our defense, which hadn't been our strong suit for much of the year, stood out. In the fifth, after Kinsler singled and a sacrifice put him at second, with the tying run on and only one out, Hamilton hit a high pop fly just past the Rangers' dugout near a temporary camera location. David Freese got over to the railing quickly, established himself, and made a nice catch. If that ball hadn't been caught, we'd have still had the dangerous hitter in there. Getting outs any way possible, especially when a runner can't advance, makes a pitcher's job easier.

So does increasing a lead. In the fifth, with Scott Feldman in for the Rangers, we tallied two runs without the benefit of a hit. We'd scored a run without a hit in Game 6 as well; I've seen lots of ball games, but I'd have to say that these two instances really benefited us. You start to believe that something is in the air when your club gets a walk, a hit by pitch, an intentional walk, a bases-loaded walk, and another hit by pitch to bring in another run.

When that kind of funky inning happens to you defensively, you come in muttering under your breath, cursing the baseball gods. In this case, we were thanking them.

That inning also showed how much we had improved our strike-zone discipline. We maintained our aggressiveness, but were getting more good hitting counts in our favor. That was something we'd been talking about and working on since spring training, and it paid dividends for us in this game and elsewhere in the postseason. It's easy to say that a walk is a result of a pitcher's wildness, but sometimes what the hitter doesn't do (swing at a borderline pitch) is just as important.

With one out in the top of the sixth, we were thanking Allen Craig for making it easier on Carp to shut them down after we'd scored. Nelson Cruz got into a fastball that Carp intended for low and on the outside corner but that went up and in a bit on Cruz. He lashed at it and hit a towering fly ball to left. Craig went back to the wall, waited, and then, timing it perfectly, jumped up to make the catch, robbing Cruz of at least a double and more likely a home run. The next hitter, Napoli, lined out hard to right.

I caught Carp as he came off the mound and said, "Great job," and shook his hand. That's the usual signal to let a pitcher know that he's done. I then told Dunc that I thought Carp had had enough. In each of those last two outs, the hitter had gotten the center of the barrel on the ball. What Carp had given us was outstanding. He'd done his job. Dunc agreed. However, Yadi, having seen all that go on, came over and said, "No, no. I've got a lot to work with." Yadi's experience and insight carries weight with us.

This would have been the ideal situation in which to take Carp out. He was due to lead off that inning. We were up only three and still had nine outs to get. I had a lot of respect for Texas and their ability to come back. Asking a bullpen to get nine outs is a tough challenge. Based on what Yadi had said, Dunc and I rethought our plan. I decided that Carp could go out there and buy us some outs, reduce the number that the bullpen was going to have to get. However many he could get was going to be good for us. Carp is a pitcher who gets stronger late into games, so he was the ideal guy to start the process of getting each of those outs. I'd never changed my mind before. That's how much I trusted those two guys—Carp and Yadi.

As it turned out, Carp gave up a leadoff double, and he was done for the night. When I went out to get him and said, "Good adjustment on three days. You did more than we could have asked for. Now get your pom-poms and cheer us on to victory."

When I brought in Arthur to get Endy Chavez, they went with Yorvit Torrealba off the bench, but it didn't matter. Arthur got him, and I turned things over to Dotel, who retired the side on a strike-out and another fly-out. I can't stress enough how important it was that those two got those three outs without that runner scoring from second. With the score 5–2, that third run in would have meant that anytime they got a runner on after that, the hitter coming to bat would be the tying run.

As often happens, when one teams fails in a chance, the other team responds. We got another run in our half of the seventh on an infield hit by Berkman, a walk to Freese, and Molina's single.

Lance Lynn came in (as expected this time) and ended his postseason on a high note by retiring the side in order. We all saw something special about what Lance brought to the mound. In that situation, looking for those next few outs, I had to consider something I thought about in every game: What did that pitcher's last good outing look like? And what did his last bad outing look like? In Game 6, Lance had been roughed up a bit by those back-to-back home runs. In other games, though, I'd seen that he had that ability to turn the page. We had other guys to back Lynn up if he got into any kind of trouble, but I trusted that he was the best option against the Rangers' three-four-five hitters—Hamilton, Young, and Beltre. They were some very tough outs who'd proven just how tough throughout their careers. That I went with Lance in that situation speaks volumes about the confidence he'd earned. That Lance retired the side in order speaks volumes about his ability to learn from his mistakes, make adjustments, and come back strong.

The changes I made in the ninth, putting our best defensive team out there and our closer on the hill even with a four-run lead, also gave those guys—Jay, Schumaker, Punto, Descalso, and Motte—a role in our eventual victory.

I was still observing closely. Only when we got to two outs did I think, *Son of a gun, we're going to do this.*

As soon as I saw the eventual final out's fly-ball trajectory, I knew the game was over and we'd done it. Suddenly, I couldn't breathe and I felt myself rising. I was in the grip of a crushing bear hug, and I saw Berk's grinning face. He set me down and took off running. His doing that meant a lot to me. I had liked him immediately, and as the season progressed and we got to know each other better, he told me that, as an opposing player, he'd gotten to the point that he wanted to punch me. "You never smiled, and you always looked like you wanted to come out and kick all our asses." As the season went on, he told me that his perception of me from the outside was radically different from what he'd experienced on the inside. I'd seen and heard that before from other players, like Mark DeRosa in 2009, but in this context, with the stadium erupting in joy, Berk's hug was memorable.

We let the players celebrate on the field, and the coaches, trainers, and equipment guys all exchanged congratulations. The look of pride and disbelief was on virtually everyone's face. Along with the players' and coaches' family members, Elaine came up out of the tunnel and into the dugout. We hugged, and she said, "I just don't believe it. This couldn't happen."

"I agree."

When I'd told Elaine at the beginning of the Series that, despite what all the experts were claiming, I thought the two teams were even, she was surprised. She had been troubled when we lost Game 5; just like me, she knew how those numbers worked against us. I'd said to her again when I got back to St. Louis and she joined me there that I still believed we had a shot.

Right then, I believed it. I still wasn't sure I could explain how it happened. There'd be time for that analysis.

One of the joys of winning a World Series is always seeing the wives and other family members and friends coming out on the field to join in the celebration. The entire infield surface was covered with people. I spent the next few minutes making sure that I got to as many guys as I could and found their families to congratulate them too, before going through the trophy presentation. After that, all the players and family members retreated to the clubhouse and continued the celebration in there.

I was concerned about one thing—being doused with cold champagne can literally take your breath away. Maybe because I'm older now, I wanted to avoid that, so I snuck past everybody and ducked into my office, hoping that I wouldn't get caught in the crossfire or corralled and chilled myself. Once in my office, I thought briefly of writing a memo to the commissioner asking that Major League Baseball require room-temperature champagne.

Instead, I visited with Elaine and some of our friends, Howard and Jordan Schultz, Rick Carlisle, Keith Grant, Jerry Reinsdorf of the White Sox, and our New York friends Nevin and Paige. Players, staff, organizational employees, and others came and went, offering their congratulations. We all enjoyed a special moment when we all went into the conference room to celebrate with Dunc, Jeanine, and their sons and their wives.

The best part of winning and the celebration afterward is seeing the elation that other people experience in being part of it, especially when you win at home. That increases my enjoyment exponentially. I was so caught up in what was going on that I ended up with one regret from the whole experience. Somehow I missed the players going out onto the field to do their victory lap for the fans. I'd wanted to be in the dugout to witness that. I'm not sure when that tradition started, but I love it. I get so much pleasure from seeing the fans' reaction to any win, but this one was obviously more special.

I thought of that '89 Series again. We'd won, but we'd celebrated privately, out of respect for the lives and property lost in the earthquake, and not as publicly as we would have otherwise. We'd won the game in San Francisco and then went across the bay to the Coliseum and had a get-together there. A small gathering of the fans and our team met a day or so later at Jack London Square as the only public gathering. Walter Haas, the owner of the team and one of the greatest human beings who ever lived, made the decision about the parade, and it was absolutely the right one. Walter rarely asked anyone for anything. He did ask this of me: win another World Championship in Oakland so that we can have a parade. Every year in spring training, I'd remind the guys that that was what we wanted to do—win and get that parade for Mr. Haas. We got close, but fell short of that goal and never made it. As someone who tries to live his life and have no regrets, not being able to do that for him has stuck with me.

Winning as we'd done, extending the Series to its full length, had put off a gathering of another kind. I was going to have to let the players know that I was retiring. I'd lived with that knowledge since July, and the reality of that choice had become like breathing— I was only rarely conscious of its presence. Only after we'd taken the team photo in the clubhouse did I even begin to consider what was next on that front.

I didn't like the idea that all of this was going to have to take place so quickly. I wasn't the one setting the timetable, but I was still uncomfortable with the thought of my retirement announcement coming so soon after the win. The players deserved to have the spotlight on them for as long as possible. I know how the media works: the victory would be fresh for only so long, and then the news cycle would churn around again.

I didn't dwell on it for long. Friday night stretched into Saturday morning, and I was busy with phone calls and getting the details about the parade. I was eager for that to happen. Back in 2006, Elaine, the girls, and I had gotten to ride on the wagon that the Clydesdales draw down the streets of St. Louis, and it was a thrill. You can have your convertibles and floats. I don't know what it is, but the sound of their hooves on the pavement just seems to be a part of the October pageantry that adds an element of nostalgic pleasure. Our daughters weren't going to be with me this time, and in this one sense that was a good thing.

When we won the Series in Oakland, Bianca and Devon, who'd been teasing me for a while about how uncool I was, suggested that if we won the title, I had to get an earring. I told them that given my job in professional baseball, I didn't think my employers and others in the game would take too kindly to that. To appease them, I said, "Next time we win it all, I'll get the earring." Fast-forward to 2006. Earrings are no longer cool, but tattoos are. The girls—and this includes Elaine—reminded me of that long-ago bet. This time I couldn't back out. I went to a well-known biker tattoo parlor in Oakland and got one done on my shoulder, where it isn't visible to the public. An appropriate spot considering my injury history with that joint.

I don't know about the cool factor in 2011 and what my girls had planned for me. I did know that we had a parade to get to. The turnout and the atmosphere were amazing. I was grateful that both times we'd won it all in St. Louis, we'd done it at home and could immediately engage with our fans. Fall days in the Midwest, with the sun shining and the sky as powder blue as a '70s road uniform, can be added to my list of things to hold on to and remember.

I knew I faced a tough task in telling the guys I was retiring, but you have to practice what you teach, so I didn't give much thought to what I had to do after the parade and rally were over. Toward the end of the parade, I did say something about it to Elaine, and she said, "You mean you're really going to do it?"

Climbing onto the podium to speak at the rally, I asked the rest of the team to close ranks behind me and gather around. I hadn't done that in 2006, they'd all kind of hung back, and maybe this spontaneous gesture was symbolic of just how strongly I felt about this group. At the end of my remarks, I shared with the fans there in the ballpark the story I've told here about Jake Westbrook and how he handled being held off the playoff roster. I said this then, and I think it bears repeating: sometimes it feels like there's no justice in our game. But Jake's getting the win in the most historic game proves that just as often there is.

Later, as we left the podium and the field and went inside the bowels of the stadium, I asked a few coaches and other members of the organization to spread the word to the players that they needed to gather in the gym. I knew that they were figuring this was me taking one last opportunity to say something to them all about how I felt about what they'd done, remind them to take good care of themselves in the off-season, and say that I'd see them again next spring. A few later told me that they were thinking I was going to bring up the magic word—*repeat*.

Right prefix, wrong word.

I knew that given how I was feeling, I had to get through this with as short and sweet a statement as I could. I didn't even really want to look around the room. I knew that Mo and Bill were there, as well as other members of the Cardinal family, the coaching staff, Elaine, and a few others.

I used the usual pat-and-pop approach. I stressed again how I felt about the season, about them, and about what they'd all done. Then I said, "Some of you are going to say, 'Good riddance.'" The guys laughed, thinking I was talking about the end of the year. Hearing that gave me the courage I needed to look at them all looking at me.

"I don't know how to do this any other way but to do it. I'm retiring."

When I saw the look of shock and surprise on some of their faces, my windpipe tightened and the tears came. I shifted uncomfortably on my feet and pursed my lips. I shrugged and couldn't say any more. This was proof again that you can't ever have a completely happy day at the ballpark.

After that, the players came up to me, and they were all so shocked and unprepared. Almost without exception, we hugged and they said some version of thanks. I responded by thanking them for all they'd done for me. A few guys added that we'd talk, and later on we did. Carp and I had grown close, as I had with a bunch of other players. I felt bad about not being able to tell them earlier. For several reasons, a few of them had asked me at the end of the year what I was thinking. This year, when that question came up, I'd said that it was too soon to talk about any of that. When Carp approached me, he said, "I had a feeling this was different."

Mo and Bill asked me privately if I would reconsider, and I declined. I told them how much it meant to be asked, but I wasn't going to change my mind.

This was an intentional walk.

The next couple of days I was in my office packing, and the players stopped by and we got to say a few of the things that we'd not been able to say when I first told them I was leaving. At one point or another I talked with all of them, and there was a lot of that "Thank you"—"No, thank you" stuff going on. We all meant the words, of course. Many of the guys thanked me for creating the environment that produced a championship, and I cut every one of them off and said that *we* had done that together. For the young guys and the veterans new to the team, my message was a variation on this. They'd taken me to a place I hadn't been before. I saw how much fun they were having. Maybe earlier in my career I'd been too focused on other things to notice my players' enjoyment, but with these guys it just jumped out at me, was as subtle as a ripped jersey. More than that, though, they were just such incredible competitors who loved and lived that simple formula: Our Side. Their Side. Keep Score.

I did have to say to Arthur Rhodes, who got his first ring after so long, that we had wanted him in our club for a long time. Arthur smiled at that and, in his velvety voice, said, "I wish you could have worked it out." No words can explain the pleasure I felt in watching Berkman, Dotel, Rhodes, and Furcal, all veteran warriors, celebrating that championship. I told Rafael that the picture I'd seen of him hugging Albert after the last out was tied for first as my favorite World Series picture. I told Berk that I was sorry that he was going to miss his moment to punch me out.

For the veterans who'd been with us for a while, the good-byes and good-lucks lasted a while longer. When Schu came in, we talked about the spring and the decision to convert him to second base, and the progress we'd seen him make from January to October. I told him that I knew he could do it because, like Mike Shannon, he was that talented and that tough. He reminded me that after he'd gotten the call from us about the move to a new position, he'd immediately called his dad. Schu's father said, "Well, then, let's go field some ground balls." A good man. A good son. We both laughed about the time against L.A. when I went to him before Game 1 of the 2009 NLDS to tell him to take ground balls at second and flies; I wasn't sure where he'd be playing. Later, when I told him he'd be in there at second, I could see a flicker of doubt in his eyes, and I told him the truth. "Dunc says you're the best second baseman we've got." When I told him that then, and reminded him again of it now, Schu shook his head slightly, like me, still wondering at the mystery of it all.

Similarly, I reminded Yadi of what I'd said about him when he struggled at the bat so early in his major league career. I told him I meant every word of that statement about him being my catcher even if he went hitless for the year. I also asked him if he understood just how much confidence we had in him—letting him take charge of the visits to the mound, what he said to those pitchers, and what all that said about him.

"Tony," he said, "I didn't understand it then, but I felt something. Now I really get it."

Yadi didn't need to tell me that. I already knew that he got it and that he had for a long time.

I wound up my conversation with Carp by telling him that anytime he wanted to, he could have his son, Sam, a spitting image of Carp by the way, sing the national anthem for me. I'll never forget how proud Carp was when he approached me one day to ask if I wanted to hear Sam sing it. There's that something special about fathers and sons. I told David Freese that I'd be pulling for him and reminded him that we all cared for him, and that extended beyond the players' entrance and exit to the ballpark.

Albert and I both knew we'd said and felt everything we could, and that this wasn't the end of our friendship. Adam Wainwright reminded me of how I was more upset—*livid* was the right word— than he was when he didn't get the Cy Young in 2010. I could feel my face flushing when I remembered how a single writer, who had looked at some metrics to downgrade his season, had left him off the ballot entirely, thus ensuring that Tim Lincecum got his second in a row. I also remember that the bullpen had mugged one on him in 2009, preventing him from getting his twentieth win of the year, a win that might have been enough so that I wouldn't have had to call Adam in the off-season and say, "You deserved it. You got robbed."

What was so memorable about that was after the 2006 season and we had won it all and Adam had worked as our closer in the late season, he came to me and said, "I can be as good a starter as Carp is."

I said, "You know how much I love confidence, but you know what I love more than that? Back it up."

He did that.

And with the season just over, we'd all done that.

So many times since that evening I've been asked to sum up my thoughts on the 2011 Cardinals' remarkable year, the end of my career, and that final victory.

Here's what I think. If there's any lesson to be taken away from our 2011 season, one in which we continued to come back over and over, it's this:

Just because you're down to your last strike, you're not out yet. You can always do more. You'll always have more at-bats to take. That's true in baseball, in rescuing animals, and in life generally.

In fact, the lesson is even more profound. As retired Lieutenant General Hal Moore, a true hero, likes to say, "Even when you have three strikes, you're still not out. There is always something else you can do."

EPILOGUE

OVER THE YEARS, TWO OF THE HALLMARKS OF MY MANAGERIAL career have been coincidence and good fortune. They've been with me every step of the way, starting with my employment in truly ideal situations—White Sox, A's, and Cardinals—and continuing all the way up until Game 7 of the World Series in 2011 as well as to my final duty as manager of the 2012 All-Star Game. As the winner of the National League pennant, the 2012 All-Star Game was my last managerial assignment ever. What I didn't realize going in was that this "last" game would share some eerie similarities with another of my "last" games—game 162. What they have in common and how each became a win was beyond spooky to the point of unexplainable. Five runs scored in the top of the first inning and three runs added with outstanding pitching defined the 8–0 wins.

I have no clue what the odds are that those games, with so much personal and team importance, could be so identical. What I do know is that they both provided a rare opportunity to enjoy the final moments. For more than 5,000 managed games, the last three innings were, almost without exception, a gut-wrenching, head-splitting experience with us grinding hard to get to the finish line. Somehow in both game 162 and the All-Star Game, though, I was able to enjoy all sorts of memories. As a result, it wasn't lost on me that the All-Star Game was part of another coincidence—my last game in a major league uniform was in the same city as my first appearance. In 1963, at the age of eighteen, I was a member of the Kansas City Athletics. To be sure the record is accurate, I need to admit that mine was not an earned roster spot. In those years, if you signed a bonus contract, the organization had to keep you on their major league roster or risk losing you to another team. Still, it felt like a fitting end.

The Kansas City All-Star Game was a terrific experience with the glaring exception of when the Reds' manager fired off a cheap shot at me questioning my All-Star roster selections. Now I always understood there's no free lunch—especially at the All-Star Game. Ever since I managed my first All-Star Game, I've recognized that part of the dues you pay for the honor of managing that game is the responsibility for some roster selections. Anybody who has that job recognizes that there are difficult choices with disappointments and criticisms that always follow. Your only objective is to do the best you can.

What I struggled with in this instance was that the ugliness was caused by attacks on my integrity. Different opinions are part of managing, but making it personal was not acceptable. Besides destroying a relationship, it simply reminded me that I had indeed made the right decision to retire. Part of the managing territory is taking the heat for your decisions and results, but these kinds of distractions were precisely what took away from the privilege of major league competition.

Despite that situation, there was nothing that could tarnish my excitement about being on the bench this one last time. Ultimately, it is being a part of the game that's the biggest turn-on, and I think it's one that all players with longevity share. Contrary to what many believe, the criteria for managers is not below-average playing ability. It is a love of the game and a desire to learn it. George Kissell made that clear to me in 1977, and it explains why star players like Joe Torre, Don Baylor, and Mike Scioscia, to name a few, were outstanding managers.

Love and learn are also true for coaches. Their importance at all levels cannot be exaggerated. In fact, because developing talent is so often rushed to the majors, teaching is as important in the majors as in the minors. Our coaching staffs over the years are only the good fortune part of the combination. There is no coincidence: it's all about my and our organizations' benefiting from their expertise and passion that contributed to our success.

ONE LAST STRIKE WAS WRITTEN TO TRY TO ANSWER THE QUESTION I've been getting since the final out of Game 7: how did we do it— how did the Cardinals pull off a historic comeback to earn the wild-card playoff spot and then win three October series as underdogs to claim the World Series Championship? The answer, as you can probably tell, is far from simple, but in the end it's about *how talent, character, the will to win, and toughness all combined in one unique and incredibly special group of players.*

Still, words fall short when it comes to describing what this final season, not to mention my entire career, have meant to my life. Increasingly, I receive questions about my "legacy." My answer is that the wins or losses happen, but they are not my legacy. I believe my legacy is defined by two things. The first is how we competed. Our preparation wasn't just getting ready to play. I believe our teams brought effort and execution to the games. The other side brought theirs. The score determined who did best. The game competition was our focus. Our priority. Our motivation.

The second part of my legacy will surprise many because they don't realize the extent and strength of its existence. Of the two legacy parts, this is the one I treasure most. From the White Sox to the A's and the Cardinals, I've developed a deep and lasting group of close relationships with just about everyone I've managed. Our players, coaches, and everyone who interacted with our teams worked that respect, trust, and caring formula that built those bonds every day of every year. It's the experiences of competing together and retaining those memories and relationships over the years that are my favorite to remember and where I feel my true legacy lies. The "how we competed" part of my legacy is best judged by our competitors. The close relationships part is reserved for those who experienced it. Their judgment is the part that matters most to me.

These relationships are so meaningful because from February until early or late October, teammates spend so much time together. But there is another side to this equation. The time spent with teammates is at the expense of our families. To allow me to pursue my baseball passion, Elaine and the girls had to do most of the heavy lifting. As a way to make this point, consider that from 1974 to 2011 we packed for some type of move fifty-six times. By any measure, that's an excessive sacrifice.

In the end, perhaps the only way to think about legacy is to recognize and appreciate the people who have helped you achieve one in the first place. During late July 2012, I paid a visit to Cooperstown to celebrate the Cardinals' history of World Championships, and while there I spent time with Roland Hemond and Red Schoendienst. Roland was my first general manager with the Chicago White Sox; Red was our special coach in St. Louis for spring training and home games. Imagine my great fortune for more than twenty years to have close personal contact with them and to experience their unique qualities. They are as beloved and respected as any men our game has ever known. It would take another book to describe what these men have meant to professional baseball for more than sixty years.

Standing there, at Baseball's Hall of Fame, with these two men who had contributed so much to my career—Roland at the beginning, Red at the end—I couldn't help but think about them and everyone like them who I'd encountered in my career. These two amazing men were the bookends, but everyone in between had been the stories. No manager has ever had it any better.

ACKNOWLEDGMENTS

Like a baseball organization, working on a book is a team effort and I have a lot of players, coaches, and managers to thank.

First of all, to my cowriter, Rick Hummel, who is already enshrined in the writers' wing of the Baseball Hall of Fame and has been covering the Cardinals for so long, his tenure makes me look like a rookie. Thank you, Rick, for all your hours of hard work even while covering this season's games.

While Rick was my starting pitcher, due to deadline pressure to get this book to the fans on a tight schedule, we also brought in our closer from the bullpen. Gary Brozek was the talented writer who worked with me to close out the win and I can't thank him enough for the crucial role he played. Gary's tireless efforts, his skill with words, his own extensive understanding of baseball, and his indefatigable enthusiasm despite an incredibly tight deadline helped to make this book what it is. Rick, I enjoyed our time in St. Louis, and, Gary, I will always remember our hours working on chapter after chapter in the Colorado mountains. My travel schedule working on this book has rivaled what it was while I was managing the Cards in the postseason. Actually, it's been even tougher.

None of this could have been accomplished without the fine skills of my team at William Morrow, a division of HarperCollins Publishers. Thanks to the captain of my book team, Lisa Sharkey, who signed me up, and to executive editor Matt Harper, who has worked around the clock to get the manuscript in shape. Much appreciation also goes to editorial assistance from Sara Partridge, publicist Danielle Bartlett, art director Richard Aquan, marketing team Tavia Kowalchuk and Megan Traynor, and the incredible sales force led by Josh Marwell, Brian Grogan, and Doug Jones. My gratitude also goes to HarperCollins president Michael Morrison, CEO Brian Murray, William Morrow publisher Liate Stehlik, and associate publisher Lynn Grady for your enthusiasm and support of this project.

On the e-book side, thanks to Ana Maria Allessi, Marisa Benedetto, and Scooter (Jeffrey Kaplan) for the hard work editing the video for the enhanced e-book, which contains some very special moments. Some of my close friends contributed to those videos, and I want to give a special nod of appreciation to Joe Torre, Tom Seaver, Brian Jordan, and Dennis Eckersley for agreeing to be interviewed for it.

My blurb brothers get a special high-five. John Grisham, thanks for finding the time in between writing your own blockbuster best sellers to write the foreword. Special shout-outs also go to Lee Child, Howard Schultz, Bob Costas, and Joe Torre for your words of praise on the jacket to help alert readers to this book.

Thanks also to the Cardinals and MLB for allowing our cameras into Busch Stadium in an effort to let fans see the incredible behind-the-scenes tour of the most beautiful ballpark in America.

At IMG, thanks to Sandy Montag and his team, including Jill Driban and Max Teller, for all your help in managing my personal postseason play.

Last, this book is as much about leadership as it is about baseball, and no book on these two subjects would be complete without mentioning the name of a man I've been privileged to work with for much of my managing career—Bud Selig. What's been accomplished in Major League Baseball during Bud's tenure—the way he has encouraged the growth of MLB and his contributions to the game—has been invaluable.

APPENDIX

ANYONE WHO KNOWS ME WOULD LAUGH AT THE SUGGESTION THAT I was one of the first "computer managers." I was mistakenly identified as one because in the early days of computer usage in baseball, I happened to be managing for the A's and the White Sox, two teams at the forefront of that movement. To this day, I've never carried a laptop or traveled with one.

What follows are examples of the tried-and-true, hands-on, paper-and-pencil notes that Dave Duncan and I used to keep track of player performances, tendencies, and game notes—some done after the fact, others kept during the actual playing of the game. I hope the fans find our scribbling of interest.

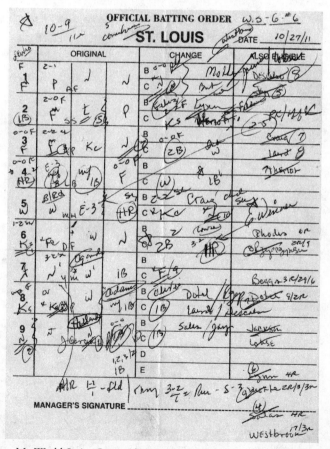

My World Series Game 6 lineup card with notes on our offense.

The back of the Rangers' lineup card, where I wrote down reminders about how we should compete: "Keep on Believing!," "Be Good Enough!!," "Self-affirmation," and "Be Tough Enough!!!"

			ORIGINAL			CHANGE				ALSO ELIGIBLE		
282 1	279	AND	0|6		B 3|9							1|3
315	290	BLr	5|22'	2|10	C 6|14		0|1 / 0|1		2|3	0|1		
					B							
2 357	290	CHr	0|1	0|1	C 4|7		4|8					
340 3	243	Cr3	1|2'	2|9	B 5|12		1|1 / 0|1	0|2				2|5
					C							
265 4	277	6Nr	0|1		B 1|3							
1|4	3|7	6rm	0|2	1|5	C							
5 260	314	HmL	0|1	0|1	C 1|6'				0|2	0|3		
262 6	252	KNS	0|6	2|9'	B 6|18"				0|1	1|2	4|6'	
					C							
234 7	266	MrL	1|1'		B 4|8'							0|1
215	296	MrP	0|2		C							0|4
					B							
8 319	320	NPL	0|3	1|4	C 1|9	0|2	0|1 / 1|1					1|5
256 9	280	TrL	2|2	0|3	B 0|6	0|1	0|2					1|1
					C							
361	330	YrL	3|12	11|27'	D 6|22		0|1		0|9	1|4		
159	242	TrJr			E		FS / mB					

OFFICIAL BATTING ORDER
ST. LOUIS   DATE

MANAGER'S SIGNATURE _____

A matchup card showing our relievers versus the Rangers' hitters.

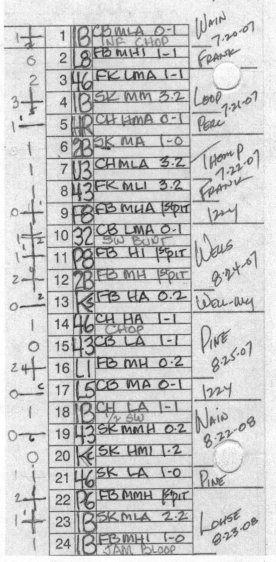

A portion of Dunc's chart tracking Chipper Jones's at-bats. Dunc distills this and other information into a strategy to get hitters out.

INDEX

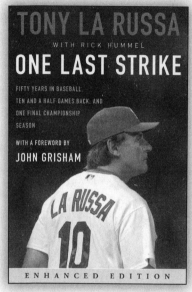